LANGUAGE AND TRAVEL GUIDE to ROMANIA

Rosemary K. Rennon

Hippocrene Books, Inc.
New York, NY

Publisher: George Blagowidow.
Editor: Tanya Shohov.
Book design by Susan Ahlquist.
Cover design by Ben Herson/Nomadic Wax.

For information, address:
HIPPOCRENE BOOKS, INC.
171 Madison Avenue
New York, NY 10016
www.hippocrenebooks.com

ISBN-13: 978-0-7818-1150-7
ISBN-10: 0-7818-1150-3

Cataloging-in-Publication data available from the Library of Congress.

Printed in the United States of America.

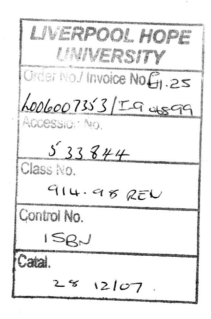

ACKNOWLEDGMENTS

Many kind people have helped me find my way during my six trips to Romania over the past 10 years. But for this last visit, in preparation for this book, there are two who allowed me to access many new places. First and always is Simion Alb of the Romanian National Tourist Office in New York City, whose direction, contacts, information resources and patience with me over the years have been invaluable. Secondly, I am extremely grateful to Răzvan Balint of Cultural Romtour for showing me every nook and cranny of rural Transylvania and Moldavia, complete with historical and folkloric details. His vast knowledge of the countryside and his boundless energy are truly staggering.

It was wonderful to see my old friends from previous visits, and have them fill me in on the enormous changes that have taken place in recent years. Many thanks to my dear friend Radu Antofi who has offered his help from the moment I met him and his lovely wife at the Bucharest telephone office in 1998; also to fellow American and longtime Bucharest resident Tim Judy, who always imparts valuable information over a bottle of Romanian *vin roşu*; to Marian of Villa Helga, who has seen me through several trying episodes; and to my first Romanian travel coordinator, who in 1996 thought I was crazy, but still arranged my requested venture into the unknown, Andrea Brezean. Finally, to my friend Nick Klepper, author of Romanian history and cookery books, for referring his publisher to me. I love you all!

ROSEMARY K. RENNON

TABLE OF CONTENTS

CHAPTER 1

INTRODUCING ROMANIA

Romania is one of those mysterious treasures, a place whose name everyone has heard, but that few know anything about. Thus the surprise when one discovers this enchanting and wildly beautiful country. It's a land of diverse regions ranging from the forested Carpathian Mountains to lush farmland and green rolling hills; from the Danube river delta, rich with bird, plant and aquatic life, to sandy beach resorts along the Black Sea. Its countryside is dotted with medieval castles, ancient fortresses, historic monasteries and quaint peasant villages where local folk still live much as they did centuries ago, weaving their own cloth and driving horse carts to their fields. Many of Romania's cities have retained their historic architecture, with centuries-old buildings still serving as civic offices, shops and homes surrounding the town square.

Located in eastern Europe, Romania shares borders with Hungary to the west, Ukraine and the Republic of Moldova to the north and northeast, and Serbia and Bulgaria to the south. The Black Sea forms its 244 km (152 miles) southeastern coastline. Romania is a mid-sized European country covering 238,391 sq. km (92,043 sq. miles), about the same size as the state of Oregon, slightly smaller than the U.K. The horseshoe-shaped Carpathian chain curves through its center, its basin covering most of central Romania with rolling hills, forests and farmland. Outside the Carpathian curve are lowlands, farms and plains that reach to Romania's bordering neighbors. The Danube River runs along the country's southern border, then turns north, to create Europe's second-largest delta and wildlife preserve at the Black Sea. The country is comprised of three historical regions: Moldavia to the northeast, Transylvania in its center, and Wallachia to the south. Within these regions are smaller, distinctive provinces.

Romania's peaceful landscape belies its turbulent history. Inhabited since the Stone Age and settled by early Greek traders and Thracians, the territory has endured constant invasions, first by Romans, later by Ottomans. In later years, the Habsburg dynasty controlled its western territory, primarily Transylvania. And most recently, the country endured 40 years of repressive domination by the former Soviet Union.

But all that changed in 1989, when the people revolted against their ruthless Communist dictator, Nicolae Ceauşescu in a remarkably non-violent uprising and took back their country and their independence. Romania now has a constitutional republic form of government, with a multi-party parliamentary system consisting of a Chamber of Deputies and a Senate. Its President is elected by the people, and his nomination for Prime Minister and Cabinet must be approved by Parliament.

Though one of the world's most isolated countries under communism, Romania is regaining its identity as a popular vacation spot for Europeans, and it is now attracting tourists from all over the world. It has something special for every type of visitor: Transylvania's medieval cities and castles to explore; skiing and hiking in the majestic Carpathian mountains; fishing or birdwatching in the Danube Delta wildlife preserve, numerous Black Sea beach resorts and famous health spas; magnificent old architecture; and tiny country villages that will take you back centuries in time. And speaking of centuries, this land is strewn with ancient historical sites that date back over 2,000 years.

The capital city of Bucharest, after enduring decades of social control and physical neglect by the ruling communists, has come back to life. Buildings damaged during the 1989 revolt have been restored and the hotels have been renovated. Communication services have been upgraded. Fashionable clothes and consumer goods are available again. Elegant restaurants once more offer the international and traditional Romanian cuisine that made the city famous back in its heyday, between the two World Wars. New pubs, jazz clubs, discos, and casinos now offer alternative night life to the classical theater, opera and philharmonic programs; and the museums and parks offer hours of quiet beauty and relaxation.

Whether you're a rugged outdoorsperson, a lover of arts and architecture, a sun and sea worshiper, a history buff, a Dracula hunter, a denizen of glitzy casinos and nightclubs, or just want to escape to someplace untouched by modernity, Romania will captivate you.

The National Flag, Emblem and Anthem

Romania's flag is a tri-color vertical stripe design of blue, yellow and red.

National Seal—The central element of Romania's national emblem is a golden eagle with an Orthodox cross in its beak, and holding in its talons the insignia of sovereignty: a scepter representing Michael the Brave (1593-1601), the first unifier of the Romanian countries, and saber, representing Moldavia's ruler, Stephen the Great (1457-1504). Traditionally, this eagle stands for the "nest of the Basarabs," the nucleus around which Wallachia was organized, the province that determined the historical fate of the whole Romania. The shield on which it is placed is azure, symbolizing the sky.

On the bird's chest there is a quartered escutcheon with symbols of the Romanian provinces (Wallachia, Moldavia, Transylvania, Banat and Crişana). In the first quarter Wallachia's coat-of-arms is repeated: an eagle with a cross in its beak, a sun on the right and a moon on the left. The second quarter holds

Moldavia's coat-of-arms: an auroch head on red with a mullet between its horns; a rose is on the right and a crescent on the left, both silver. The third quarter features the coat of arms of Banat and Oltenia: a golden bridge (symbolizing Roman Emperor Trajan's bridge over the Danube), and a lion holding a broadsword in its right forepaw. The fourth quarter shows the coat–of–arms of Transylvania with Maramureş and Crişana: a shield parted by a narrow fesse; on the azure upper, an eagle accompanied by a golden sun on the right and a silver crescent on the left; on the base are seven towers. At bottom center, two dolphins represent the country's Black Sea Coast.

National Anthem—Romania's anthem is "Awaken Thee, Romanian," lyrics by Andrei Mureşanu (1816-1863) and music by Anton Pan (1796-1854). It was originally a march of the revolutionaries of 1848.

Awaken Thee, Romanian!

Wake up, Romanian, from your deadly slumber,
In which barbaric tyrants kept you so long by force!
Now or never is the time for you to have a new fate,
Which should command respect of even your
cruel enemies.

Now or never is the time for us to prove to the
entire world
That in these arms Roman blood still flows,
And that in our hearts we proudly keep a name
Triumphant in all battles, the name of Trajan.

Behold, glorious shadow, Mihai, Ştefan, Corvin,
This is the Romanian nation, your own great-grandsons,
With weapons in their hands, your fire in their veins,
All shouting, "We want to live in freedom, or else die!

Priests carry the cross on high! Our army is blessed,
Its banner is called freedom and its ideal is sacred,
We'd rather die in battle, and in a blaze of glory,
Than live again like slaves in our beloved land!"

The Economy

Romania is a lower-middle income country with a gross national income per person of only US$2,310 in 2003. A full 25% of the population lives below the poverty line and 60% of the poor live in rural areas, despite the country's substantial potential in agriculture, forestry, and fisheries.

In 1989, after 40 years of Communist central planning that emphasized self-reliance, excessive focus on heavy industry, and large, uneconomic infrastructure projects, Romania's economy was on the verge of collapse. The new democratic government resisted imposing tight fiscal constraints and the privatization of large loss-making enterprises. Then, in the late 1990s, attempts to impose macro-economic stability without full structural support led to negative economic growth, and poverty increased sharply.

The last four years have shown progress in consolidating the macro-economic stability, while lowering inflation. At an average rate of about 5.6% per year, GDP growth was among the highest in the region, with investment and private consumption the main drivers in 2003 and 2004. In 2004 the GDP grew by 8.3%, and 2005's growth is estimated to be 5.5%–6%.

Beginning January 1, 2005, the government introduced a new 16% flat tax rate that applies to both income and to corporate profit. This is a reduction from the previous 18 to 40% progressive income tax and the 25% on corporate profits. The measure is aimed at encouraging private entrepreneurship and foreign investment, while consolidating the Romanian capital, thus creating new jobs and increasing the purchase power of the population.

Romania now appears to be right on track to become a member of the European Union on January 1, 2007. The country's Accession Treaty was signed on April 25, 2005, but the EU Commission will monitor Romania's compliance with its commitments very closely. Despite economic growth in the past three years, more structural reforms are crucial to produce a competitive market economy capable of withstanding the pressures of EU integration. These include:

- Streamlining the legislative process and improving the integrity and efficiency of the judiciary
- Eliminating administrative barriers to improve the business climate; completing privatization, and implementing a transparent and predictable tax system
- Reforming public services to benefit the population
- Developing the rural areas and reducing poverty
- Reforming the energy sector and eliminating subsidies

These measures must be complemented by a no-tolerance attitude to corruption and fiscal evasion. If the EU Commission finds that Romania has not met its reform commitments by 2007, the country's accession to the European Union may be delayed. It's a tall order for a country still learning to adapt to its first ever democracy.

The People

Romania has 22 million people, 89.5% of whom are Romanian, 6.6% Hungarian, 2.5% Roma or Gypsy, .3% Germans, .3% Ukrainians, .3% Turks, .2% Russians and .3% all others. Religions represented here are: Eastern Orthodox 87%, Protestant 6.8%, Catholic 5.6%, other (mostly Muslim) 0.4%. The country has a very high 98.4% literacy rate.

The Romanians

Romanians are descendants of two ancient peoples: the Dacians and the Romans. The Dacians were the original inhabitants of this rich land, but in AD 106, the Emperor Traianus crossed the Danube River and conquered the territory for Rome. Many Roman soldiers remained there and intermarried with the Dacians, creating a new mix of peoples who were called Romanians. The Romans' Latin language was adopted and evolved into today's Romanian. (Traianus's Column in Rome was built by the emperor to commemorate his great victory over the Dacians.)

The Minorities

Hungarians (Magyars), the largest minority in Romania, numbering 1.4 million, have always lived in Transylvania. The region's control has been in dispute between Romanians and Hungarians for centuries, but has belonged to Romania since the demise of the Austro-Hungarian Empire after World War I. And for the most part, except for a few hot political issues (usually about language and education), the Hungarians live peacefully among their Romanian neighbors.

Transylvanian **Germans** have a two-tiered history. The first German colonists—the Saxons—came to Transylvania in the 12th century. They were industrious, skilled tradesmen and they built prosperous communities during the Middle Ages. They also built beautiful cities throughout the region, such as Sibiu, Sighişoara, Braşov. The second wave of German colonists was the Swabians, from southern Germany, who settled in the southwestern Banat region in the late 18th century, when Transylvania and Banat were still part of the Austro-Hungarian empire. After the region returned to Romanian rule in 1920, they became subject to Romania's political problems. Tragically, after eight centuries of productive living in Transylvania, today only 66,000 Germans remain in Romania. Most of them fled back to Germany to escape communism or left after the borders reopened in 1989. Nevertheless, their influence remains strong throughout western Romania.

Romania's 56,700 **Turkish** residents live in the southeastern province of Dobrogea, near the Black Sea coast. The first Turks in Romania were the Pechenaks, who arrived in the late 9th century. In 1057 the Pechenaks were defeated by invading Kuman Turks, who dominated Dobrogea for two centuries. In 1241, the Tatars merged with the Mongols and invaded the region. Then, in the 14th century, the Ottoman Empire expanded into the Balkans and ruled for nearly 300 years, despite fierce battles with Romania's greatest heroes (including Vlad Dracula). Ottoman rule ended in the mid-1800s after several defeats by occupying Russian troops. Today, most of the Turkish minority in Romania is composed of Roumelian Turks (immigrants from former Ottoman territories in the Balkans) and Tatars (from the Crimea). The majority of Turks live in Constanţa. Their beautiful mosques there and in Mangalia are a major tourist attraction.

The 64,000 **Ukrainians** live in the northernmost region of Romania, near its border with Ukraine. They are renowned for their elaborately painted Easter eggs, an age-old Ukrainian tradition that has been adopted by Romanians in Moldavia.

A **Russian** minority of 36,600 lives in the Danube Delta. They call themselves "Lipoveni" (from Leipzig) and are very different from the typical Russians. They fled Russia over religious differences and, due to the remoteness of the area, lost all contact with Russia. The Lipoveni are traditionally fishermen and are masters of the intricate maze of canals in the Delta.

About 23,000 **Serbs** live in the southwestern province of Banat, in and around the cities of Arad and Timişoara. The Serbs have about 15 churches and 5 monasteries in Romania. They are known for their traditional costumes and music.

There are 500,000 Roma (also called *Ţigani*, Romanian for Gypsies) living in Romania. They have representation in the Romanian Parliament. However, in keeping with their old ways, they still have their own emperor and king.

CHAPTER 2

A SHORT HISTORY OF ROMANIA

Ancient

The lands of Romania have been inhabited since the Paleolithic, or Stone Age, as evidenced by carved stone tools unearthed there. Some flint implements, found in the Carpathians, date from 600,000 BC. The first known art consists of cave paintings in northwest Transylvania dated to 10,000 BC; and Neolithic pottery and art from the 4th to 3rd millennia BC have been found all over Romania. In the 3rd millennium BC an Indo-European migration throughout the Carpathian and Danubian territories began, and from the Bronze Age in the 2nd millennium BC, Thracian tribes occupied the lands. Called Getae by the Greeks, and Dacians by the Romans, the Geto-Dacians have lived in the area since the Iron Age of the 1st millennium BC. The Greeks arrived in the 7th to 6th centuries BC; they settled the land near the Black Sea and Danube Delta, and established the cities of Histria, Tomis (now Constanţa) and Callatis (now Mangalia).

Constantly beset by intruders, in 514 BC the Geto-Dacians fought off Persian invasions, and in 335 BC they turned back the Macedons of Thrace. Their civilization reached its zenith in the 1st century AD under the great ruler Decebalus. In AD 106, the Dacian ruler was slain by Roman Emperor Trajan's legions, who crossed the Danube River and conquered, and then colonized the territory. Dacia became a Roman province, the Dacians assimilating with the Romans and adopting their language. After fighting off the barbarian Goths for 100 years, Roman troops finally abandoned the land in AD 271; but years of intermarriage with the Dacians had created the Daco-Roman people of Romania. From the 4th century on, nomadic tribes from all over Europe and Asia invaded Dacia. These included the Goths, Visigoths, Ostrogoths, Vandals, Tatars, Lombards, Slavs, Avars, Huns, and Bulgars. In AD 840-890, Magyars descended on the Danubian plains, eventually moving into Transylvania and Hungary. By the 10th century, Romanian states were beginning to form. These led to the principalities, called voivodates, of Wallachia, Moldavia, Transylvania and Dobrogea, established in the 14th century.

Medieval

The first mention of Romanians appears in Byzantine documents of 1160 when the Wallachians and Byzantines fought the Hungarians. The Hungarians defeated Bulgar-Romanian forces in 1230 and took over Wallachia; and in 1241, Mongolian Tatars seized the coastal region of Dobrogea. In the 14th century, Prince Basarab established a semi-independent principality in Wallachia. Then Dobrogea, the region bordering the Black Sea, gained its independence and united with Wallachia. At the same time, Prince Bogdan created the principality of Moldavia. Wallachia and Moldavia then united to fight back the Hungarians. Transylvania, however, remained under Hungarian rule from the 11th century until 1526 but it was allowed administrative autonomy, even under its later Turkish rule.

14th–19th Centuries

During the late 14th century the Ottomans began their invasions from the Black Sea and pushed east as far as Hungary. Romanian rulers Mircea the Old of Wallachia (1386-1418), Dan II (1420-1431) and Vlad Dracula (1456-1462) fought against the Turks but were defeated, and Vlad was killed. Up north, in Moldavia, Alexander the Good (1401-1431) and Stephen the Great (1457-1504) defended their province against Turks and Poles. Stephen built over 50 monastery-fortresses to shelter his people from invaders; many of them are still in use. In Transylvania in 1514, a Peasant Uprising against the Hungarians ended in bloody defeat with the torturous execution of its leader, Gheorghe Doja. Soon after, the Turks took control of Transylvania and Hungary, ruling until 1688, when the Habsburgs ran them out. In the late 16th century Michael the Brave (1593-1601) became Voivode (Prince) of Wallachia and united with Transylvania to cast out the Turks; but after he was assassinated in 1601, the alliance fell apart. The Turks regained control and held Wallachia from 1716-1821. Greek Phanariots bribed the Turks for high positions and ruled the area, but they allowed Wallachia and Moldavia to set up their own law codes. Greek became the language of law and of the Orthodox church.

In 1718 Austria took the Banat region in the southwest. Tsarist Russia and Austria both fought for the north territory in Moldavia, and in 1775 the Habsburgs took Bucovina; Bessarabia went to Russia in 1812. In 1821 and again in 1848, popular uprisings occurred down in Bucharest in an attempt to expel the Greeks and Turks, but were defeated. Back in Transylvania, Saxons and Romanians fought the Magyars (Hungarians), but this region remained under Austro-Hungarian control until 1918.

After Russia's defeat in the Crimean War in 1856, the Congress of Paris proclaimed a joint protectorate of Wallachia and Moldavia by Great Britain, France, Prussia, Austria, Russia and Turkey. The Paris Treaty returned Bessarabia to Moldavia. Then, with the support of France, in 1857 the assemblies of Wallachia and Moldavia decided to unite, electing Alexandru Ioan Cuza as their ruler. In 1862 the state of Romania was officially proclaimed. When Cuza resigned in 1866, Prussian Prince Karl of Hohenzollern-Sigmaringen, the cousin of Kaiser Wilhelm I, was named as ruler of the union and moved to Romania. He submitted a constitution, which was ratified by the convention, and took the title of Prince Carol I. His Prussian wife, Elizabeth, was also known as the poet Carmen Silva. In 1877 Romania proclaimed its independence. Carol I then led Romanian forces to join with the Russians and finally defeat the Turks at Plevna. In 1878 the Congress of Berlin recognized Romania's independence and restored the Black Sea region of Dobrogea. At the same time, it forced Romania to cede Bessarabia to Russia, once again. In 1881 Carol was crowned king.

20th Century

In the First Balkan War in 1912-1913, Romania remained neutral; but in the Second Balkan War in June 1913, it joined Greece, Serbia and Turkey against Bulgaria. In 1914 King Carol I died and, having no son, named his nephew, Prince Ferdinand of Hohenzollern-Sigmaringen, as successor. He became Ferdinand I and ruled from 1914-1927 with his wife, the beloved Queen Marie. Born Princess Marie of Edinburgh, she was the granddaughter of Queen Victoria and the cousin of Tsar Nicholas II. Queen Marie became known as "the Warrior Queen", commanding her own cavalry detachment and visiting cholera-stricken troops in Bulgaria during the Second Balkan War. She died in 1938.

During the first two years of World War I Romania again remained neutral, but in 1916 it joined the Allies against Germany, Hungary, Turkey and Bulgaria. Their armies were defeated in Transylvania by the Germans, who pushed farther into the Wallachia and, with the Turks and Bulgarians, into Dobrogea. The Romanians held out in Moldavia, but were forced to sign the Treaty of Bucharest in 1918 and exit the war. They reentered later in 1918 and their forces returned to Transylvania, pushed into Hungary in 1919 and captured Budapest, occupying it for a short time. On December 1, 1918, the national assembly met in Alba Iulia where Transylvania voted to become part of Romania, as Bessarabia and Bucovina had previously done, forming the union of Romania. In 1920 the Treaty of Trianon redrew the Hungarian border awarding Transylvania, the Banat, Maramureş and Bucovina to Romania.

During Ferdinand's reign, Romania had been governed by the National Liberal Party, but after his death they were dismissed and replaced by the conservative National Peasant government, led by Iuliu Maniu. The Romanian Communist Party was formed in 1921, but outlawed in 1924. In 1930, Ferdinand and Marie's son, Carol II took the throne. He broke a promise to end an affair with Magda Lupescu, his divorced Jewish mistress, leading Iuliu Maniu to resign in protest, after which the government fell apart. Carol II then abolished the constitution, banned all political parties but his own, and set up a royal dictatorship. His government was totally corrupt, fixing elections and then dismissing them at will. Strikes in the rail and oil industries were met with military force.

In the meantime, a Fascist movement called the Legion of the Archangel Michael had been founded in 1927 by Corneliu Zelea-Codreanu. His Nazi-backed Iron Guard grew in strength during the 1930s with the support of King Carol II. But when the Iron Guard turned against Carol because of his liaison with the Jewish Lupescu, Carol had Codreanu shot in 1938 and imprisoned thousands of his followers. In retaliation, the Legionaires killed sixty-four officials of Carol's regime, burned synagogues, and raped and killed hundreds of Bucharest's Jews. By the time the Iron Guard was finally eliminated in 1941, it had assassinated four prime ministers.

World War II–Communism

In 1939 Germany demanded a monopoly on Romanian exports in exchange for the guarantee of its borders. In 1940, following the Nazi-Soviet Non-Aggression Pact, Stalin annexed Bessarabia and northern Bucovina. Carol II turned to Hitler for help but, angry about Carol's murder of Iron Guard leaders, Hitler instead demanded Northern Transylvania for Hungary and southern Dobrogea for Bulgaria. Disgraced, Carol and his mistress Lupescu fled Romania in 1940, taking with them its gold and art treasures. His nineteen-year-old son Michael was left behind to take over the throne. Nazi-backed General Ion Antonescu, known also as "Red Dog" for his red hair, led the country for several years hence. He appointed Iron Guard legionnaires to his cabinet and allied Romania with Hitler. Romania entered World War II marching with German forces against the Soviets. The Soviets proved the stronger, however, and entered Romania in August 1944. King Michael, engineering a royal coup, had Antonescu arrested and ordered a stop to the fighting. The country then changed sides and joined the Soviet forces against Germany. On August 31, the Russians took over Bucharest without opposition.

The Yalta Agreement of 1945 made Romania part of the Soviet system and Dr. Petru Groza was named Premier. By 1947 the communists had taken control of the government. King Michael was forced to abdicate and the monarchy was abolished. Following the Communist takeover, industries, banks and transportation systems became nationalized. In 1952 Gheorghe Gheorghiu-Dej became leader of communist Romania and after Stalin died in 1953, he began developing heavy industry and attempting to improve relations with the West and Asia.

After Gheorghiu-Dej died in March 1965, Nicolae Ceauşescu took over. He was originally well thought of by the people, challenging the Soviet right to dictate to members of the Warsaw Pact and maintaining an independent foreign policy. But in the 1970s Ceauşescu became obsessed with building a strong national work force through population growth; he forbade birth control and abortions for any woman under 40 with fewer than four children. He penalized unmarried people and couples without children with higher taxes and required mandatory gynecological examinations. He was also obsessed with repaying the national debt, and all but the minimum food supplies were exported.

Ceauşescu discriminated against all minorities, insisting that they assimilate with the Romanian population. The ethnic Germans, Hungarians, and Jewish citizens all felt the pressure to give up their language and customs. Peasants were forced out of their houses and into concrete bloc-apartments to discourage independence. Germany and Israel purchased thousands of exit visas from Romania so that ethnic Germans and

Jews could leave the country. The Romanian people were also under severe restrictions. People were not allowed to speak to foreigners. Censorship laws required that all typewriters be registered with the police. Everyone feared their neighbor was a spy who would report any infraction of the law. Living standards declined for everyone, with shortages of food and consumer goods. Despite a failing economy, Ceauşescu proceeded with his megalomaniacal building plan, erecting new government buildings and apartment blocs all over the city. The gigantic House of the People was to be the seat of his communist empire.

In December 1989, local protests against the internal exile of a Hungarian priest in Timişoara sparked the national uprising that finally ousted the dictator and his hated wife Elena. After the military was ordered to fire at the demonstrators in Timişoara, Romanians united in protest. Factories went on strike, and on December 21st and 22nd huge crowds gathered in Bucharest to shout down Ceauşescu's speech with angry reminders of Timişoara. The Securitate (secret police) fired on the crowd but could not contain them. The rest of the country saw the chaos on television before their TVs went blank. Recognizing the end of his power, Ceauşescu and his wife fled Bucharest by helicopter but were caught the next day in Târgovişte. They were quickly tried and executed on Christmas Eve, abruptly ending 45 years of communist dictatorship.

Democracy since 1990

Two days after Ceauşescu's execution, the National Salvation Front (FSN) headed by Ion Iliescu, assumed power, announcing the dismantling of the communist structures, the switch to the market economy, and free elections. The country's historical political parties (the National Peasant Party, the National Liberal Party and the Social Democratic Party) quickly resumed activity and new parties were created. In the country's first ever democratic elections in 1990, former communist Iliescu was made Romania's president. Romania's new 1991 constitution (amended in 2003) proclaims Romania a democratic and social republic, deriving its sovereignty from the people. It also states that "human dignity, civic rights and freedoms, the unhindered development of human personality, justice, and political pluralism are supreme and guaranteed values."

In late 1991, a descent on Bucharest by angry coal miners forced the ousting of FSN Prime Minister Petre Roman just a few months before the 1992 elections. The FSN party split in two, and Iliescu's supporters formed a new party called the Democratic National Salvation Front (FDSN). The 1992 elections revealed a political rift between major urban centers and the countryside, with rural voters, grateful for the restoration of agricultural land to farmers but fearful of change, strongly favoring Iliescu and the FDSN, while the urban electorate favored the quicker reform offered by the CDR (Democratic Convention of Romania, a coalition of several parties and civic organizations). Iliescu was reelected over five other candidates.

But in the electoral campaign of 1996, the disgruntled opposition hammered away on the need to eliminate rampant corruption and to launch economic reform. This resulted in a victory for the CDR coalition and the election of centrist Emil Constantinescu as president. More problems over the next four years resulted in the changing of prime ministers three times. After continued slow progress and high inflation, Constantinescu lost the 2000 elections and Iliescu, with his new party, the Romanian Social Democratic Party (PDSR), was reinstalled.

Nevertheless, public confidence in both governmental institutions and politicians suffered considerably in 2002, influenced by a series of corruption scandals involving leading government officials. Public opinion polls conducted between November 2001 and July 2002 indicated that distrust of the government was increasing by 2.5% each month during this period. Romania had also seen more than one million of its people leave the country by 2002. One bright moment was

Romania's invitation to join NATO at the November 2002 Prague Summit; the following May its NATO membership became official.

In December 2004, Bucharest's populist mayor Traian Băsescu, running on a reformist, center-right ticket, was elected Romania's new president by a narrow margin. His new government cut taxes and actively began encouraging foreign investment.

In April 2005 the European Union and Romania signed a provisional treaty inviting Romania's entry to the EU on Jan. 1, 2007. The EU has reserved the right to delay the entry of Romania until 2008, however, if it fails to make the required reforms, which include bringing its laws into line with the 25-country bloc, enforcing antitrust rules, and the establishment of an independent judiciary. It's a tough challenge for a bureaucracy still trying to shed a lifetime of corrupt communistic practices and adapt to the ways of democracy.

CHAPTER 3

ROMANIAN CULTURE

Romanians are great lovers of art, music and literature. They revere their cultural heroes and have named many streets and institutions after them. Several of these illustrious artists have been instrumental in shaping the direction of arts endeavor around the world.

Musicians

George Enescu (1881-1955)—Enescu was a composer, violinist, pianist, director, teacher, and one of the most important musicians from the end of the 19th century and the first half of the 20th century. He was born in a Moldavian village and, influenced by his parents, amateur musicians of violin, piano and guitar, and by the folk music of his region, he composed his first music at the age of five. As a young boy he fashioned a violin from shingles. On the advice of composer Eduard Caudella, his parents took seven-year-old George to Habsburg Vienna and enrolled him in the Vienna Conservatory. There, he studied under Jules Massenet and Gabriel Fauré, and alongside Maurice Ravel and Jean Roger-Ducasse. He also met Johannes Brahms, whose symphonies he admired. After graduating in 1893, young George moved to Paris, where he first performed his "Poema Română" ("Romanian Poem") in 1898. His love of folk music continued to inform his compositions, and in 1901 he completed his famous "Romanian Rhapsodies." He also collaborated with Romania's Queen Elizabeta, a poetess who called herself Carmen Silva. Working together at her Peleş Palace in Sinaia, Enescu set several of her poems to music. He also wrote arrangements for *doine*, Romanian folksongs, and composed numerous sonatas and symphonies.

Yehudi Menuhin took violin lessons from Enescu in Paris in 1927, and again in 1928 at Romania's mountain resort of Sinaia, the same town as Queen Elizabeta's palace, Peleş. In 1931, they played Bach's Double Concerto together, Enescu on cello, Menuhin on violin. That year he also completed his only opera, *Oedip* (*Oedipus*), which debuted in Paris in 1940, but not until 1958 in Romania.

Enescu was conductor of the New York Philharmonic from 1937-1938. He married Romanian Princess Maria Cantacuzino in 1939, and she bought him the beautiful Cantacuzino palace on Calea Victoriei in downtown Bucharest. But he preferred to work in two small rooms by the gardens. The palace is now the Museum of Romanian Music.

Dinu Lipatti (1917-1950)—A prodigy from a musical family, Lipatti made his public debut as a pianist and composer at age four. He played violin and piano and won second prize at the Vienna Piano Competition in 1934. Afterward, he moved to Paris and studied under Alfred Cortot and Nadia Boulanger. He became renowned throughout Europe for his charming interpretations of Bach, Chopin, Ravel, Schubert, Schumann and George Enescu. His final concert, which luckily was recorded, was in September 1950, just two months before he died of leukemia at age 33.

Gheorghe Zamfir (1941-)—Born in a village 60 km (40 miles) north of Bucharest, Zamfir studied pan-flute (or panpipe) under Fănica Luca at the Bucharest Academy of Music. He was discovered in Bucharest by Swiss folklorist Marcel Cellier, who recorded Zamfir's music and broadcast it on his radio show. In 1969 he invited Zamfir to Switzerland. When Cellier played a Romanian *doina* (folksong) for him on an organ, Zamfir joined in with his soprano panpipes. This collaboration led to an international concert tour together. Zamfir has since infused many Romanian folk songs and Classical compositions with his spellbinding melodies. Some of his recordings are *Solitude* (1973), *Lonely Shepherd* (1988), and *Romance* (1984). In 1981 he played at Carnegie Hall. He has also written music for films.

Dramatists

Ion Luca Caragiale (1852-1912)—Romania's foremost dramatist was born in Haimanale, near Ploieşti. After finishing school there and in Bucharest, he worked as a copyist, editor, bartender and merchant. He also worked as the director of Bucharest's National Theatre for a while. He joined the Junimea Literary Society, writing dramas and tragedies. After receiving an inheritance, he moved to Berlin to concentrate on his writing. Known for his humor and sarcasm, he was fascinating, yet controversial. He was a satirist and keen observer of social realities. His plays are brilliant satires on 19th-century Romanian society. Most famous are "*O noapte furtunoasă*" ("A Stormy Night," 1879) and "O scrisoare pierdută" ("The Lost Letter," 1884). Other plays include "Carnival Adventures" (1885) and "False Accusation" (1889), a tragedy. He also wrote short stories and novels. He died suddenly on June 9, 1912 in Berlin. His body was returned to Bucharest and buried in Bellu Cemetery in Bucharest, not far from Eminescu's.

Eugène Ionesco (1909-1994)—Ionesco is one of the most prominent dramatic playwrights of the 20th century, known as an innovator of dramatic techniques and creator of the "Theatre of the Absurd." He was born in Slatina to a Romanian father and a French mother. Most of his childhood was spent in France, but during the 1920s he returned to Romania and attended the University of Bucharest. He was part of Bucharest's artistic, bohemian crowd, disgusted with the bourgeois conventions of post-WWI society. He returned to France in 1941, where he wrote *La Cantatrice Chauve* (*The Bald Prima Donna*) employing the themes of self-estrangement and the difficulty of communication. His plays combined farce and tragedy with surrealism, as they mocked and denounced bourgeois society and the mechanical nature of modern civilization. He followed with "*La Leçon*" ("The Lesson"), "*Les Chaises*" ("The Chairs"), "*Le Nouveau Locataire*" ("The New Tenant"), "*Le Roi se meurt*" ("Exit the King"), and "*La Soif et la Faim*" ("Thirst and Hunger"). His most famous play, "Rhinoceros," portrays a character trying to preserve his humanity in a world where humans are mutating into beasts. Ionesco's plays were banned in Romania during the Communist regime.

Writers

Ion Creangă (1837-1890)—Ion Creangă was Romania's most celebrated storyteller. He was born in the village of Humuleşti, near the ruin of Neamţ Castle, one of eight children of Ştefan of Petrei, the shoemaker, and his wife Smaranda. Self-described as "smart and nasty," he attended the church school until his mother sent him to her father David Creangă, who took him to Broşteni in Bistriţa valley to study. He later attended the Princely school in Târgu Neamţ, (his teacher became the hero of his story "Popa Duhu"). The school registered him as Ştefănescu Ion.

But his mother wanted him to become a priest, and in 1854 he was sent to the Catechist school in Fălticeni, the "priest factory" where his name was changed to Ion Creangă. When the school was abolished, Creangă went to Iaşi, where he lived and studied at the theological seminary "Veniamin Costachi." In 1859 he married Ileana, daughter of a priest from Iaşi and on December 26 he was ordained deacon at the "Sfânta Treime" church. In 1860 they had a son, Constantin.

After 12 years as a servant of the church, in 1872 he was expelled from the clergy for shooting crows that dirtied the Golia church roof and for having cut his hair like a civilian. Shortly thereafter, his wife left him. He remained a teacher for 25 years, co-authoring four school manuals, despite also being expelled from the educational system. (After 122 years, a decision was made in 1993 to reinstate Creangă as a deacon in the clergy.)

In 1873, after a long legal battle, Creangă won custody of his son Constantin, then 12, and moved into the *bojdeuca* (mud house) in Ţicău, a suburb of Iaşi, along with a housewife, Tinca Vartic. They lived together, unmarried, for the rest of his life.

In 1875, Creangă met Mihai Eminescu and they became close friends. The poet discovered Creangă's talent as a story teller and he convinced Creangă to write and introduced him to Junimea literary club. At 36, Creangă's first story, "*Soacra cu trei nurori*" was published in *Convorbiri literare*. This began his brilliant literary career, charming all generations of readers. The most famous of his many books is: "*Amintiri din copilărie*" ("Memories of my Childhood").

In 1883 Creangă became ill and wrote very little. He suffered epileptic seizures for six years (his mother had died from epilepsy). After learning that his friend, Eminescu, was also ill, his condition worsened. It got even worse after learning that his brother Mihai had died, and that a beloved friend of Eminescu's had poisoned herself at Văratec Monastery. After falling in front of his pupils and missing many classes, he checked into to Slănic Moldova for treatment.

Back in Iaşi on New Year's Eve 1889, his school children ran through streets reciting congratulation verse. Creangă joined the celebration, eating donuts and drinking brandy with a fellow teacher, and returned home with joyous wishes for a Happy New Year. But that very night he died.

His friend built him a coffin, but was unable get it out of the house. The coffin was too big, the doors too narrow. So they demolished the wall, and took him to Eternitatea cemetery, where he was buried on January 2, 1890. His little house in Ţicău is now open to visitors.

Mihai Eminescu (1850-1889)—Romania's greatest poet was born in Botoşani, the seventh of eleven children of Gheorghe and Raluca Eminovici. His father Gheorghe was a collector of duties on spirits and worked as bailiff on an estate in Dumbrăveni. Mihai spent his childhood in Botoşani and traveled with his parents to their Durneşti estate. He had a charmed childhood in Ipoteşti, but was later sent to the Austro-Hungarian empire, to attend the *National-Hauptschule*. He was homesick and did not do well, and ran away several times. In 1864 he joined a theater troupe and became its prompter, traveling with it on tour to Braşov. After that, he found work as a copyist in Botoşani County administration until March 1865.

He composed his first poem, "*La Mormântul lui Aron Pumnul*" in homage to his favorite teacher. When a poem about his first love was published, he changed his name from Eminovici to Eminescu. He traveled a lot on foot wearing torn boots, earned little money and lived in attics. But he read avidly, gathered folklore and wrote lyrics in the parks.

In 1869, he went to Vienna, where he enrolled in University where he was an extraordinary student, despite never having finished high school. He immersed himself in philosophy, law, economics, Roman languages, anatomy, and he wrote. In 1871, he met the beautiful Veronica Micle, on treatment in Vienna.

In 1872 Eminescu left Vienna and went to Iaşi, where he read his poem *Egipetul* and his short story *Sărmanul Dionis* at Junimea society. Impressed, the members of the society decided to support his studies at Humboldt University in Berlin;

but he left Berlin suddenly, without taking his exams and went to Königsberg (Braşov) to search through documents about Romanian history. In the summer of 1874 he returned to Iaşi without his doctorate title. Nevertheless, he was appointed director of the Central Library, and sworn in by Stefan Micle, the rector and husband of Veronica Micle. He began attending her literary evenings and fell in love with her.

In 1875 he met and began his longtime friendship with Ion Creangă. During this period he was a journalist at *Curierul de Iaşi*, but left the newspaper after a conflict with a staff member. He then left Iaşi to become a writer for the conservative newspaper *Timpul*. From the years 1876 to 1883 he created his greatest body of work: *Făt-Frumos din tei*, *Călin, Lacul, Dorinţa, Peste vârfuri* and his masterpieces: *Luceăfarul, Scrisorile*, and *Doina*.

His exhaustive work on the news articles and his poems, his disorderly life and his bohemian nature all contributed to his breakdown, which began with severe headaches in 1883. That summer, Eminescu declared that he wanted to learn the Albanian language and become a monk. Another time, he went to a Capşa coffee house, took out a revolver and cried out that the king must be shot because he is on the liberals' side. He once locked himself in a public bath for eight hours, allowing the water to overflow. Guards finally broke the door down and put him in a straitjacket. He was interned in the Sutu sanatorium in Bucharest. He was just 33 years old.

From then until his death, he would stay in a series of hospitals and madhouses, living off public charity and a life annuity. In November 1883 he

And If . . .

And if the branches tap my pane
And the poplars whisper nightly,
It is to make me dream again
I hold you to me tightly.

And if the stars shine on the pond
And light its sombre shoal,
It is to quench my mind's despond
And flood with peace my soul.

And if the clouds their tresses part
And does the moon outblaze,
It is but to remind my heart
I long for you always.

Mihai Eminescu
(Translated by Corneliu M. Popescu)

went to Vienna for a stay at OberDöbling Sanatorium. While there, the first edition of his poems was published.

Over the next six years Eminescu lived in Iaşi, and traveled in Italy and to the baths at Liman near Odessa. In 1886, he was interned in the madhouse at the Neamţ monastery, where Ion Creangă visited him. Upon returning to Botoşani, his paralytic sister Harieta tended him. In 1888 he left Botoşani for Bucharest, where Veronica Micle took him for medical care, and the following year he was again interned in Sutu sanatorium. To him, the stones there looked like diamonds, the leaves looked like money. He believed he was Voivode Matei Basarab. On June 15, 1889, a fellow patient hit him in the head with a stone, but his death came from an old endocarditis. Eminescu was buried in Bellu with national honors.

Painters

Nicolae Grigorescu (1838-1907)—Considered Romania's greatest painter, Nicolae Grigorescu was born to a poor family in the village of Pitaru in Dâmboviţa County. At age ten he began painting icons to help support his family. Later he was commissioned to paint the interior walls of the church of Agapia Monastery in Moldavia. Impressed by the young artist, Mihail Kogălniceanu helped him go to Paris to study art. Later he moved his studies to Barbizon near Fountainebleau. He developed into a skilled impressionist and worked with France's celebrated artists, Corot, Millet, and Courbet. Napoleon III purchased two of his paintings at an exhibition in 1867. Grigorescu briefly returned to Romania, but then traveled in Italy and Greece.

In 1877, Ion C. Brătianu called him back to Romania and commissioned him to paint scenes from the War for Independence. There, together with Theodor Aman, he founded the Romanian School of Art. Grigorescu's paintings include numerous portraits and scenes of rural life. He is called the "father of modern Romanian painting."

Ion Andreescu (1850-1882)—Romania's second most famous painter, Andreescu was born in Bucharest in 1869. He entered Theodor Aman's Fine Arts School and in 1872 he became a teacher of linear drawing and calligraphy at a school in Buzău. Toward the end of 1878 he went to Paris, where he took courses at the Julian Free Academy. Summers would be spent painting at Barbizon (where he met Nicolae Grigorescu) and elsewhere in the countryside. As a teacher of drawing in a small, repressive town, Andreescu feverishly took to painting. His passion found a release in his artwork. For a young man living alone, painting was a cry for dialogue and expression. His talent being fueled by strong feelings and attitudes, his art was introspective and strenuously self-asserting. In his painting, he used colors with a master's technical dexterity. But his life was uneventful, bordering on poverty, racked by illness and much too short. Nevertheless, he left behind a creative work not only extensive, but complete, mature and without a need for probing. Equally versatile in multiple painting genres, Andreescu painted landscapes, portraits and still life.

Ştefan Luchian (1868-1916)—This great painter was born in Ştefăneşti, Botoşani, amid vineyards on the Prut river banks and green river meadows. Inspired by the works of Grigorescu and Andreescu, he went to Bucharest to study at the Fine Arts School. Later he spent a year in Munich at the Academy of Fine Arts and two years in Paris at the Julian Academy. Back in Romania, he was a founder of the "*Ileana*" Artistic Society. After his participation in the 1892 Artistic Youth Exhibition, his reputation as a painter was well-established. Luchian painted with an impressionistic touch, concentrating on the intensities of light. His art portrays the simple joys of a drab everyday life. He painted landscapes and portraits, compositions and still life. His landscapes show picturesque nature scenes, but with human interaction. Painting flowers was one of his favorite occupations, as were compositions showing Romania country life around 1907, the year of peasants' uprisings. One of his paintings, "The Washing" (Lăutul, 1912), is a beautiful representation of how the painter could elicit strong emotion from a seemingly simple composition.

Sculptor

Constantin Brâncuşi (1876-1957)—Born in the peasant village of Hobiţa, in the southern province of Oltenia, the future sculptor left home at age eleven and found menial work in nearby Târgu Jiu. After five years, he moved to Craiova and enrolled in the School of Arts and Crafts, where he graduated with honors in 1898. Then he went to Bucharest, attended the School of Fine Arts and won several prizes for his work. After taking a year off to travel around Europe, Brâncuşi settled in Paris in 1904, where he studied at the École des Beaux Arts. There he mixed with Max Jacob, Apollinaire, Picasso and Modigliani. He worked in Rodin's sculpture studio for a while, but then moved on to develop his own style, which included simple shapes that held symbolic meaning.

Around 1908, Brâncuşi created his famous sculpture *The Kiss*, which resides in the Art Gallery of Craiova. In 1937 he was commissioned to create a memorial for the Romanians of Târgu Jiu who died defending the city against the Germans during World War I. The memorial consists of a ninety-eight foot tall column entitled the Column of Endless Gratitude, along with a Garden of Meditation in Parcul Tineretului, west of the town center. The column consists of an iron core with 15 steel "beads" stacked upward reaching 30 meters (98 ft.) high. Neglected and rusting, the column was almost destroyed during the Communist era; but in 1996 it was disassembled, refurbished and reassembled for Romania's 2001 designation of "Brâncuşi Year." Two other sculptures stand in a small park beside the Jiu River: his stone table, known as the Table of Silence (*Masa Tăcerii*) with its twelve hemispheric stools, and his travertine arch known as the Gate of the Kiss (*Poarta Sărutului*). Brâncuşi died in Paris. The traditional, three-room house of his birth in Hobita has been turned into a memorial house and is open to visitors from Tuesday–Sunday.

Architecture

The blending of eastern and western architectural influences in Romania has produced a distinctive design that has become uniquely Romanian.

The medieval architecture of Transylvania owes its western influence to the early Saxon settlers, craftsmen who built many fine cities and fortified churches. The most significant representations of the Gothic style are the 14th-15th-century Black Church in Braşov; the 14th-century Bran Castle in Braşov County; and the 15th-century Corvineşti Castle in Hunedoara. Also specific to Transylvania was the Saxon's unique style of town planning and the fortification of their cities. The city's layout was based on functionality, with a central square and church, surrounded by narrow streets of shops and houses linked by archways. The towns were protected from invaders by massive fortress walls with multiple bastions, each built by one of the town's trade guilds. The medieval cities of Sighişoara, Sibiu and Braşov are marvelous examples. Later architecture includes the characteristics of the Hungarian culture, as well as Germanic and Romanian styles.

The most unique architectural style belongs to the group of churches built throughout Moldavia under the rule of Stephen the Great (1457-1504). Of these, the graceful church of Neamţ Monastery became a paragon of Moldavian religious architecture, characterized by slender silhouettes, harmonious facades, and the picturesque roofs of folk inspiration. This synthesis was carried on during the next century, during the rule of Stephen the Great's son, Petru Rareş, the main innovation being the porch and the exterior wall painting (as on the churches of Voroneţ, Humor, Suceviţa and Moldoviţa monasteries).

The 17th century brought the development of elaborate lay constructions, such as the elegant boyars' mansions, the opulent princely palaces and the Renaissance-style castles in Transylvania. During this era, the Trei Ierarhi Monastery was built in Iaşi, a truly unique monument due to the lavishly carved geometric motifs, colored in lapis lazuli and golden foil, that cover its entire exterior. This architectural style developed in Wallachia under the reigns of Matei Basarab and Constantin Brâncoveanu. The distinctive Brâncovan style integrates both Baroque and Oriental features into the local tradition with lavish decoration of stone carvings, stucco work and paintings. Outstanding examples are the Horezu monastery in Oltenia and the princely palace of Mogoşoaia (Brâncoveanu's home).

The 18th century, during the Phanariot rule, brought elements of Oriental influence to Wallachia and Moldavia, primarily in their urban civil architecture. In Transylvania, the Baroque dominated both the religious (Roman Catholic churches in Timişoara and Oradea) and the lay architecture (Bánffy and Brukenthal palaces in Cluj and Sibiu, respectively).

The first half of the 19th century, with its rapid growth of urban life and a Western-type modernization policy, introduced a combination of Romantic and Neo-Classical elements. But in the second half of the century, there was a national reversion to the use of elements and forms from the old folk architecture. Ion Mincu (1852-1912) was the promoter of this trend and the founder of the Romanian school of architecture. His works, the Lahovary House or the Central Girls' School in Bucharest, are among the achievements of this movement.

Opposition to this trend, however, led to new administrative buildings being designed in the spirit of French eclecticism (the Palace of Justice, the Central Post Office) or Rococo (the House of the Men of Science or the Cantacuzino Palace in Bucharest). Such lavish styles inspired Bucharest's nickname "Little Paris." Other important architects, like Peter Antonescu (1873-1960), Horia Creangă (1893-1963) and Duiliu Marcu (1885-1966) rejected such elaborate adornments and opted for simple lines and functional forms.

By the early 20th century, the opulent downtown buildings of Romanian towns and cities contrasted sharply with their almost rural outskirts, while the villages remained—architecturally speaking—medieval. Shortly thereafter, the first signs of central town planning appeared in some urban districts, resulting in the first one-family houses on two levels, and the first two- and three-story apartment flats.

The forced industrialization and its resulting urban growth in the latter decades of the communist era, introduced a series of lackluster (if not outright hideous) architectural projects and pre-fabricated technology in the construction of huge blocks of residential flats, and a leveling of the traditional townscape. Simultaneous with the demolition of long-established urban centers and the replacing of picturesque rural settlements with drab block flats, was Ceauşescu's plan for building monumental public buildings of a dull neo-classical solemnity. The most profound example of this communistic architectural style is Ceauşescu's gigantic House of the People in Bucharest, now renamed the Parliament Palace, for which an entire section of the old city was destroyed.

Luckily, most of Romania's magnificent old buildings suffered only the ravages of neglect, rather than total destruction, and post-revolutionary Romania quickly got busy restoring them to their original grandeur.

Structure, Protocol, Formality

Structure—During the communist era, the 45 years prior to 1990, Romania was very much orientated on the collective manner. All property belonged to the State and all of the people had the same rights. The communist regime organized everything and the people were discouraged from taking initiative. Private businesses were forbidden because they were too individualistic and contradicted the collectivist system. Information was tightly controlled to prevent the public from thinking too broadly and forming educated ideas that might lead to dissent. Anyone who dared to express opposing ideas might be reported to the authorities as a potential rebel. As a result, Romanians focused all their energies on their families, whom they trusted.

Romanians are very closely attached to their families; even after a young couple gets married, the parents of either the husband or wife may live with the couple. Most Romanians over age 50 are not particularly interested in attaining status or financial riches, nor are they much interested in business. The saying "One works to live" fits them aptly, and time off from work is taken as often as possible. The country's low salaries and unpaid overtime likely influence their lethargic attitude towards work, but a lifetime with no control over their destiny surely has contributed. Under communism, a favorite saying was: "They pretend to pay us, and we pretend to work." It's a hard habit to break.

Today's younger generation of city dwellers, however, is becoming much more independent and self-reliant. They are excited about the opportunities that the new market economy has opened up. They are quickly learning the ways of free enterprise. Some work more than one job, while others try starting new businesses, willing to risk all they've got in hopes of achieving success. All this new ambition leaves little time to sit home with family, but Romania's future relies on this young, active generation.

Protocol—Another remnant of communism's heavy hand, and one that hinders the country's progress in both governmental reform and in business dealings, is the entrenched bureaucracy in Romania. This system serves as a control tactic that protects big shots from the working people, installs unqualified cronies in prominent positions, and bogs down progress by adhering to cumbersome procedures and creating unnecessary channels and paperwork that allow ideas and decisions to stagnate. But being all they've known during 45 years of communism, the people feel a strong need for predictability and rules. Thus, the inefficient rituals and protocols are held and adhered to, even if they make business development slower and more difficult. Proposing a new idea or more efficient method, however, could threaten the hierarchy and get a lower level worker fired. Clearly, style over substance is the rule here.

Romanian office relationships are also quite formal, especially toward older persons and any higher management position in the company. People are addressed formally (Mr. or Mrs. and surname), even within the same job level. It is considered impolite to address a business colleague by their first name, although higher management may use non-formal language with persons that are under them. Meetings also tend to be very protocol oriented; lower-level staff remaining quiet, while those in higher-level positions may be rather loud and quick with their opinions. Office communication is usually face-to-face or by telephone conversation; rarely do Romanians leave notes or e-mail or phone messages.

But these days, people are trying to make the system of laws easier and to cut down the bureaucracy. Young people are learning to "think outside the box," to question old standards and search for new and better ways to achieve goals. While recognition of the youthful, open mind certainly benefits business, it does cause some employment issues. For instance, most private businesses request an age range between 18 and 35 when hiring new personnel, leaving older workers with fewer job opportunities.

Another major change in recent years is the emancipation of Romanian women. These days many educated young women prefer building a career instead of doing household work. But women still encounter a substantial dose of chauvinism, particularly by men over 35. According to the Romanian Constitution and the new Romanian Labor Code in effect since March 1, 2003, "discrimination based on race, nationality, ethnic origin, language, religion, sex, opinion and political allegiance, wealth, or social background is forbidden." In practice, however, the Government has little interest in enforcing these provisions, and women and other minorities are still exposed to various forms of discrimination. The unemployment rate for women is higher than for men, and women occupy few influential positions. Being a woman in Romania is especially challenging because a woman must divide her time between her family (children, husband, home) and her profession. Romanian men are not prone to sharing household chores—yet.

Formality

There are a lot of rules regarding communication between people, such as showing respect for elders or superiors by not raising the tone of the voice while speaking with them; it's also considered impolite to use large hand gestures, to keep your hands in your pocket, or to have your arms crossed. In Romanian communication the message is often sent indirectly, through passive conversation based on suggestions through the use of metaphors. If the message was not understood correctly, however, a direct conversation would be held. Eye contact between people is also important to Romanians, who believe that, "the eyes are the window to the soul." To not look directly at the person with whom you are talking is deemed disrespectful and also suggests that you are hiding something, or even lying. On the other hand, it's not considered rude to ask personal questions, if asked politely. Romanians normally ask how old you are, how much you weigh, whether you are married, how much money you make and how much things cost. To Americans, this is considered extremely rude and inappropriate, no matter how politely one asks. It is disrespectful, rude and impolite to make a person wait longer than 15 minutes—anywhere.

In Romania, personal space is minimal. It is quite normal for two persons to stand very close to one another. It is also normal to see women walking arm-in-arm with one another. Romanians, being of Latin descent, like to spread kisses around, and it is common to see two men, after greeting by shaking hands, kiss each other once on each cheek. It is also considered an act of courtesy for a man to kiss a woman's hand when they are introduced to each other. Such a man would be thought of as well-educated and of high class. Women can also initiate a kiss on the cheek to another woman or to a man, if they know each other, in a simple, friendly gesture.

Private space such as property, however, is considered very important. Romanians are protective of their private space, and guests in a Romanian home should not go looking around the house without being invited to, or accompanied by their host.

Even in the most informal situations, Romanians always expect good behavior and manners, a certain formality in gestures, stature positions, and language, as well as servitude. This may present a huge challenge to Americans and other westerners for whom equality and efficiency are more important than hierarchy and ceremony.

Romanian Folklore: Superstitions and Traditions

Romanians are a very traditional and superstitious people. Vestiges of their Thracian-Dacian origins date back to the 7th century BC, and the myths and traditions accumulated since then were passed down through generations and still exist today. These include family customs, religious rituals and many myths and superstitions. The most well-known, of course, is that of the vampire.

Vampires

Dracula is not the only vampire haunting Romania. In fact, he is not a vampire at all, but rather an esteemed, albeit cruel, national hero. Nevertheless, Romanians do believe in the roamings of the undead. A real vampire is one who physically returns from the dead, leaving its tomb at only night to suck the blood of mortals in order to extend its posthumous existence, and must return to its tomb before the cock crows. Its victims, drained of blood, will become vampires after their own deaths and also rise at night in search of blood. Vampires fear holy water—since sacred water is the source of life—as well as the symbol of the cross. The fear of vampires was at its height during the early 1700s, provoked by two infamous cases, a Hungarian named Peter Plogojowitz and a Frenchman named Arnold Paole, whose stories spread throughout France, Germany, and the Austrian empire.

Anyone might become a vampire after death, but certain people are believed to be more susceptible, victims of violent death, the stillborn, suicides, witches, and those who were excommunicated or did not have a Christian burial. People born with red hair, very dark eyes or very clear blue eyes, and those born with teeth or with spots on their bodies are believed especially vulnerable. When such people died, certain precautions had to be taken before their burial to prevent them from rising from the dead: in Romania, a nail was driven into a corpse's forehead or the body would be pierced with needles; or to prevent the body from leaving its tomb, it was nailed to the bottom of the coffin. To block the soul of an alleged vampire from rejoining its body, a clove of garlic would be placed in its mouth. The execution of these rituals is referred to in Romania as the "great reparation." The popular conception of garlic as a useful protection against vampires is specific to Romania; strings of garlic would be hung in every room, and garlic was rubbed on the doors, windows, chimneys and keyholes.

The rationalism of the Enlightenment in the 18th century diminished the legend of the vampire, but it could not totally banish it from one's imagination. A Romantic rebellion against this new atmosphere of material positivism, and a nostalgia for an intriguing and magical past, soon revitalized the vampire through new literature. Thus, some Romanians still practice rituals to protect themselves and their families from a return of the undead.

Superstitions

A belief in mystical powers nourishes people's need for some control over their life and their reality. In Romania, the ancient myths and superstitions of ancestors are passed on from generation to generation through the retelling of old tales of ghosts, apparitions, witches and werewolves. Many people, especially the secular, who don't surrender their minds fully to the church, struggle with fatalism and superstitions. If a simple gesture—or the avoidance of such—can prevent or assure a turn of luck, one feels a bit of control over a situation. Some of the many common superstitions in Romania are:

- If someone spills salt on a table, it means that he or she will get into trouble, a fight or an argument; the person must put a bit of the spilt salt on their forehead to receive protection.
- If a matchbox is dropped, that means good luck.
- If you drop a fork on the floor, a man will visit you; if you drop a spoon, a woman will visit you.
- On a person's birthday cake, an extra candle is added for the next year to come.
- Two siblings getting married in the same year will bring death to one of them.
- A mother should not attend her child's baptism because of bad luck.

Some other Romanian superstitions about dreams are:

- If you fall asleep while counting, you will dream something.
- All dreams between Saturday and Sunday will come true.
- In order to stop dreaming, don't tell anyone your dreams.
- If someone dreams they are flying, they will grow in honor.
- If you dream about beating someone, you will have guests.
- It is said that if you tell someone your dream, it will come true.
- The snake in dreams shows wind; the fish, rain; the eggs show snow.
- When you wake up, do not look out of the window, or you will forget the dreams.
- If someone dreams he/she is crying, he/she will be happy.
- Dreaming about ploughland, new graves, turbid waters, non-burning candles, slaughtered cows or people in mourning anticipates death.

White and black magic are also still widely practiced in Romania. Many people believe that witches can tell the future, cure illnesses and bad habits, cast love-spells and even cause death. Often, particularly in isolated villages, people will go to a witch before they go see a doctor; but it's not only in villages that witches are consulted.

In urban areas, as well, gypsy women are known for their skill in witchcraft, and they make good money from it. Many of the people who visit witches are young girls in search of their true love; but adults also go for all sorts of different reasons. Many witches pretend that, besides "reading" the future in playing cards, they can also breakup marriages, cast spells and even cure alcoholism. There is no shame to visiting a witch in Romania; although, like a doctor's appointment, it's not a thing people want to broadcast publicly.

Traditions

All of Romania's traditions and holidays are founded on either family-based customs, calendar-based customs or religious customs, and are marked by the three major life changes: Birth, Marriage and Death. Some of these holidays are celebrated throughout the whole country; while others are unique to specific regions of the country. Nevertheless, they have common threads running through them.

The focus of most Romanian spirituality is found in each village. Rural Romanians traditionally were (and still are) farmers, who worked the land, kept vineyards, raised cattle or lived as shepherds. Each village still functions in harmony with its natural environment. Traveling throughout rural Romania, you may notice how one county's villages vary from another's. Each embodies the cultural influences of their particular location and the natural landscape surrounding their village. Villagers are steadfast observers of the feasts for the earth, their cattle, the flowers and crops, and of living.

This same unity can be found in the traditions and customs throughout the country, including the Christian holidays. Since

Romania is mainly an Eastern Orthodox country, this form of Christianity permeates the spirit of the holidays, with other themes, such as the seasons or common trades, being blended within the religious themes.

Family-based Traditions

Birth—A birth signifies its own customs. During pregnancy, a prospective mother must observe some interdictions that will protect the baby from supposed evil spirits. The birth itself represents the transition from the unknown to the known world or from the "blackness" to the "whiteness."

The ceremony of the "first bath" is one of the most important Romanian traditions. Only the women can assist in the bathing of the newborn child, and the oldest woman related to the father of the baby is in charge of the event. Fresh, clean water enriched with flowers, money, honey and milk are thought to purify and join the newborn to the family. The elder woman gives the cleansed baby to the mother with wishes for the child's moral, spiritual and physical integrity. She wishes for the child to marry, to be good-looking and healthy, to be respectful of his or her parents and to be a patient person. She wishes that the child thrives, grows to maturity, and becomes hard-working.

The second important moment related to birth is the Christening, a ceremony in which the child is named. In the Eastern Orthodox church, the spiritual parents, or "Godparents" of the child have an important ceremonial function. Usually, the child will be named after the Godfather, or after a close family member. Later, the Godparents will play an important role in the wedding ceremony of the child.

Weddings—According to Romanian tradition, prior to a marriage is the betrothal, which is followed by a long process of acceptance towards the prospective couple by those already married. A wedding is a performance with well-established rituals. Poetry, song, dance and ceremonial costumes all play a detailed role in the wedding ceremony.

The ceremony begins when the spokesman of the bridegroom comes to the bride's home to woo her. During this time, the best men go throughout the village inviting the relatives and friends to the wedding. Then, before closed gates guarded by the bride's relatives, the bridegroom's best man tells the story of a young emperor who gathered a great army and went hunting. While hunting, he saw a fairy and sent his warriors to look for her. Following the fairy's trail, they arrive at the bride's house. They were told that there is a certain flower in the garden that cannot bear fruit because of the unsuitable soil in which it grows. The warriors came to pick the flower and plant it in the young emperor's garden. There, the soil was known to be good and provide the nutrients enabling the flower to bear fruit.

In Bihor, in western Transylvania, the bridegroom must also pass a test of cleverness by solving a series of riddles in order to prove that he is able to be part of the married community.

For her wedding, the bride wears a ceremonial costume and flowers in her hair. During the ceremony, songs are performed by musicians. A varied melody is "*A miresei*" (of the bride), sung either at the solemn moment when the bride takes leave of her parents and her home, or when she changes her maiden head-gear for that of a wife. (The entrance of the bride into the community of married women is marked by a change of her hair style and the covering of her head with a scarf, the symbol of a married woman.)

The wedding meal provides an opportunity for singing, dancing and listening to epic hero songs. Dancing is an essential part of the wedding. One dance, the "hora," marks the decisive moments of the ceremony—the seal of the marriage contract. Traditional weddings last for three days. The final day ends with a "dance of masks."

Funerals—Romanians believe that for each man, there exists a star and a tree. The falling of the star marks the death of a person. The fir, the tree of life, is placed at the head on the grave of a deceased person. The fir is brought from the forest by a group of young men, who are met at the entrance of the village by a group of women. The women sing the song "*Cântecul bradului*" ("The Song of the Pine") about the link of the man with the tree of life, and of lament of the fir-tree who complains that it believed it would be used in the building of a house, when instead, it will be left to wither at the head of the grave of the deceased person.

Another funeral custom is the Dawn Song, or Great Song. It is sung by an appointed group of old women at the dawn of the two days between a death and a funeral and announces the death to the village. Their faces turned eastward, sometimes with lighted candles in their hands, the group implores the dawn to delay its coming until "the sweet wanderer" will get everything he needs ready for the long journey he undertakes. This song advises the dead person and describes the journey that he or she will make into the land of their ancestors. (In northern Moldavia and Transylvania, death is announced to the village by the sound of alphorns.)

Preparation of the funeral consists of greeting the relatives, making the funeral objects, such as the coffin, the veil that will cover the body, the funeral candle and the carriage with bulls, as well as the preparation of food for relatives and friends after the funeral. Throughout the preparations, there is a wake for the deceased. The body is never left alone, and those at the wake tell stories about the deceased. A group of old women mourn the body as well.

The most important burial songs are the *bocete* (dirges), sung by female relations and close friends of the dead. They are "a melodic overflow of sorrow" at the dead person's bedside, in the yard, on the road, in the church-yard during the burial and subsequently on certain dates destined for the commemoration of the dead.

The Calendar-based Holidays & Festivals

The calendar-based holidays are divided by the four seasons. Winter is designated as the season of rest, gatherings and spiritual expressions. Spring represents the rejuvenation of nature and the beginning of the farming season. It is the season of birth and blooming. Summer is dominated by the busy farming season. Fall is the season of wealth, the harvest and beginning preparations for the long winter ahead.

Spring Holidays

The Plowman is a celebration of the man who first plows the fields in the spring. Celebrated by song and dance, it represents hope at the end of winter and the beginning of a new and prosperous year.

The first day of March is the celebration of ***Mărtişor*** (mar-tsi-shor), a day when gifts of small objects—plants, shells, flowers, animals, snowmen or tools, and a red and white ribbon symbolizing life and purity—are given to young girls and women. It is believed that the gifts bring good luck during the month of March and throughout the year ahead. Mărtişor signifies the end of winter and the arrival of spring.

In the Orthodox faith, if a person is named after a saint, it is customary to celebrate on the anniversary of their respective saint's feast day. Those people whose names have no religious meaning celebrate on March 9 by enjoying some traditional cookies. The Sunday before Easter Sunday is called *Flowers' Sunday*. On that day, a special celebration takes place for all who have names associated with flowers. A fish meal is eaten on that day.

Easter is the second largest religious celebration in Romania. A six-week fast precedes the holiday, and the rituals of traditional food preparation resemble those of Christmas. The egg represents the miracle of creation. A ritual coloring of the eggs takes place to express this symbolism. The first egg colored for Easter belongs to the children and it must be colored red. It is placed in the children's room to protect them from evil. The second egg is colored blue, representing the "love of young women" and is meant to bring good luck in marriage. On the first day of Easter, one egg is placed in a pot of water, along with a silver coin and some fresh basil. All household members will wash their faces with this water. Easter Mass takes place at midnight, preceeded by a candle-lit procession to the church. Easter Eve is marked by total fasting and the first Easter meal takes place that night, following the Mass. Lamb, feta cheese, colored eggs and cheesecake are part of every Easter dinner.

Another Spring tradition celebrates the shepherds as they head for the mountains. All villagers who plan to send their sheep to the mountains with the shepherds gather on a particular Sunday. Each person milks a sheep, and afterward a meal, songs and dances take place.

Summer Holidays & Festivals

Drăgaica (or ***Sânzienele***) is an important Midsummer Day festival and fair which takes place on the 24th of June, when a specific Romanian lively folk dance is performed. When the harvest is almost ripe, the girls from the village gather together to choose Drăgaica. This is the name given to the most beautiful and hard-working peasant girl who is selected to lead the dance. A procession is formed, sweeping through the fields. A wreath is plaited of grain stalks and put on Drăgaica's head. The practice has auspicious and benefic functions.

To the tune of a lad playing the flute or the bagpipe, the girls dance a jig from house to house, while singing ironic verse: "*Jig, Drăgaica, jig/For in winter you will spin/Till your fingers will grow thin.*" Drăgaica or the procession of lasses is an agrarian midsummer custom in preparation for reaping.

Summer, a season of intensive field work, has relatively few traditional customs taking place. ***Paparuda*** is an augural agrarian custom concerned with preventing drought. A little girl clad in a dress made of leaves or shoots of willow goes dancing and singing a rain-invocation through the village lanes, together with other children, until an older woman comes along and sprinkles the Paparuda with cold water. The incantation should release rain and save the harvest. "*Paparuda, Paparuda,/ Come and sprinkle water,/Sprinkle from a pail/Until we cry hail./Let the rain pour down/ From dusk till dawn.*"

Fairs occur during the summer, including the well-known **Maiden's Fair on Găina Mountain** in Hunedoara County. This is a traditional festival where villagers don traditional costumes and walk up the mountain for dancing and feasting. The fair has a dual purpose: as a time for the exchange of goods, and as an opportunity for match-making between young maidens and men. The chance to meet and fall in love at a fair was a highly anticipated event each year.

Caloianul, Romanian Rainmaker, is a figure used in Romanian villages' rainmaking rite. In summertime, women and children from the dry regions model this "Caloian." He looks like a man and is adorned with flowers. Everybody gathers at the border of the village and together they adorn a young tree. They use fresh fruit, pretzels and candies. Afterward the group simulates the funeral of the "Caloian." First they walk him over the dry fields. Throughout the procession, the children and women cry and mourn, and the village priest says prayers for invoking the rain. At the end they bury the "Caloian" by throwing it into a river. The waters of the river must carry it far away, thus bringing rains. In some regions, dancing and singing accompany this ritual. On several occasions the invoked rain appears a day or two after this ritual. The popular belief is that only the "Caloian" can unfastened the rains.

Autumn Festivals

Harvest time also celebrates Romanian wine-making. Since 1992, the **International Festival of Vineyard and Wine** has been held in the Vrancea region, the first winemaking region of Romania. It celebrates local wines and helps wine makers take advantage of the country's new commercial opportunities. This event has become increasingly popular each year with over 252 types of wine from 28 producers participating. The festival offers several programs, such as the Showroom of Vineyard and Wine, a specialized information session for wine producing and viticulture activities, and cultural events with a vineyard theme, such as painting exhibitions, folk concerts, book launches, poetry and limericks contests. It is held during the last 10 days of October.

Winter Holidays & Festivals

Winter brings an abundance of music festivals and customs. The Christmas and New Year celebrations become merged, and elements of the Christian faith are blended with traditional hopes for a prosperous New Year. These customs originated with the ancient ancestors of the Romanians.

Saint Nicholas Day, when Old Saint Nicholas arrives in Romania every year on the 6th of December, announces the beginning of the winter holidays. On the evening of December 5th, people put their newly polished boots near the entrance door, waiting for presents. Saint Nicholas takes care of each member of the family, putting a little present into everyone's boots. This custom is very old in Romania, and Saint Nicholas Day is one of the most important festivals of the year, especially for the children.

The winter solstice, "the birthday of the invincible Sun," had been celebrated for centuries with songs and dances, greetings, presents and wishes of prosperity. Later, the feast of the Christian Christmas was established at this same time of the year. The clergy have long struggled to abolish the old pagan customs and replace them with religious ones, but their efforts have failed. They did succeed in adopting a series of religious songs, the *Cântece de Stea* (Star-songs), and nativity plays that have been incorporated into holiday celebrations, but the traditional Romanian songs and customs have proved too strong to suppress.

These customs begin on Christmas and last until Epiphany. The most important is ***colindatul*** (the carolling). Carollers go from house to house and sing ancient songs of greeting, called "*colinde*" (carols) at the windows. The true aim of the carols is to greet and to praise in an allegoric way those to whom they are sung. But the religious *Steaua* (Star-songs) have joined the celebration, with groups of children who carry a star made of wood and colored paper, and adorned by gold and silver tinsel, representing the star that guided the Magi to the manger of Bethlehem. These children sing the Star-songs, poetical carols inspired by the scriptures.

New Year's Eve is animated by colorful pageants, some specific to a particular region. Costumes, songs and dances all contribute to these happy traditions that bring together groups of children and teenagers who go from house to house wishing everybody a bountiful new year, and peace and prosperity. The children, who symbolize purity and hope, usually receive apples, nuts and home-baked bread. There are several unique customs involved in the celebration of the New Year.

Sorcova is a bouquet made of fruit-tree branches (apple, pear, cherry, or plum tree) that are put into water in a warm place on November 30th, in order to bud and blossom on New Year's Eve. Children wish the people a Happy New Year while touching them lightly with this bouquet.

Pluguşorul (the little plough), a ritual common around the country, comes from ancient times when farmers dedicated the fruits of their labor to their gods in gratitude for their benevolence. Today it is a traditional procession on New Years' Day with a decorated plough. The "ploughmen" are teenagers and children carrying whips, bells and pipes. A recitation of verse representing the work of the field, from the ploughing to the kneading and baking of rolls of pure cornflower is intoned against a background of sounds produced by the bellowing of a friction drum called *buhai* (bull) and the melody of the pipes and bells.

Among the masked dances performed during the winter feast, the most remarkable is *Capra* (the Goat), emblem of fecundity. This custom, whose magical significance has been lost over the course of time, consists of a dance by a masked man who represents a goat or a stag. The muzzle of the mask is made of two pieces of wood covered with hare-skin. A noisy group of children accompany the mask. The goat jumps, jerks, bends and turns, clattering the wooden jaws. This celebration is famous for its originality of costumes and for the "animal's" choreography.

For all Romanian celebrations, song is an essential component. The songs reveal all sides of the Romanians' sensitive hearts. There are the *Doinele*, songs of sorrow, melancholy, love or rebellion that evoke either a longing for loved ones, or social injustice. Romanian ballads, or epic songs, represent various human experiences. They may describe such events as the sunrise, or historical events, heroism, or the death of freedom fighters. Occasionally they involve the trades of the people. Love songs, lullabies and party songs are also part of Romanian folklore.

The Handicrafts of Romania

While Romania has many fine artists, the real zest for life here is best expressed in the traditional arts and crafts of its peasants. Their beautiful and durable products are crafted by the same methods their ancestors used: hand-woven and dyed threads, exquisite hand-sewn embroideries, fabrics and rugs woven on home-made looms, hand-thrown pottery, blown glassware, and festival masks made from all manner of natural elements.

Ceramics—Most Romanian pottery is still made on traditional kick-wheels with simple finishing tools. Their shapes, sizes colors and patterns are unique to the different clays, cultures and regions where they are produced. Colored glazes and decorative motifs vary from strong geometrics to delicate florals, animals and humans. There are about 30 pottery centers throughout Romania, each producing wares in its own distinctive style, but the main ceramics areas are Horezu in Oltenia, Corund in eastern Transylvania and Rădăuţi and Marginea in Moldavia.

Embroidery—The elaborate needlework on folk costumes worn for holidays and special occasions follows strict regional patterns. Sibiu uses black and white graphic motifs, reflecting its Saxon heritage; the southern regions of Argeş, Muscel, Dâmboviţa and Prahova use red, black, maroon, yellow, gold, and silver threads, reflecting influences of the Ottoman Empire. Buzău's color is terracotta; Oaş uses green, and Moldavia combines orange with the Voroneţ-blue made famous by the exterior paintings of its Voroneţ monastery. Especially beautiful is cut embroidery on white or ecru linen and cotton, sewn throughout the country. The embroidered peasant blouses and skirts are made of cocoon silk, cotton or linens; sheepskin waistcoats also bear decorative embroideries. A wonderful place to view this extraordinary needlework on traditional costumes is in Bucharest's **Museum of the Romanian Peasant**, *Muzeul Ţăranului Roman*.

Glass—The oldest preserved Romanian glass dates back to the Roman Empire. Currently, there is a renewed passion for creating art in blown glass and several contemporary Romanian glass artists enjoy world renown. Most of the professional glass artists are clustered in the northeast, near Botoşani. Glass artisans are also employed in factories located in Avrig, Turda and Buzău, turning out molded, hand-carved and hand-blown pieces, many of which are museum quality. But you can also find glass-blowers tucked into a workshop in Bucharest's historical district, on Strada Şelari, between Strada Iuliu Maniu and Strada Lipscani; the street is lined with glassware galleries.

Festival Masks—Elaborate and rather grotesque masks are linked to folk festivals held predominantly in Maramureş and Moldavia. Typically made from the hides of sheep, goats or cows, the masks are decorated with fabric, feathers, beans, straw hats, and animal horns to represent bears and goats. They are traditionally worn to welcome in the New Year during the winter festivals.

Painted Eggs—The painted eggs of Moldavia may be the most recognizable examples of Romanian folk art. The painting of hollowed-out eggs has always been an integral part of preparations for the Eastertime festival of renewal and rebirth. Women and children would gather in a home and spend the day painting intricate designs, said to be secret languages known only to residents of the regions where they are painted. The original decorated eggs were painted with aqua fortis (nitric acid) on a traditional red background. Today, the multicolored eggs can be purchased in many shops and street markets.

Textiles—Textile weaving is the most widespread craft in Romania, handed down from generation to generation using distinctive family patterns, mingled with motifs specific to different provinces. Looms are still common fixtures in homes and women weave and embroider from childhood through old age. Wool and cotton are woven into rugs, wall hangings, table covers and clothing. Some Romanian weavers and embroiderers still produce their own threads and yarns, but the younger ones usually purchase their raw materials. They weave and embroider just about every cloth article used in their homes, from colorful linen and cotton towels, to window draperies, bedspreads, rugs, wall hangings, furniture throws and clothing.

At the edge of the outdoor market adjacent to Bran Castle, there is a peasant cottage with a window, behind which sits an old woman at her loom, weaving and watching the passing scene. She'll invite interested visitors into her home, where her English-speaking daughter will explain that she's in her seventies and has been weaving since she was seven years old. She still weaves with thread she spins herself from sheep her family keeps in their tiny enclosed courtyard. On display in her tiny weaving room, which is also her bedroom, is a selection of magnificent throws and spreads that she has woven. Not for sale, they are priceless examples of this enduring way of life.

In the village of Botiza in Maramureş, lives *Doamna* (Mrs.) Berbecău, the woman who revived the traditional natural color dyes used on spun wool. There you may also be able to see a local weaver hard at work on her traditional loom.

Rugs—Romania's hand-made rugs vary as dramatically as the regions of their origin. Most are flat-weave kilims, introduced centuries ago by the Ottoman Empire. But today's hand-weavers mix the traditional vegetable-dyed yarns with commercial aniline-dyed yarns to produce vibrant accents within the traditional patterns and colors. Rugs from Oltenia are characterized by their bright colors, red and blue predominating, and their nature designs of flowers, trees and birds. Those from Moldavia have more subdued coloring, woven in patterns of little branches to create a "Tree of Life." Rugs from Maramureş tend to have geometric shapes, resembling those from Turkey and the Caucasian mountains.

Wood—Maramureş is the best place to see the fine art of Romanian woodwork. The local houses are trimmed in elaborately carved designs, and their tall wooden gates display carved decorations in complex patterns that hold meanings beyond the purely decorative; their "trees of life," twisted rope, moons, stars, flowers and wolf teeth are all associated with ancient myths and superstitions. Historically, in this region, a family's community status was displayed through their gate—the more elaborate, the more important the family.

The ageless techniques and designs in wood have been cherished and preserved with their regional variations for centuries. These skilled artisans also create decorative household items such as spoons, kitchen wares, cupboards, keepsake chests, and furniture, as well as walking sticks and even musical instruments like flutes, fiddles and shepherd's pipes.

Another wonderful example of Maramureş wood carving is the "**Merry Cemetery**" of Săpânţa, near Sighetul Marmaţiei, where the grave markers portray fanciful carved scenes and anecdotal verses (in Romanian) about the deceased. It's open all year and is well worth a visit, as there is nothing quite like it in the world. More about Romanian cultural is available at the Institute for Cultural Memory (CIMEC) website: http://cimec.ro/e_default.htm.

Gastronomy

Romanians have long done without all of the international ingredients that we in the West have at our disposal. Cut off from the outside world during the Soviet years, they had to rely on their own home-grown meats, vegetables, fruits, grains and dairy products. Nevertheless, their food is hearty and quite delicious. The prevelant meat is pork, although beef and chicken dishes are also available. The national dish, called ***sarmale***, are rolls of minced meats, rice and onions stuffed into cabbage or vine leaf wraps and cooked in broth on a bed of tomatoes. During the Lenten fast (called *Post*) when the eating of animal products is forbidden, a vegetarian filling made of mushrooms, rice, onions, carrots and walnuts is substituted for the usual meat sarmale.

Another local favorite is ***mămăliga,*** a heavenly (and heavy) corn meal polenta, which may be served in a variety of ways, though usually as a side dish with creamy smântână on top, or with cheese or bacon, or with a hot pepper buried within its mound.

Tangy soup broths, called ***supă*** or ***ciorbă*** (pronounced chorba) are always popular, and are generally served after the starter course and followed by cheese and a salad. ***Borş*** (pronounced borsh, but not the Russian beet soup) is a sour soup made from a wheat-bran stock of the same name. Variations of borş are: Bukovina's borş de sfeclă, a beetroot borş, which includes vegetables, herbs and a dab of smântână (sour crème); Danube Delta's borş de peşte, a delicious fish soup; and Transylvania's supă de păstăi made with beans and paprika.

A favorite of Romanians are the spicy, sausage-shaped patties called ***mititei*** (wee ones). These small ground meat skinless sausages are grilled over charcoal and best eaten with a hunk of fresh bread and some mustard and accompanied by beer. You'll find them at any outdoor gathering or festival, as well as in restaurants.

A traditional Romanian breakfast consists of sliced cold meats (ham and salami), one or two kinds of cheese, ripe tomato wedges and fresh round bread. Hard-boiled eggs often accompany the meal, and hotels now often provide omelets, as well. Coffee—either Turkish-style or Western—completes the meal.

It must be said that, because Romanian produce is always farm fresh and contains no preservatives, it is far more delicious than any to be found in American supermarkets. Of course, these days foreign investment in restaurants has brought food from around the world to Romania (including many McDonalds), but they are found mainly in the cities. Still, you would be well served to try the local fare!

Romanian Wines

Romanians have been producing exceptional wines for thousands of years. The main winegrowing regions are: Moldavia (red and white wines), Dobrogea (red and white), Transylvania (white), and Muntenia (principally red) and Oltenia (red and white) provinces. Maramureş (white), Crişana (red and white) and the Banat (principally red) have fewer vineyards, but their wines are of equally fine quality.

Moldavia's ***Cotnari*** vineyard was making wine for Stephen the Great in the 15th century. Stephen commissioned bridges and paved roads for wine transport, as well as deep cellars to keep it nice and cool. The leading wine of the vineyard, *Grasa de Cotnari*, is described as having the bitterish taste of a nutshell and a strong flavor; it is an excellent wine, whose aging enhances its noble qualities. At the World Exhibition in Paris in 1900, *Grasa de Cotnari* was awarded the gold medal; it has since acquired the name "Romania's Bloom."

Huşi vineyard is known for its flavored high quality wines, among which *Busuioaca de Bohotin*, of a traditional Romanian stock, holds pride of place. Varieties of regional table wine are *Zghihara de Huşi*, *Aligoté*, *Feteasca regală*, and the higher quality white wines *Feteasca Alba* and Italian Riesling. Other red table wines include Băbeasca Neagră and Porto; higher quality red wines are *Feteasca Neagră*, Cabernet Sauvignon and Merlot.

Odobeşti vineyard, near Focşani, is one of the largest and oldest in Romania. It is renowned for its table wines from traditional Romanian varieties, like *Galbena de Odobeşti*, *Plavaie* and *Feteasca regală*. Vine-growers in the area have drawn old distillates of varieties like *Mustoasa de Maderat*, *Feteasca regală* and *Galbena de Odobeşti*.

Transylvania's vineyards are mainly on the slopes of the Târnava Mica and Târnava Mare rivers.

Târnave vineyards produce white wines with a fragrance of pine resin and lime blossom, and the transparency and sweetness of acacia honey. It is known for its Feteasca Alba, Pinot Gris, Traminer Rosé and Sauvignon (dry or medium). It also produces flavored wines of the Muscat Ottonel type and sparkling wines like Feteasca Regala, Feteasca Alba and Italian Riesling. The vineyard has won over 100 gold medals.

Alba Iulia vineyard has been known since the 1st century B.C. Its old cellars have catacombs designed for grape processing and wine depositing, and are a tourist highlight. Alba Iulia vineyard produces Fetească Alba, Furmint, Traminer, Grasa, Riesling, Sauvignon, Pinot Gris and Muscat Ottonel. These pleasant, golden yellow wines are light and slightly soft.

At ***Sebeş-Apold*** vineyard, the bulk of production is in the sparkling wines, Feteasca Alba, Feteasca Regala, but it also produces Sauvignon Blanc, Pinot Gris, Furmint, and Muscat Ottonel.

Wallachia's ancient vineyards have produced many award-winning vintages. ***Dealu Mare*** vineyard, stretching 70 km (44 miles) across Buzău and Prahova counties, is the cradle of the red wines, whose special taste and flavor are credited to its local soil and climate. Its vines yield high quality red wines like

Feteasca Neagră, Burgund Mare, Merlot, Pinot Noir, Cabernet Sauvignon, as well as high quality white wines, i.e. Feteasca Alba, Feteasca Neagră, Feteasca Regala, Pinot Gris and Muscat Ottonel. (Dealu Mare's *Premiat* label can be found in selected wine shops in New York City and around the USA.)

Muntenia's wine-growing center of ***Pietroasa*** deserves special mention; its Tămâioasa Românească wines have been awarded many gold medals at both Romanian and world competitions.

Stefăneşti vineyard is 10 km (6 miles) from the town of Piteşti. First mentioned in 330 BC in a writing of Greek historian Diodorus Siculus, the vineyard was also referred to in several medieval chronicles of Wallachia since 1388. It mainly produces high quality white wines like Feteasca Alba, Sauvignon, Italian Riesling, and the red wines Fetească Neagră, Cabernet Sauvignon, Merlot and Burgund Mare, as well as flavored wines like Tămâioasa Românească and Muscat Ottonel.

Sâmbureşti vineyard is situated in a hilly area in the south of the country and is known for its Cabernet Sauvignon, Fetească Neagră, Pinot Noir and Merlot. The Sâmbureşti Cabernet stands out for its strength and color, as well as by its pleasant taste and flavor.

The ***Drăgăşani*** vineyard's history can be traced back to the Geto-Dacians, who lived in the Olt river valley some three thousands years ago. Tonic, slightly frothy, with a long-lasting flavor, they acquired world recognition at the wine competitions in Bordeaux (1898) and at the World Exhibition in Paris (1900), being awarded an Honorary Diploma and a Gold Medal, respectively.

The ***Segarcea*** vineyard, also in Oltenia, is near the city of Craiova. It is a smaller vineyard, but its local soil and climate allow the production of high quality red wines like Pinot Noir, Merlot, Burgund Mare, Cabernet Sauvignon, as well as white wines. Segarcea vineyard is also known for its golden and pink Chasselas, Muscat Hamburg and Muscat de Adda table grapes.

In **Dobrudja**, the ***Murfatlar*** vineyards are one of Romania's finest wine producers. Its vineyard was first mentioned in the writings of the Latin poet Ovid, but was officially acknowledged since 1907. Vine growing has always been a major occupation in this area. The vineyard is renowned for its sweet wines made of grapes with a high sugar content, because they are reaped after they have already dried up. Wines produced by the Murfatlar vineyard include Pinot Gris, Sauvignon, Italian Riesling, Chardonnay, Muscat Ottonel, Pinot Noir, Merlot, and Cabernet Sauvignon. The Murfatlar vintage has been awarded more than 350 gold medals over the last 15 years at international competitions. (www.murfatlarwinery.com)

Ostrov vineyard, outside Călăraşi, at Romania's border with Bulgaria, specializes in table wines and high quality red wines like Burgund mare, Merlot, Pinot Noir, Cabernet Sauvignon. The Ostrov wines do not differ much from the Murfatlar ones, and have been awarded gold and silver medals.

The ***Sarica-Niculiţel*** vineyard is in northern Tulcea County and is renowned for its red wines, but its white wine Aligoté is considered to be the best of its kind in the country. Dry, strong and properly acidulated, it has a pleasant taste and a special bouquet.

Several tourism companies offer regional **vineyard tours**, with wine-tasting and overnight accommodation. One such is Cultural Romtour, with English and German-speaking guides; www.culturalromtour.com. (See Appendix for more tours.)

More and more of these excellent wines are being exported to the United States and other countries now, so it's also possible to sample them at home.

Liqueurs

In Moldavia, there are two delicious sweet liqueurs: ***Afinată***, made from the local afine (berries), and ***Zmeurată***, made from red raspberries. Heavenly!

Every country has its own special liqueur and Romania's is ***ţuica***. This is a clear plum brandy that will knock your socks off. Occasionally a variety of ţuica will also be made from pears or apples. Drinking a shot of ţuica before a meal is a traditional gesture, so it's impolite to refuse. But a friendly warning: if your host offers you a small glass (or two) of ţuica, make sure you don't have to drive anywhere. It's powerful stuff and Romania has a zero-tolerance law.

Romanian hospitality is warm and open. They might not have much by western standards, but they are very generous and may offer you food and drink in their homes. If you accept such a gracious invitation, bring along some candy or flowers for your hostess; an odd number of flowers is the rule, except for sad occasions like funerals, when bouquets should have an even number of flowers (more superstition).

It is not necessary to finish everything on your plate to please your hosts. In fact, if you do, you will likely be given more food, as your host will assume you are still hungry. Likewise, with wine—if you empty your glass, they will pour you more. So leave a little behind on your plate or in your glass to indicate that you are full. A less charming tradition is smoking. Many Romanians are heavy smokers. Nevertheless, it is considered poor manners to light up while others are still eating, although some locals do it anyway.

Private space, such as property, is also considered very important to Romanians, so guests in a Romanian's home should not go and look around the house without being invited to or without being accompanied by their host.

CHAPTER 4

PLANNING YOUR TRIP

One of the first things on your To-Do list should be to contact the Romanian National Tourism Office and request an information package of brochures, maps and tour schedules. Ask for both a national map and Bucharest street and metrou maps, as they are hard to find over there. Be sure to mention if you have any specific interests, such as castles, ancient ruins, mountain sports, spas, Saxon, Hungarian or Jewish history, Dracula, wine tours, etc. as they may have special booklets pertaining to your special interest. (See Appendix for international RoNTO contact locations or check www.romaniatourism.com/worldwide.html.)

Arriving & Departing

By Plane: Austrian Airlines offers daily connections to Bucharest, Timişoara and Cluj from several cities in the USA and Canada. Bucharest is no more than 2 hours by plane from most cities in Western Europe. Other cities in Romania, including Timişoara, Cluj, Sibiu, Oradea, Arad, and Bacău, are connected with destinations in Austria, Germany, Italy and Hungary by flights with Austrian Airlines, CarpatAir and Tarom.

By Train: Traveling by train from other European countries to Romania takes from 6 hours (Budapest to Timişoara) to about 46 hours (London to Bucharest). Most train tickets allow several stopovers en route, so trains are a great way to include Romania in a multi-country trip.

Romanian National Railways (SNCFR) operates service from Bucharest to many European cities. First- and second-class sleepers are available for journeys longer than 10 hours and for overnight trains. For information on train schedules and fares go to www.CFR.ro. For advance ticket reservations, visit www.RailEurope.com or www.wasteelstravel.ro.

By Car: Border crossing between Romania and its western neighbors is just a formality. If renting a car in Europe, check with the car rental agency about its policy regarding taking the car across national borders. Insurance can be purchased at any Romanian border crossing point. Documents required by Romanian Customs are the vehicle's registration, proof of insurance (Green Card) and a valid driver's license from the driver's home country. If not a member of the EU, you must also have a valid passport. (See below for visa requirements and driving information.)

There are six European highways that enter Romania at nine locations: from Hungary: **E60** from Budapest via Borş or **E64** from Mako, via Nădlac; from Serbia: **E70** via Moraviţa to Timişoara; from Bulgaria: **E79** via Vidin and Calafat, or **E70/E85** via Giurgiu to Bucharest, and **E60/E87** via Vama Veche to the Black Sea coast; from the Republic of Moldova: **E580** via Albiţa & Huşi; from Ukraine: **E70** via Siret to Suceava or **E81** (from Warsaw) to Satu Mare.

By Bus: There are many bus routes that connect Bucharest and Romania's main cities with Athens, Berlin, Budapest, Copenhagen, Frankfurt, Istanbul, London, Milan, Munich, Paris, Rome, and Vienna.

The bus terminals in Bucharest are: Filaret Bus Terminal, Strada Cuţitul de Argint 2B, sector 4, Tel: (021)336.06.92; fax: (021)337.36.12; transfer to city tram #7. Băneasa Bus Terminal, Bd. Ionescu de la Brad 3-5, Tel: (021)230.56.45; transfer to city buses #205 or 131. Griviţa Bus Terminal, Şoseaua Chitilei 221, Tel: (021)667.59.70; transfer to city bus #645. Militari Bus Terminal, Bd. Iuliu Maniu 141, Tel: (021)434.17.39; fax: (021)434.17.51. Rahova Bus Terminal, Şoseaua Alexandriei 164,

Tel: (021)420.47.95; transfer to city bus #303, trolleybus #96, or trams #2, 32, 15. Obor Bus Terminal, Bd. Gării Obor 5, Tel: (021)252.76.46; transfer to city trolleybus lines #85 or 69.

By Boat: Several river cruise companies based in Germany or Austria offer cruises on the Danube River through to Romania's Danube Delta and the Black Sea Coast. They are: Value World Tours, www.rivercruises.net; Vantage Deluxe World Travel, www.vantagetravel.com; Uniworld, www.uniworld.com; and Scylla Tours, www.scylla-tours.com.

Sailing on the Danube in privately owned boats is allowed for the entire Romanian section of the river. The only requirements when sailing from Vienna, Budapest or Belgrade are a passport check and a yacht/boat technical inspection. No inoculations are required, no visa for Americans, Canadians and citizens of the European Union countries.

There are two Danube Border Checking Points: Orşova and Drobeta Turnu Severin. Required documentation: a passport and the yacht/boat proof of ownership and registration. There is a yacht/boat fee of $15.00 to $30.00 depending on the size of the boat. For more information please contact the Orşova Danube River Authority (40-252)36.12.95 or the Drobeta Turnu Severin Danube River Authority (40-252)31.64.93.

Passports, Visas & Customs: American, Canadian, Norwegian and Swiss passport holders do not need a visa for visits up to 90 days. European Union citizens do not even need a passport, so long as they have their valid Identity Card. All other international visitors are required to have a passport and a visa issued from a Romanian embassy before arriving. Extensions of visits beyond 90 days can be arranged in Bucharest or at a local passport office. If your visa (or your 90-day grace) expires, you may be detained for a very long time before being allowed to leave the country. If planning a visit longer than 90 days, procure your visa before leaving home, if possible. There is no entry or departure tax and no vaccinations are required or necessary.

Americans can contact the Romanian Consulate in New York City: (212)682-9122; fax: (212)972-8463, E-mail: office@romconsny.org, www.romconsny.org., in Chicago: Tel: (312)573-1315; fax:(312)573-9771, E-mail: office@roconschicago.org, www.roconschicago.org, or in Los Angeles: Tel: (310)444.00.43; fax: (310)445.00.43, E-mail: consulat@consulateromania.net, www.consulateromania.net.

Canadians can contact consulates in Ottawa, Toronto, or Montreal: Tel: 514-876-1792; fax: 514-876.1797, E-mail: romanian.consulate@bellnet.ca. British travelers can ring their Romanian Embassy in London for visa information: (020)7937 9666. Australians should phone the embassy in Canberra for information: Tel: 00-61-26-286.23.43; fax: 00-61-26-286.24.33, E-mail: roembassy@roembau.org, www.roembau.org. For more visa information and a list of all Romanian diplomatic offices abroad go to www.mae.ro.

Customs Regulations: You can enter and leave Romania with up to $10,000 in cash or traveler's checks. Amounts over $10,000 must be declared at Customs.

Import allowances: Tobacco: 200 cigarettes (one carton) or 40 cigars; Liquor: 4 liters of wine or 2 liters of liquor; 20 rolls of camera film; a reasonable quantity of gifts; medicines for own use. Customs officers do not usually check the baggage of individual travelers or tour groups. They do, however, have the authority to check passports and to conduct enforcement examinations without a warrant, ranging from a single luggage examination to a personal search. For more information on customs regulations go to www.customs.ro.

VAT: A 19% sales tax is included in the prices posted in stores, hotels and restaurants. As in many countries, hotels charge an additional tax (0.5% to 5% depending on the class of hotel). VAT refund: Keep your original receipts and ask for a store-identified VAT refund form. VAT refund offices can be found at any Romanian border crossing point.

Practical Information

Disabled visitors: Romania is not an easy place for travelers with disabilities. City sidewalks are bumpy and many small hotels and tourist sites do not have elevators or ramps. Access to tourist attractions has improved somewhat, but it is advisable to check with all service providers prior to your visit to find out whether they are able to meet your particular needs. Advance notice and reservations will also help ensure that you receive the best possible assistance.

Driving: There are eight national highways extending to/from Bucharest, going to/from different corners of the country; they continue into other countries in the north, east, south, west and center of Europe:

DN1 = Bucharest - Ploieşti - Braşov - Sibiu - Alba Iulia - Cluj-Napoca - Oradea - Borş [E60 to Hungary]

DN1A = Bucharest - Ploieşti - Braşov - Sibiu - Deva - Arad - Nădlac [E64 to Hungary]

DN2 = Bucharest - Urziceni - Buzău - Focşani - Bacău - Suceava - Siret [E85 to Ukraine or Bulgaria]

DN3 = Bucharest Lehliu - Călăraşi - Ostrov - Constanţa

DN4 = Bucharest - Olteniţa

DN5 = Bucharest - Giurgiu [E70] [E85]

DN6 = Bucharest - Alexandria Craiova - Drobeta-Turnu Severin [E70 to Hungary or Serbia]

DN7 = Bucharest - Piteşti - Ramnicu Valcea - Sibiu - Deva - Arad - Nadlac [E70-81-64]

Driving speed conversion:
Kilometers divided by 1.6 = miles

KmPH:	10	30	50	60	80	90	110
MPH:	6	21	31	39	50	56	70

Rules of the Road

- Minimum driving age is 18.
- U.S. and Canadian driver's licenses are valid for driving in Romania.
- Driving is on the right side of the road.
- Passengers in the front seat of a car must wear seatbelts at all times. Children under 12 years of age may not ride in the front seat.
- Speed limits are 50 km/h (31 mph) in cities, 90 km/h (56 mph) on main roads and 110 km/h (70 mph) on highway, unless posted otherwise. Driving above these limits will result in fines with the possibility of losing your license.
- Pedestrians have priority at all times at crossings without traffic lights.
- Bring your car to a full stop at railway crossings without traffic lights.
- Unless otherwise indicated (stop or yield sign) traffic coming from the right has the right of way.
- The use of cellular phones while driving is not allowed.
- Driving while under the influence of alcohol is a criminal offense and penalties are severe. Blood alcohol level should be 0.00 while driving. We strongly advise you not to drink and drive.
- In case of a car accident call the police and be sure that you get a copy of the police report.

Electricity—Electrical current is 220V AC, 50Hz. Outlets take plugs with two round prongs. Bring a transformer and adapter for any western appliances requiring 110 V.

Health—No immunizations or unusual health precautions are necessary. Romania has no infectious risks and there are no poisonous insects. During the summer months there are mosquitoes, particularly in the Danube Delta. Always pack some mosquito repellent if traveling during summer season.

Tap water is safe to drink, but bottled water is available everywhere. Romania has more than one-third of all the natural mineral springs in Europe, and some Romanian bottled water is rated the best in the world for purity and taste.

Take along your own medicines and first-aid items. While in Bucharest and other large cities you can usually find what you need, that is not so in the countryside Bucharest has greatly reduced the incidence of wild dogs roaming the streets in recent years, but still be wary of loose, barking dogs. They are less likely to bite if you don't act afraid.

Internet Access—There are lots of Internet Cafes in Romania's main cities. Most young people can probably tell you where the nearest Internet cafe is located. The better hotels have business centers where you can access the Internet. Also check the free tourist booklets and newspapers in each city for listings of cybercafes and other services.

Money—Romania's currency is called the *Leu*: plural is *Lei* (*lay*)—ROL. On July 1, 2005, Romania dropped four zeros from its national currency. The old 25,000 Romanian *lei* now equals 2 new *Lei* and 50 *bani* (*bah-nee*) or 2.50 new *Lei*. New Romanian banknotes have been issued in 1, 5, 10, 50, 100 and 500 Lei denominations; the new coins are in 1, 5, 10 and 50 bani pieces. Old lei banknotes were issued in the following amounts: 2,000, 10,000, 50,000, 100,000, 500,000 and 1,000,000 Lei. Old coins are in denominations of 1, 100, 500, 1,000 and 5, 000 Lei. Both the old and new coins and banknotes will be in circulation until December 31, 2006. On January 1, 2007 the old currency will be withdrawn from circulation. Romania is still primarily a cash economy. The larger cities are quickly adapting to credit card purchasing (American Express, Diners Club, JBC International, Euro-Master Card, VISA.), but while most city hotels, travel agencies, airlines, car rental companies and some shops and restaurants do accept credit cards, travelers are advised to use cash for goods and services due to an increase in credit card fraud. A few venders have been known to make illegal purchases on customers' accounts. VISA is the preferred card in

Romania. It is advisable to check in advance about card acceptance. Credit card processing fees are 1%–5%.

Foreign currencies may be exchanged for lei at the international airport, at larger hotels, banks or authorized exchange offices (called *casa de schimb* or *birou de schimb valutar*). Exchange rates are clearly posted, as well as commissions charged, if any. You'll need your passport, and save your receipt to prove you changed the money legally. Never change money with someone who approaches you on the street. It's always a scam and it's illegal!

Travelers' checks are of limited use as they are still not accepted for purchases in shops. They may, however, be accepted for payment of hotel, airline, car rental and railroad bills. Traveler's checks can be cashed for US dollars or Euros for a fee in Bucharest at Banca Comercială Română or at most commercial banks and exchange houses. (Agencies and banks prefer VISA traveler's checks, and may not accept American Express checks). Outside of Bucharest you should go to their local branches. Some banks will also give cash advances on credit cards, but they will charge a commission.

American Express travelers checks can be cashed in Bucharest at some Exchange Offices or at the American Express representatives at the Marshal Travel Agency, Bd. Unirii 20, Tel: 335.12.24, or at the Bd. Magheru 43 office.

ATMs (called *Bancomate*) are now at the airports, the main banks and at shopping centers in major cities. But don't expect to find ATMs in smaller towns or villages. The countryside still relies primarily on cash, so make sure you always carry sufficient lei to cover your needs.

To transfer funds to Romania commercially, there are two methods. Your bank abroad can wire money to the Romanian Bank for Foreign Trade (BRCE), Strada Eugen Carada 1-3 (corner of Strada Lipscani), or your bank abroad may get in touch with Chase Manhattan Bank (American), which has a branch in Bucharest at Str. Vasile Lascar 42-44, Tel: (40-21)210.76.46; fax: (40-21)210.31.37.

In-bound cash remittances for individuals visiting or residing in Romania may be sent via any Western Union. After the transfer has been made, the recipient may go to any branch of Banca

Românească (an associate of Western Union) and collect the transfer. No bank account is needed either by the remitter or beneficiary. Fees are prepaid, so the beneficiary in Romania gets full payment in cash, settled in US dollars or in lei. Proceeds will be available the same day. The recipient needs only to complete a form identifying the sender, his/her address, the amount expected, and provide an ID in the beneficiary's name. In cases of emergency only, money can be transferred via the State Department, to be disbursed by the American Embassy in Bucharest.

When Romania officially joins the European Union its currency will change to the Euro, thus the Euro has surpassed the American dollar in importance. Most price conversion lists now show lei-to-euro, rather than lei-to-dollar equivalents. Check the conversion rate at the time of your visit and carry a calculator.

Packing—First off, Romanians don't use washcloths, so bring your own. Also pack enough medicines to last your stay. You'll want a calculator or metric converter for converting measures (distance, weight, volumes, etc.), as well as for money conversions (from lei or Euros to dollars). If you like your coffee light, take along some powdered creamer. Using milk in coffee is relatively new to Romanians, who prefer theirs Turkish-style, and some places may not provide it. Candy is best brought from home too; it's better quality and it makes great gifts for the locals, especially in rural areas where they don't have access to any. (It may win you access to peasant homes or other normally inaccessible local treats.) If you're planning to explore the countryside independently, take along a compass, too.

Post Office—Mail boxes in Romania are red (or yellow) and marked "Poşta Română." One slot is for Bucharest addresses; the other for all other destinations. Main post offices are open Monday through Saturday until 8pm and Sunday until noon. To locate a branch Post Office, look for signs with the postal logo, or check the Poşta Română website: www.posta-romana.ro. A postage stamp is called "*timbru*." Postcards are "*vederi*." Delivery times for postcards and letters to western Europe are

4 to 6 days. Ordinary post to North America takes from 7 to 20 days. You can send international faxes from a main post office for about $5 per page. The Romanian Post is the sole provider in Romania for Western Union home delivery money transfer.

To receive mail in Bucharest, the letter or package must be addressed to your name, c/o Poşta Restantă, Poşta Română Oficiul Bucureşti 1, Strada Matei Millo 10, RO-70700 Bucharest, ROMANIA. *Poşta Restantă* mail can be collected at the Central Post Office on Strada Matei Millo (near the Telephone building on Calea Victoriei), in the room with the post office boxes. Collection times are weekdays from 7:30am to 8pm, and Saturday from 8am to 1pm. Incoming mail will be held for one month. In other Romanian cities, check with the main Post Office in that town.

Public Holidays—January 1 & 2 (New Year); Orthodox Easter Monday; May Day; December 1 (National Day); December 25 and 26 (Christmas).

Restrooms—There are few public restrooms, so your best bet is large hotels, department stores or fast-food restaurants. Use of some public restrooms may be subject to a small fee (including McDonalds). Public facilities in crowded areas, including in trains and train stations, often have no toilet paper or might not be clean, so always carry a packet of tissues (or a roll of TP) with you. Restrooms signs will indicate Femei (Women) or Bărbaţi (Men). For more information about restrooms on the road, checkout www.thebathroomdiaries.com.

Smoking Policy—It seems like everyone in Romania still smokes. The Romanian government has passed legislation banning smoking in all public places, including hospitals, concert halls, and theaters (but not restaurants or bars). Currently smoking is also prohibited on airplanes, buses and on some trains. Luxury hotels have designated no-smoking rooms, but very few restaurants have established no-smoking sections. Unfortunately, most smokers have little respect for non-smokers and for smoking laws.

Standard of Measurement—Romania uses the metric system (so take a conversion table).

Telephones—Romania's country code is: **40**. To call Romania from abroad, dial the international access code, then 40 and then the area code of the locality of the receiving party, i.e. (Bucharest=21), e.g.: international access code + 40 + (21) + seven-digit telephone no. or international access code + (3-digit area code) + 6-digit phone no. Dialing from abroad to any other city in Romania: International Access Code + 40 + (3-digit area code) + six-digit phone no. (See a complete list of Romanian area codes in the Appendix.)

International direct dialing service is available throughout Romania; if for some reason IDD by dialing 001 is not available, dial 971 for the international operator. To place an international call from Romania, dial: 00 + 92 country code + (area code) + telephone no.

Dialing within Romania: To call anywhere in the countryside, dial: 0 + (3-digit area code) + 6-digit telephone no. To call a number in Bucharest from elsewhere in the country, dial: 0 + 21 + 7-digit telephone no. Special 3-digit telephone numbers are local toll-free numbers for emergencies or businesses (i.e. taxis). A general emergency phone number, 112, now operates all over Romania.

Public telephones are orange or green and require Rom-Telecom phone cards, called ***cartelă telefonică***, which are sold in three different values (paid in Lei) and can be purchased at the Telephone Center, most Post Offices, some hotels, or at labeled kiosks on the street. The amount of talking time allowed on the cartela will vary depending on whether you make local calls or long-distance calls. Bucharest's old Telephone Center is on Strada Matei Millo at Calea Victoriei; it has the talking times allowed per cartela to all international destinations posted on a large board. You can make your calls from one of its many telephone booths.

Most Romanians now use cell phones; the two providers are Connex-Vodafone and Orange. Their phone cards can also be purchased at the street kiosks or at storefront offices. It is very easy to rent or buy a cellular telephone in Romania.

Emergency Contacts in Bucharest: US Embassy: (40-21)210.40.42; Embassy of Canada: (40-21)222.98.45; Embassy of the United Kingdom: (40-21)312.03.03; Embassy of Australia: (40-21)320.98.02. For a listing of all diplomatic offices in Romania, visit: www.mae.ro or www.embassyworld.com.

Time—Romania is 7 hours ahead of USA time, 2 hours ahead of GMT, and 1 hour ahead of CET. Daylight saving time (GMT+3) runs from the end of March until the end of September.

Transportation—Airports: Romania has international airports in Bucharest and Timisoara, and fifteen domestic airports in cities throughout the country. In Bucharest, **Henri Coandă International Airport** (formerly Otopeni) has two terminals: one for arrivals and one for departures. It has a currency exchange desk, an ATM, luggage check, and an information desk. It is 17 km (10.5 miles) from downtown Bucharest. Tel/Fax: (40-21)201.40.00, (40-21)204.10.00. Arrivals Infoline: (40-21)204.12.24, (40-21)204.12.20; Departures Infoline: (40-21)204.12.10, (40-21)204.12.00. Romania's international airline is TAROM, www.tarom.ro. (See Appendix for international airlines that fly to Romania.)

Băneasa Airport handles mainly domestic flights and charter flights, but some international flights land here. The airport is 4 km (2.5 miles from downtown Bucharest). Tel: (40-021)232.00.20; (40-021)232.01.30; fax: (40-021)232.36.87. Airport bus #783 runs from both airports to Piaţa Romană, Piaţa Unirii and Colţea in the city center (centru). Buy an airport bus card – good for two rides.

Trains—SNCFR (*Societatea Naţională Căilor Ferate Române*) is the national railway, covering over 11,000 kilometers (6,800 miles) throughout Romania. (See route map on page 94.) The trains are generally old and shabby, but they are inexpensive and very efficient; one third are electrified. There are three speeds of regular trains: *Rapid, Accelerat* and *Personal* (the slowest). There are also the shiny, new InterCity trains: shorter, with a bullet-like exterior and metrou-like inside. They have smoking and non-smoking cars, clean lavatories and even coffee vending machines.

CFR timetables are posted on large overhead boards in the stations (*gara*), along with the track number (linia) for your train. If planning a lot of train travel throughout Romania, find and buy the current timetable book called *Mersul Trenurilor* at the station or at CFR offices; it lists all routes, foreign and domestic, their schedules and train numbers (updated each May).

Buying a 1st-class ticket assures you an assigned seat in an enclosed cabin for six or eight persons; it costs only a little more than 2nd class. First-class (clasa întâi) and second-class tickets are usually purchased at separate windows. If traveling at night, reserve a *vagon de dormit*, a sleeping cabin with two bunks and a (usually non-working) sink. (If riding alone, to avoid sharing sleeper with a stranger, you might consider buying tickets for both places; it's worth it for the privacy.) It's a good idea to take along some food and water, too. Smoking is not permitted inside the cabins, but you may smoke in the corridor. Beware: train toilets are often very dirty, especially on the slower trains; carry your own toilet paper or tissues.

In Bucharest's *Gara de Nord* the 1st-class ticket windows are in a separate hall just left of the terminal entrance off Calea Griviţei. You will be charged a few lei to enter the station by a red-jacketed security person. This is part of the city's effort to keep out the unsavory characters that once lurked inside the station. Gara de Nord is 5 km (3 miles) from the city center. Tickets can only be purchased at the station two or three hours prior to departure. You can, however, buy them a day in advance at CFR ticket agencies. International tickets must be purchased in advance at a CFR office.

In Bucharest, the ***Agenţia de Voiaj CFR***, is at Strada Domniţa Anastasia 10-14, off Strada Brezoianu, just south of the Bulevardul Regina Elisabeta McDonald's, Tel: (021)313.26.42/43 or (021)311.08.57 (domestic); (021)314.55.28 (international);

also offices at: Bd. Ferdinand 96., Tel: (021)252.94.57; Bd. Nicolae Grigorescu 2, Tel: (021)340.35.30 or (021)340.53.00; Şoseaua Griviţei 139, Tel: (021)212.89.47 (international); and Bd. Obregia 25-29, Tel: (021)460.96.00. If you have trouble communicating with the window attendants, ask a young person for help; they probably speak some English and are happy to assist foreigners.

Domestic tickets are usually tiny cardboard stubs—sometimes 2 or 3 per trip if you require transfers; your wagon number and seat number will be written on the backside. Note: CFR agencies are closed on weekends.

Some train language: Arrival = *Sosire*, Departure = *Plecare*, ticket = *bilet*, 1st class = *clasa întâi*, to = *la* or *spre*, from = *din* or *de la*, seat = *loc*, car = *vagon*, sleeping car = *vagon de dormit*, track = *linia*, station = *gară*, connection = *legatura*, trip = *călătorie*.

Bucharest Metrou—There are three *metrou* lines crossing the city from north-south (M2-blue), east-west (M3-yellow), and a circular route (M1-red). The system is very efficient and the stations are clean and well marked, each having a unique design. You must buy a metrou card for either 2 rides or 10 rides; they are very cheap, the equivalent of about 50 cents a ride. Metrous operate from 5am until 11pm. (Check the metrou map in this guide for routes and stops) Note: photographing on the metrou platform is not allowed. (See route map on page 117.)

Buses and trams generally run from dawn until 11 pm and travel everywhere, but are difficult to figure out, as there are no route maps. Tickets are sold at yellow kiosks near some stops until early evening. They're cheap, so buy two or three to be safe. When you get on the bus, validate your ticket by punching it in the little box on board.

In Bucharest, a special bus, #783, runs to Henri Coandă Airport from Piaţa Romană and Piaţa Unirii in the city center (*centru*). Buses #79, 86 and 133 run from various stops around the *Gara de Nord* train station to Piaţa Romană. The buses are old and very crowded so, as in most other big cities, be especially aware of pickpockets.

Taxis are usually picked up on a street corner where the cabbies hang out, rather than hailed on the street. Try to use only licensed metered taxis that have a lighted sign on top and their name, number and rate on the car door. They will likely try to overcharge you, so watch the meter or agree on a price before you drive off. Most city trips should cost between $3.00-6.00, paid in lei; pay with small bills and don't expect any change back. In most cities you can also phone for a taxi at various 3-digit numbers; Bucharest's are: 941, 946, 953, 954 and 956. Concierges will call for you if asked. Just so you know, the official airport taxis at the Bucharest airports charge about triple the regular rate.

Travel Agencies—There are plenty of tourism agencies in Bucharest and other large cities to help you plan trips to the countryside. They will make hotel reservations for you and book domestic airline flights, if you choose not to ride the trains. Some arrange group bus tours to the most popular touring spots. If you prefer to travel independently, they may be able to arrange for an English-speaking guide and car at your destination. Your hotel will likely carry several English-language brochures and touring magazines listing local agencies. You can also just walk in to any store-front travel office; at least one of their representatives will speak English.

Traveling with Pets—Documents required to bring your pet into Romania include a Veterinary Health Certificate and proof of a rabies vaccination not older than six months. Translation of documents is not needed if they are in English, French or German. Pets are allowed on trains and buses; however, large dogs must wear a muzzle. In general, pets are allowed in hotels and restaurants, but each hotel or restaurant has its own pet policy. Hotels will usually charge a bit extra for guests with pets.

Weather—Romania has a temperate climate, much like the USA, with four distinct seasons. In Bucharest, the average summer temperature is 75° Fahrenheit (24° Centigrade), but

July and August often reach 100 °F (37° C). In winter it can hit freezing, 32° F (0°C). Springtime is beautiful with gardens and flowing trees blooming in the cities. It is always much cooler in the mountains, especially at night, so take along a warm sweater, even in summer.

Last, but not least, bring your camera. You'll want to capture the majesty and mystery of this beautiful country that, while hurrying to catch up with the modern world, still keeps one foot firmly entrenched in its past.

Rural Tourism

Much of Romania is comprised of undeveloped farming and herding villages that have not changed much in the last centuries. This presents an opportunity to step back in time and experience the rural lifestyle of our ancestors. For visitors who want a taste of authentic countryside living, the **National Association of Rural, Ecological and Cultural Tourism** (ANTREC), has developed a large network (30 branches) of village homeowners all over the country who will host tourists in their homes. This is a fabulous way to see and experience some of the most gorgeous and interesting parts of Romania. ANTREC has strict standards that their registered hosts must adhere to regarding facilities, cleanliness, privacy, and services. Some hosts will cook for you or offer you transportation to local sights (sometimes in their horse-carts); others may allow you to participate in the farm chores if you wish. These types of rural accommodations are especially popular in the areas around Bran Castle in Transylvania, and near Bucovina's painted monasteries, both areas of high tourist interest, but few hotels. ANTREC also has a few 4-5 day organized programmes to rural villages with unique historical sights or activities (hiking, bird-watching). Contact ANTREC online at www.antrec.ro or at their main office in Bucharest to arrange a tour or a rural guest-house. ANTREC Bucharest address: Strada Maica Alexandra

7, sector 1, Tel: (40-21) 223.70.24; fax: (40-21) 222.80.01 E-mail: antrec@antrec.ro, antrec@xnet.ro or office@antrec.ro.

There are also many owner-operated *pensiuni*, where locals have converted their houses into small inns, with a guest dining room and bedrooms with private bathrooms. Some tourism agencies offer their own countryside tours with a driver/guide and overnight stays in a charming and comfortable *pensiune*. Check the rural programmes at www.culturalromtour.com.

Active Tourism

Romania has lots of outdoor activities for visitors interested in pursuing rugged adventures in an extraordinary environment. There's hiking, biking, camping, caving, climbing, and skiing in the majestic mountain ranges; or golf, horseback riding, river rafting and parachuting in lush valleys; to fishing and bird watching in the pristine Danube Delta. One can even join the lumberjacks on their steam train journey into the northernmost forests of Maramures. You can sleep under the stars (beware of bears in the mountains), or have ANTREC set you up with a comfortable room in a country home; www.antrec.ro.

Alpinism/Mountaineering

Mountain climbing is a popular sport in Romania's Carpathians, which are part of the greater Alpino-Carpato-Himalayan chain that begins in the north of Bratislava and ends in Timok Valley. The center of climbing, or Alpinism, in Romania is the town of Buşteni, between Sinaia and Predeal in Prahova Valley. Club Alpin Roman is based there.

The Carpathians have three independent groups: the Oriental Carpathians; the Meridional Carpathians and the Occidental Carpathians. Among the most important and interesting *massifs* (mountain ranges) are: the Rodna, Căliman, Ceahlău, Harghita, and Ciucaş in the Oriental Carpathians; the Bucegi,

Piatra Craiului, Făgăraş, Parâng, and Retezat in the Meridional Carpathians; and the Bihor, Vlădeasa, and Trascău in the Occidental Carpathians.

Bucegi Mountains—These mountains are the center of Romanian tourism and rock climbing, comprising the most and the longest alpine routes. The Eastern mountainside of Bucegi, above Prahova Valley, is commanded by Caraiman, Coştila and Jepii Mici peaks, and it forms an exquisite precipice that reaches 1700 m (23,000 ft.). Morarul and Bucşoiul peaks drop toward the north and northeast, while Guşanul, Grohotişul (Detribus) and Strungile Mari (Big Cloughs) have craggy areas above Bran-Rucăr passage. The town of Buşteni, capital of the Romanian mountaineering world, sits at the foot of Caraiman Mountain. It is the main access point for the climbing routes of the Bucegi mountains.

Caraiman, with the **Heroes' Cross** perched on its peak overlooking Buşteni, Caraiman mountain, 2,384 m (7,820 ft.), is a distinct landmark of Prahova Valley. It is bounded by Jepilor Valley to the south and Alba Valley to the north. The many valleys and mountain paths that cross Caraiman are recommended mountaineering routes for beginners.

Coştila is the favorite Romanian alpine destination. It rises 2,490 m (8,170 ft.) and has 150 alpine routes in all grades of difficulty. Its starting point is in Buşteni. On the way up one might choose Coştila shelter as a base for your climb. The face of Coştila includes the four walls of four valleys: Alba, Policandrului, Coştilei, and Gălbenelelor.

The area around Braşov attracts many climbers, mostly for the routes on the southern mountainside and *Cheile Râşnovului* (Râşnovului Gorges), easily accessible in any season. Rock composition: limestone.

Piatra Craiului Mountains—This is Romanians' second favorite climbing area in the Carpathians, after Bucegi. Mountaineers love it because of the beauty of its routes and landscapes. Its highest peak reaches 2,238 meters (7,342 ft.). The best routes are on the northwestern and western faces. Popular areas for climbing include Diana Towers, Poiana Închisă, Orga Mare, Marele Grohotiş Wall, Şpirla, Prăpăstiile Zărneşti, Acul Crăpăturii, Padina lui Călineţ, Ciorânga, Umerii, Gălbenoasa Wall. Piatra Craiului is recommended for all types of climbing, with a difficulty level of 1-10 UIAA.

There are dangers, however. Winter lasts from November through May or June in the mountains, with heavy snows obliterating paths and winds pushing temperatures below freezing. Only experienced and well-equipped alpine mountaineers should venture up the Piatra Craiului during the winter. Avalanches can be fatal here. The mountain rescue teams are not equipped with hi-tech equipment, and mobile phones will only operate on high peaks and a few others places. Also, beware of snakes; viper bites can be fatal if proper first aid is not applied immediately.

Bicaz Gorges—The Gorges were carved by the waters of the Bicaz River into the Jurassic limestone of Hăşmaş massif over a length of 6 km (3.7 miles) and a depth of 300m (984 ft.). This is the third most popular area for climbing after Bucegi and Piatra Craiului, and it has the most difficult routes.

Căpăţânii (Buila-Vânturăriţa) Mountains—Buila-Vânturăriţa is a limestone massif in the southeastern side of Căpăţânii. It stands over the gorge of Cheia Valley.

Cerna Valley—In Cerna Valley in southwestern Wallachia, near the Băile Herculane spa, the limestone walls that surround the spa offer climbers several routes that are comparable in difficulty to those in Piatra Craiului or Postavaru. The most frequented walls are Şoimului, Domogled and Grota Haiducilor.

Făgăraş Mountains—The Făgăraş are the highest mountains in Romania but, while popular for summer hiking, they lack the large vertical walls like those in Bucegi, Bicaz Gorges or Piatra Craiului. But though their summer routes are relatively modest, they present an outstanding challenge to the winter climber due to the problems that weather presents.

They are formed of metamorphic or crystalline rocks, jagged with long ridges on the south side. They are major endeavors that require complex technical and physical training, as well as good equipment.

Biking

Romania has outstanding potential for cycle-touring and mountain biking. You'll encounter magnificent scenery on trails through woods or riding through the traditional farming villages. The mountain trails offer varying levels of difficulty, from easy tracks on forest roads to more dangerous long ridge paths. Some of the most interesting areas for mountain biking are Bucovina, the Neamţ areas of Ceahlău and the Bicaz Gorge, the Apuseni Mountains, the mountains between the Olt and Jiu rivers, and the Banat Mountains. Mountain biking is the best way to see the more remote villages throughout Transylvania. There are few bike repair facilities, however, so be prepared to carry your own tools and spare parts, along with your camping gear.

Biking follows the same rules as mountain climbing, as well as the rules specific to cyclists regarding the training, equipment, and knowledge. In the mountains, the weather is moody, requiring cyclists to always be prepared for changes. There are no posted signs for mountain bikers yet, but many of the hiking routes are also used by cyclists. A map and a compass or GPS is recommended for orientation. Keep in mind that items noted on maps or guidebooks may differ from the reality of the moment. Occasionally, a marked chalet or road may be gone or destroyed. It helps to check multiple reference sources before heading to secluded mountain areas, because Salvamont (the Mountain-rescue squad) is often difficult to reach.

All routes—path, forest or tractor road—are open to cyclists, with a few exceptions (scientific reserves, border areas, etc.). On the forest roads, be especially careful of foresting traffic, logs and the cutting of trees, since these are not public roads. On narrow paths, vehicles have first priority. The principles of the international ethic code apply to bikers. For instance, the cyclists must respect other types of travelers and avoid scaring the animals. He/she must protect nature, the natives and all other things around them. Bikers must be cautious, paying close attention to trucks and tractors, and avoid traveling at night. Mountain roads can present many obstacles (such as potholes, animals, horse-carts, vehicles etc.), requiring cautious behavior and sharp awareness, especially on the slopes and winding curves.

International transport of bicycles—By Train: International trains do not have luggage wagons, so your bike should be dismantled and packed in the class carriage or the sleeping carriage. **By Bus**: Many international buses drive daily routes to Romania from other European countries. Some have non-specialized trailers allowing bikes to be taken on board, if they are properly packed. **By Airplane**: Flights from European countries to Bucharest, Timişoara, Cluj-Napoca, Sibiu, and Constanţa are daily operated by Tarom and Carpatair, but you should call to ask if the type of airplane used has enough space to carry a bike on board. Domestic airplanes are usually small and do not have space to transport bikes, but check with the flight to be sure.

Transport of bikes within Romania: Transporting bikes to and from your starting point can be done either by a car or by public transport, especially by train. However, not all trains have a luggage wagon. You can usually bring a bike on the slow, Personal trains, but they are very crowded. In some fast trains, including the new Intercity trains, there are usually empty spaces where the bike can be placcd, but you may be charged a fee. It is highly recommended that the bike be dismantled, if possible. Inter-urban buses usually do not have a trailer or a specialized trunk and will transport bikes only if the driver agrees. Groups should rent a shuttle with a specialized trunk or a trailer.

Tourism agencies with biking programs: Cultural Romtour combines bicycling with local culture on its group tour through

Transylvania, Bucovina and Maramures, www.culturalromtour.com. Green Mountain Holidays, Cluj County, www.greenmountainholidays.ro. Sources for mountain biking: www.mybike.ro, www.bike-world.online.ro, or www.alpinet.org.

A map of mountain biking routes in Prahova Valley was published by Prahova Mountain Tourism Association, and a general map of Romania was edited by BikeRomania and Napoca Mountain Biking Club.

Bird-watching

The Danube Delta is home to hundreds of species of birds—at least from late Spring until mid-Fall. Bird-watchers do not need any equipment (although binoculars help), no license is required, and there are plenty of locations throughout the Danube Delta to watch fowl in their natural habitat. Most bird-watchers are lucky enough to spot black pelican colonies. Just a few of the other birds to be found in the Delta are purple herons, spoonbills, ospreys, cranes and cormorants. *Ibis Tours* specializes in bird-watching trips to the Danube Delta, www.ibistours.net; ANTREC also organizes bird-watching programs in the Delta, www.antrec.com or E-mail: tulcea@antrec.ro.

Bungee Jumping

The second highest bungee jumping place in Europe is in Râşnoava Gorges, one of the tallest gorges in Romania. There is a properly equipped setup for this activity there. Râşnoava gorges are in the Postăvaru mountains, southwest of Braşov, by the medieval village of Râşnov.

Camping

Get really close to Romania's natural splendor by spending a few nights camping beside one of its many rivers or one of its magnificent mountains. From late Spring until early Autumn nature lovers flock to Romania's camping areas to enjoy an abundance of nearby attractions. For more information on the 69 camping sites licensed by the Romanian Ministry of Tourism or to request a camping site map, please contact the nearest Romanian Tourist Information Office. (See Appendix.)

Caving

Caving is a hugely popular sport in Romania and there are more than 12,500 known caves in Romania. Rocks favorable to the development of the caves (limestone, marble, dolomites, sandstone, salt) cover 6,320 sq.km (3,927 sq.miles) of Romania, about 2.6% of the country; and Romania's caves are filled with incredible natural riches.

The first topographic plans in the world were made of Romania's **Veterani Cave** (Almăj Mtns.) in 1692. The skeletons of hundreds of *Ursus spelaeus* (cave bears) were discovered in **Zmeilor Cave** in Onceasa (Bihor Mtns.). Four of Romania's caves were first prepared for tourism in the 19th century; these are: **Ialomiţa Cave** (Bucegi Mtns.), **Meziad Cave** and **Vadul Crişului Cave** (Pădurea Craiului Mtns.), and **Scărişoara Glacier** (Bihor Mtns.). And in 1920, Romanian Emil Racoviţă, a former Antarctica explorer, founded the first Speleology Institute in the world in Cluj-Napoca, making it an international center for biospeleological research. In 1965, a team from the Speleology Institute discovered an ancient human in **Ciur-Izbuc Cave** (Pădurea Craiului Mtns.).

Romania's longest cave, spanning 50 km (31 miles) is **Vântului Cave** (Pădurea Craiului Mtns.). The deepest difference of levels is in the hollows under **Colţii Grindului** (also Piatra Craiului) descending 540 m (1,772 ft.), while the largest positive difference of level—405 m (1,329 ft.), is in **Şura Mare Cave** (Şureanu Mtns.).

The largest vertical cave, reaching 121 m (387 ft.), is **Clocoticiul din Cârca Păreţilor** (Vâlcan Mtns.) and the largest underground waterfall—52 m (170 ft.)—is in **Găvanului Cave** in Gura Cerului (Someş Plateau). Romania also has caves of salt, the largest at **Mânzăleşti**, in the Buzău Mountains. It is 3,234 m (6,593 ft.) long, and crossed by two salty brooks.

In 1978, a team from Emil Racoviţă Club discovered the first Paleolitic paintings in Central and Southeast Europe in the cave at **Cuciulat quarry** (Someş Plateau): a horse, a cat, and a human silhouette. The researchers from the Archeology Institute dated them from 12,000 years ago. **Adam's Cave** in the Cerna Mountains, has two galleries: one has a thick layer of bat guano, while the other one is crossed by a warm air current (40°C /104°F) charged with hot water vapors.

Ten caves with underground glaciers were discovered in Romania in the Bihor and Făgăraş Mountains. Scărişoara Glacier (Bihor) has a volume of 50,000 m3. In the deepest part of this natural underground glacier, the temperature never falls below the freezing point. You can find cave beetles here, depending on the seasonal fluctuations of the ice.

Movile Cave in Dobrogea is supplied by thermal waters (20°C / 68°F) rich in sulfide hydrogen. This compound enables the chemosynthetical process which, along with its diverse fauna, makes Movile Cave unique. The animals living in this cave include 30 new troglobiontic or stygobiontic species, some from groups with no other cave species.

The Racoviţă Club also discovered caves at more than 2,000 m altitude. The highest is in the Făgăraş Mtns. at 2,517 m (8,258 ft.). In some areas of Apuseni Mountains there are over 200 caves to explore.

A few caves have been fitted with electric lights: **Urşilor** cave at Chişcău (Bihor), **Muierii** cave (Parâng Mtns), **Ialomiţa** cave (Bucegi), and **Vadul Crişului** cave (Pădurea Craiului). More information about Romania's caves can be found at the Emil Racoviţă Club, Bucharest, and via www.muntiicarpati.alpinet.org; E-mail: muntiicarpati@pcnet.ro; Tel: (021)311.28.22 or malex@customers.digiro.net.

Fishing

The best fishing areas in Romania are: the Danube Delta, with more than 160 species of game fish; the waters in the hilly areas of southeastern Romania (Călăraşi, Giurgiu, Constanta, Galaţi counties); the central region (Braşov and Timiş counties); and the mountainous waters in Maramureş, Suceava, Hunedoara, Sibiu, Covasna or Harghita counties. Trout can be found in the mountain water. Catfish, carp, pike, sturgeon, zander, and sheatfish live in Romania's hundreds of lakes and rivers. Fishing is permitted in any lake or river year round, except from April 1 until May 31. Every two years, a world fishing cup is organized in Săruleşti, near Bucharest. More information is available from www.fishing-resource.com and AGVPS, Tel: (021)313.33.63; fax: (021)313.68.04, E-mail: agvpsrom@pcnet.ro.

Golf

"***Lac de Verde***" (Lake of Green) in Breaza, Prahova County, is the first deluxe private golf club in Romania, and is located in one of the most beautiful, towns of the sub-Carpathians, Breaza, 75 minutes by car from Bucharest and 20 minutes from Peleş Castle in Sinaia.

Lac de Verde is the first official golf course in Romania. The course sits at 700 m (2,300 ft.) altitude, a unique landscape for its 9-hole course (par 32). Its design is in accordance with PGA standards. Club services include: a clubhouse with 4 suites, a conference room, a fitness center with jacuzzi, a massage and sauna, a swimming pool, billiards, and terraces; a mini-hotel with 4 suites, a studio, a meeting room, sauna, jacuzzi, massage, terraces; a 9-villa resort, each with balcony and hydromassage shower; a 600 sqm driving range, covered and heated in winter, with 20 training areas and computerized swing analysis. The complex also has a workshop for assembling irons, a restaurant with terrace, and two professional tennis courts. Its 14 golf carts were imported from the USA.

Equipment rental consists of: a bag with 14 clubs, golf shoes, a glove, a pair of trousers with a special golf T-shirt. Equipment usage is included in the training price. The green-fee includes the cost of the personal trainer. Tel: (40-244)34.35.25, E-mail: contact@lacdeverde.ro, www.golfromania.com.

In Bucharest, the **Diplomatic Club**, founded in 1929, is located near Herăstrău Lake and offers excellent conditions for golf. The golf course has 9 holes and a driving range. It offers a 40-minute class and bag rental. The Club also has two swimming pools—one Olympic size and one for children; eight outdoor tennis courts and two covered courts; facilities for basketball and football. Tel: (021)224.29.41, fax (021)222.84.16, E-mail: diplclub@fx.ro.

Pianu de Jos golf course is in Alba County, amid a gorgeous landscape. The course has 9 holes over 35 hectares (86 acres); route length is 5,830 m (6,376 yd.) for men, and 5,092 m (5,569 yd.) for women. Equipment can be rented from the owners. Tel/fax: (0258)73.54.66, E-mail: strajan@cristalsoft.ro.

Hiking

There are hundreds of great hiking trails in Romania's mountains and nature reservations, with a every type of terrain, for every level of skill, from rugged and challenging to easy day walks. The routes introduce you to rare species of flora, offer glimpses of mountain animals, and present spectacular vistas.

The **Apuseni mountains** or "Green Mountains" west of Cluj, are ideal for hiking. Bordered by the Crişul Repede River to the north and by the Aries to the south, they are home to the limestone **Turda gorge**, 3 km (1.8 miles) long with 300 m (985 ft.) cliffs, and cave systems including **Peştera Urşilor** (Bear Cave) and the exceptional **Scărişoara Ice Caves**, with stalactites and stalagmites, subterranean rivers, and igneous mountains. The Apuseni's are host to the famous "**Maidens' Fair**" folk festival held on Mount Găina; they also preserve the traditional culture of the Moţi, ancient inhabitants of this isolated region. Flora and fauna in the Apuseni's include bears, wolves, eagles, chamois and many endemic plant species. Green Mountain Holidays in Izvoru Crişului specialize in Apuseni mountain adventures such as hiking, caving, mountain biking, horse cart trips and kayaking with experts of the Apuseni. Tel: (0264)41.86.91, E-mail: gmh@cluj.astral.ro, www.greenmountainholidays.ro.

The **Făgăraş** are a favorite of local hikers, for their wild ruggedness and their stunning views. They are the highest mountains in Romania, running east to west, separating southern Transylvania from Wallachia in the south, and have more than 60 glacial lakes. But these mountains can be dangerous and should be approached only by experienced and highly-skilled hikers. The hiking season lasts only from July to mid-September, and snowstorms can begin as early as August. Most of the mountain is very open and snow covers the highest slopes all year. Some of the trails can take up to 12 hours to complete, so good maps and careful planning are essential. The mountains are also home to the big brown bear; and there are not many cabanas or campsites in the Făgăraş, so overnight hikers should be prepared to camp, in the wild if necessary. There are countless trails, but most start in the Olt Valley, on the railroad from Sibiu to the south. Most hikers enter the ridge at *Avrig Lac*, a glacial lake reachable by the red cross and blue dot trails from Avrig, a small town 30 km (20 miles) from Sibiu.

The **Retezat mountains** are one of the most beautiful mountain ranges in Romania, covering 800 sq. km (500 sq. miles) and with more than 80 high, rocky peaks. Located in western Romania, near the cities of Deva and Petroşani, this is hiking heaven with over 100 clear glacial lakes, many unique mountain flower and plant species, and animals such as bears, lynx, and chamois. It is also the site of Romania's only National Park, and a biosphere reserve.

There are two main ridges: the northern one with the highest peaks, and the southern one, formed by short ridges which lead down into the Petroşani Depression. Retezat is best accessed from the north, where a trail leads up to the **Pietrele chalet**; from there, a strenuous hike will take you to **Bucura lake** at the center of the range (or massif). The view is spectacular, and it's an ideal spot for camping, with Peleaga peak on one side of the lake, and the Retezat peak on the other. From there, a one-day hike will take you to the mountain's major attractions. Heading east, past the Peleaga peak, go through a spectacular passage at *Porţile Închise* and on to beautiful **Galeşu lake**. On the opposite side of the valley is the National Park. Entering the park requires a special pass, but the hike is worth it. You'll see fabulous wildlife, including the rare mountain goat or chamois, and unique mountain flowers.

Retezat is also popular with rock climbers. Like the Făgăraş, granite rock is scarce in the Retezat, but they provide ideal conditions for winter climbs, with lots of trails spanning all levels of difficulty, and unforgettable views.

Piatra Craiului Mountains are Romania's most loved mountains. They are wedged between Bucegi on the east and the Făgăraş mountains on the west. Their limestone ridge is only 25 km long, but they have the greatest bio-diversity in the country; and their white peaks create one of the most beautiful scenes in the Carpathians. They also offer magnificent views of the surrounding countryside below. Braşov sits conveniently at the eastern foot of the mountain ridge. A funicular runs up **Mount Tâmpa**; at the top, you'll find a spectacular birds-eye view of Braşov.

A two-day hike along the north–south ridge trail might begin at Plaiul Foii in the northwest or Curmătura in the northeast. Hikers must climb up to the ridge before reaching the path that runs along the mountain's narrow spine. The descent on the southern end leads into a karst landscape of deep gorges and pitted slopes, where water penetrating the rock has carved a series of caves. The town of **Zărneşti** (between Bran and

Râşnov) is the best approach from the north, lying at a distance of 28 km from the city of Braşov, by road or by railway. From Zărneşti, an 11-km-long road connects with **Plaiul Foii**; a forest road starts from the southwestern part of the town, going through Prăpăstiile, Valea Cheii and Valea Valea Vlăîduşca.

Rock-climbing enthusiasts should head for the main rock-climbing gateways: Buşteni, Sinaia, Zărneşti and Petroşani.

Horseback Riding

Explore the rural countryside by horseback on mountain roads and secluded paths. Spend evenings in front of a fire camp. Romania's National Committee for the Equestrian Tourism (CNTE), trains specialized guides for equestrian tourism. All the equestrian centers have tourism programs that include trips on horseback or by carriage, and offer riding lessons. There are routes for different levels of riding skill: beginners can enjoy long slow rides in among attractive natural scenery, while experienced riders can run in larger spaces.

For those who love horses, but don't want to ride, carriages are available. On the overnight adventure trips, tourists can choose to stay in a guesthouse, under a tent in the camp near the horses, or sleep under the open sky. All programs include a specialized guide. Groups are accompanied by a car or carriage transporting the luggage. Programs are all-inclusive, and prices range from 70 to 100 euros per person, per day. For more information on the equestrian tourism check www.daksa.ro, E-mail: daksa@mobius.ro; www.riding-holidays.ro; www.merlelor.com.html; and www.ridingholidays.com.

Hunting

Romanian hunting offers both big and small game. Big game includes brown bear, wild boar, roebuck, chamois, wolf, and lynx. Small game are the birds (pheasant, grouse, geese, ducks), and hare. The Carpathians are home to the greatest population of chamois in the world. The world record of this species was established in1934 in the Făgăraş Mountains. The roebuck is another valuable game, scoring 180 CIC (the International Hunting and the Preservation of the Game International Council) points. Romania has the largest population of brown bear in Europe.

To bring your own hunting gun to Romania, legal papers are mandatory. You can rent guns from any subsidiary of AGVPS (General Association of Hunters and Fishermen), but you must provide proof as a hunter in your country of origin, and you'll pay about 25 Euros for a gun with small shot, or 30 Euros for a gun with cartridges.

Hunting tariffs vary depending on the species: roebuck (male season is September 1 to November 15; female from November 1 to February 15) has tariffs ranging from 550-8,800 Euros, depending on its weight; chamois (male and female, from September 15 to December 15) tariffs run 1,100-2,860 Euros; wild boar (August 1 to February 15) tariffs range from 250-750 Euros; small game tariffs are priced by piece, varying between 6 to 125 Euros.

Parachuting

Romania has over 40 places for parachuting. The most popular are Prahova Valley's Bucegi Mountains, the Hăşmaă Mountains at Bicaz Gorge, the Apuseni Mountains, Vatra Dornei, and the areas along the northern seacoast. Parachuting in Romania requires a valid pilot licence. If using your own equipment, it must have an ID certificate and a paper issued by Romania's Airclub. Get additional information at: www.airclub.rdsnet.ro, E-mail: ultrausoare@apropo.ro, or at www.parapanta.ro and www.skysport.com.

In Vatra Dornei, flights are performed using parachutes in two places; the tourists are accompanied by highly experienced pilot-instructors. Transport to the mountain peaks is by special 6x6 vehicles. The mountains surrounding the Dorna Basin are perfect and safe for taking off, as they have soft ridges, grass and good wind speed. Dorna Basin has many excellent thermal currents. Check with the Adventure Tourism Centers at the Sport Hotel, Strada Republicii 33, Vatra Dornei, Tel/fax: (0230)37.15.67, mobile: (0723)82.93.01.

Paragliding

The northern slope of the Bucegi and Postăvaru Mountains, north of Bucharest, as well as several other ranges such as the Parâng (southwestern Romania), the Rodna and the Ciucas, provide the best conditions for taking off downhill paragliding.

Rafting and Canyoning

Rafting on fast mountain rivers can be organized in many regions in the country: Mureş Valley and Olt Valley (the center of the country), the Nera and Crişurile rivers in western Romania, the Dâmboviţa in the south, or the Bistriţa, one of the fastest rivers in the country, in the north. Some of them can be covered in a single day (Dâmboviţa valley) or in a few days (the Olt or Mureş). The most popular rafting rivers are Criş and Olt.

There are a lot of good places for canyoning, too. Piatra Mare Mountains, near Bucharest, as well as the Rodna, the Cerna Mountains and other ranges provide good conditions for this type of activity. For more information on rafting and canyoning tours visit www.turismaventura.ro or www.foruminternational.com.

Narrow-gauge Railway Riding

Vaser Valley—The narrow gauge railway in Vaser Valley is one of the last remaining forestry railways in Romania, and the only one still hauling timber down from the forests. The railway runs 43 km through Vaser Valley, one of the most beautiful areas in Maramures. The valley was developed in the 18th century as a forestry center and remains one of the wildest areas in Romania. Jagged rocks and gorges alternate with dells and mineral springs. The train carries the wood and loggers back and forth from Vişeu de Sus to Coman, near the Ukrainian border. Along the way it may pick up some shepherds, hikers or kayakers in its one passenger car. The route up to Coman point is 43 km (26 miles) and passes through tall forests and dark tunnels, and looks down on the rushing river. Its destinations are the sunny call stations of Novăt, Cozia, Bârdau, Botizu, Suliguli, Faina and Comanu. Several times during the trip, the train must stop and refuel with water from the Vaser River. These are ideal times to have a bite to eat, because the ride to Faina will climb more than 400m high, amid cliffs and brooks, for almost 5 hours, averaging only 10-15 km/hour.

To plan a Vaser Valley rail trip contact: RG Holz Company SRL, Tel: (0262)35.20.34; fax (0262)35.24.17, E-mail: rgholz@gmx.net, Leopold Langtaler, mobile (0744)98.62.42; or Vasertour travel agency, Tel/fax: (0262)35.22.85, E-mail: proviseu@mail.alphanet.ro, mobile: (0745)59.57.18, in Sabău.

You can also ride the steam trains through Transylvania. **Ronedo** offers a 7-day **History and Steam tour** that begins in Bucharest and includes Piatra Neamţ, Bucovina's painted monasteries, Sighişoara, Sibiu, a steam train ride to Făgăraş, Braşov, Bran and Sinaia. www.ronedo.ro, Email: office@ronedo.ro.

Another trip by small train offers a picturesque route from **Târgu Mureş to Band** that includes an iron bridge over the Mureş River, Cenan lakes, Moreşti archeologic site of a Roman castrum from A.D.1, and Sântioara Hunting Reserve. www.beyondtheforest.com, Email: travel@beyondtheforest.com.

Skiing & Snowboarding

Romania has many terrific places to ski in the Carpathian mountains. **Prahova Valley**, just 125-135 km (80 miles) north of

Bucharest, has four famous ski resorts. **Sinaia** has ski tracks up to 2,000 m (6,562 ft.) altitude in the Bucegi mountains, for both advanced skiers and beginners; season is December–March; elevation 1,400 m (4,593 ft.), snow layer is 50 cm (20 in.); its chair-lift & drag-lift operate 9am–5pm, Tel: (0244)31.16.74. It has the Trăistaru ski school: (0722)31.52.31; and the Association of the Monitors (0244)31.45.10. Salvamont mountain-rescue squad: (0244)31.31.31.

Azuga is a little farther north and the newest ski resort in Prahova Valley, at the foot of the Baiului Mountains. It has two medium-difficulty slopes at 561 m (1,840 ft.) and 801 m (2,628 ft.); two ski-lifts to 153 m (515 ft.) and 166 m (545 ft.), and one chair-lift to 561 m (1,840 ft.).

Buşteni, at the base of the Caraiman Mountains, claims to be the best place for extreme skiing in Romania. It has 11 trails, offers cross-country skiing, snowboards and night skiing. The Buşteni-Babele car-lift goes to 1,238 m (4,062 ft.); Peştera's car-lift goes to 138 m (453 ft.); the Kalinderu chair-lift goes to 282 m (925 ft.).

Both resorts have a snow depth 50 cm (20 in.) with an average winter temperature of 4.5°C (40°F); ski season is December until April. These resorts are between 800 m (2,625 ft.) and 950 m (3,117 ft.) high, while their tracks cover 2,000 m (6,562 ft.). They can be easily reached by train from Bucharest, or by driving along the DN 1 road.

Predeal resort is about 145 km (90 miles) north of Bucharest, between Postăvaru and the Piatra Mare Mountains. It is the highest urban settlement in Romania at more than 1,000 m. Predeal is the most popular ski resort and offers both daytime and nighttime skiing. The resort also can make artificial snow if necessary. Its season is December–March; altitude 1,040 m (3,412 ft.)–1,520 m (4,989 ft.); with a snow layer of 45 cm (18 in.); its chair-lift and drag-lift operate from 8am–4pm;. Tel: (0268)45.63.12. For info in Predeal, visit Strada Teleferic 1, Tel: (268)45.57.24, fax (268)45.54.63.

Poiana Braşov ski resort is just 13 km from Braşov, at the foot of the Postăvaru mountains. This resort has great snow conditions and 13 tracks for beginners and professionals. There are 9 km (5.6 miles) of cross-country trails, plus snowboarding. Its season is December–March with a snow layer of 50-60 cm (20-24 in.); altitudes from 1,020m (3,346 ft.)–1,799 m (5,902 ft.); an average winter temperature: -3°C (27°F); three chairlifts and 8 drag lifts operate from 8am–5pm;. Tel: (0268)55.04.43; (0268)26.21.31, Salvamont (mountain-rescuers): (0745)0.196.45; (0722)52.32.98. Buses run from downtown Braşov to Poiana Braşov every day. And within 30 km (19 miles), you can also visit the fortified churches of Prejmer and Harman; Bran Castle, 25 km (15 miles) or the peasant fortress at Râşnov, 10 km (6 miles).

Vatra Dornei, farther north in the Bistriţei mountains of Suceava County is one of the best winter sports resorts in northern Romania at an altitude of 800 m (2,625 ft.)–1,300 m (4,265 ft.); its snow layer is 45 cm (18 in.); ski season lasts December–March; the chair-lift and drag-lift operate from: 8am–4pm; Tel: (0744)85.15.50. Salvamont: Tel: (0230)37.27.67. Vatra Dornei is also famous for its spas.

Borşa resort is in the Rodnei Mountains in eastern Maramureş, an area of unique beauty and long-preserved traditions and folklore. Skiing has been popular here since the late 19th century. Its slopes rise 1,200 m (3,937 ft.)–1,500 m (4,921 ft.), are of medium difficulty, and have a natural ski jumping hill 50 m (164 ft.) high, unique in Europe. It has a sub-alpine climate and a snow depth average of 50 cm (20 in.). The tourist compound is linked by rope-chair (1,920 m in length, 500 m grade) to *Poiana Ştiol*, and further on, by ski lift (790 m in length), to *Ştiol* peak (1,611 m). Borşa's ski season is from December to April. Lifts: Slalom to 495m (1,624 ft.), Sub *telescaun* to 495 m (1,624 ft.), Ştiol to 180 m (590 ft.). The resort can be reached by driving the DN18 road or DN17, or by train to Vişeu de Sus, where you must switch and take the bus.

Păltiniş, at an altitude of 1,400 m (4,593 ft.) in the Cibin Mountains, in Sibiu County, has the best conditions for skiing and snowboarding, as well as randonnee (walk/ski in shorter skis) in the area. Its altitude is 1,430 m (4,692 ft.)–1,912 m (6,273 ft.); the snow layer is 50 cm (20 in.); with a chair-lift and drag-lift. Ski season is from December–March. Tel: (0269)21.43.77; Salvamont: Tel: (0269)44.36.14 (Păltiniş resort is covered by Salvamont Sibiu).

Stâna de Vale in the Apuseni Mountains (Bihor County) and **Semenic** in the Banat Mountains (Caraş-Severin County) are two smaller resorts located in the west of Romania. They do not have the modern infrastructure of other resorts, but offer good skiing and beautiful nature. Their altitude is between 1,100 m (3,609 ft.) and 1,400 m (4,591 ft.), inducing a mild climate (especially in Semenic) and huge quantities of snow (especially in Stâna de Vale).

Skiing facilities can also be found in: Aries Valley or Băişoara Mountains in the Apuseni Mountains; Bran in the Bucegi Mountains, Sugaş near Sfântu Gheorghe (Covasna County), Harghita Mădăraş and Izvoru Mureşului in Harghita County. More information on Romania's ski resorts can be found at www.skiresorts.ro.

Water Sports

The Black Sea offers all manner of water sports. In Mamaia there are eight designated water sports zones, four on Lake Siutghiol and four on the seaside, where you can go parasailing, jet skiing, water biking, scuba diving, sailing (and take sailing lessons), tube riding, and waterskiing and windsurfing. The other resorts along the seaside offer some of the same activities.

For information about Black Sea diving, contact Delphi S.R.L., Bd. Mamaia 16 in Constanta, Tel/fax: (40-241)64.60.21, (40-722)33.66.86, E-mail: delphi@rdslink.ro, www.divingdelphi.ro; their Bucharest office is at Unirea Shopping Center, etaj

3. Olimp also has a scuba diving facility, Respiro Dive Center, at the Hotel Belvedere, Tel: (40-722)32.51.35, E-mail: respiro@respirodiving.ro, www.respirodiving.ro (in Romanian).

It is possible to scuba dive in Romania's lakes, as well, including the southern Carpathians' crystal clear **glacial lakes**; or go **cave diving** through the galleries of some of Romania's ancient caves. In Bucharest, stop by the ScubaDiver Center, Şos. Stefan cel Mare 52, Sector 2, Tel: (40-21)610.46.02, Mobile: (40-723)01.64.67; Fax: (40-21)610.46.02, Web: E-mail: office@scuba-diver.ro, www.scubadiver.ro (in Romanian). If you need—and have time for—lessons, there are NAUI (National Association of Underwater Instructors) credentialed scuba diving courses at the Carpatica Dive Center**,** Str. Mihail Moxa 9, etaj 1, sector 1, in Bucureşti, Tel: (40-21)212-7546; fax: (40-21)212-7547, E-Mail: office@diving.ro, www.scubadiver.ro, www.naui.org.

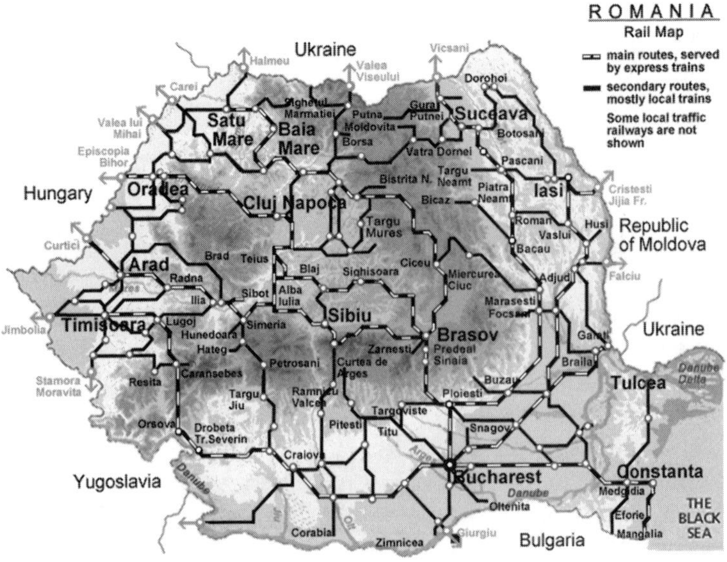

CHAPTER 5

WALLACHIA

History

The medieval territory south of the Carpathian mountains and north of the Danube River, was the first independent principality of the Romanians. Wallachia (land of the Vlachs or Wallachs) was founded in 1290 by Radu Negru as a feudal state with allegiance to Hungary. But in 1310, Romanian Duke Basarab I took advantage of the ending of Hungary's Arpad dynasty and refused to continue paying vassalage tributes to the kingdom. In 1330, Hungary's King Charles I (Charles Robert of Anjou) led his army into the territory in an attempt to reclaim it, but Basarab's forces defeated Charles' army at Posada. Basarab was named Prince (*Voivode*) Basarab I, and the state became the independent principality of Wallachia.

In the mid-14th century, the expanding Ottoman Empire had gained a foothold in southern Europe, and by 1396 they had reached the south bank of the Danube River. Eventually, the entire Balkan Peninsula became Turkish territory and, after the fall of Constantinople to Mehmed II in 1453, the Romanian principalities had to accept the suzerainty of the Ottoman Empire.

The Ottoman's controlled the regions of Easter Europe for more than three centuries, but local leaders continued their fight to regain their independence. Mircea the Elder (1386-1418) and Prince Vlad Dracul (1456-1462) of Wallachia led fierce battles against the Turks, but were defeated.

In 1593 Michael the Brave became Voivode of Wallachia and joined forces with Transylvania to cast out the Turks. In 1600, he managed to unite the three principalities and was proclaimed prince of Wallachia, Transylvania and Moldavia. However, Michael made enemies within, and in 1601 was killed while sleeping. After that, the alliance fell apart and Wallachia and Moldavia reverted to Turkish suzerainty, while Transylvania fell under Austria's Habsburg rule.

In the north, Alexander the Good (1401-1431) and Stephen the Great (1457-1504) of Moldavia, and Janos Hunyadi, prince of Transylvania (honored by both Romanians and Hungarians), also fought many defensive battles against the Ottomans, preventing them from expanding into Central Europe.

Over the centuries, a tribute paid to the Turks allowed Wallachia to maintain their autonomy. But in 1611, during Turkish battles with the Habsburgs over the region, the Turks installed Radu Mihnea as ruler of Wallachia. He appointed Greeks from the Phanar section of Istanbul to high government posts.

In 1632 until 1654, Matei Basarab ruled Wallachia. He promoted art and culture, and brought stability to the region. But after his death, infighting among the Romanian ruling families lasted fifteen years, ending with Şerban Cantacuzino's crowning and rule from 1678-1688. He was followed by Constantine Brâncoveanu until 1714. Brâncoveanu's tenure brought great economic progress and cultural development. He opened schools, brought in the first printing press, and built many churches, monasteries and other buildings in the region. He also introduced a new style of architecture that combined western and oriental designs, and became known as the Brâncoveanu style. But during his reign, the Ottomans began appointing Greek tax farmers from Istanbul (Phanariots) as princes for the purpose of getting as much money out of the land as possible. While negotiating a treaty with Czar Peter the Great of Russia for support in ousting the Turks, Brâncoveanu was betrayed by the Cantacuzinos and taken to Istanbul, where he was tortured and executed, along with his sons. His successor, Stephen Cantacuzino, was executed two years later, and Wallachia became governed by Turkish-appointed Phanariots.

The Phanariot regime lasted 106 years and was a period of corruption and decadence. The rulers lived lavishly and taxed heavily. They lost Oltenia (western Wallachia) to the Austrians in 1718, but under the Treaty of Belgrade, Oltenia was returned in 1739. The Austrians had introduced tax reforms to help the overburdened peasants, and in 1741 Phanariot Governor Constantine Mavrocordat adopted the Austrian's reforms and installed some of his own. He further abolished serfdom. Succeeding governors continued with reforms until 1782. The last two Phanariots raised the taxes again, a move that led to the 1821 revolution.

In 1768 Turkey was at war with Russia over control of Moldavia and Wallachia. Romanians aided Russia, and the Turks were pushed south of the Danube. From 1769-1774 the provinces were under Russian occupation, despite the Turkish suzerainty; but to appease Austria, who had supported the Turks, Russia returned the provinces. In the deal, Austria was given Bucovina, in northern Moldavia.

The Turks fought two more wars with Russia in 1787 and from 1806-1812, when the Russians occupied Wallachia and Moldavia. The latter ended with the Treaty of Bucharest, and Russia's annexation of Bessarabia.

In 1821 Greek Christian merchants from Russia organized another revolution to oust the Ottomans from Romania. They allied with Tudor Vladimirescu, the vice-governor of Oltenia, but later killed him for negotiating with the Turks. The revolt failed, but it resulted in abolishment of the Phanariot regime and both Russia and the Turks agreeing to allow Wallachia and Moldavia to elect their rulers from local nobility.

In 1827 Russia was at war with Turkey over Greek independence and they again occupied Wallachia and used it as a battlefield. But they forced Turkey to sign the Treaty of Adrianople in 1829, recognizing the two Romanian provinces and terminating their economic control of them.

Russia's General Pavel D. Kiseleff, head of Administration, oversaw repairing the war damage, and controlling famine and disease. He drew up constitutions for the two provinces and organized the rebuilding of the social and economic infrastructures. During the occupation Romanian princes again ruled their provinces, and the first Romanian newspapers appeared.

In 1859, Wallachia voted to unite with Moldavia to form the state of Romania, under the rule of Alexandru Ioan Cuza.

Geography

The historic region of Wallachia covers 76,581 sq km (29,568 sq mi) in southern Romania. It is one of Romania's three original regions (along with Moldavia and Transylvania). The Transylvanian Alps separate it in the northwest from Transylvania and the Banat; the Danube River separates it from Serbia in the west, Bulgaria in the south, and northern Dobrogea in the east. In the northeast it adjoins Moldavia. The Olt River divides the western Oltenia province from the eastern Muntenia province of Wallachia; Dobrogea province is east of the Danube River to the Black Sea.

Wallachia's main city is **Bucharest**. The rich oil fields at Ploieşti and the industrialized area near Bucharest make Wallachia the most economically developed region of Romania. Its industries (mainly chemicals, heavy machinery and shipbuilding) provide employment for about half of the country's labor force. Wallachia is also a rich agricultural area. An overwhelming majority of the region's population is Romanian, but there are also some Bulgarians, Serbs and Turks.

The **Danube River** flows 1,075 km along and through Wallachia; from the southwestern border town of Baziaş, along 468 km (290 miles) of Romania's southern border to just below Călăraşi, where it turns north on its way to Galaţi and the creation of its 2,590 sq km (1,000 sq miles) delta, before emptying into the Black Sea. It is the second largest river in Europe—2,850 km (1,770 miles) long—and a major source of transportation connecting seven countries: Germany, Austria, Slovakia,

Hungary, Serbia, Bulgaria and Romania. Since the 19th century, the river has served as a major commercial link between the industrial centers of Europe and the agricultural areas of the Balkan Peninsula. In 1896, the **Sip Canal** was opened at ***Porţile de Fier*** (Iron Gates) gorge to bypass its rapids and allow large ships to pass through the narrow gorge and continue all the way to the Black Sea.

BUCHAREST—ROMANIA'S CAPITAL

History

Founded on the banks of the Dâmbovița River in 1459 by Prince Vlad Dracula, Bucharest is Romania's largest and most prosperous city. Its name means gladness, something its two million inhabitants were deprived of for 45 years. A whole generation never knew the pleasures of a gentle, prosperous society; they were just trying to survive under the harsh austerity of Ceaușescu's dictatorship.

Dubbed the "Paris of the East" between the two World Wars for its architectural beauty, its sophisticated, international social scene and its extravagant aristocracy, the city's elegance crumbled during the communist years of megalomaniac Nicolae Ceausescu. He destroyed an entire community of historic homes and 26 churches, relocating 40,000 people, in order to erect an elaborate Civic Centre, crowned by the gigantic 12-story palace he called the "House of the People." Ugly, poorly constructed apartment structures were erected next to the city's classical buildings, and all were left to deteriorate from pollution, earthquakes and general neglect. The city's shops were bare and food was scarce, heat and running water only sporadically available, as nearly all of Romania's food and production were exported. Fear and mistrust permeated the city, lest someone report a minor infraction of their neighbor, in order to gain favor with the authorities. A smile was the rarest of sights.

But the city has finally come back to life. Its grand old buildings and tree-lined *bulevards* are being restored, and new shops, restaurants and entertainments are appearing, filled with goods from around the world, and its international visitors are returning.

Bucharest's recovery has taken longer than other former communist cities, partly because the post-revolution government, comprised of former Communists, was reluctant to proceed with total reform. But Romania's new democratic government welcomes western influence, avidly promoting private business and international investment. Today there are more than 8,000 "expats," foreign residents living and working in the city.

Bucharest's future relies on its young people who have the freedom, energy and open-mindedness needed to restore their city to greatness. It is well on its way!

Sightseeing

Bucharest has many outstanding museums, galleries, and architectural jewels. Glimpses of its regal and turbulent history can be seen in these monuments and exhibits. It's an easy walking city, but it also has an excellent underground metrou system and bus/tram service to help you get around.

Arcul de Triumf, Şoseaua Kiseleff. A replica of Paris' Arc de Triomphe, this one honors Romania's World War I dead. It stands in the middle of Şoseaua Kiseleff at the foot of Herăstrau Park.

Atheneul Roman (Romanian Atheneum), Piaţa Revoluţiei. Grand concert hall and headquarters of the George Enescu Philharmonic. Built in 1888 by French architect Albert Galleron in neo-classic style, its magnificent interior includes a rotunda of six masonry columns and four monumental staircases; a round concert hall of 600 seats and 60 boxes; and a huge fresco depicting 25 episodes in Romanian history.

Cercul Militar, Calea Victoriei 27. A military officers' club, it also has an art gallery open to the public, a restaurant and an outdoor cafe by the fountain.

Civic Centre, the area along Bulevardul Unirii, west of the *piaţa*, where it meets the Parliament Palace. This is the neighborhood where thousands of houses and churches were demolished by Ceauşescu in order to create his monument to communism, the House of the People, and where many government ministries are located. It was completed in 1989, just before Ceauşescu's overthrow.

Curtea Veche (Old Court), Strada Franceză 31. The ruins of the palace built by Prince Vlad Dracula from 1456-1462, and the court of several Wallachian princes. Destroyed by the Turks and by earthquakes, it now consists of only a few walls and an archway which were once the ambassadors' reception hall and the guard room. Next door is the Princely Church, built in 1546 by Prince Mircea Ciobanu, where the princes of Wallachia were anointed. It is the oldest church in Bucharest and open to the public.

Hanul lui Manuc, Strada Franceza 62-64. Built in 1808 by Manuc-Bey, an Armenian trader, as a caravansary for traveling merchants. The building and its timbered balcony surround a large inner courtyard with an outdoor cafe. Inside, there's a charming restaurant with wine cellar plus a hotel.

Historical District, a winding maze of narrow streets in Bucharest's oldest section, nestled between Calea Victoriei and Bd. I.C.Brătianu. Spanning the district is Strada Lipscani, a bustling bazaar of shops, outdoor vendors and cafes. Among its cross-streets you will find clusters of glassware stores, wedding shops, bakeries and boutiques. The Curtea Veche, Stavropoleos church, Hanul lui Manuc, and Caru cu Bere restaurant are all in this district. Its south end opens onto Splaiul Independenţei and the Dâmboviţa River near Piaţa Unirii. (See City Walk #4, p. 115.)

Kreţulescu Church, Calea Victoriei at Piaţa Revoluţiei. This tiny Orthodox church, built in 1725 by Iordache Kreţulescu in the Brâncovenesc style, rests at the south end of the former Royal Palace. It has an intricately carved entry and a worn, but interesting, fresco of the Apocalypse.

Lens-Vernescu House, Calea Victoriei 133. Built in 1820 and restored in 1887; its interior painting is by F.D. Mirea. It now houses the Palace Casino and the Casa Vernescu restaurant and garden.

National Theatre, Bd. Bălcescu 2, at Piaţa Universităţii. Completed in 1970, it has two main halls and hosts all types of productions. It is also home to the Opereta Theatre, Artexpo and Dominus Art Galeries, and the Lăptăria Enache jazz cafe. Tel: (021)614.71.71.

Opera Româna, Bd. Kogălniceanu 70, at the west end of the boulevard, where it meets Splaiul Independenţei and the Dâmboviţa River. Presents a classical repertoire at inexpensive prices. Note: Romanians still dress up for the opera, so don't show up in your jeans and T-shirt. Closed in summer. Tel: (021)313.18.57.

Palace of Justice, Strada Splaiul Unirii 6. Built between 1890 and 1895 in the French Renaissance style, on the south bank of the Dâmboviţa River.

Parliament Palace, Calea 13 Septembrie, at the west end of Bd. Unirii. Built by Nicolae Ceauşescu, his "House of the People" (*Casa Poporului*) was intended as headquarters for his communist government. It is the second largest building in the world, after the U.S. Pentagon, at 1,181,100 square feet (360,000 sq. meters), and standing 84 meters (275 ft.) high.

More than 400 architects and 20,000 workers constructed the palace, which contains 1,100 rooms and halls of 100-2,600 sq. meters (330-8,500 sq. ft.). There are 480 colossal rooms on the second floor alone. It is built and furnished entirely from Romanian materials including local marble, cherry wood and walnut paneling, crystal chandeliers, regional tapestries, carpets and draperies. It is now used as an international conference center and as home of the Romanian Parliament. There is also a theater, art gallery and restaurant inside. Guided tours are conducted between 10am and 4pm daily in summer, but only on Fridays, Saturdays and Sundays when Parliament is in session; call ahead to schedule a tour in your language. Entrance is on the south side. Well worth a visit to see its opulent interiors. Tel: (021)311.36.11, 311.36.13; fax: (021)312.09.02, E-mail: cic@camera.ro. (Izvor or Unirii *metrou*)

Patriarchal Cathedral and Palace, Strada Dealul Mitropoliei, atop Mitropoliei Hill, just south of Piaţa Unirii. Built in 1655-1668 in classic Romanian style, the relics of Bucharest's patron saint, St. Dumitru are kept here. Next door is the guarded Chamber of Deputies, the former house of Parliament I in 1907.

Piaţa Revoluţiei, on Calea Victoriei. Scene of much of the fighting during the 1989 uprising, this was the location of Ceauşescu's Communist Party Central Committee building, with the balcony where he gave his final speech before fleeing the city. Across the street, the beautiful University Library, gutted during the events of 1989, has been restored. Across the piaţa, the former Royal Palace now houses the National Art Museum. At the north end stand the historic Athenée Palace hotel and the Atheneul Român concert hall. At its south end is the tiny Kreţulescu church.

Piaţa Romană, this busy intersection marks the beginning of the city's most commercial strip along the multi-named Bulevardul Gen. Magheru–N. Bălcescu–I.C. Brătianu, which leads south to Piaţa Unirii. Just east of the piaţa, along Bd. Dacia, are some lovely old mansions that house many international embassies. Northward, Bd. Lascăr Catargiu leads to Piaţa Victoriei. Piaţa Romană is a metrou stop on the north–south blue line and a major stop on the bus routes.

Piaţa Unirii, a vast open green at the southern tip of the commercial area along Bd. Brătianu, surrounded by stores and businesses. This flat, sunny park has benches for relaxing, flower beds, and a magnificent display of mosaic fountains at the southern end. Beneath the piaţa, all three metrou lines link. To the west, along Bd. Unirii, is the Civic Center and Parliament Palace.

Piaţa Universităţii, a main center of activity, with the University of Bucharest and its bookstalls and flower vendors on one side, and the National Theatre and the Intercontinental Hotel across Bd. Bălcescu. Below is an underground concourse of shops and eateries that leads to the metrou station and also passes under the crossroads to their opposite sides.

Piaţa Victoriei, a large open expanse of roadway at the north end of the city centre dominated by the government building, Victoriei Palace. Calea Victoriei begins here, as does the tree-lined Şoseaua Kiseleff heading north toward Herăstrău Parc. The long multi-named Bulevardul (L. Catargiu, G. Magheru, N. Bălcescu, I.C. Brătianu, D. Cantemir) also begins here. A major metrou transfer station is underground.

RomExpo, at Piaţa Presei Libere, north of Herăstrău Parc. This is Bucharest's contemporary, domed exhibition hall, where various trade shows are held year round. It is located north of the centre, next door to the World Trade Center and Sofitel Hotel. Many shows are open to the public for a fee.

Royal Palace, on Calea Victoriei in Piaţa Revoluţiei. Erected in 1927-1937 in the neoclassical style, it consists of a wide central section and two lateral wings. It was home to King Carol II and his son King Mihai I until 1947, when the monarchy was abolished. Since 1950, it has housed the National Art Museum.

Stavropoleos Church, Strada Stavropoleos, off Calea Victoriei. Built in 1724-1730 in the Brâncovenesc style (a combination of Romanian and Byzantine) with elaborate wood and stone carvings, this tiny church with its courtyard is one of the city's oldest. The church is open daily until 6pm; services are held Sunday morning at 9:30 and 10:30am, Wednesday at 4:30pm, and Friday and Saturday at 5pm.

Village Museum (*Muzeul Satului*), Şoseaua Kiseleff 30. A wonderful outdoor exhibition of authentic rural houses and work buildings brought from all regions of the country into a re-created village setting. It's the countryside in Bucharest. (See Museums below.)

World Trade Center Plaza, at Sofitel hotel, north of city center and next door to RomExpo. There is a swanky shopping gallery and exhibition hall open to the public, plus a convention center, reception rooms, and 300-seat amphitheater with video and interpreting facilities.

Museums

Most of Bucharest's museums are open from 10am until 6pm, and closed on Mondays. There will be a small entry fee to see the exhibits. Most museum attendants speak little or no English, so ask your hotel concierge to call, if necessary.

Arts Collection Museum (*Palatul Romanit*), Calea Victoriei 111. Contains all art genres including fine paintings, Romanian folk art and painted-glass icons. Tel: (021)650.61.32.

Bucharest History & Arts Museum, History Section, Bd. I.C. Brătianu 2. The former Şuţu Palace, a boyar mansion built in 1835, now houses collections of archeology, Neolithic art, old coins, photos, weapons, furniture and old costumes relating to the history of the city of Bucharest. A 1459 document by Vlad the Impaler (Dracula) names Bucharest for the first time. (Piaţa Universităţii metrou) Tel: (021)313.85.15, fax: (021)315.68.58, E-mail: mistorie@sunu.rnc.ro.

Ceramics and Glass Museum, Calea Victoriei 107. Housed in the former Ştirbei Palace (1856), this neo-classical museum displays exquisite mirrors, chandeliers, a Tiffany lamp, oriental tiles, porcelain, pottery and even tapestries, carpets and furniture. Tel: (021)615.43.94.

Cotroceni Palace and Museum (former Royal Residence), Bd. Geniului 1, west of city centre. Exhibits 17th and 18th century art; hosts special exhibitions and concerts. This former palace was erected for Princess Marie, niece of Queen Victoria, who married King Ferdinand and became the Queen of Romania. After renovations following the 1977 earthquake, Ceauşescu made it an official guest house. In 1991 one wing of the palace became the residence of the President of Romania. Visits must be pre-arranged by phone; tours in English are available. Tel: (021)222.12.00, 430.44.85. (Eroilor metrou; then walk west on Bd. Eroii Sanitari, then around the block to the front entrance)

Geological Museum, Şoseaua Kiseleff 2. Unusual collection of crystals; rocks that glow in the dark. Closes at 3 pm. (Piaţa Victoriei metrou)

George Enescu Museum/Cantacuzino Palace, Calea Victoriei 141. Composer and violinist Enescu (1881-1954) married the Princess Maria Cantacuzino, but chose to live in three simple rooms rather than in her French-baroque style palace. The ornate building now contains the personal objects, musical scores and instruments of the composer. Music performed some evenings. Tel: (021)659.63.65.

History Museum of the Jewish Community in Romania, Strada Mămulari 3. Documents the lives and destiny of the Jewish community beginning from the year AD 100. Tel: (021)311 08 70; E-mail: auroras@antipa.ro. Open Wed and Sun, closed Saturdays, 9am-1pm.

Museum of Natural History "Grigore Antipa," Şoseaua Kiseleff 1. Built in 1904, its 30,000 zoological and mineral exhibits include a 15-foot high dinosaur skeleton, a Peruvian mummy, a re-created cave with stalactites, and a rare butterfly collection. Tel: (021)312.88.62, fax: (021)312.88.86, www.antipa.ro. (Piaţa Victoriei metrou)

***Muzeul Ţăranului Român* (Museum of the Romanian Peasant)**, Şoseaua Kiseleff 3. Outstanding exhibits of traditional, regional clothing on life-size mannequins, hand-made textiles, wooden and iron objects, ceramics, paintings, drawings and photos. The museum contains an authentic Oltenia house and a room full of very large farm machinery. Tel: (021)650.53.60; fax: (021)312.98.75, E-mail: muztar@rnc.ro, www.itcnet.ro/mtr/index_en.html. (Piaţa Victoriei metrou)

National Art Museum, Calea Victoriei 49-53 (in the former Royal Palace). Contains 100,000 exhibits of European and Asian art dating from the 1st century. One hall displays international artworks (paintings by Corot, Delacroix, El Greco, Manet, Rubens, Rembrandt & Sisley); the other is dedicated to Romanian artists, including sculptures by Brâncuşi. Tel: (021)313.30.30; fax: (021)314.81.10, E-mail: national.art@art.museum.ro, http://art.museum.ro/museum.html. Closed Monday and Tuesday.

National History Museum of Romania, Calea Victoriei 12. In the old neo-classical Postal building, over 600,000 items from prehistoric times through the modern period, including exhibits of Romania's Greek and Roman history and the royal treasury of silver, gold and jewels located downstairs. Closed Monday and Tuesday. Tel: (021)315.70.56; fax: (021)311.33.56, E-mail direct@mnir.ro, www.mnir.ro.html. Also visit: http://cimec.ro/e_default.htm.

National Military Museum, Strada Mircea Vulcănescu 125-127. One million exhibits representing guns and combat equipment, anti-aircraft artillery, uniforms, medals, flags, maps and plans, harness and horse racing accessories, luggage carriages, mobile kitchens, royal carriages and even a steam railway engine used in World War I. There is a section dedicated to the army's role during the 1989 revolution. A hangar displays airforce planes, helicopters and the Soyouz-40 space capsule from 1981. Tel: (021)637.76.35, 638.76.30.

Technical Museum "*Dimitrie Leonida*," in Carol I Park, Strada Gen. Candiano Popescu 2. Founded in 1909 by engineer Dimitrie Leonida (1883-1965), this is a hands-on museum where visitors can view and operate mechanisms that illustrate the mechanics, electricity and magnetism laws. Over 5,000 exhibits from all the fields of activity, including an 1894 electrical tram engine, 1924 aerodynamic motor car, two 1880 Brush dynamos; the 1884 Edison dynamo, the cylinder of the first steam machine, and the Gogu Constantinescu sonic engine. Tel: (021)623.77.77, www.cimec.ro/muzee/mteh/mteh_eng.htm.

Village Museum (*Muzeul Satului*), Şoseaua Kiseleff 28-30, in Herăstrău Parc. If you can't get out to the countryside, you must visit this fabulous outdoor museum, where more than 60 rural houses, workshops, mills and churches have been brought from all regions of the country and arranged in a re-created village setting. "Peasant" workers in traditional costume portray life in the 16th and 17th centuries. Traditional crafts are for sale, and there is often folk music on Sundays at 11am. Tel: (021)222.91.10, fax: (021)222.90.68, E-mail: contact@muzeul-satului.ro, www.muzeul-satului.ro. (Buses #131, 205, 331, 335, or 783 to Arcul de Triumf/Muzeul Satului; Tram: #41 to Institutul Agronomic; Aviatorilor metrou to Herăstrău Parc; then walk west to Şoseaua. Kiseleff, and north to entrance.)

Parks

Botanical Gardens, Şoseaua Cotroceni 32. West of the city center, in the residential area called Cotroceni, the gardens occupy 42 acres and display over 10,000 plants and flowers from around the world. Open daily from 7am to evening, there is a small admission fee. The greenhouse and museum are open on Tuesdays, Thursdays, & Sundays from 9am-1pm only. Follow Splaiul Independenţei west to Şoseaua Cotroceni on the left. Tel: (021)638.44.50. (Eroilor metrou, then walk west to Şoseaua Cotroceni, and turn left)

The huge glasshouses are open Tue, Thr, Sat, Sun, 09:00-13:00. Take bus 336 from Universitate to get there. Admission 10,000 lei (5,000 for children).

Grădina Cişmigiu, Bd. Regina Elisabeta. For 150 years Cişmigiu Garden has been the perfect escape from the hubbub of downtown Bucharest with its lovely manicured gardens and tree-shaded paths. It was designed in 1845 by German landscape architect Carl Meyer, and completed in 1860. More than 30,000 trees and plants were transplanted from the Romanian mountains; and the more exotic plants were brought from the botanical gardens of Vienna. There's a lake with rowboat rentals, a Roman Garden including busts of Romania's most famous writers, and Ion Jalea's French memorial in Carrara marble, commemorating French troops killed on Romanian territory during the Great War. There is also a beer garden, a gazebo where music is sometimes played, a children's playground, and numerous park benches lining the paths for relaxing and people watching. In the northwest section you'll find a small plaza where the old men gather to play chess, remi and other board and tile games. The garden's south entrance is a short walk west of Calea Victoriei on Bd. Regina Elisabeta; it is also bordered by Str. Ştirbei Vodă to the north and Bd. Schitu Măgureanu on its west side (Izvor metrou).

Parcul Herăstrău, Şoseaua Kiseleff 32. Bucharest's largest park has broad lakes, beautiful gardens, tree-lined walking paths, fountain pools, and even a kiddie amusement park. Its 187 hectares (462 acres) surround Herăstrău lake, at the north side of which are boat rentals, a sailboat launch, a go-cart track, and several outdoor lakeside cafes. The park is also home to the **Village Museum** (*Muzeul Satului*). Herăstrău is located north of the city center along Şoseaua Kiseleff, beginning at the Arcul de Triumf at Bd. Mareşal Prezan; its east entrance is at Piaţa Charles de Gaulle (Aviatorilor metrou).

Parcul Kiseleff, Soseaua Kiseleff. A small patch of greenery just north of Piaţa Victoriei on Şoseaua Kiseleff, this park begins the way to the stretch of mansions leading north toward the Arc de Triumf and Herăstrău Parc. (Piaţa Victoriei metrou)

Parcul Carol I, Calea Şerban Vodă. Lesser-known to visitors, this large park is one of the loveliest in the city. It is located south of Piaţa Unirii and west of Bd. Dimitrie Cantemir. The park has tree-lined paths, a lake and is home to the Technical Museum. A massive monument once held the remains of communist leader Gheorghe Gheorghiu-Dej, but now contains artifacts and furniture that belonged to Nicolae Ceausescu, but unfortunately, it is not open to the public. The park also contains the "eternal flame" marking the grave of the unknown soldier. (Carol I Parc can be reached via trams no.15, 23, 30 or bus no.232; get off at the Parcul Libertăţii stop. You can also walk south from Bd. Unirii along Bd. D. Cantemir, then turn right onto Bd. Mărăşeşti which goes directly to the park's northern entrance.)

Piaţa Unirii, Not exactly a park, this large green piaţa, with its park benches and flower beds, is an oasis at the southern tip of Bucharest's busy commercial area. It is surrounded by stores, businesses and vendors, and sits above two metrou transfer stations. At the south end are the fabulous mosaic fountains from which one can see the huge Parliament Palace a mile to the west. (Piaţa Unirii metrou)

Băneasa Forest, 10 km (6 miles) north of Bucharest's center is a wonderful forested park with the city zoo, plus picnic grounds, food kiosks and beer gardens serving traditional grilled mititei sausages. Zoo admission is about 30 cents. It's open daily from 8am-8pm. (Take bus #301 from Piaţa Romană.)

City Walks

Seasoned travelers know that the best way to get to know a city is by foot. The following walks are designed to guide you around the four central areas of Bucharest, pointing out distinctive places and special sights along the way. Stray from the routes as you wish, as you're bound to find other interesting places on your walk that are not mentioned here. Allow approximately three hours for each walk.

Walk #1 North of Center

This beautiful walk takes you through the quiet area north of the city center. Begin at **Piaţa Victoriei** with the government's **Victoriei Palace** on its east side. Cross the piaţa carefully, and walk north along tree-lined **Şoseaua Kiseleff**. On your left are the **Museum of Natural History** and the ***Muzeul Ţăranului Român*** **(Romanian Peasants Museum)**; across the street is the **Geologic Museum**. After passing through **Parcul Kiseleff**, stroll northward along the grand mansions that line the shaded avenue. (The U.S. Ambassador's residence is on the west side of the avenue.) You will soon come to Romania's own **Arc de Triumf**. At this point the lovely **Herăstrău Parc** begins (on the right), with its large lake, gardens and outdoor restaurants. If you stay on the avenue, you will reach the entrance to the wonderful open-air **Muzeul Satului (Village Museum)**; take time to stop in and admire the authentic peasant houses and artifacts.

Continuing to the north end of Herăstrău park, off Piaţa Presei Libere you'll see the domed **RomExpo** convention center and the **World Trade Center Plaza** at Sofitel Hotel. There's a fancy shopping arcade inside and a very nice coffee shop in the hotel where you can get a bite to eat. Catch bus #335 back to Piaţa Charles de Gaulle for the Aviatorilor metrou stop, or take bus #331 back to Piaţa Romană. (Near hotels Flora, Helvetia, Parc, Sofitel and Triumf.)

Walk #2 West-Central

This walk follows the route of Bucharest's most famous historic avenue, Calea Victoriei. Beginning at **Piaţa Victoriei**, stroll south along **Calea Victoriei**. You will pass **Casa Vernescu**, the **George Enescu Museum** in **Cantacuzino Palace**, the **Art Collections Museum** and the **Ceramics and Glass Museum**.

Two blocks south of Bd. Dacia, detour left onto **Strada Piaţa Amzei** where you'll come upon the colorful **open-air produce market**. Then return to Calea Victoriei and turn left to resume the walk south, stopping in the many designer **fashion boutiques** and shops along the way.

Upon reaching **Piaţa Revoluţiei** you will find the **Athenée Palace Hotel**, the **Atheneul Român** concert house (ask for an inside tour), the **National Art Museum** in the former **Royal Palace**, the elegant **University Library** (totally restored after being gutted during the 1989 revolution), the former **Communist Party Central Committee building** where Ceauşescu gave his last speech, and finally, the small **Kreţulescu Church** built in 1725. Continuing south on Calea Victoriei, you'll pass more shops and hotels; note the **Teatreu Odeon** sitting back from the street on the left. On the right you'll come to **Cercul Militar** which has an outdoor cafe and an art gallery.

Turn right (west) at the corner onto **Bd. Regina Elisabeta** and follow it past the McDonald's to **Cişmigiu Gardens**, the last stop on this walk. Stroll around the lake, watch the chess games, or just relax watching the rowboats. The beer garden or the boathouse cafe may be open for a snack or refreshment. (Near hotels Bucureşti, Bulevard, Capitol, Central, Continental, Hilton Athenée Palace, Majestic and Opera.)

Walk #3 East-Central

This walk takes you along Bucharest's busiest commercial and shopping area. The bulevard changes names five times, but on this walk you will cover the length of only three of its five sections: Bd. General Magheru, Bd. N. Bălcescu and Bd. I.C. Brătianu. Starting from **Piaţa Romană**, you might first want to walk east on **Bd. Dacia** for a look at some of the **embassy mansions**; then return to Piaţa Romană.

Next, head south on **Bd. Gen. Magheru**. You'll soon spot the stairway down to the Piaţa Romană **metrou station** and **bus stop**. The small kiosk is a good place to buy a *cartelă de telefon* (RomTelecom phone card) or stock up on bus tickets (*bilete*). The street is filled with clothing boutiques, sidewalk vendors, pastry shops and cafes (*cofetării*), cinemas, stationary stores (*papetărie*), and antique shops. You'll soon spy the KFC and McDonalds eateries, the Everest café tucked in between. Their patios are very popular gathering places. Continuing, across Strada George Enescu are **Teatru Nottara** and the **Galeria de Artă**. Stop into the charming bookstore (*librărie*) **Cărtureşti**, set back a bit from the street on your left, and browse the many wonderful picture books about Romania. Several tourist agencies and international airline offices also line this little square. **Cinema Patria**, across the street, shows top American films with sub-titles. The Hotel Ambassador is along this stretch, too.

At Strada Rosetti, the bulevard's name changes to **Bd. N. Bălcescu,** where you'll find more boutiques, pass *Biserica Italiană Sfântul Giulgiu* (Catholic church), the two Comfort Suites hotels, and come upon the ***Librăria Noi*** bookstore, which has a nice selection of American picture books and English novels. There are even more boutiques and several **art and antique galleries**, including two in the **National Theatre** which is next to the modern high-rise **Intercontinental Hotel**. The **American Consulate** and the **American Library** are located on the streets behind the hotel. Reaching **Piaţa Universităţii**, on the west side of the street you'll see **Bucharest University** and the sidewalk book and flower vendors; sit a moment at the fountain in the adjoining piaţa and watch the activity. To cross the bulevard, use the underground passage, rather than deal with the street traffic above; the **concourse** is also your access to the Piaţa Universităţii **metrou** and has shops, newsstands with American magazines, and several fast food eateries.

The west side of Bd. Bălcescu has the western boutiques Nautica, Timberland and Sephora among others, the Orizont art gallery, a *bancomat* for cash, the **Carlton Café**, Bar, and patio Brasserie, **Pescarul** restaurant and the **Princess Casino**.

South of Piaţa Universităţii the street name changes again, to **Bd. I.C. Brătianu**. On your right is the **Bucharest History Museum**, in the former **Sutu Palace**, built in 1835. Farther down, on the east side will be **St. Gheorghe cel Nou** church, built in 1707. The eastern end of **Strada Lipscani** meets the bulevard on the west side. (This is the city's historical district, Walk #4.) Continuing south, you will end this walk at **Piaţa Unirii**, a large grassy park with benches to rest on and an enormous complex of **fountains** at its south end. Alongside, there is a McDonalds and a department store. Underground, Piaţa Unirii's two metrou lines link with all other metrou stops. (Near hotels Duke, Minerva, Grand Plaza, Ambasador, Lido, Comfort and Intercontinental.)

Walk #4 South

This route weaves through a tangle of colorful side streets in Bucharest's historic district. Be extra alert here, as you will do some back-tracking. Begin at the crossroads of **Calea Victoriei** and **Bd. Regina Elisabeta**. Walk south on Calea Victoriei, along the east side of the street. Duck into **Pasajul Villa Cross** (also called *Pasajul Bijuteria*), a golden skylit arcade of boutiques, **Café Villacross** and the **Blues Cafe**. Follow its U-shape back to Calea Victoriei and walk south a block, to the beginning of **Strada Lipscani**.

Stroll Strada Lipscani to see the vendors and shops. Sample the cheese, fruit and meat pastries sold under the yellow awning while viewing the fabulous 100-year-old **CEC Palace** (Savings Bank), across the avenue. Strada Lipscani runs through to Bd. I.C. Brătianu (Walk #3). At its half-way point, however, you might turn onto **Strada Smârdan** and walk south to **Strada Stavropoleos** and visit the tiny **Biserica Stavropoleos,** built in 1724, a combination of Romanian and Byzantine architecture; it has a beautiful façade, delicately-carved columns and a scene of Samson fighting the lion fret-worked into the rail of the porch. Attached is its peaceful garden and courtyard. Farther down the street at no. 3-5 is the **Caru cu Bere** restaurant. If you can't stop in for a beer or snack, at least peek inside to see its magnificent interior.

Heading south again on Strada Smârdan, you will come to **Strada Franceză** (formerly Str. Iuliu Maniu) where you will find the remains of ***Curtea Veche*** (the Old Court) of the real Prince Dracula and his **Princely Church**, the oldest in Bucharest. Just across the road is the former caravansary **Hanul lui Manuc**, now a restaurant and inn. Go inside the courtyard for a look at its timbered design, or stop there for some food or a drink.

Another tiny street, **Strada Şelari**, runs from Strada Iuliu Maniu back up to Strada Lipscani; this is the street of glass, lined with **glassware galleries,** shops and the **glass-blowing** courtyard workshop **Curtea Sticlarilor**. If you take the narrow street south, you'll exit the neighborhood at the Splaiul Independenţei and the **Dâmboviţa River**.

Another option is to take Str. Franceză back to Calea Victoriei, where the **National History Museum** holds the crown jewels and other precious artifacts from royal times.

Across the river you can see the 100-year-old **Palace of Justice**. Cross the bulevard to reach the broad, green **Piaţa Unirii**. Here you can rest while watching the fountains and the people. There are several places to get a snack along the piaţa's west side.

From the south end of Piaţa Unirii, looking west, you can see Ceauşescu's huge **House of the People**, now **Parliament Palace**. Walk west along Bd. Unirii toward the Parliament Palace; this area is the **Civic Center**. When you reach the building, turn right, and walk north, back to the river.

Cross the Dâmboviţa River again at the **Izvor bridge**. Walk a block north to Bd. Regina Elisabeta, then turn right and you'll wind up across the street from **Cişmigiu Garden**. To end this walk, continue east on Bd. Elisabeta to Calea Victoriei; or go a little farther, toward Piaţa Universităţii and its metrou station. (Near hotels Bulevard, Capitol, Central, Continental, Majestic and Opera.)

City Transportation

Bucharest Metrou There are three metrou lines crossing the city from north-south (M2-blue), east-west (M3-yellow), and a circular route (M1-red). The system is very efficient and the stations are clean and well marked, each having a unique design. You must buy a metrou card for either 2 rides or 10 rides; they are very cheap, the equivalent of about 50 cents a ride. Metros operate from 5am until 11pm. (Check the metrou map below for routes and stops.) Note: photographing on the metrou platform is not allowed.

Bucharest buses and trams run from dawn to 11pm and travel everywhere, but are difficult to figure out as there are no route maps. Tickets are sold at yellow kiosks near some stops until early evening. They're cheap, so buy 2 or 3 to be safe. When you get on the bus, validate your ticket by punching it in the little box on board. A special bus, **#783**, runs to Henri Coandă

Airport from Piaţa Romană and Piaţa Unirii in the city centre (*centru*). Buses #79, 86 and 133 run from various stops around the Gara de Nord train station to Piaţa Romană. The buses are old and very crowded so, as in most big cities, be especially aware of pick-pockets.

Bucharest's Main **Bus Terminals** are: Filaret Bus Terminal, Cuţitul de Argint Street 2B, sector 4, Tel: (021)336.06.92.12, transfer to public tramway no.7; Băneasa Bus Terminal, Bd. Ionescu de la Brad 3-5, Tel: (021)230.56.45, transfer to public buses nos. 205 and 131; Griviţa Bus Terminal, Şoseaua Chitilei 221, Tel: (021)667.59.70, transfer to public bus no.645; Militari Bus Terminal, Bd. Iuliu Maniu 141, Tel: (021)434.17.39; Rahova Bus Terminal, Şoseaua Alexandriei 164, Tel: (021)420.47.95, transfer to public bus no. 303, trolleybus no. 96, or trams nos. 2, 32, 15; Obor Bus Terminal:, Bd. Gării Obor 5, Tel: (021)252.76.46, transfer to public trolleybus lines nos. 85 and 69.

Shopping

Bucharest now has many international boutiques and stores. The most exclusive designer shops are on Calea Victoriei, followed by those on Bd. Magheru/Brătianu. The new shops offer a wide selection of clothes, shoes, accessories, jewelry, watches, sportswear, lingerie, perfumes and gifts. Shops open at 9 or 10am and close at 6 or 7pm on weekdays, possibly earlier on Saturdays; most stores are closed on Sundays.

Department Stores: Bucharest's old department stores in are in a transition period. Though still not as polished and fancy as western department stores, they are now well stocked with ready-to-wear fashions, cosmetics, electronics, luggage items and appliances; some even sell delicatessen foods. Along with their specialized departments, they may also contain small private-vendor "bazaar" type sections. Bucharest department stores offer low- to mid-quality products. There is usually a food court or café in or adjacent to the premises.

Art: Apollo Gallery Bd. Balcescu 2 (right side of National Theatre) Romanian paintings, sculpture, graphic and decorative art. Tel: (021)613.50.10, open Mon-Sat, 10am-6pm; **ArtExpo Gallery,** Bd. Balcescu 2 (3rd and 4th floors of the National Theatre), Tel: (021)613.91.15, open Tues-Sun; **Căminul Artei Gallery,** Strada Biserica Enei 16, paintings, sculpture, decorative art. Tel: (021)614.18.18, open Mon-Fri; **Cercul Militar National Gallery,** Strada Constantin Mille 1, Tel: (021)613.86.80; **Dominus Art Gallery**, Bd. Balcescu 2 (ground floor of National Theatre), Romanian paintings, sculpture, sketch and graphic art. Tel: (021)614.22.86, open Mon-Fri; **Graphis Gallery**, Bd. Balcescu 23A, Graphic art. Tel: (021)615.38.27, open Monday-Friday, and Saturday morning; **Hanul cu Tei**, Strada Blănari 5-7 (Lipscani Arcade, near Bd. Brătianu), paintings, sculpture, jewelry, graphic art, decorative art, antiques. Tel: (021)615.38.27, open Monday-Friday, and Saturday morning; **Orizont Gallery**, Bd. Balcescu 23A, sculpture, ceramics, glass decorative objects. Tel: (021)615.89.17, open Monday-Friday, and Saturday morning.

Antiques: A A Antiques, Strada Quinet 4; **Craii de Curtea Veche**, Strada Covaci 14; **Da Vinci**, Calea Victoriei 118; **Galateea**, Calea Victoriei 134; **Galeria Djaburov**, Strada Popa Tatu 28; **Galeria de Arta Dorobanti**, Strada Tudor Stefan 13; **Hanul cu Tei**, Strada Lipscani 63; **Palas Antiques**, Calea Victoriei 100; **Quasar Antiques**, Calea Victoriei 63-81.

Books, Music, Computers: Cărtureşti, Bd. Magheru at Str. Pictor Verona, books, tea and music, Tel: 212.19.22; **Galeria La Calu' Bălan**, Str. Halelor 3 at Splaiul Independenţiei, good selection of English literature and travel guides; **Librăria Eminescu**, Strada Edgar Quinet, by the University, carries some English literature; **Librăria Noi**, Bd. Balcescu 18, large bookstore carries English literature and picture books, Tel: 311.07.00; **Librăria Muzica**, Calea Victoriei 41-43, CDs and cassettes, instruments, scores; **Swing Music**, Bd. Expoziţiei 2, at the World Trade Center, original CDs and videos, classical, jazz, pop, rock, folk and international music; **Computerland**, Bd. Unirii 15, computers, software, mobile phones; **A&S Computer Center**, Strada Academiei 18-21, Canon, Corel, Hewlett Packard, Microsoft, et al.

China & Crystal: Camina, Piaţa Romana 9; **Leu**, Bd. Unirii 11; **Sticerom**, Strada Şelari 9-11; and at **Unirea Shopping Center**, Piaţa Unirii 1.

Fashion: The poshest international designer boutiques, like **Boss, Cerutti, Ferre, Hechter** and **Mara** cluster along Calea Victoriei. But Romania has its own fine designers with boutiques worth checking out: **Alb & Negru (Agnes Toma)** in Unirea Shopping Center; **Atelier Cătălin Botezatu**, Str. Londra 42; **Atelier Levintza**, Str. Constantin Prezan 4A; **Dan Coma**, within **Agila Gallery**, Bd. Ion Mihalche 113; **Ingrid Vlasov**, Str. A. Constantinescu 41; **Irina Schrötter**, in Bucharest Mall; **Lilliana Turoiu Udea** within **Mihai Albu**, Calea Victoriei 102-110; **Rita Murisan**, Allee Alexandru 7A; **Venera Arapu**, within **Griffes**, Calea Dorobanţiilor 170; **Wilhelmina Arz**, Bd. Bucureştii Noi 139. Other fine shops are **Alsa Boutiques, Bliss, Ellis, La Femme, Stefanel** and **Yokko**, all on Calea Victoriei. Calea Victoriei 25, Men's designer clothes (Boss, Hechter, et al.), Tel: 312.10.61.

Bulevard Magheru-Bălcescu-Brătianu is lined with jewelry and fashion boutiques like **Brutus, Cellini, DIKA, Eva, Fiorangelo, Ken Velo**, **LaCoste, Leonardo, Micri Gold, Naf Naf, Steilmann, Timberland** and **Yokko.**

Women's clothing size equivalents:

Mic/small	38 - 42	(38 = 8 US)
Mediu/medium	44 - 48	(46 = 12 US)
Mare/large	50 - 54	

Shoes:

Mic 33 - 35, *Mediu* 36 - 38 (37 = 7 US), *Mare* 39 - 41.

Bucharest Mall, 55-59, Calea Vitan, 1 km west of Bucharest's centre. A new four-story, 50,000 sq m (164,045 sq. ft.) mall with 70 stores, a supermarket, over 25 restaurants and cafes, a ten-screen cinema multiplex, a bowling alley, a child-care center, a video arcade, a public library, and an exhibition space for young artists, all surrounding an airy atrium under a translucent dome and central fountain. Take the M2 subway to Piaţa Unirii and then the M1 to Dristor; then catch trolley 15, which stops beside the Mall, Tel: 327.61.00, www.bucurestimall.com.

Plaza Romania, Bd. Timisoara 26, the newest and largest shopping center, in a rather rundown area of the city. It has lots of big name stores not found anywhere else in Bucharest, including Sunglasses Hut and Zara, Tel: 407.84.16; fax: 319.50.51; www.plazaromania.ro. (Take bus no. 137 from Piaţa Rosetti or Bd. Balcescu at Pta. Universităţii.)

Unirea Shopping Center, Piaţa Unirii 1, over 250 shops on four levels, plus cafes, Tel: (40-21) 303.0.208; fax: (40-21) 303.02.36; www.stoptoshop.ro.

World Trade Plaza—Shopping Gallery, Bd. Expoziţiei 2, north of the center. An upmarket selection of shops selling perfume, leather, antiques, watches, electronics, glass, lingerie and souvenirs, Tel: 202.44.50.

Handicrafts: Artizanat, Strada Academiei 25 and Strada Anastasie Simu 6, Unirea Shopping Center; Bucur Obor department store; embroidered clothing and decorations, hand painted eggs, pottery, carpets, carvings, dolls and masks. **Covorul**, Bd. Unirii 13; **Eva**, Bd. Magheru 9; **Mioriţa**, Strada Ion Câmpineanu 18; **Romarta**, Bd. Unirii 8; **Romartizana**, Calea Victoriei 18-20 and World Trade Center shopping gallery; **UniversalCoop**, Calea Victoriei 16-20.

Supermarkets: The new grocery stores usually offer a complete range of food products. Many international brands, from European to American, Arabian and Asian, are also available. Prices may vary slightly due to the location of the store or the availability of products. If buying food, especially from an outdoor market or small bakery, carry your own plastic or net bags.

La Fourmi, Piaţa Unirii, east side, local and imported foods. **Unic**, Bd. Bălcescu 33, general grocery. **Nic**, Piaţa Amzei 15, Intrarea A, no. 10-22, Strada Radu Beller 5-7, and Strada Sf. Elefterie 47, www.nic.ro; **Carrefour Orhideea**, Splaiul Independenţei 210-210B Grozăveşti; **Vox Maris**, Strada G. Enescu (east of Bd. Magheru), mostly imported food.

Sports & Leisure

Billiards & Bowling: Club Champion, Şos. Kiseleff 32 (next to the Village Museum), has billiard/pool tables, a bowling alley, a bar and restaurant, Tel: (021)222.93.217; **Texas**, Spl. Independenţei 290 (west of the center), has billiards and bowling, a bar with TVs, and a restaurant, Tel: (021)220.76.68.

Bodybuilding & Aerobics: Health Complex, Piaţa Chişinău (Bd. Chisinau 2) and Strada Ştirbei Vodă 156, weights, exercise room, sauna and massage; **Pit Gym Club**, Strada Popa Marin 2, fitness and bodybuilding, sauna and massage.

Cycling: The Cycling Society, Str. Academiei 2 Tel: (021) 615.91.94.

Go-Carting: Herăstrău Racing Team Şos. Nordului 9-11, at the north side of Herăstrău Lake; beer garden, open 3 pm-midnight, Tel: (021)232.01.20.

Rowing: Canotaj Rowing Club, Tel: (021)211.55.66 and the **Kayak Canoeing Club**, Tel: (021)211.55.76 are both headquartered at the Ministry of Sports, Strada Vasile Conta 16; **Cişmigiu Garden** and **Herăstrău Parc** offer rowboat rental on their lakes.

Swimming: Bucharest Water Park, DN1 (255A, Calea Bucureştilor), nr. 255A, Otopeni, 20 km from the city center.

The largest water park in Romania, it covers 40,000 sm and has 9 swimming pools, 43 water slides (10 just for children) and a dance floor. Use of sunbeds, umbrellas, life buoys, and all kinds of inflatable things is free. There are fast-food areas, two bars, a restaurant and a discotheque located within the park.

The park is open every day from 10am-8pm. Entrance fees vary on weekdays, evenings and weekends (children under 5 years old get in free). By car, take route DN1 to Otopeni, near the airport; the park has a large parking lot. There is an Express bus from Piaţa Presei Libere to the Waterpark, as well as city bus no. 449. There is also a Water Park shuttle from Piaţa Presei Libere every half hour that will leave you right in front of the park. Tel: (021)266.48.80/83.

Bucureşti Hotel, Calea Victoriei 63-81, has an indoor pool, sauna, massages, and exercise room open to the public, entrance is on Strada G. Enescu, Tel: (021)312.70.70; **Lido Hotel**, Bd. Magheru 5, has an outdoor pool with an artificial wave system, Tel: (021)614.49.30; **Parc Hotel/Turist Hotel Complex** Bd. Poligrafiei 3-5, has an indoor pool behind the hotel, Tel: (021)618.09.50; in summer visit the **beaches** on **Lake Floreasca** and **Lake Tei**, northeast of the center.

Tennis: Arenele Progresul, Strada Dr. Lister 37, west of the center, in the Cotroceni district, Tel: (021)638.33.80 (Eroilor metrou); **Club Ilie Năstase**, Bd. Mircea Eliade 1, overlooking Herăstrău Lake, Tel: (021)679.63.85; **Diplomatic Club** in Herăstrău Parc, Tel: (021)618.35.25; **Complex Parc Herăstrău** Şos. Nordului 7-9, lots of tennis courts, fitness, massage, sauna, and billiards, open 24 hrs., Tel: (021)232.21.28.

Services

ACR (Automobile Club of Romania)

Offers motorists touring information, car rental and road service; rents Eurodollar cars. Offices in Bucharest at Strada Cihoschi 2, Tel: (40-21)611.04.08, fax: (40-21)312.04.34, and at Henri

Coandă Airport (40-21)679.52.84). Branch offices in Braşov, Sinaia, Timişoara and in summer at Black Sea coast resorts. For road assistance call Tel: 927 in Bucharest; anywhere else in Romania, call Tel: 12345 preceded by the local area code.

American Express, the official AMEX Travel Service representative in Bucharest is Marshal Tourism at Bd. Magheru 43; they handle replacement of lost or stolen traveler's checks, emergency check cashing on American Express cards, payments of monthly credit card bills, replacement of lost, stolen or damaged credit cards, bookings, clients' mail and worldwide customer care. Tel: (40-21) 335.12.24; fax (40-21) 335.66.56. Lost or stolen traveler's checks can also be reported at the American Express Travel Service Representative, Str. Ghe. Manu 2-4, next to the Minerva Hotel, Tel: (40-21) 312.39.69; fax: (40-21) 312.27.38.

Banks

Banca Comercială Română (BCR), Bd. Regina Elisabeta 5, Tel: (40-21)312.47.05 and at Piaţa Victoriei. Changes traveler's checks and gives Visa and MasterCard cash advances; has **ATMs** all over town.

Banc Post, Bd. Libertăţii 18, Tel: 400.14.31. Branch offices have ATMs.

Banca Comercială Ion Ţiriac (BCIT), Strada Doamnei 12, Tel: (40-21)638.75.60.

Chase Manhattan Bank, Strada Vasile Lascăr 42-44, Tel: (40-21)210.76.46; fax: (40-21)210.31.37. (Business only)

Citibank Corp., Bd. Iancu de Hunedoara 8, Tel: (40-21)210.18.50; fax: (40-21)210.06.59.

ING Barings, Soseaua Kiseleff 13-15, Tel: (40-21)312.89.44; fax: (40-21)312.75.44.

Société Générale, Strada Ion Câmpineanu 11, Tel: (40-21)311.16.40; fax: (40-21)312.00.26.

MoneyTips

- New Romanian banknotes have been issued in 1, 5, 10, 50, 100 and 500 Lei denominations; the new coins are in 1, 5, 10 and 50 bani pieces.
- Romania uses periods rather than commas to denote thousands, thus 10.000 means 10,000.
- Many small vendors cannot change large bills, so it's best to carry several small denomination *lei* and coins (*bani*). Don't expect change back for less than one lei, either.
- Tipping is welcome, as Romanians earn very low wages. 10% is standard for restaurants, beauty parlors, etc.

Business Centers

Intercontinental Hotel, (2nd floor) computer and copy center; secretarial and telecommunication services. Tel: (40-21) 210.73.30/ ext.7222; fax: (40-21)312.10.17.

Negoiu, Strada Ion Câmpineanu 16, rents unfurnished offices with phone facilities, Tel: (40-21)311.13.07; **Plaza Bucharest**, rents furnished offices and 25-person conference room, secretarial and translation services, legal consulting, telecommunications, Tel: (40-21)211.26.40, fax: (40-21) 211.06.79; **World Trade Center**, (at the Sofitel Hotel) rents furnished offices and offers 24-hour business services, trade assistance, communications facilities, two conference centers, trade fair and exhibition space, Tel: (40-21)212.50.60; fax: (40-21)222.48.70.

Car Rental

Most international driving licenses are accepted in Romania, but check with the rental company to be sure. Some rental car companies will also provide a driver with a hired car. Several car rental companies have counters in the Arrivals hall at Henri Coandă Airport and at upscale hotels, as well as their storefront offices. Major cities in Romania are also covered for both pick-up and collection services. Rates are high and cars generally cannot be taken out of the country. Most cars have manual transmission. A blood alcohol level of any kind is not tolerated, and talking on a cell phone while driving is prohibited.

AAA Autorent Hertz, Str. Ion Bianu 47, Tel: (021) 222.12.56, fax: (021)222.12.57, E-mail: reservations@hertz.com.ro, www.hertz.com.ro; also at Crown Plaza hotel (closed weekends) Tel: (021)202.10.57, E-mail: robuc62@hertz.com.ro; Marriott Grand Hotel, Tel: (021)403.29.56, fax: (021)403.29.57, E-mail: robuc63@hertz.com.ro; and Henri Coandă Airport, Tel: (021)201.49.54, fax: (021)201.49.55, E-mail: robuc51@hertz.com.ro, www.hertz.com.ro.

Autorent, Reservations: Tel: (021)319-0432; fax: (021)319-0431, partner of **Dollar** and **Thrifty** car rentals, office@autorent.ro, www.autorent.ro.

Avis, Str. Mihail Moxa 9, Tel: (021)210.43.44, 210.43.45; fax: (021)210-69.12, E-mail: reservations@avis.ro, avis.ro@pcnet.ro, www.avis.ro; hotel offices at Hilton, Tel: (021)312.20.43, Intercontinental, Tel: (021)314.18.37; Minerva, Tel: (021)312.27.38, and at Henri Coandă Airport, Tel: (021)201.19.57, www.avis.ro.

Budget, Str. Polonă 35, etaj 1, ap. 4, Tel: (021)210.28.67, 212.26.51, fax: (021)210.29.95, E-mail: budget@pcnet.ro, www.budgetro.ro; at Henri Coandă Airport, 24 hours, Tel: (021)204.16.67, Liberty Agency, Str. Batiştei 5, Tel: (021)33.70.70; and World Trade Center – Mara Agency (weekdays only), Tel: (021)224.40.26. Offices also in Braşov, Constanţa, Neptun and Timişoara. www.budgetro.ro.

Europcar, Bd. Magheru 7, Tel/fax: (021)314.39.10, E-mail: europcar@ont.ro, www.europcar.com.ro; also at Intercontinental hotel (closed weekends), Tel: 314.04.00, ext. 365, and Henri Coandă Airport (closed weekends), Tel: (021)312.70.78.

FrancRoCar, Str. Louis Blank 2, (Closed Sunday), Tel. 230 47.89, fax 230 04 39, E-mail: rent.a.car@francrocar.com, www.francrocar.com.

International Car Rental, near Henri Coandă Airport, Tel: (021)232-66.79, (0788)48.32.49, fax: (021)233.12.19, sales@intcarrental.ro, www.intcarrental.ro.

Mega Taxi, Str. Institutul Medico-Militar 11, Tel. (0722)49.59.00, (0722)49.59.01, E-mail: megataxi99@yahoo.com. Cruise Romanian roads in true style in a revamped Pontiac Firebird (US$25 a day). Also rents out a big and cozy shuttle bus that can seat up to 25 people. Reservations required.

Sixt, Str. Horia, Cloşca şi Crişan 17, Main office Tel: (021)233-22.22, (0788)00.88.08, fax: (021)233.23.53, E-mail: email@sixt.ro, www.sixt.ro; also at Henri Coandă Airport (closed weekends), Tel: (021)201.46.26.

Thrifty, Reservations: Tel: (021)319-0432; fax: (021)319-0431, www.thrifty.ro.

Dry Cleaners

Called *Nufărul*, they are few and far between. Best to hand wash yourself or pay hotel personnel for the service. Some locations: Calea Moşilor 276, open 10am-6pm and Ştirbei Vodă 2-4, open 10am-6pm. Sofitel and Bucureşti hotels also have good dry cleaning services.

Embassies/Consulates

American Embassy, Strada Tudor Arghezi 7-9 (located behind the Intercontinental Hotel), Tel: (021)200.33.00. **Consulate**, where you go for passport problems, is on Strada Filipescu 26, open Mon-Fri, 9am-5pm; Tel: (021)200.33.00. Cultural Center & Library is located on nearby Strada J. Calderon 9, Tel: (021) 319.41.36 (closed in August); **Australian Consulate**, World Trade Center, Regus Centre 10, Montreal Square, Tel: (021) 316.75.58; **British Embassy**, Strada Jules Michelet 24 (east of Bd. Magheru), Tel: (021) 201.72.00, The British Council Library is at Calea Dorobanţilor 14; **Canadian**

Embassy, Strada N. Iorga 36 (off Bd. Dacia, west of Piaţa Romană), Tel: (021)307.50.00.

English language newspapers & TV

Local English language newspapers are the daily **Nine O'Clock** and the weekly România **Liberă**, **Business Review**, **Bucharest Business Week** and monthly **Romanian Business Journal** found at English bars and most hotels; all are free. Better hotels may carry the *Wall Street Journal* and *International Business Tribune*. The magazine vendors often carry *TIME*, *Newsweek* and the *Economist*.

On Bucharest cable TV, the **EuroNews** channel has continuous coverage of world events. American TV programs are shown on the **ProTV** channel (check listings in *Nine O'Clock*); EuroNews runs 24 hours.

Express Mail & Freight Forwarding

DHL, Calea Victoriei 63-81, at Bucureşti hotel, 2nd flr. Tel: (021)312.26.61; fax: (021)312.84.89 and through **Kamino Transport**, Cargo Terminal Henri Coandă Airport, Tel: (021)312.80.79, 312.78.95. (18 locations throughout Romania.)

FedEx/International RomExpress, Strada Mihai Eminescu 47, Tel: (49-69) 698.03.140.

UPS/Romtrans, Calea Rahovei 196, P.O.Box 13-11, Tel: (021)336.17.31, 337.20.19; fax: (021)337.32.30, 337.28.40.

TNT, Bd. Magheru 16-18, 4th floor, Suite 35 Tel: (021)212.12.10; fax: (021)210.59.00.

Exposition Centers

RomExpo S.A, Bd. Mărăşti 65-67, Tel: (021)233.11.60, 233.11.61; fax: (021)312.84.00, 222.61.69. International trade shows, fairs and exhibitions.

Gas/Petrol Stations—24 Hour

Intercontinental, Strada Tudor Arghezi 7; **Cotroceni**, Splaiul Independenţei; **Dorobanţi**, Calea Dorobanţilor 180; **Shell**, Bucharest-Ploieşti Road 2.

Internet Cafes

Access Internet, Bd. Catargiu 6, open 24 hours, Tel: (021)650.78.79; **Biblioteca GDS**, Calea Victoriei 120, open 24 hours, Tel: (021)314.14.71; **Brit C@fe,** Calea Dorobanţilor 14, Tel: (021)210.03.14, E-mail: britcafe@britshcouncil.ro; **Cyber Espace**, Bd. Dacia 77, at the French Institute, Tel: (021)211.38.36; **eNET**, Bd. Nicolae Balcescu 24, open 24 hours, Tel: (021)315.48.71, www.enet.ro; **Extremis**, Str. Academiei 9, open 24 hours; **FX**, Bd. Magheru 8-10, open 10am-midnight; **Internet Cafe**, Bd. Carol I 25, at Piaţa Rosetti, open 24 hour, Tel: (021)313.10.48, E-mail: icafe@icafe.ro; **PC-Net Café**, Calea Victoriei 136, open 24 hours, Tel: (021)650.42.14; **Silence Café**, Str. Căderea Bastiliei 19, open 24 hours, Tel: (021)659.40.89.

Medical & Dental Assistance

Medical care in Romania is not up to Western standards and basic medical supplies are limited, especially outside of major cities. Still, foreigners can receive very good services in Bucharest, in either university or private clinics. Ask friends or colleagues for recommendations for good doctors or clinics. Doctors and hospitals often expect immediate cash payment for health services. But if you just want information about a condition, send a detailed E-mail message to office@medsana.ro.

AMBULANCE (24 hours), Tel: **961** or 212.04.02.

Medical Centers

Aesthetic Line Clinique, Clinique of Plastic, Esthetic and Reconstructive Surgery, Bd. Dacia 51, Sector 1, Tel/fax: (40-21)211.44.16, 211.29.98, E-mail: aestheticline@home.ro, http://aestheticline@hom.ro; **American Medical Center**, Strada Dragoş Vodă 70, Sector 2, a multi-disciplinary medical center; Unique clinic of preventive medicine; Laser ophthalmologic therapy and surgery; Dental implantation. Home medical assistance, Tel: (0722)64.18.45. Kineto-therapy with Japanese massage, Tel: (40-21)210.27.06, 210.05.64, fax: (40-21)210.49.23; **Bio-Medica International**, Str. M. Eminescu 42, Romanian-American center. All specialities also air ambulance, Tel: (40-21)211.96.74, 21.17.13, Emergency only: (0722)33.83.83, E-mail: biomedical@totalnet.ro, www.bio-medica.ro; **Clinical Hospital for Children "Marie Curie"** (BUDIMEX), Strada Constantin Brâncoveanu 20, Tel: (40-21)682-3025, 682-4735, http://mscuriehosp.home.ro; **Colţea Hospital** (General), Bd. I.C. Brătianu 1, Tel: (40-21)311.01.53 or 614.27.44, www.coltea.ro; **Emergency Hospital**: Calea Floreasca 8, Tel: (40-21)230.49.53 or 230.01.06, http://urgenta.sfos.ro; **Emergency Neurosurgery Hospital "Prof. Dr. Bagdasar**," Şos. Berceni 10, Tel: (40-21)683.21.30, 683-2410; **French Village Clinic,** gen. practice, family medicine and emergencies, Şos. Nordului 119, Tel: (40-21) 232-3580; **MEDICOVER Center**, Calea Plevnei nr. 96, Tel: (40-21)310.44.10 or 310.40.66, www.medicover.com; **MEDSANA Bucharest Medical Center**, Str. Dr. Nanu Muscel 12, Sector 5, over 20 medical specialties, laboratories, computerized tomography, digital radioscopy, echography, in-vitro fertilization, prenatal assistance, Tel: (40-21)410.8643, 410.8543, 410.8459, 410.8403, E-mail: office@medsana.ro, www.medsana.ro; **Psychological Clinic ESA**, psychotherapy and hypnosis, Tel: (40-21)212.40.46, (40-722)77.99.76; **Spitalul Clinic de Urgenţă**, Calea Floreasca 8, Tel: (40-21)212.01.07 or (40-21)212.24.68; **Unirea Medical Center I**, Unirii Blvd, Bloc E4 57, Bucharest, all specialties, Tel: (40-21)327.1.88, 327.11.89;

fax: (40-21)327.11.95, E-mail: cmu@fx.ro; **Unirea Medical Center II,** Str. Batiştei 9, 8th Floor, general practitioner, Tel: (40-21)211.59.42; fax: (40-21)211.59.42, cmu@fx.ro; **"Victor Babeş" Medical Center**, Şoseaua Mihai Bravu 281, internal medicine, infectious and tropical diseases, pneumology and phthisiology, pediatric, endocrinology, cardiology, gynecology, neurology, psychiatry, ophthalmology, urology, surgery, immunizations, laboratory assistance for hematology, immunology, tumoral markers, bacteriology and virology, parasitology, Tel: (40-21)322.92.50, 323.14.88, 323.14.89; **PULS Medical Center and Ambulance**, Str. Turda 127; Str.Teiul Doamnei2, Bucharest, emergency, allergology, internal medicine, cardiology, dermatology, endocrinology, ENT, gynecology-obstetrics, neurology, opthalmology, rheumatology, urology. Tel: **973**, (40-21)224.44.32, 242.13.76; fax: (40-21)211.17.55.

Dentists

Biodent, Piaţa Amzei 10-22, Tel: (021)312-3752; **Dent-A-America - American Dental Clinic,** Str. Varşovia 4, Sector 1, Dr. George Danciu, DMD, Tel: (021)230-2826; **Novident**, Str.Apolodor 13-15, entr.B, apt. 52: Dr. Camelia Cornell, Tel: (021)336-1223.

24 Hour Pharmacies

Farmacia No. 26	Şos. Colentina 1	Tel: (021)252.50.10
Farmacia No. 70	Şos. Alexandriei 104	Tel: (021)420.27.4
Farmacia No. 5	Bd. Magheru 18-20.	Tel: (021)659.61.15
Farmacia No. 14	Şos. Iancului 57	Tel: (021)250.21.72
Farmacia 1	Strada Edgar Quinet 6	Tel: (021)613.59.94
Farmacia No. 20	Calea Şerban Vodă 43	Tel: (021)336.76.47
Farmadex	Bd. N. Titulescu 19	Tel: (0744)650.078
MedFARM	Bd. I.C. Brătianu 34	Tel: (021)315.23.09
SENSIBLU	Calea Dorobanţilor 65	Tel: (021)211.11.27 or 312.83.25

Post Office

The main post office at Strada Matei Millo 10 (behind the telephone center, off Calea Victoriei) is open from 7:30am-8pm. Besides buying stamps and posting letters, you can also send telegrams and receive letters addressed to you c/o **Poşta Restant, Poşta Română Oficiul Bucureşti 1, Strada Matei Millo 10, RP-70700 Bucureşti, ROMANIA**. Open Mon-Fri, 8am-7pm, Sat 8am-1pm.

Telephone Numbers

Romania's country code is **40**; the code for Bucharest is **21** (prefix 40-21).

International Operator: 971; overseas country codes dialing from Romania to the USA: 001; to the UK: 0044; to Ireland: 00353; to Canada: 001; to Australia: 0061.

Directory inquiries: Domestic numbers A-L: 931 and M-Z: 932. Business numbers: 930.

Taxis: To phone for a taxi, dial 922, 941, 945, 946, 953 or 956.

Police: 955; **Fire**: 981; **Ambulance**: 961; **Emergency hospital**: 962.

Tourism Agencies

Agencies can arrange city tours and excursions throughout the countryside, airline and hotel accommodations; they also provide international ticketing and reservations.

ANTREC (National Association of Rural, Ecological and Cultural Tourism), Strada Maica Alexandra 7, sector 1, Tel: (40-21)22.370.24, fax: (40-21)22.280.01, E-mail: antrec@antrec.ro, antrec@xnet.ro, office@antrec.ro, www.antrec.ro, specializes in rural accommodations in private homes; **Cultural Romtour**,

Bd. Burebista 4, specializes in guided tours of Romania's historical, cultural and traditional gems, Tel: (40-21)316.67.65, fax: (40-21)316.67.64, E-mail: office@culturalromtour.ro, www.culturalromtour.com; **Marshall Turism**, Bd. Unirii 20 or Bd Magheru 43, American Express onsite representatives will cash and replace lost or stolen traveler's checks, process emergency check cashing on AMEX cards, payments of monthly credit card bills, replacement of lost, stolen or damaged credit cards, Tel: (40-21)335.12.24, fax: (40-21)335.66.56, E-mail: office@marshal.ro, www.marshal.ro; **Paralela 45 Turism**, Bd. Regina Elisabeta 29-31, specializes in Black Sea resorts; offices throughout Romania, Tel: (40-21)311.19.58, fax: (40-21)311.10.64, E-mail: office@paralela45.ro, www.paralela45.ro; **Peter Express**, Bd. Magheru 32-36, flr.A, Tel: (40-21)212.95.66, fax: (40-21)212.95.67, E-mail: peter@kappa.ro, www.turism.ro; **Romantic Travel**, Str. Prof. M. Georgescu 24, Tel: (40-21)326.04.35, fax (40-21)314.30.56, E-mail: romantic@fx.ro, www.romantic.ro; **Touring ACR**, Strada Take Ionescu 27, agency of Automobile Club Romania, Tel: (40-21)650.25.95, fax: (40-21)312.04.34.

Train Tickets

The ***Agenţia de Voiaj CFR*** (Domestic and International), Strada Domnita Anastasia 10, Tel: (40-21)223.04.55; ***Gara de Nord***, Calea Grivitei 139, Tel: (40-21)650.72.45.

Translators

Central European Translations, 19, Unirii Blvd., Tel/fax: (40-21)336.2825, 336.27.24, 335.01.56, E-mail: info@babelmaster.de; **Pro Tours International**, 83, Calea Victoriei, Tel: (40-21)310.28.90, 310.28.91, fax: (40-21)310.28.91.

Restaurants

Bucharest has very many good restaurants, with new ones opening up all over town; and international cuisines are rapidly expanding their once meager presence. Some restaurants still do not accept credit cards though, so carry plenty of local currency when dining; VISA is the most accepted card. Look for the free weekly booklet called "*Şapte Seri*" (Seven Days). It lists many more restaurants, their hours, reservation numbers, CC acceptance and atmosphere (some in English, some in Romanian).

The bill is called a ***nota de plată***; your receipt, a ***chitanţă***. A 10% tip is the standard. It's best to call ahead for reservations, though not always necessary. Because most Romanians still smoke, there are few designated non-smoking sections. Hopefully, this will change soon, so ask the maitre d' if they have a smoke-free area. (*Aveţi secţie pentru nefumători?*) Price ranges are indicated by: Expensive=$$$, Moderate= $$, Inexpensive=$. Some pubs and bars also serve moderately priced food. (See Night Life, page 137.)

Traditional Romanian specialties include *mititei*, small, spicy sausage-like burgers; *sarmale*, stuffed cabbage; and *mămăligă*, a corn polenta. *Ţuica*, a plum brandy, is the national firewater. If ordering steak, be sure to tell the waiter how you want it cooked; they won't ask. If you don't like sugar in your coffee, specify "*fără zahăr*"; for milk added, say "*cafea cu lapte.*" A few new and old favorites are:

Bistro Atheneu $$, Strada Episcopiei 3 (next to the Atheneul Român), a small cozy bistro with a friendly atmosphere; Romanian food and bar. Tel: (021)613.49.00, open 10am-midnight; **Becker Brau** $$, Str. Rahovei 155, German food. Tel: (021)335.56.50; **Bucur** $$, Strada Poenaru Bordea 2 (near Parliament Palace), Lebanese and Romanian food in a warm, comfortable setting. Casino attached. Tel: (021)336.15.92; **Capşa** $$$, Calea Victoriei, 36, Romanian food. Built in 1852, it is representative of the city's past elegance. Brasserie attached. (Closed Sunday.).

Tel/fax: (021)313.40.38; **Caru cu Bere** $$, Strada Stavropoleos 5 (off Calea Victoriei in the historical section), Romanian specialties; folk music. Magnificent German-gothic décor, Tel: (021)613.75.60; **Casa Doina** $$$, Şos. Kiseleff 4. Romanian cuisine in a 19th-century villa with a beautiful dining room; folk music. CC accepted. Tel: (021)222.31.79, open 10am-2am; **Casa Veche** $$, Strada G. Enescu 15-17, off Bd. Magheru. Charming rustic restaurant serving 40 varieties of pizza; wine list. Has a nice terrace and attached pastry shop. CC accepted. Tel: (021)312.58.16; **Casa Vernescu/Grădina Vernescu** $$$, Calea Victoriei 133 (in historic Lens-Vernescu house), Romanian and continental cuisine; elegant restaurant with piano and violin music. In summer there is dining in the lovely canopied garden with strolling musicians. CC accepted. Valet parking. Tel: (021)231.02.20, www.casavernescu.ro; **Count Dracula Club** $$$, Splaiul Independenţei 8A, on the Dâmboviţa River. Elegant restaurant with three unique salons—Medieval, Transylvanian and Hunting, plus a Dungeon bar; authentic Transylvanian menu. CC accepted. Tel: (021)312.13.53; **Edgar's Pub** $$, Str. Edgar Quinet 9, between the Universităţii Piaţa and Calea Victoriei, an elegant English pub with relaxing music and very good food. Tel: (021)314.18.43; **Hanul lui Manuc** $$, Strada Iuliu Maniu 52-54. Romanian food; balcony and courtyard dining; salon for receptions; wine cellar. Credit cards accepted. Tel: (021)613.14.15; **L' Harmattan**, $$$, Str. Franceză 56, next to Curtea Veche, French and Moroccan cuisine, separate rooms for parties. Tel: (021)314.12.50, (0723)248.810, E-mail: restaurant_lharmattanfx.ro. **Kiraly Csarda**, Calea Dorobanţilor 177, Austro-Hungarian cuisine. Tel: (021)230.40.83, E-mail: rezervari@kiralycsarda.ro, www.kiralycsarda.ro; **La Premiera** $$, Bd. Nicolae Bălcescu 2 (behind the National Theatre, near U.S. Embassy), German/Bavarian specialties and Romanian food. Terrace dining. Tel: (021)312.43.97, open 10am-1am; **Piccolo Mondo** $$, Strada Clucerului 19 (south of Arcul de Triumf, off Şoseaua Kiseleff, via Strada Docenţilor). Lebanese and international food; garden dining. Tel: (021)665.57.55; **Trattoria il Calcio** $$, Strada Tache Ionescu at Str. Mendeleev,

Cucina Italiana, cozy wood and brick interior; **Vatra** $$, Strada Brezoianu 23-25, traditional rural-style décor and cuisine, Tel: 315.83.75, (0721)20.08.00, E-mail: vatra@vatra.ro, www.vatra.ro; **Volubilis** $$, Sofitel Hotel, Bd. Expoziţiei 2. Classy cafe in hotel offers a different ethnic buffet and music each weeknight, plus regular menu. Also serves breakfast, lunch and Sunday brunch. CC accepted. Tel: (021)223.40.00, open 6:30am-11pm.

Casual Dining

Some of the best snacks are the cheese pastries (*pateuri cu brânză*) sold by little streetside vendors; others may also contain fruit or meat. Best eaten immediately, you can also take it away wrapped (*paquet*). Carry your own napkins. Sidewalk soft ice cream (*îngheţată*) vendors will serve you a cone (*cornet*) or a cup (*pahar*).

Cafes, Pastry Shops & Fast Food

Patiseria Ana, Bd. Magheru, Calea Dorobanţilor and on Şoseaua Titulescu. French-style bakery with croissants, pastries and finger foods and cake; **Caffe Damirco,** Bd. Magheru 18, **Cofetăria Ema,** Bd. Golescu 24, by the train station. Delicious sweets, charming café; **Everest Café**, Bd. Magheru, tucked between KFC and McDonalds, sandwiches, pizza, etc., with a large outdoor patio; **Gioia Café**, Bd. Kogălniceanu 35, a charming Italian café, Tel: 315.82.92; **Panipat,** locations at Calea Victoriei 204, Bd. Magheru 44, Bd. Brătianu 44, Strada Rosetti 15, and at Gara de Nord. Pastries, breads and take-out pizzas; **Patiseria Emi**, Bd. Magheru, fresh, delicious treats; **Patisserie Parisienne,** Piaţa Romană and Piaţa Victoriei. French pastries, cakes, pies; **Picasso Café**, Strada Franceză 2-4, Tel: 312 15 76; **Pizza Hut**, 4 locations: Piaţa Romană, Bd. Regina Elisabeta 15-19, Calea Moşilor 219 and Calea Dorobanţi 5-7, indoor dining or patio; beer and wine, www.pizzahut.ro; **Quattro Stagioni**, Mareşal Prezan 1, pizza and pasta; drinks,

Tel: 222.7222, (0723)19.63.80; **Salzburg Café**, Str. Brezoianu 19, elegant little Austrian café serving special coffees, desserts, sandwiches and salads, Tel: 312.07.14; **Sheriff's**, Bd. I.C. Brătianu 40, burgers, pizzas and other fast food.

Night Life

Pubs & Bars

Amsterdam Grand Cafe, Strada Covaci 6 in the historical section. Popular, sophisticated bar and restaurant that also has private rooms and a basement dance club. Tel: (021)313.75.80, E-mail: info@amsterdam.ro, www.amsterdam.ro; **Cotton Club**, Pasajul Victoriei. American bar upstairs from shirt shop. Bistro menu, music from '50s and '60s. Tel: (021)613.02.44; **Dubliners Irish Pub**, Bd. Nicolae Titulescu 18, west of Piaţa Victoriei. Friendly English-speaking pub where expatriates meet, hang out, play darts. Guinness Stout on tap; sandwiches and meat pies served. Tel: (021)222.94.73, open 7 days, noon-2am; **The Harp**, Piaţa Unirii 1 (south side). Elegant two-level Irish pub and restaurant; open late, 24 hours on weekends. Tel: (021)410.65.08; **The Office**, Strada Tache Ionescu 2. Elegant downstairs lounge bar, private club 6pm-9pm; opens to public after 9pm. Dress well; **Terminus**, Strada George Enescu 5. Popular expat cellar bar with streetside tables as well. Open 10am-5am; **White Horse Inn**, Strada George Călinescu 4A. English pub and restaurant; wide-screen sports TV, Tel: (021)679.77.96, open noon until late.

Jazz Clubs

Art Jazz Club, Bd. N. Bălcescu 23A. Sometimes packed, sometimes near empty, the club hosts three or four pretty good concerts every week; drinks are well priced; the entrance is via a small door beside a park lot behind the Senate, rather than on Bd. Bălcescu. Tel: (0723)52.06.43; **Big Mamou**, Splaiul

Independenţei 2A, live jazz and blues in a thick fog of smoke, a swell place to contract lung cancer, Tel: (0724)67.11.08; **Blues Club**, Calea Victoriei 16-20 (in *Pasajul Villacrosse*), a tiny cafe that plays only (recorded) jazz, with tables in the passage, Tel: (0723) 52 06 43; **Cafe Indigo**, Strada Eforiei 2 (off Calea Victoriei, near National History Museum). Live jazz and blues on weekends, international cuisine, American bar. Tel: (021) 312.63.36; **Daily Café**, Strada Eforie 2, snooty café on three levels, around a central staircase; wait to be seated by the staff; menu includes 200 cocktails, cigars, cheap soggy pizzas and Romanian dishes, but good jazz and blues concerts on Tuesday and Friday. Tel: 312.63.36; **Green Hours 22 Jazz Café**, Calea Victoriei 120. Trendy, atmospheric jazz club with terrace; best to reserve a table in advance. Live jazz on Thursdays and 'off-off Broadway' theatrical performances every Monday, Tel: 314.57.51, open 24 hrs; **Jazz Bar Café**, Ştefan cel Mare 6, an Italian bistro, sandwiches, salads, grills and drinks to a background of jazz, call for live jazz, Tel: 212.32.33; **Lăptăria Enache**, Bd. Bălcescu 2 (in the National Theatre, 4th floor, north entrance), live jazz on Friday, Saturday and Sunday. Bohemian ambiance; sandwiches served; rooftop terrace. Tel: 315.85.08, open 9pm-2am; **Lobb's**, Bd. Expozitiei 2 (inside the World Trade Center). This Italian restaurant hosts Bucharest's finest jazz musicians every Friday night. Tel: 224.27.13, open 8pm-2am; **Piano Café**, Strada Ion Câmpineanu 33 (behind the National Art Museum). Live piano music nightly; cozy atmosphere; business lunch and dinner; weekend brunch. Tel: 312.10.68, open 8am-2am; **Swing House**, Strada Gabroveni 20, cellar bar on *Pasajul Francez* just off Strada Lipscani; live music begins at 9:30pm.

Clubs & Discos

Bucharest is such a happening place that no one needs to spend an evening alone. Many new clubs have joined the older classics, and all draw good crowds, dancing or otherwise.

Allure Club, Calea Floreasca 110, trendy, lavishly decorated, with a rare non-smoking section, Tel: (0722)654.423;

Armadillo Club, Str. Piaţa Amzei 6, underground club with great music, Tel: (0722)195.813; **Backstage**, Str. Gabroveni 14, a popular downstairs dive with a chic young clientele; expensive drinks, but good, retro rock music and occasional live music, Tel**:** 312 39 43, www.backstage.ro; **Club A**, Strada Blănari 14, one of the first and best with great classic dance music, often live on weekends, and a young, unpretentious crowd. Tel: 315.68.53, www.cluba.ro; **Coyote Café**, Calea Victoriei 48-50 (*Pasajul Victoriei*), a loud bar, good rock music and a fun crowd, Tel: 311.34.87; **Escape,** Strada Turturelelor 11, the former Why Not? disco, still popular with locals; it can be reserved for private parties, open Fridays and Saturdays only, Tel: 323.14.50, E-mail: office@escapeclub.ro; **Event Club**, Str. Icoanei 2, a good cabaret presenting a variety of live acts, including jazz bands and stand-up comics; live Dixieland jazz every Friday at 11:30pm, Tel: 210.59.21, www.eventclub.ro; **Exit**, Str. Covaci 6, downstairs at Amsterdam Café, every Friday and Saturday night the DJ mixes cool music like Bossa Nova and New Jazz for a hip mature crowd, Tel: 313.75.80, www.amsterdam.ro; **Mirage Club**, Bd. Nicolae Balcescu 3-5, great decor, great music, a good crowd and smack in the middle of town; **Monaco Lounge Café**, Str. Covaci 16, upmarket lounge in the cellar of Monaco French restaurant for trendy, well-dressed crowd; has a giant screen TV for watching sports events. Tel: 314.00.79, www.monacolounge.ro; **Music Club**, Str. Baratiei 3, possibly the best live music venue in town, a great house band plays favorite classic hits, often joined by leading Romanian musicians, Tel: 314.61.97; **Oldies Club**, Calea Mosilor 91, popular bar and crowded weekend dance club attracting lovers of the great 1980s tunes. Tel: (0723)66.65.51; **The Office**, Str. Tache Ionescu 2, expensive and pretentious, it's best during early evening; good music, an exclusive clientele, and a line to get in, Tel: (0745)11.00.64, E-mail: party@theoffice.ro; **Planter's**, Str. Mendeleev 8-10, most popular night-time destination, but difficult to get into on a weekend night. Sexy leather sofas, small dance floor, and some of the most expensive drinks in town, Tel: (0723)55.99.08; **Prometheus Club**, Bd. Natiunile Unite

3-5, classy interior and good music, with regular live music and comedy, Tel: 336 66 38, www.prometheus.ro; **Salsa III**, Str. Mihai Eminescu 89, the third and best location of this Salsa club is spacious, stylish and in the city center, Tel: (0723)53.18.41; **Space**, Str. Academiei 35-37, top dance club in the center of town, known for a tasteful crowd and cutting-edge tunes, big international names play sets here occasionally, www.rights.ro/space; **Spago,** Str. Mendeleev 1, a classy restaurant and nightclub, excellent food, but later tables are moved out for dancing; attracts a slightly older, more sophisticated crowd, Tel: 310 24 19; **Stuf Vama Veche**, Str. Berzei 25A, good pub and club with a back terrace, playing good dance tunes; popular with an older crowd, Tel: 224.89.25; **Temple**, Splaiul Independentei, good music until very late, with talented barmaid goddesses, Tel: (0727)29.76.10, E-mail: temple@baracademy.ro; **Tipsy**, Bd. Schitu Măgureanu 13, popular with a well-dressed pre-dinner drinking crowd, reservations recommended for dinner; afterward the downstairs party begins, Tel: (0745)20.06.11; **Tunnel Club**, Str. Academiei 19-21, huge club with a maze of large rooms, plays house and dance music, Tel: 312 69 71; **Underworld**, Bd. Mihail Kogalniceanu 3, one of the best venues in town, with top house music on Saturday nights, and live acts during the week, Tel: (0741)949.085, www.underworld-club.ro.

Casinos

Bucharest, Bd. Balcescu 4 (*Intercontinental Hotel*), European style. Bar; lounge. Tel: 310.20.20, ext. 7592, www.casinobucharest.ro; **Fortuna**, Str. Anastasie Panu 26, World Trade Center, 10 tables, 28 slots, Tel: 227.43.00, www.casinofortuna.ro; **Grand**, Calea 13 Septembrie 90, 10 tables, 22 slots, Tel: 403.08.01; **Lido**, Strada C.A. Rosetti 13. Players' bar and buffet, Tel: 311.0101, www.casinolido.ro; **Mirage**, Bd. Magheru 8-10, 12 tables, 60 slots, Tel: 313.89.52, www.miragecasino.ro; **Palace**, Calea Victoriei 133 (*Casa Vernescu*), 25 tables, 75 slots, Players' bar; lounge. Tel: 231.02.20, www.casinopalace.ro; **Partouche** (*Athenée Palace Hilton*),

Str. Episcopiei 1-3, 8 tables, 5 slots, Tel: 3314.72.00, www.bucharest.hilton.com; **Perla Princess**, Bd. Regina Elisabeta 9, 10 game tables and 50 slots; floor show. Tel: 312.90.91; **Plaza Casino Club**, Calea Victoriei 163, 9 tables, 10 slots, Tel: 310.24.80.

Concert Halls

Tickets are available at theater box offices. Shows begin between 6-7pm.

Opera Română, Bd. Kogălniceanu 70. Classical repertoire; tickets best purchased in advance at box office, open Tues-Sun. Closed during summer until October. Tel: 313.69.80. **Philharmonic "George Enescu" Atheneul Roman**, Strada B. Franklin 1 (on Piaţa Revoluţiei), beautiful concert hall with terrific acoustics; often hosts special guest performers, Tel: 315.25.67. **Radio Concert Hall**, Strada G. Berthelot 62-64, classical programs by the National Radio Orchestra, Tel: 314.68.00.

Theatres

Teatrul Bulandra, Sala "Toma Caragiu," Strada D. Geronta 75A, Tel: 314.75.46, 212.05.27; **Teatrul de Comedie**, Str. Sfântul Dumitru 2, Tel: 315.91.77; **Teatrul Ion Creangă,** St. Piaţa Amzei 13, Tel: 212.85.90; **Teatrul Evreiesc** (Jewish Theatre), Jewish plays with Jewish actors; performances on weekend days, in Yiddish with Romanian translations via headphones, Str. Barasch 15, Tel: 323.39.70. **Teatrul Mic**, Strada Constantin Mille 16, Chekov, Kundera, etaj, Tel: 314.70.81; **Teatrul Odeon**, Calea Victoriei 40-42, avant-garde, Tel: 314.72.34; **Teatrul Naţional "I.L. Caragiale,"** Bd. Bălcescu 2, three auditoriums, Tel: 314.71.71; **Teatrul Nottara**, Bd. Magheru 20. Tel: 212.52.89, 212.85.44, Classics.

Cinemas

Movie houses show American and English films with Romanian subtitles.

Patria, Bd. Magheru 12-14., American films in a refurbished 1,000-seat theater with marble halls and air conditioning, in the city center, Tel: 211.86.25; **Scala**, Bd. Magheru 2, nice inside and show top western films, Tel: 211.03.72; **Studio**, Bd. Magheru 29, near Piaţa Romană, Tel: 212.81.57; **Cinemateca Eforie**, Strada Eforie 2, old classics, Tel: 313.04.83; **Bucuresti**, Bd. Regina Elisabeta 6, Tel: 315.61.54; **Corso**, Bd. Regina Elisabeta 5, air-conditioned, dolby sound, Tel: 315.13.34; **Elvira Popescu**, Bd. Dacia 77, French Institute's petite cinema/theater showing French films, plays or concerts, Tel: 210 02 24, www.ifb.ro; **Europa**, Calea Moşilor 127, Tel: 314.27.14; **Festival,** Bd. Reg. Elisabeta 34, old and cruddy, Tel: 315.63.84; **Lumina**, Bd. Reg. Elisabeta 12, Tel: 314.74.16; **Scala**, Bd. Reg. Elisabeta 2-3, Tel: 21.03.72; **Hollywood Multiplex**, Bucharest Mall, Calea Vitan 55-59, 10 screens, popcorn, comfortable seats; located on the top floor of Bucuresti Mall, Tel: 327.70.20, www.hmultiplex.ro; **Movieplex Cinema**, Bd. Timisoara 26, sector 6, within Plaza Romania mall, Tel: 407.83.00.

Hotels

Bucharest has a huge selection of hotels in every price range and standard. Many new hotels have opened in recent years, and older ones have undergone renovations to accommodate their influx of international business travelers and new tourists. Many offer international direct dialing, fax, Internet access and meeting rooms, if not full business centers. Guest services usually include phone, cable TV, and often a mini-refrigerator in rooms; lobby services often have an exchange office (hard currency to lei only), concierge or tourism office, restaurant and bar.

Most Romanian hotels also include breakfast (*mic dejun*) in the price, but ask to be sure. They also now accept credit cards, but few take travelers' checks. Prices can change quickly in Romania due to its rapid inflation rate, so only star status is mentioned here. In general, hotel rates are now on par with other European cities. English is spoken at all hotels in Bucharest.

★★★★★

Casa Capşa Hotel, Calea Victoriei 36, entrance on Strada Edgar Quinet, near museums, theaters, restaurants and shops. Combines classic 19th-century elegance with modern services. The hotel has 61 guestrooms: singles, doubles and suites. All have cable TV, international direct phone, radio, minibar, Internet, air conditioning. Amenities include a lobby bar, room-service, reserved parking, sauna, fitness and massage, mail, laundry, courier, phone/fax, a safe for valuables; full services for banquets and conferences in four elegant salons (40-90 seats). Historic **Casa Capşa restaurant** is the most famous in Romania, offering extraordinary traditional and international cuisine. Tel: (40-21)313.40.38, www.capsa.ro.

Hilton Athenée Palace, Strada Episcopiei 13, next to Atheneul Roman in Piaţa Revoluţiei. Built in 1914, Bucharest's most luxurious old hotel has been restored to its past elegance. Steeped in historical intrigue, it offers full guest services, three restaurants and the famous English Bar; a health club and pool; a ballroom; a casino; meeting and banquet facilities, a business center with translation service and computers. 272 rooms, Tel: (40-21)303.37.77, fax: (40-21)315.38.13, E-mail: hilton@hilton.ro, www.hilton.com.

Marriott Bucharest Grand, Calea 13 Septembrie 90. Located west of the Parliament Palace and Civic Center, it caters to the business traveler. Huge parking space. Spacious rooms for living/working environment; many suites. Smoking and non-smoking rooms. World Class Health Academy with indoor pool, sauna, and jaccuzzi. Five food and beverage outlets. Swanky shopping arcade. Multi-lingual staff. Largest hotel conference facilities: 12 flexible meeting rooms total 2,000 sq.m; 633 sq.m Grand Ballroom, divisible into four sections, that accommodate up to 800 guests; 350 sq.m Constanta Ballroom, accommodates 400, Ballroom Foyer perfect for receptions. Ten medium to small meeting rooms featuring natural day light, Internet access and modern equipment. 402 rooms, Tel: (40-21)403.00.00, (from USA: 888-236-2427), fax: (40-21)411.29.70, E-mail: marriott.bucharest@marriotthotels.com, www.marriotthotels.com.

Sofitel, Bd. Expozitiei 12, at the World Trade Center, north of city center. Next to Romexpo and Herăstrău Parc, this modern high-rise hotel offers full guest services plus an elegant shopping gallery and detached sports club; office and apartment rentals; parking and airport shuttle. 203 rooms. Tel: (40-21)314.90.22, fax: (40-21)211.56.88, E-mail: sofitel@sofitel.ro, www.sofitel.com.

****

★★★★

Bucharest Comfort Suites, Bd. N. Balcescu 16, near Piaţa Universităţii, new small hotel in center, suites with kitchen or jacuzzi, satellite TV, Internet access, room service, secretarial service, airport transfer; Tel: (40-21)310.28.84, fax: (40-21)310.28.87, E-mail: relax@comfort-suites.ro, www.comfort-suites.ro.

Continental, Calea Victoriei 56. Located in the city center, across from Cercul Militar and near the Royal Palace. This 150 year-old classical-style building has an aura of old elegance; with 53 rooms (14 single, 33 double and 6 apartments). There is a travel agency, a confectionery and parking in the hotel, plus two restaurants, a summer terrace and a cocktail lounge; four conference rooms for 20, 30, 50, and 100 people; simultaneous translation in 6 languages available, flipchart, video projector, TV and projector screen. Tel: (40-21)313.36.94, fax: (40-21)312.01.34, Email: bucuresti@continentalhotels.ro, www.continentalhotels.ro.

Crown Plaza, Strada Poligrafiei 1, north of city center, near Romexpo and Herăstrău Parc. Contemporary four-level hotel in a garden setting offers full guest services, conference rooms, gym, tennis courts and indoor pool; beauty parlor/barber; English newspapers. 155 rooms, Tel: (40-21)224.00.34, fax: (40-21)224.11.26, E-mail: bucharest@crowneplaza.ro, www.bucharest.crowneplaza.com.

Golden Tulip Hotel, Calea Victoriei 166, at Bd. Dacia, in city center. New high-rise hotel; 83 single/double rooms and suites, all with individual climate control, room safe, minibar, sprinkler system, hair dryer. Services include 24-hour room service, free parking, free high-speed Internet access, 4 meeting rooms, restaurant. Tel: (40-21)212.55.58, fax: (40-21)212 51 21,

E-mail: goldentulipbucharest@rdslink.ro, www.goldentulip.com/goldentulipbucharest. (Piaţa Romană & Piaţa Victoria metrous)

Howard Johnson Grand Plaza Bucharest, Calea Dorobanţilor 5-7, east of Piaţa Romană, walking distance to shopping, nightlife, fine dining and some of city's best sightseeing. Totally renovated high-rise building with air-conditioned rooms, room service, satellite TV; rooms for disabled guests, parking; 8 meeting rooms for 20 to 80 people with state-of-art technical equipment. Laundry and dry cleaning, indoor parking, high-speed Internet access, shuttle bus services, doctor on call, car rental, secretarial service, IT assistance. The hotel's fitness center has sauna, solarium and massage. There's a multifunctional ballroom, lobby bar and lounge and Japanese restaurant and sushi bar. 285 rooms, Tel: (40-21)201.50.00, fax: (40-21)201.18.88, E-mail: sales@hojoplaza.ro www.hojoplaza.ro. (Piaţa Romană metrou)

Intercontinental, Bd. Nicolae Balcescu 4, in city center next to the National Theatre. Modern high-rise; 390 rooms, 13 suites (16 connecting rooms, non-smoking rooms, 2 rooms for disabled guests). All rooms with balconies and satellite TV, pay TV, direct-dial telephones, bathroom phone, bathrobes, minibar and in-room safe. Ballroom, conferences rooms and banquets for up to 300 people. 21st floor restaurant with spectacular view. English newspapers. Tel: (40-21)310.20.20, E-mail: marketing@interconti.com, www.intercontinental.com. (Piaţa Universităţii metrou)

Lebăda, Strada Biruinţei 3, 10 km (6 miles) from central Bucharest; a former 18th-century princely palace on an island in Pantelimon Lake amidst a 52,000 sq. meters (11 acre) park; 250 rooms in suites, single and double rooms with air conditioner, satellite TV, telephone, international phone lines. The hotel has tennis courts, an indoor pool, solarium and sauna, billiards, arcade games, and a wine cellar. There's a 150-seat restaurant, breakfast salon, a snack bar, a coffee shop and a bar; two conference rooms, 80 seats and 40 seats, both equipped with TV, video, overhead projector and flipchart. 127 rooms, Tel: (40-21)255.02.84, fax: (40-21)255.00.41, E-mail: reservations@lebadahotel.com, www.lebadahotel.ro.

Lido, Bd. Magheru 5-7 in city center. Elegant hotel in city center. Hotel has 12 suites, 30 double rooms and 78 single rooms, all equipped with satellite TV, telephone and air-conditioning. Facilities include swimming pool, beauty salon, parking, currency exchange, safe and laundry service. There is a breakfast hall, day bar, and two restaurants, plus conference facilities for up to 50 people. Tel: (40-21)614.49.30, fax: (40-21)312.65.44, E-mail: hotel@lido.ro, www.lido.ro.

Majestic Hotel, Strada Academiei 11, set back from Calea Victoriei. A favorite of business travelers, with 74 guest rooms, 4 suites, and special rooms for disabled guests; also non-smoking rooms. All have adjustable air-conditioning, TV and Pay-TV system, minibar, direct telephone with message, automatic wake-up system, in-room safety deposit box; 24- hour room service. The Fitness Center includes sauna, massage and beauty salon. Restaurant serves Romanian, Turkish and International cuisine. Snack-Bar open from early to late night for light meals, snacks and drinks. Conference Center seats up to 150 with video projector and overhead projector, flipchart and screen; sound installation and translation installation, I.S.D.N. high-speed Internet access, computers, TV and video player. Tel: (40-21) 311.32.12, fax: (40-21) 310.27.99, E-mail: reservations@majestic.ro, www.majestic.ro.

Parliament Hotel, Strada Izvor 106, sector 5, next to the Parliament Palace. Charming hotel caters to business guests; close to main business areas and surrounded by government ministries; 20 modern, spacious guestrooms: 12 deluxe rooms and 8 suites, with jacuzzi, king-sized beds, two TV sets, bathrobes, large bathrooms. Hotel has a terrace restaurant and bar with view; laundry service, 24-hour room service, guarded free parking, interpreters on request, doctor and dentist on call, international newspapers; 24-hour rooftop restaurant and bar with view over Parliament Palace serves international cuisine and Romanian and Turkish specialties; fully equipped meeting/business room for up to 60 persons. Tel: (40-21)411.99.90, fax: (40-21)411.99.91, E-mail: info@parliament-hotel.ro, www.parliament-hotel.ro.

Relax Comfort Hotel, Bd. N. Balcescu 22. Charming new small hotel in the city center; credit cards accepted. Tel:

(40-21)311.02.10, fax: (40-21)311.02.13, E-mail: relax@comfort-suites.ro, www.comfort-suites.ro.

****

★★★

Ambassador, Bd. Magheru 8, in city center. Large hotel with art deco design; full guest services, however lobby and some rooms not air-conditioned; cabaret and disco; conference rooms; fax and copy service. Credit cards accepted; no traveler's checks. 216 rooms, Tel: (40-21)315.90.80, fax: (40-21)312.35.95, E-mail: hotelaambasador.ro, www.ambasador.ro.

Best Western Parc, Bd. Poligrafiei 3-5, north of the center, near Romexpo, Herăstrău Parc and the World Trade Center. Newly renovated. The top five floors host the business-class rooms, each with a data port. Rooms are air-conditioned, with 30-channel color TV, international direct-dial telephone, hair dryer, in-room safe deposit box, minibar, data port, info-center. Conference facilities for 6–300 persons; four with Internet line. Hotel has swimming pool and tennis courts. Restaurants serve Romanian and international cuisine. 275 rooms; 5 km from the Henri Coandă International Airport. Tel: (40-21) 224.20.00, fax: (40-21) 224.29.84, E-mail: bestwest@parc.ro, www.parch.ro. (Bus #331 to city center)

Bucureşti, Calea Victoriei 63-81, north of Piaţa Revoluţtiei. Large, modern state-run hotel, caters to business clientel. Full guest services; conference rooms; gym and pool; Avis car rental, DHL office; English newspapers and international time clocks. Credit cards and travelers checks accepted. 454 rooms, Tel: (40-21) 312.70.70, fax:(40-21) 312.09.27.

Bulevard, Bd. Regina Elisabeta 21, at Calea Victoriei. Old elegance, Louis XIV decor, lobby bar and restaurant; not air-conditioned; limited guest services; TV and radio; fax and copier service. Visa and MC accepted; no travelers checks. 89 rooms Tel: (40-21) 315.33.00, fax: (40-21) 312.39.23, E-mail: athenee@fx.ro.

Capitol, Calea Victoriei 29, in the heart of Bucharest. Renovated back to original elegance, just minutes from metrou and theaters, large rooms, restaurant, conference rooms, breakfast and

VAT included; 79 Rooms. Tel: (40-21) 315 80 30, fax: (40-21) 312 41 69, E-mail: reservations@hotelcapitol.ro, www.hotelcapitol.ro.

Central, Strada Brezoianu 13, off Bd. Regina Elisabeta, near Cişmigiu Garden; 62 refurbished rooms with phone, TV, air conditioning and minibar. International telephone, fax, mail, storage for valuables and luggage, room service, conference room and contemporary lobby bar. Breakfast included. Tel: (40-21)315.56.37, fax: (40-21)315.56.37, E-mail: info@centralhotel.ro, www.centralhotel.ro. (Izvor metrou)

Dalin, Bd. Mărăsesti 70-72, just south of Piaţa Unirii. Small 2001 hotel near the city center; 16 rooms, 4 suites, all modern, air-conditioned, satellite TV, some non-smoking rooms, Internet access; airport transfer; breakfast included. Tel: (40-21)335 55 41, fax: (40-21)336.62.84, www.hoteldalin.ro.

Dan, Bd. Dacia 125. A small friendly hotel in city center, nice rooms are all well-sized and well-equipped; wheelchair access. Breakfast and VAT included. 15 Rooms, Tel: (40-21)210.39.58, fax: (40-21)210.39.17, Email: office@hoteldan.ro, www.hoteldan.ro.

Duke, Bd. Dacia 33, west of Piaţa Romana in city center. New small hotel with 38 air-conditioned rooms and suites, cable TV, direct-dial telephone, Internet data port, minibar, hair dryer, bathroom phone, room service, laundry/dry cleaning, car rental. Breakfast buffet and lounge bar. Tel: (40-21) 212.53.45, fax: (40-21)212.53.47, E-mail: office@hotelduke.ro, www.hotelduke.ro.

Euro International, Strada Gheorghe Polizu 4, charming new hotel near Gara de Nord; large rooms with air conditioning and TV; not the best area of town, however. Breakfast and VAT included; 30 rooms. Tel: (40-21)212. 88.39, fax: (40-21)22.83.60, E-mail: office@euro-hotels.ro, www.euro-hotels.ro.

Euro Hotels & Suites, Calea Plevnei 10, Piaţa Kogalniceanu, west of Cişmigiu Gardens. Small, elegant, old-style, hotel in nice area with international phone, fax, Internet cable connection in each room, TV cable, air conditioner, room service, minibar, dry cleaning, hair dryer; suites have kitchens; restaurant; 19 rooms, north of Parliament Palace. Tel: (40-21) 315.57.90, E-mail: res.kogal@eurosuites.ro. (Izvor metrou)

Flanders, Strada Stefan Mihailescu 20. Flanders is a traditional Belgian hotel in an old aristocratic-style house that was fully refurbished in 2001; located in a quiet neighborhood close to the city center; caters to all business travelers, 7 rooms, 1 suite furnished in Scandinavian-style, with extra-large beds, office desk, safe in room, cable TV, air-conditioning, room service, direct-dial international telephone; bar, restaurant with two terraces and live jazz on Wednesdays; laundry service, complimentary airport transfers, parking. Tel: (40-21)327.65.72, fax: (40-21)327.65.73, E-mail: office@flandershotel.ro, www.flandershotel.ro.

Helvetia, Piaţa Charles de Gaulle 13, north of the center. Lovely, small hotel across from Herăstrău park; air-conditioned rooms, satellite TV, room service; restaurant and lobby bar. Credit cards accepted. 29 rooms. Tel: (40-21)223.05.66, fax: (40-21)223.05.67, E-mail: helvetia@ines.ro, www.helvetia.netvision.net.il. (Aviatorilor metrou)

Ibis Bucureşti Gara de Nord, Calea Griviţei 143. A new hotel near Gara de Nord train station. The hotel provides 200 standard rooms, 38 double rooms, 8 apartments. All rooms have air-conditioning, Internet access, satellite TV, direct-dial telephone and minibar. Non-smoking rooms available. Breakfast included. Tel: (40-21) 222 27 22, fax: 021-222 27 23, E-mail: reservations@ibisaccor.ro, www.ibishotel.com.

Minerva, Strada Gheorghe Manu 2-4, off Bd. Lascăr Catargiu. Popular hotel near city center; air-conditioned, cable TV and radio; room service, minibars in rooms, business center and meeting facilities, Avis car rental, parking, 24-hour lobby bar; Nan Jing Chinese restaurant; safe boxes. Credit cards accepted. 83 rooms. Tel: (40-21)311.15.50, fax: (40-21)312.39.63, E-mail: reservation@minerva.ro or minerva@minerva.ro, www.minerva.ro.

Opera, Strada Brezoianu 37, west of Calea Victoriei, near Cişmigiu Garden. Beautifully renovated hotel tucked behind the Royal Palace complex. 33 rooms, all with balconies: 4 "Junior Suites," 3 apartments, 20 double rooms, and 6 singles, tastefully furnished, suitable for business or leisure; fully air-conditioned, satellite and cable TV, high-speed Internet access, minibar, international telephone, modern bath with hair dryer; a room with facilities for guests with disabilities. Services include buffet breakfast, room-service, lobby bar, rent a car, parking, storage for valuables and luggage, mail distribution. Tel: (40-21) 312.48.55; fax: (40-21)312.48.58, Email: info@hotelopera.ro or hopera@kappa.ro, www.hotelopera.ro.

Rembrandt, Strada Smârdan 11, in the historic section. New small business-class hotel in the historic section, fully refurbished 1925 building, 15 spacious, rooms with cable TV, CD, DVD, Internet access, 24-hour room service; fax, Xerox, international newspapers in the Klein Bar and Bistro (open to the public). Tel: (40-21)313.93.15, fax: (40-21)313.93.16, E-mail: info@rembrandt.ro, www.rembrandt.ro.

Tempo Hotel, Strada Armand Călinescu 19, off Bd. Carol I, a 5 minute walk from Piaţa Universităţii. Rooms have bright décor, minibar, cable TV, bathtub or hydro-massage shower system, hair dryer, individual climate control, electronic key-card system, electronic safe box, fire alarm system. Hotel has one conference room accommodating up to 120 people. Breakfast included. 33 rooms. Tel: (40-21)310.12.16, fax: (40-21)310.12.41, E-mail: info@tempohotel.com, www.tempohotel.com.

****

★★

Astoria, Bd. Dinicu Golescu 27, by the train station. Elegant old hotel; just 100 m from Gara de Nord train station. Hotel provides fax, copy service, safe luggage deposit room, guarded parking place. All rooms have cable TV, international phone; some rooms have air conditioning and refrigerator. Conference room with audio-visual, seats 30. Breakfast room, lounge bar. Breakfast included; 166 rooms. 25 minutes from Henri Coandă International Airport. Tel: (40-21)637.52.25, fax: (40-21)638.2690. Visa and MC accepted. (Bus #133 to the center.)

Banat, Piaţa Rosetti 5, east of Piaţa Universităţii. A grand old 1930s building, completely renovated; rooms have a TV, minibar, air conditioning; international phone and spacious bathrooms. If there's a group of you, then the apartments are good value. Casa Ţărănească Elite restaurant; credit cards accepted, 19 rooms. Tel: (40-21)313.10.56, fax: (40-21)312.65.47, E-mail: reservation@hotelbanat.ro or office@hotelbanat.ro, www.hotelbanat.ro.

Hanul lui Manuc, Strada Franceză 62-64, near Curtea Veche. Built in 1808 as a caravansary, its wooden balconies surround the courtyard, a truly charming place; TV and radio; not air-conditioned; courtyard and balcony dining. Amex and Visa accepted; no travelers' checks. 32 rooms. Tel: (40-21)613.14.11, fax: (40-21)312.28.11, www.hanulmanuc.ro.

Triumf, Soseaua Kiseleff 12, north of Piaţa Victoriei. Handsome brick building in beautiful garden setting along tree-lined avenue; cable TV; not air-conditioned; beauty parlor and barber; restaurant and outdoor wine garden. Visa accepted; no travelers' checks. 100 rooms. Tel: (40-21) 222.31.72, fax: (40-21)223.24.11. (Piaţa Victoriei metrou)

****

★

Bucegi, Strada Witing 2, near Gara de Nord train station. A favorite of backpackers, though most rooms are small; some doubles have a TV and private bath, some rooms without private bath; a helpful staff. 57 rooms, restaurant. Tel: (40-21)212.71.54, fax: 212 66 41. (Bus #79 to the center)

Carpati, Str. Matei Millo 16. Good place for bargain hunters: central, clean and quite modern with friendly, multilingual staff; six different size and facilities of rooms, some with shared (clean) bathrooms; larger rooms have en suite facilities and TVs; air conditioned; breakfast and VAT included; credit cards accepted. Tel: (40-21)315.01.40, fax: (40-21)312.18.57, E-mail: rezervari@hotelcarpatibucuresti.ro, www.hotelcarpatibucuresti.ro.

Cerna, Bd. Golescu 29, by the train station. Rooms with or without private bath; better rooms also have TV and telephone; air conditioned; data ports; restaurant; disabled accessible. Tel: (40-21)311.05.35, fax: (40-21)311.07.21. (Bus #133 to the center)

Marna, Strada Buzeşti 3, east of train station. Rooms with or without private bath. Tel: (40-21)212.83.66, fax: (40-21)312.94.55, E-mail: hotelmarna@hotmail.com. (Bus #79 to the center)

Muntenia, Strada Academiei 21, west of Piaţa Revoluţiei. Budget hotel in great location, TV and phone; rooms with or without showers; bar; not air-conditioned. Cash only. 116 rooms. Tel: (40-21)314.60.10, fax: (40-21)314.17.82.

Hostels

Backpacker's Lodge Hostel, Radu Beller 9, etaj 2, apt. 8. Situated in a beautiful residential area near German, Dutch, Spanish, Finnish, Portuguese and Swiss embassies. Buses #182 and #282 from Bucharest's Gara de Nord train station stop across the street from hostel (Piaţa Dorobanţi); or take the metrou one stop from Gara de Nord to Piaţa Victoriei station and walk 10 minutes on Strada Paris to the hostel. There are three six-bed mixed dorms, a fully equipped kitchen, cozy living-room and Internet access. Tel: (40-21) 23.13.43, Email: office@backpacker.ro, www.backpacker.ro.

Casa Hostel, Strada Lugoj 52. Located near Gara de Nord, 2 minute walk from Basarab metro, many restaurants and pubs nearby, close to Univ. of Bucharest dormitories. Clean, renovated in 2004, with one 2-bunk bedroom with a private bathroom; a 4-bed room (2 bunk beds) with shared bathroom; and 8-bed mixed dorm; 2 bathrooms (tub and shower); has a pub-style bar. Access to fully equipped kitchen. Open all year, no curfew, no lockout. Cash only. 24-hour reception; checkout at 12:00pm. Kind staff will help you with information (tours, train/bus timetable, entrance fees, etc.). Tel:(40-21) 260 04 08, fax: (40-21) 260.04.08, Email: info@hostelcasa.ro, www.hostelcasa.ro.

Dida House, Strada Albinelor 32, Bloc 32, Scara 4, Apt. 62, Interfon 62. Near Parliament Palace and Piaţa Unirii. A friendly Romanian family house with single or double room in a private atmosphere. Free continental breakfast, kitchen use, hot showers, hair dryer, washing machine, iron and ironing board, international TV, high-speed cable Internet. Linen and towels provided. Romanian home cooking (sarmale, ciorbă, tochitură cu mămăliguţă), Romanian wine. There is a barbeque area and baggage storage. English and Italian speaking staff. No curfew. Checkout time is 12pm. Car rental is available; call for airport and railway pick up. (Book via Internet.)

Elvis's Villa, Strada Avram Iancu 5, free laundry, Internet access and breakfast; from Piata Universităţii, take any trolleybus three stops east on Bd. Carol I, walk past the roundabout and the Acropolis-like building and turn right. Tel: (40-21)312.16.53, E-mail: Elvis@elvisvilla.ro, www.elvisvilla.ro.

Funky Chicken Hostel, Strada General Berthelot 63, behind Cişmigiu Garden, another great house by the Villa Helga group. Tel: (40-21)312.14.25, Email: funkychickenhostel@hotmail.com, www.funkychickenhostel.com.

Hostel Miorita, Str. Lipscani 12, an upmarket hostel in the center of town, where €44 per night per room gets you a very comfortable room with a huge bed, breakfast, cable TV and all modern conveniences. 6 rooms €44 per room per night. Prices include VAT and breakfast. Tel: (40-21)312 03 61, fax: (40-21)312 03 28, E-mail: hostelmiorita@hostel-miorita.ro, www.hostel-miorita.ro.

Villa Gabriela, Strada Mărgăritarului 18, Vila A104. Close to the Bucharest airport, with convenient access to the city and the surrounding area. This is ecotourism in traditional Romanian style, but in convenient proximity to the city. It's a 4-apartment house; guests have access to two of them. One has dining area and a bedroom; the other has 3 bedrooms, maximum 10 people. Traditional Romanian meals are cooked by Carmina. You also have full access to the kitchen to cook your own food. Activities and tours (including skiing, Transylvania, the Black Sea and the Carpathians) can be arranged upon request. (Book via Internet.)

Villa Helga Hostel, Strada Salcâmilor 2, Sector 2, off Bd. Dacia. Bucharest's first hostel, run by friendly English-speaking staff, in city center near Piaţa Romană, markets, restaurants and the main sights; breakfast included; kitchen privileges; patio, laundry; Internet service; no curfew (buses #79, 86 or 133 from train station to Piaţa Gemini). Tel/fax: (40-21)610.22.14, E-mail: helga@rotravel.com.

Hotel Tips

- Some hotels expect you to leave the hotel key at the front desk when going out; check the policy where you stay. They may also hold your passport, but if you need it to exchange currency, just ask for it.
- When in your room, keep your key in the door. The maids don't knock before entering; they just try their key and if it opens the door, they will enter the room unannounced.
- Washcloths are not used in Romania so bring your own; toilet paper is very rough, so bring some if you're picky about softness.

Places of Worship

Orthodox: Patriarchal Cathedral, Aleea Mitropoliei 1, Tel: 615.67.72; Colţea Church, Bd. Bratianu; Stavropoleos Church, Strada Stavropoleos, in the historical section; St. Nicholas Russian Church, Strada Ion Ghica; Kretzulescu Church, Piaţa Revoluţiei; Armenian Church, Bd. Carol 43, Tel: 613.90.70.

Roman Catholic: St. Iosif Cathedral, Strada Gen.Berthelot 19 (behind Bucuresti hotel), Tel: 312.12.08; Italian Church, Bd. N. Bălcescu 28, Tel: 614.18.57; Bărăţiei Church, Bd. Bratianu 16 (open Sundays only); French Church, Strada Cpt. Demetriad 1-3, Tel: 633.43.01.

Protestant: Anglican Church, Strada Xenopol 2, services 10am Sundays, Tel: 312.29.38; Reformed Church "Calvineum," Strada Luterană 13, Tel: 614.44.96; Evangelical Church, Strada Luterană 2, Tel: 613.31.65.

Greek-Catholic: Maica Domnului Church, Strada Sirenelor 39, Tel: 781.73.56.

Neo-Protestant: Christian Baptist Church, Strada Popa Rusu 15, Tel: 623.10.84; Seventh-Day Adventist Church, Strada Plantelor 12, Tel: 312.20.54.

Jewish: Coral Temple Synagogue, Strada Sfânta Vineri 9-11 (east of Piaţa Unirii), services 7pm Friday, 8:30am Saturday, and 8am Mon-Thurs.

Moslem: The Mosque, Strada Constantin. Mănescu 4, Tel: 641.11.33, services Friday at 12:30 in winter and 1:30 in summer.

THE WALLACHIAN COUNTRYSIDE

Snagov

Just 40 km (25 miles) north of Bucharest, this is a popular lake resort on summer weekends. A perfect day-trip, there are water sports and a water plants reserve. The lake also protects an island and monastery built in 1408 where the headless body of Vlad the Impaler, Dracula, is said to be entombed. Visitors can ferry to the monastery, but the monks insist upon respectful attire for entrance. A train to ***Plaja Snagov*** (Snagov beach) leaves early weekend mornings and returns in the evening. ONT Carpaţi arranges 5-hour day trips. It's a good idea to pack a snack, though there is a restaurant at the Hotel Măgurele in the village.

Mogoşoaia

Another good day-trip is a visit to Mogoşoaia Palace, just 14 km (9 miles) northwest of Bucharest's center. In 1672 Prince Constantin Brâncoveanu built the brick and stone palace for his son in a park on the shores of a lake. In 1688, he built a small church in honor of St. George. It is one of the finest examples of Brâncovenesc architectural style, combining Byzantine decorative features with elements characteristic of both the Italian Renaissance and the Baroque, as evidenced in its arcades, ogee arches, columns with capitals and a vaulted porch. Since 1957 it is the **Museum of Brâncovan Art** with collections of silverware, sculptures in wood, fabrics, including gold and silver thread embroideries, parchments, rare printed works and miniatures. Mogoşoaia can easily be reached by local trains, bus or by car from Bucharest. ***Palatele Brâncoveneşti Mogoşoaia***, Calea Valea Parcului 1, Mogoşoaia, Ilfov, Tel: (021)490.42.37. Open daily except Sunday. http://bucharest.8k.com/mogosoaia/.

PRAHOVA VALLEY

A couple of hours north of Bucharest lies Prahova Valley, a corridor that connects the regions of Wallachia and Transylvania, and cuts through the Bucegi mountains. In winter the mountain resorts lining the valley cater to skiers; in summer, its many hiking trails and quiet relaxation make it a popular getaway from Bucharest. There are numerous trains from Bucharest stopping in the valley every day on the route to Braşov.

Sinaia

Known as the "Pearl of the Carpathians" for its beautiful mountain scenery, it is both a popular ski resort and the setting for the magnificent **Peleş Castle**, the summer residence of King Carol I and his wife Queen Elisabeta. Sinaia was named by 17th-century boyar Mihail Cantacazino who, in 1695, built a monastery on a forested hillside of the Bucegi mountains after returning from a visit to the Holy Land. In August 1866, Carol I took refuge at the remote monastery. In 1872 he bought 1,000 acres nearby and began the building of Peleş Castle.

The castle was built and expanded over the next 20 years, employing three different architects before its completion. Its exterior is German neo-Renaissance style, with tall, slim towers and multiple spires, an asymmetrical shape, and a fragmented composition of facades, displaying decorative carvings and timbered designs. It stands atop a broad sloped clearing, surrounded by the peaks of the Bucegi Massif.

Its interior has 160 rooms on three floors and combines a multitude of styles, including Italian and English Renaissance, German baroque, Roccoco, Moorish and Turkish elements. The rooms are designed with masses of elaborately carved woodworks, cast bronze doors, gold-plated stucco, Cordoba leather paneling, Carrera and Paunazio marble, hand-made embroideries from Vienna, and 400 stained-glass windows.

They are filled with Aubusson tapestries, paintings by Klimt, chandeliers of Murano glass, armor and weaponry displays, musical instruments and a rich variety of furniture and statues collected by the royal family. Tours are given Wednesday to Sunday, between 10am-4pm, for an admission fee.

Next door is the smaller palace called **Pelişor,** where Carol I's nephew and heir, Ferdinand and his wife Marie stayed beginning in 1903. Marie was an artist and poet who wrote several books and children's stories. She had a strong eclectic, personal style and mixed Art Nouveau elements with Byzantine and Celtic influences in the decoration of Pelişor. Many of the paintings hanging in the palace were gifts to Marie from young painters whose work she had supported. After King Carol's death in 1914, Ferdinand and Marie both became monarchs. They never moved into the grander Peleş Castle, however, which was given to the state.

You must buy a ticket to be allowed entry to the palaces. Guided tours are conducted in various languages from Wednesday to Sunday until 3pm. There is restaurant and café in separate buildings on the grounds.

Midway along the walking path through the fir forests to the castles, you come to the 17th-century **Sinaia Monastery** that Cantacazino built. Go inside the monastery's inner courtyard to see its Brâncovan-style architectural details. Its museum has the largest collection of religious art and icons in Romania.

Sinaia is also a winter **ski resort** with various lifts to transport skiers to its 10 downhill tracks, 3 cross-country trails, 3 sleigh slopes and bobsled slope. There is a ski school and a sport gear shop at the cable car terminal, behind the Montana hotel. In summertime, the cable car will lead you to several hiking trails adjacent to the ski runs. There are also many footpaths that lead into the mountains.

The town also has a lovely park at its north end, across from the train station. The **Casino**, a grand white building, stands at the park's north end. The elegant **Palace Hotel**, founded in 1911, borders the park a few yards from the Casino at Strada Octavian Goga 8, Tel: (0244)31.20.51; fax: (0244)37.46.33).

Across the park, the **Hotel Caraiman**, built in 1881, has a more intimate atmosphere; it's at Bd. Carol I 4, just above the train station, Tel: (0244)31.35.51, fax: (0244)37.46.33. Other hotels are: the totally renovated **New Montana**, on Bd. Carol I 24, Tel: (044)31.27.50, fax: (0244)31.40.51; and the **Sinaia**, at Bd. Carol I 8, Tel: (0244)31.15.51, fax: (0244)31.40.98. Both are modern hotels that cater to skiers. There's also the **International**, at Strada Avram Iancu 1, at the southern end of the boulevard, Tel: (0244)31.38.51, fax: (0244)31.38.55. All of the restaurants in Sinaia are within the hotels.

Buşteni

Eight kilometers (5 miles) north of Sinaia, the town of Buşteni sits at the foot of Caraiman mountain, 2,384 m (4,860 ft.), in the Bucegi range, the most visited mountains in Romania. At the top of Caraiman, the steel **Heroes' Cross**, commemorating Romania's lost WWI heroes, overlooks Buşteni; it is a distinct landmark of Prahova Valley. This is the main access point for hiking and climbing routes in the Bucegi mountains. There is a vast network of well-marked trails and mountain cabanas where hikers can get food and shelter. A one-day hike requires no special equipment. The Bucegi are known for their colorful diversity in plants and strange erosions. Hikers can take the Buşteni-Babele cable car up to **Cabana Babele** at 2,206 m (7,533 ft.), where the wind-modeled stone shapes of **Babele**, resembling old ladies talking, and **Sphinx** are found. From that point hikers can follow blue trail markers for a 5-hour hike that ends in Sinaia. Or one can hike to **Omu peak**, at 2,505 m (8,218 ft.), and return through the beautiful nature reserves. Visitors are always amazed at the variety of wild plants and flowers here, including several kinds of orchids, gentians, and campanulas. A second cable-car from the top of Caraiman mountain links Buşteni with **Peştera (the Cave) Hotel** where you can see the unique **Monastery in the Cave**.

The valleys and mountain paths that cross Caraiman are the recommended mountaineering routes for beginners. These mountains are the center of Romanian rock climbing, comprising the most and the longest alpine routes. The eastern mountainside of the Bucegi, dominated by Caraiman, Coştila and Jepii Mici peaks, it forms an exquisite steep that reaches 1,700 m (23,000 ft.) above Prahova Valley. Morarul and Bucşoiul peaks drop toward the north and northeast, while Guţanul, Grohotişul and Strungile Mari have craggy areas above the Bran-Rucăr passage. You can get a map of mountain routes in town or in Sinaia; it's unadvisable to trek or climb without one.

If camping in the mountains, take some food, water and warm clothing. It gets very cold at night in the mountains, so a tent would help protect against the elements, and the animals, which include the brown bear and black goat.

Buşteni also has several **ski runs**, some perfect for extreme skiing. Ski season begins in December and lasts until April.

Accommodations in Buşteni include: **Hotel Alexandros**, Bd. Libertăţii 153, newly renovated with 20 double rooms, 6 suites, with color TV, cable, minibar, and phone. The hotel has a restaurant, conference room, sport courts, sauna, fitness center, bar, parking; **Caraiman** hotel at Bd. Libertăţii 89, Tel: (0244)32.01.56; the **Silva**, Strada Industriei 39, Buşteni, (0244)32.14.12; **Vadul Cerbului**, Dn, Buşteni, (0244)31.23.91. You might also inquire at the tourist office at Str. Libertăţii 202, 150 m (500 ft.) north of the train station, about available private rooms and cabana in the mountains, Tel: (0244)32.00.27. Both the Silva and Caraiman hotels have good restaurants.

A good resource for comprehensive ski resort info and conditions (in Romanian, but still helpful) is: www.skiresorts.ro.

Azuga

Azuga is 6 km (4 miles) north of Buşteni and is a relatively new ski resort. It too sits at the foot of the Bucegi mountains and shares some facilities with Buşteni. Azuga has the longest ski run in Romania, Sorica slope, as well as Cazacu slope, which are both accessible by chair-lift. At the bottom of the run there are bars, restaurants, ski rentals and cottages.

To the northwest there is Clăbucetele Predealului Massive (highest peak Clăbucetul Azugii, 1,586 m); to the southeast are Baiului and Gârbovei mountains, with peaks over 1,700 m (5,578 ft.).

Accommodations: **Cabana Sorica**, at the foot of the slopes, has 24 rooms, some with private bathrooms, Tel: (0244)32.64.44; **Pensiunea Casa'n Casă**, 100 m from the end station of the maxi-taxis near the lifts, has 5 double and 2 triple rooms with TVs and showers. It also has a good restaurant serving Muntenian cuisine. Its annex across the street has five more rooms, but you must book well in advance, Tel: (0292)60.94.54. There's also **Pensiunea Serena**, Tel: 094-983073; and **Pensiunea Căprioara**, Tel: (0244)32.63.18; **Hotel Azuga**, Tel: (0292)32.74.06; and **Pensiunea Topaz**, Tel: (0292)32.69.84. Romenergo Bar is a small bar and fast food joint at the bottom of the slopes, Tel: (0244)32.71.50. You can rent skis in the same building, around the corner. Mountain bikes can also be rented in Azuga.

The **Azuga campsite** is set between Azuga and Buşteni, along route DN1, but it is near the train line and can be quite noisy. http://azuga.8k.com

Predeal

Technically, Predeal marks the beginning of Transylvania, but because it's a ski resort in Prahova Valley, it seems appropriate to include it with the other ski villages. Six kilometers (4 miles) north of Azuga, Predeal is the most popular ski resort in the country. It is the highest town in Romania at 1,100 meters, and it has 15 ski runs. Two cable and four teleskis, plus five baby-teleskis operate until evening. The slopes have varying degrees of difficulty and there is a ski school for beginners. Cross-country skiers and hikers have many marked trails through pine-covered mountains to explore. Snowboarders are also welcome here. Equipment can be rented at the Clăbucet Sosire Chalet, Ambulance/Emergencies, Victor Babes 21, Tel: (0268)961, (0268)41.09.99. More info at: www.brasovtravelguide.ro.

Some *hotels* in Predeal are: **Orizont**, Strada Trei Brazi 6, has an indoor pool, gym, massage and sauna, Tel: (0268)25.51.50, fax: (0268)15.23.90; the **Predeal**, Strada Muncii 6, Tel: (0268) 25.64.83, fax: (0268)15.21.35; the **Cioplea,** Bd. Libertăţii 102, has a sauna and gym, Tel: (0268)25.68.70, fax: (0268)25.68.71; both also have discos. Other hotels are: **Carmen**, Bd. Mihail Săulescu 121, Tel: (0268)25.65.17, fax: (0268)15.22.06; the **Carpaţi**, Strada Nicolae Bălcescu, Tel: (0268)25.62.73, fax: (0268)15.20.80; and the **Porumbiţa**, Strada Eroilor 71, Tel: (0268)25.63.64, fax: (0268)25.68.94. There are several restaurants in the village, as well as at all the hotels.

Local tourist chalets offer day trips to sights within the surrounding 25 km, including Sinaia's Peleş Castle, Braşov's old city, and the Bran castle or Râşnov fortress.

All of the resorts in Prahova Valley are easily reached by several trains a day from Bucharest or Braşov.

MUNTENIA

Târgovişte

Târgovişte is 80 km (50 miles) northwest of Bucharest, on the right bank of the Ialomiţa River, below the southern Carpathians. The county seat of Dâmboviţa County, it was the capital of feudal Wallachia from the 14th to the 17th century. The modern city of 89,000 grew up around its production of oil-related equipment and machinery. Nevertheless, remnants of past glory still permeate the old town. There's the ***Curtea Veche*** (The Old Court), a huge complex on Calea Domnească 221, where the medieval palace of the king once stood. Remnants of its fortress walls are still visible. The 16th-century watchtower, ***Turnul Chindiei*** (the Sunset tower), built by Vlad Ţepeş, is now a museum commemorating his defense of the town from invaders. The 16th-century **Princely Church** contains beautiful frescoes portraying the life of the region's great leader Matei Basarab. The town's 17th-century Byzantine-style **Stelea Monastery**, founded by King Vasile Lupu, is toward the south end of town, between Strada Stelea and Strada Bălcescu.

Târgovişte is also a cultural center. Beloved modern painter Gheorghe Petraşcu had his workshop here. At the **rare-books museum** (former residence of Princess Safta) you can learn about the history of printed books in Romania from 1508 to the present; the museum preserves manuscripts and maps, as well as the early books. The town's **Archaeological Museum** houses Greek, Roman and Dacian artifacts from the Stone and Iron ages.

Târgovişte was also the site of the trial and execution of Nicolae Ceauşescu and his wife Elena in December 1989 that ended the Communist era in Romania.

Târgovişte can be reached by train or by bus. The train station and CFR ticket agency are at Bd. Castanilor 2. The bus station (*autogara*) is about 1 km (2/3 mile) west of the center and north of the train station, off Strada Constantin Brâncoveanu.

Hotels are: the **Dâmboviţa**, Bd Libertăţii 1, Tel: (40-245)21.33-70, fax: (40-245)21.33.74, E-mail: office@hoteld-ambovita.ro; **Walachia** at Bd. Libertatii 7; and **Phoenix Muntenia** at Strada Unirii 20B.

Curtea de Argeş

One of the most beautiful churches in all of Romania is in ***Curtea de Argeş*** (the Court of Argeş). It was built in 1517, under the rule of Prince Neagoe Basarab on the site of the first Mitropolia of Wallachia, which Vlad Ţepeş build in the 15th century. Inside are the tombs of Neagoe Basarab and Prince Radu de la Afumaţi. It also holds the **royal tombs** of Romania's kings Carol I and

Ferdinand, and their wives, the Queens Elizabeth and Mary. The remains of Saint Filofteea are also kept here. It is currently the home of the **Episcopal Palace** of Argeşului.

A city with a great past, Curtea de Argeş succeeded Câmpulung as capital of feudal Wallachia. The ruins of **St. Nicoară** church (late 13th century) and the **church of St. Nicholas**, one of the oldest churches in Wallachia with an exceptional ensemble of interior frescoes, are witnesses to the rich history of the area. (See "The Legend of Manole" next page.)

A place of pilgrimage for many Romanians, Curtea de Argeş is 130 km (80 miles) northwest of Bucharest, via route E70 to Piteşti, then north on route 7C. The **Hotel Posada**, Bd. Basarabilor 27-29, in the town center, has a restaurant, international direct-dial phones, TV, room service, laundry service and access for the disabled.

Giurgiu

Giurgiu is a city of 88,000 people in southern Romania, on the **Danube River**. First mentioned in a historical document dated 1403, Giurgiu developed primarily as a port. Roads and railroads link it to Bucharest, about 60 km (37 miles) directly north. The **Danube Bridge**, a two-level highway and railway structure built in 1954, connects Giurgiu with the Bulgarian town of Ruse across the river. The **port** at Giurgiu still handles much of the trade on the Romanian side of the Danube. The city is also a chemical manufacturing center. It became an industrial center during the 1980s, when chemical plants were built along the Danube. Pollution from these plants is an ongoing problem in the area.

Olteniţa, between Giurgiu and Călăraşi, is the ancient Constanţiola, which was the seat of the first bishopric established in ancient Dacia. In the Crimean War the Turks forced their way across the river here, and inflicted heavy losses on the Russians.

The Legend of Manole

The legend goes that the king wanted to build a church unmatched in beauty throughout the world. For this great task he hired the best builders. The chief of these master builders was Manole. They started building, but everything they erected during the day, fell apart during the night. Then they knew there was a curse upon them. One night Manole had a dream. A man appeared in his sleep and told him that in order to complete the building successfully, the builders had to build someone dear inside the wall of the church. Manole woke up and told his fellow workers about the dream. In great sadness, they agreed they had to do this. They decided to wait for their wives, who brought them food everyday at noon. The first one to come was to be built alive in the wall. But Manole's fellows cheated on him and told their wives not to come to bring them food the next day. Manole kept his word and didn't tell his wife, so Ana was the only one to come at noon. Devastated, Manole started asking God for mercy. He implored for a strong wind to blow and stop his wife on her way. A storm started, but the gusting wind, rain and lightning didn't stop his faithful wife.

When she arrived to the spot, Manole pretended he wanted to play a game and build a wall around his wife. Amused, she accepted. He started building, and as the wall grew taller, she realized he wasn't going to stop and it was not a game. She started crying and imploring him to spare her. In great grief, Manole finished the wall. When the building was done, the king came and realized that indeed, it was the most beautiful church on the face of the Earth. He congratulated the master builders and asked them if they thought they could erect an even more beautiful church. Conceitedly, they said they could. Then the king, fearing that another ruler could hire them to make that church, took away the ladders, leaving the builders on the roof, with no food, no water and no way to come down. After a few desperate days, they started building wooden wings, hoping they could fly to the ground, but they all crashed and died. The last one to jump was Manole himself. He died and on the place where he fell, a spring of salty water emerged, from the tears cried for his lost beloved wife. Nowadays, the story says, if you listen carefully, you can still hear Ana crying from inside the wall.

Călăraşi

Călăraşi is the capital of Călăraşi *judeţ* (county), at Romania's southeastern border with Bulgaria, where the Danube River turns north into Romania. It is 100 km (60 miles) southeast of Bucharest, along **Lake Călăraşi**. Călăraşi was first documented in 1593, during the reign of Michael the Brave (Mihai Viteazul). A river port and trading center, its chief industries are food processing (particularly fish), flour milling, and pulp and paper making, the latter based on reeds from local swamplands. It's not an attractive city and there isn't much to do here, but the town has an archaeological museum, **Muzeul Dunării de Jos**, at Str. Progresului 4, Tel: (0242) 313 161, fax: (0242) 311 974. The nearby town of Discheni is a former Roman settlement. Călăraşi city has railway and road connections to Feteşti and Slobozia. More info at: www.cimec.ro/Arheologie/calarasi/calarasi.htm

Accommodations: **Hotel Perla**, Bd. 1 Mai 12, Tel: (0242) 11.59.80.

OLTENIA

The most interesting part of Wallachia is its western half, known as Oltenia, which spans countryside west of the Olt River to the Banat, and from the southern Carpathians south to the Danube.

Râmnicu Vâlcea sits on the Olt River at the foothills of the meridional Carpathians. It is the capital of Vâlcea County, and an example of an older settlement that was "systematized" by the communist regime prior to 1989. Nevertheless, it has some lovely historic churches. The oldest is the 15th-century ***Biserica Cetăţuia***. ***Biserica Paraschiva*** is a good example of 16th-century architecture. There is also the 19th-century **Episcopal cathedral**, built atop its original 16th-century ruins. A **memorial house** dedicated to the writer Anton Pan is at Strada Ştirbei Vodă 18.

Accessible by train, the city's station is on Strada Cozia; the CFR ticket agency is on Calea lui Traian, Tel: (0250)73.46.50. Hotels include **Hery** at Strada Fabricii 14, Tel: (0250)74.56.03 and the **Complex Turistic Alutus** at Strada Praporgescu 10, Tel: (0250)73.66.01. You might also contact Vâlcea County's ANTREC office to arrange accommodations in local guest-houses, Tel: (0250)73.32.40, or make arrangements at the Bucharest office before you begin your trip to the Olt valley, Tel: (40-21) 223.70.24.

Just 28 km (17 miles) north are the two **spa** villages **Călimăneşti** and **Căciulata**, in the sub-Carpathian valley of the Olt River, 15 km north of Râmnicu Vâlcea. Their sulphurous waters were used by ancient Romans and by Napoleon III. The **Călimăneşti Field Centre** is operated by the University of Bucharest. This part of the Olt valley has been used for the generation of hydro-electric power and contains several fairly new HEP dams. Their hotels include the **Traian,** at Calea lui Traian 953 in Căciulata, Tel: (0250)75.05.21; the **Motel Tour-Imex,** at Călimăneşti-Căciulata 1079, Tel: (0250)75.11.79; and the **Complex Turistic,** at Strada Calea lui Traian 409 in Călimăneşti, Tel: (0250)75.02.70.

Cozia Monastery is on the bank of the Olt River, a few kilometers north the Călimăneşti-Căciulata. Its founder was Mircea cel Bătrân (Mircea the Wise), who ruled Wallachia in the 14th century and was the first to defeat the invading Turks. The monastery was built in 1388 in the Byzantine style. Its interior frescoes were painted in 1707. Across the road from the monastery, is the lovely little bolniţa, the infirmary church, built in 1542. Its vivid interior frescoes indicate that this chapel is not heavily used by the local worshipers. Immediately to the north is the **Olt pass**, a deep, twisting gorge that cuts through the Carpathians en route (E81) to Sibiu.

West of Râmnicu Vâlcea, 2 km (1.2 miles) north on a dirt road, off main route 67, is the quiet **Roma** (gypsy) village of **Costeşti**. Every year during the first week of September the village holds the largest **Roma festival** in Romania. There is music and dancing, and selling of wares and horse-trading by the thousands of Roma who come to celebrate, most arriving via their horse-drawn carts. At the fair, business deals will be struck and marriages will be arranged. The Romanian Roma king will face his rival, the self-proclaimed Emperor of Roma worldwide.

On the southern side of the main road to Târgu Jiu, on hills covered with oak forests, there is a series of little white churches, all part of the **Govora monasteries**. Built in 1491 and cared for by monks, its peaceful flower gardens are a perfect place for rest and reflection. Govora monastery has 10 beds to accommodate overnight guests, but they must be booked prior to arriving; Tel: (0250)77.03.42.

The largest and most beautiful of the medieval monasteries is in **Horezu**, the creation King Constantin Brâncoveanu in 1694. Brâncoveanu is a brilliant figure of Wallachian history; he was a man of great culture and knowledge, and during his reign the country experienced unprecedented development in the arts and crafts. Many impressive buildings in southern Romania were built during Brâncoveanu rule, and the carved stone decorations specific to that time are now referred to as Brâncovenesc. At Horezu, delicately carved stone leaves and flowers that adorn the church's exterior columns complement the stark whiteness of its walls. The monastery's art collection includes a rich collection of icons, a photography museum, Brâncovan silver, and a library with over 4,500 volumes. Horezu is one of the most important monasteries in Romania, and many writers, poets and painters come here in search of inspiration.

Horezu is also renowned for its **pottery**. An age-old craft developed on the hills of Oltenia, modeling clay has become a true art at the hands of the master potters in and around Horezu. Their work is famous both in Romania and abroad. To find the potters, you must locate their houses, which serve as their workshops. Everything about this craft is a family secret, from the choice of clay used, to the modeling, to painting, baking and glazing. The resulting plates, mugs, pitchers, and even toys and flutes, display specific colors (especially white, rich browns and grays, and sometimes green) and a specific design. Often symbolic drawings appear on these works. One of the most popular is the Rooster, and another one is the Fish. These motifs also appear in the other artifacts traditionally made in the region (rugs, painted Easter eggs). But most of the earthware is decorated in delicate, yet powerful geometric patterns, skillfully painted by the masters' wives using age old tools such as cow's horns and goose feathers.

Horezu Monastery is 1 km east of the village; watch for signs off the main road D North 67, Horezu, (0250)76.02.20. You may be able to stay **overnight at the monastery**; they have ten double rooms, and three rooms with four beds each. Tel: (0250)86.00.71.

Târgu Jiu

Târgu Jiu is located on the Jiu River in Gorj County, at the foot of the southern Carpathians that separate Wallachia from Transylvania. The valley is rich with coal deposits, making it of great strategic importance. For this reason, it was the scene of heavy fighting during World War I and World War II. To celebrate the memory of thousands of Romanian soldiers who died here during the war, abstract sculptor **Constantin Brâncuşi** (1876-1957) built a unique memorial complex in Târgu Jiu's **city park**. Brâncuşi, who was born in a neighboring village, imagined the whole scene as a temple of meditation. First, you sit at his round ***Table of Silence***, then walk along his ***Alley of the Stools***, and then pass through his ***Gate of the Kiss***. The path continues in a straight line across town to the Church where the "enlightened spirit" takes off at the ***Infinite Column***.

Târgu Jiu also has a **Country History Museum** on Strada Geneva, and an interesting **Art Museum**, on Strada Stadion, open Tues–Sun.

Târgu Jiu can be reached by train; its train station is at Strada Republicii 2. The CFR office is at Strada Unirii 2, Tel: (0253)21.19.24. The bus station is just south of the train station, off Strada Titulescu. Hotels include the **Gorj**, at Calea Eroilor 6, Tel: (0253)21.48.14; the **Parc**, at Bd. Brâncuşi 10, Tel: (0253)21.59.81; and the **Sport,** at Bd. Brâncuşi 7, Tel: (0253)21.44.02. ANTREC has a local office that arranges guesthouse accommodations, Tel: (0253)21.69.64.

The monastery of **Tismana**, is a peaceful oasis nestled in the foothills of the mountains, not far west from the town. It was founded in the late 14th century. The Romanesque-style complex of white buildings with red roofs surrounding the white church is surrounded by slopes of dense green trees. Tismana holds an annual pottery fair in March and a dance festival every August. Tismana monastery has twenty rooms to accommodate overnight visitors, Tel: (0250)37.43.17.

To the North, in the gorges of the Jiu River, is the mining town of **Petroşani**, mentioned by the French fiction writer Jules Verne in his "The Castle of the Carpathians." For information on the many **Gorj County festivals** throughout the year, visit a local tourism office or contact *Centrul de Creaţie Populară*, at Strada Vladimirescu 36, in Târgu Jiu, Tel: (0253)21.37.10. Contact Gorj County's ANTREC office to arrange accommodations in local guesthouses, Tel: (0253)22.30.81 or (0722)54.27.64.

Craiova

Situated 185 km (53 miles) west of Bucharest, on the Jiu plain of Dolj County, the modern city of Craiova is the second-largest city in Wallachia with 303,000 residents. It began as the Roman fortress *Pelendava* in the time of Emperor Traianus. Craiova reached its high point between the late 15th to 18th centuries, when it was the seat of the Bani, the governors of the region. Mihai Viteazul, Michael the Brave, the medieval leader who united the three Romanian kingdoms for the first time in 1600, was once the Ban of Craiova. During this time, the city prospered as a regional trading center despite earthquakes, plagues and foreign threats. A tourist attraction, the oldest architectural monument in town is the **St. Dumitru Church**, originally built in 1652.

The modern city is an important industrial center for the construction of locomotives and machinery. It is also a cultural center. It has a **University**, the **National Theatre**, the **Lyric Theatre** (Opera), a **Children's Theatre**, the **Oltenia Philharmonic**, an **Art Museum** and a rich regional **Museum of Oltenia**, www.craiova.ro/muzist.htm.

Craiova can be reached by train line on the Bucharest/ Timişoara line. Its train station is on Bd. Republicii, north of the center. The *Agenţia CFR* ticket office, at Calea Bucureşti 2, is open weekdays, Tel: (0251)41.16.34. TAROM's office is at the same address, (0251)41.10.49. Craiova main bus station is on Bd. Republicii, by the train station.

Some of Craiova's *hotels* are: the **Bavaria**, Strada Caracal 3, 15 minutes from the city center, Tel: (40-251)41.44.49, fax: (40-251)41.48.86, E-mail: bavaria@icnet.ro, www.bavaria.icnet.ro; **Helin**, Calea Bucureşti, U10, near the center, Tel/fax: (40-251)46.71.71, E-mail: hotel@helinstrading.com, www.helinstrading.com; the **Jiul**, Calea Bucureşti 1-3, in the center, Tel: (40-251)41.56.55; **Parc**, Strada Bibescu 16, in the center, Tel: (40-251)41.72.57; **Minerva**, Strada Mihail Kogălniceanu 3, Tel: (40-251)251-13.33.00; **Palace**, Strada Alex, Ioan Cuza 1, Tel: (40-251)251-11.69.32; **Hanul Doctorului**, Calea Bucuresti, E 70, Km 220, Tel: (40-251)251-14.40.13; and **Emma**, Calea Bucureşti 82A, 10 minutes from the center.

Băile Herculane

Herculane spans the Cerna River in a lush green valley of the **Domogled massif** (range). It sits at 152 m (500 ft.) altitude, just 40 km (25 miles) from the town of Drobeta Turnu Severin, and even closer to the Danube. It is the oldest spa in Romania, dating back to Roman times. Legend tells us that Hercules came here to heal his battle wounds and enjoy its famous mineral water springs. Archaeological discoveries have proven that the rich mineral waters at Herculane were known of long before the Romans conquered the region in the 1st century AD. But it was the Romans who developed the region, building public baths for everyone to enjoy. Today, little remains of their original constructions, but the tradition of taking to the waters for health has continued. In the 19th century, Herculane was popular with the Austro-Hungarians, and Emperor Franz Joseph and the Empress Elisabeth both frequented the spa.

Modern Herculane sits amid majestic mountain scenery. Its thermal waters spring from a depth of 1,676 to 1,981 meters (5,500 to 6,500 ft.) with temperatures ranging from 40°C to 60°C (104°F to 140°F). The waters are sulphurous, calcic, magnesian, chloride-sodic, oligo-metallic and radioactive. They have metabolic benefits and are used for both baths and internal cures. They are recommended for the treatment of rheumatism, sciatic and brachial neurologic traumas and chronic myositis, tendonitis and synovitis.

The resort also offers recreation: indoor and outdoor swimming pools, sports, hiking, fishing, and boat trips on the Danube. It has a nightclub, casino, theater, cinema and discotheque. Herculane has first-rate hotels and well-equipped camping sites, as well as restaurants and shops. A large **statue of Hercules** given by Carol I in 1847 stands in the square.

Băile Herculane can be reached by train or road from Timişoara or via Craiova. Hotels include: **Afrodita,** Băile Herculane, (40-255) 56.07.30; **Ferdinand** Hotel, Băile Herculane, (40-255) 51.61.21; **Diana,** Parc Vicol 1, (40-255) 56.01.31; **Roman**, Roman Str, (40-255) 56.03.90; **Hercules** Hotel, Strada Izvorului 17, (40-255) 56.00.30; **Minerva**, (40-255) 56.07.70.

Drobeta-Turnu Severin

The Danube River forms Romania's southern border for 468 km (291 miles) before turning north, on its way to its delta and the Black Sea. From where the river enters Romanian territory it meanders through what is called "**the Iron Gates**," the narrow, natural gorges of the Danube between Serbia and Romania. After passing through the gorges, it winds its way to the town of Drobeta-Turnu Severin.

An ancient settlement surrounded by hills, this early Dacian town was made a *castrum* (fortified place) by the Romans, as described by 2nd-century Greek geographer Ptolemy of Alexandria. It rose to the rank of *municipium* by the emperor Hadrian in 124, then to *colonia*, by emperor Septimius Severus (AD 193-211). In this period Drobeta was a prosperous town, with numerous monuments, several being uncovered by archeological investigations. Other remnants of the town's ancient past are the ruins of a Roman fortress and its baths. But the town's most impressive features are the vestiges of the **great bridge** built across the Danube by architect Apollodorus of Damascus for Emperor Traianus. The bridge was an extraordinary achievement of 2nd-century engineering, and it carried the army of Traianus across the Danube to conquer Dacia.

The town was destroyed by Huns in the 5th century, but later rebuilt by Justinian (AD 527-565). In the Middle Ages, its name was changed to Turnu Severin, after the tower that emperor Severus built to commemorate a victory. In the 13th century it became the political center of the Banat of Severin.

Drobeta-Turnu Severin is on the European route 70, 353 km from Bucharest, 210 km from Timişoara and 113 km from Craiova. Its hotels include: the **Continental Parc**, Strada Caro 2, located in the center of the city, within walking distance of the main railway station and close to the Danube River; air conditioning, TV, hair dryer, laundry service, minibar, restaurant, shopping. Tel: (40-254)31.28.51, fax: (40-254)31.69.68; the **Severin**, Strada M. Eminescu 1, near Bd. Republicii, Tel: (40-254)21.20.74, Tel/fax: (40-254)31.81.22; the **Traian**, Bd. Vladimirescu 74, Tel: (40-254)31.17.99, Tel/fax: (40-254)31.17.49.

The Danube River

The Danube is Romania's most important river for transportation and for the production of hydroelectric power. In 1896, the **Sip Canal** was opened, allowing large ships to pass through the narrow gorge (170 m/550 ft. wide, 3.2 km/2 miles long) and continue all the way to the Black Sea. In 1971 a hydroelectric project that included a huge dam called ***Porţile de Fier*** **(the Iron Gates)** was completed at Orşova to harness the power of the Danube River. At the same time, one of Europe's largest hydroelectric stations was built between Orşova and the Iron Gates gorge, just upstream of Dobreta-Turnu Severin, where the river breaks through the Transylvanian Alps. This was a joint effort between the former Yugoslav government and Romania, and it now produces electricity for a large part of Romania's southern region and for parts of Serbia and Montenegro.

The Danube is navigable for river vessels along its entire Romanian course, and for seagoing ships as far as the inland port of Brăila. One problem with the use of the Danube for inland transportation is its remoteness from most of the major industrial centers. Others are its marshy banks and perennial flooding that impede navigation in some areas. But in 1984, the 64 km (40 miles) **Danube-Black Sea canal** was completed, running from Cernavodă to Agigea, creating a direct route to the Black Sea and shortening the trip by 370 km (230 miles).

The Danube is also the only major river in Europe to flow from west to east. It receives more than 300 tributaries, including the Inn, Drava, Tisa, Sava, and Prut rivers. It was once a fabulous eco-system with hundreds of species living in its waters or on its banks. Today, the populations of local species have decreased to a point where several of the mammals, birds, and fish are endangered. This is due to overuse and pollution, particularly waste from factories and bilge oil from ships. In January 1999, a 5 km (3 miles) long oil slick floated down the Romanian-Bulgarian stretch of the river. This followed a 55 km (34 miles) slick that came from the Yugoslavian section a week earlier. Now, there are urgent measures being taken to protect the areas along the Danube.

CHAPTER 6

TRANSYLVANIA

The most famous area in Romania, thanks to the legend of Dracula, this is a picturesque region of medieval towns and hilly pastures nestled among the Carpathian mountains in the center of the country. Its name inspires romantic visions of mountain forests, imposing castles and a mysterious history.

While under Hungarian rule in the 13th century, Transylvania was settled by Saxons from Germany who were invited by King Geza II. They brought with them an advanced civilization and skilled tradesmen who built seven fortified towns in the region, which became known as the *Siebenburgen* (seven fortresses). Their communities organized guilds and became prosperous in the Middle Ages. Today these charming cities and towns are still intact and their original buildings still in use. Sadly, most of the Saxons' descendants fled Romania during Ceauşescu's communist rule or immediately thereafter, but their influence is still dominant in the region. Likewise, German is the most common language spoken in Transylvania after Romanian, followed by Hungarian. Few people speak English here.

SOUTHERN TRANSYLVANIA

Braşov

Nestled at the foot of Mount Tâmpa, Braşov is Romania's second most important city. An industrial center with over 323,000 inhabitants, Braşov's old section is a picturesque relic of its historic beginning. The first documentary mention of the town was in 1234, when it was named *Corona*; but when the Saxons settled here in the 13th century, they renamed the town *Kronstadt*. The colorfully painted and ornately trimmed buildings that line the streets of the old city are distinctively Germanic.

The center of the old town is ***Piaţa Sfatului***, surrounded by restaurants and outdoor cafes. It is to this spot that the legendary Pied Piper is to have led the children of Hamelin. The piaţa is a wonderfully charming and busy place, where the locals work and play, shop, socialize and enjoy food and drink at outdoor cafes. In the middle of the piaţa, at no. 30, stands the **Council House (*Rathaus*)** or **Old Town Hall,** built in the 15th century and combined with the 13th-century **Trumpets Tower,** a remnant from the old fortress of Brasov. Today it is the **Regional History Museum** with exhibits representing Brasov County history, from ancient times to the present. Its collections include tools made from stone (Paleolithic age), painted ceramics discovered at Arcus (Neolithic age), tools of bronze and iron, medieval weapons and armor, farming implements, the original loom mechanism made of wood (1823), and Romania's first lathe (1868). The museum is open from Tuesday to Sunday 10am-5pm.

On the east side of the piaţa is **Casa Hirscher**, also called **Merchants' Hall**, built in 1542, where the Saxon trade guilds used to meet. This golden arcaded building now houses the ***Cerbul Carpatin*** (Carpathian Stag) restaurant and terrace.

Just off the southeast corner of the piaţa is the impressive 14th-century gothic **Black Church**, so named because its exterior was blackened by smoke from a fire set by the Austrian army on April 21, 1689, during their conquest of Transylvania. (The fire destroyed most of the town and killed 3,000 of its people.) The church's interior, however, is astoundingly white and beautiful. Built from 1385-1477 as Saint Maria Catholic Church, it became Lutheran in 1542. Its altar is surrounded by nine arched stained-glass windows and has six Ionic stone columns reaching 89 meters (292 ft.) to the vaulted ceiling. At the rear of the church is a 4,000-pipe organ from 1839 that spans half the height of the church. Dark wooden pews have sliding backrests so visitors can face the altar during services or face the back of the church, toward the organ, during concerts which are held several evenings a week at 6pm. The church is lined with balconies on both sides, above side pews that face the center of the nave. Italian Renaissance-style murals and more than 100 Anatolian carpets, acquired in the 17th century, adorn the walls.

Casa Mureşenilor is a family museum dedicated to the talented artistic family of Iacob Mureşanu, a composer, who in 1838 became the founding editor of "Gazeta de Transilvania". Its exhibits include 19th-century furniture, paintings, heirlooms and keepsakes, photographs, rare books, letters, and newspapers of the musical and literary members of Mureşanu's family. The museum is housed in the family home just across the street from the main square at Piaţa Sfatului 25, Tel: (0268)47.89.64, E-mail: casa_muresenilor@yahoo.com.

Leading away from Piaţa Sfatului toward Bd. Eroilor is ***Strada Republicii***. This pedestrians-only street is lined with shops, cafes and bakeries in colorful medieval buildings; it is the favorite place for leisurely strolling and meeting friends. At its north end, at Bd. Eroilor, are some hotels and restaurants, and across the boulevard are the old Post Office and City Hall.

Next door to the Post Office is a gravesite **memorial park** honoring the people who died during the December 23, 1989, revolt which helped lead to Romania's overthrow of communism. On each gravestone is a photograph of the person and their age at death; most were students. To the left of City Hall, within the peaceful **Parc Central**, is a children's playground and a long promenade lined with park benches that runs along the center rose garden.

A couple of blocks east of the northern end of Strada Republicii, at Strada N. Bălcescu 62, is the large, three-level department store **Star** (open until 5pm). It is well-stocked with clothing, cosmetics, handicrafts, ceramics, glass, suitcases, appliances, hardware, sporting goods, food, drinks and home supplies. Next door is an open-air produce market.

Behind the store you'll find a woodsy path to **Mount Tâmpa**. Follow the pathway along the mountainside to the cable car that takes passengers to the summit. Exiting at the top, if you hike about .4 km (a quarter-mile) to your right, along the lower path, you'll reach the lookout point revealing a wonderful birds-eye view of Braşov. The **Panoramic** restaurant (open evenings until 10pm) and an outdoor cafe also sit atop Mount Tâmpa. You can also access the cable car via Strada Castelului, then Strada Romer. The Telecabina Tâmpa cable car operates from 10am to 6pm daily, except Mondays.

Near the lower cable car terminal stands what's left of the 15th-century **fortress wall** that was built to protect the city against Turkish invasion. The wall originally had seven bastions, each built by one of the local trade guilds. Of these, the best preserved is the **Weavers' Bastion**, a few blocks south at Strada George Coşbuc 9, now the **Museum of the Bârsa Land Fortifications,** open Tues-Sun., Tel: (0268)14.45.90. Inside there are three levels of galleries displaying weaponry and historical documents from the Medieval Age, including armor, artisans' tools, statues, the guilds' flags, the wood mechanism of Brasov's ancient horologe on top of the old Town Hall (1512), a medieval safe, a 16th-century street lamp, pieces of an aqueduct and rare books. In the center of the main room are models of the old Cetatea and Schei districts. Nearby, along **Poarta Schei**, are Braşov's only **Synagogue**, built in 1901, and the **Schei Gate**.

During Saxon rule, the Romanian people were forced to live outside the fortress walls in the **Schei district**, south of the town center. They were allowed to enter only at certain times to sell their goods, and were required to pay a toll at **Ecaterina's Gate**, erected in 1559 at Strada G. Bariţiu and Strada Beethoven. At **Piaţa Unirii,** the Schei district's **Church of St. Nicholas** was the **first Orthodox church** in Transylvania, built by Wallachian princes in 1495.

The yellow building to the left of the church is the country's first Romanian-language school, ***Şcoala Românească***, built in 1495 and now a **museum** holding the first printed

Romanian-language books—printed at the school in 1556, by the Deacon Coresi. The school shelters **4,000 rare books**

> Until the 17th century, the official language of Romania was Greek, written in Cyrillic. In the late 1700s, Transylvanian scholars recognized the Latin origin of Romanian and adapted the Italian alphabet to the Romanian language. The Cyrillic alphabet remained in use (gradually decreasing) until 1860, when Romania's Latin-based alphabet was made official.

(many of them printed here); 30,000 historic manuscripts, including 80 princely charters engraved on parchment; Varlaam's Homiliary written in Cyrillic (Iaşi, 1643); a 1688 Bible from Bucharest (printed on goat skin); the first Romanian-language hymnbook, catechism book, philosophy handbook, grammar, Romanian almanac and calendar from 1731. In addition to its book collection, the museum still retains its original **printing press** from 1556. The school's "Anton Pann" classroom is also preserved intact with its original furniture. (Pann was a frequent visitor and his books are here, too.) For a tour of the **Museum Complex of Schei**, contact professor Vasile Oltean, Tel: (0268)49.59.04, (0268)14.38.79, who will proudly show you the museum (he doesn't speak English). He will also guide you through the **Junii Museum**, behind the church, which holds several traditional costumes worn by the Schei men, as well as many old household items.

Just north of Bd. Eroilor and Parc Central is *Dealul Cetăţii*, **Citadel Hill**, topped by the well-preserved ruins of Braşov's 14th-century citadel. It is now a restaurant and party complex. Located farther west, at Strada Lungă 247, is the oldest building in Brasov, the 13th-century gothic **Church of St. Bartholomew**. It stands at the foot of **St. Jacob's Hill**, where Vlad Ţepeş impaled his victims on stakes in 1460.

Braşov's Art Museum is at Bd. Eroilor 21; with exhibits of Romanian and international artists, including paintings by Grigorescu, Aman, Tătărăscu, Luchian, Tonitza; European crystal and porcelain; a large collection of Oriental vases and statuettes from China, Tibet and Old Persia. Tel: (0268)14.43.84.

For entertainment, there's **Opera Braşov/Liric Theatre** at Str. Bisericii Romane 51, Tel: (0268)41.72.71, and the **"Gheorghe Dima" Philharmonic** at Str. A. Hirscher 10, Tel: (0268)47.30.58. The ticket agency (*Agenţie de bilete*) for the Opera and Philharmonic is at Str. Republicii 4. The **Teatre Arlechino** presents puppet shows at Str. A. Hirscher 10, Tel: (0268)47.52.43. **Cinemas:** the **Modern** at Str. Grivitei 47 and **Patria** at Bd.15 Noiembrie 50; movies are shown in the original language with Romanian subtitles.

Every May, Braşov hosts the **Springtime Jazz Festival** at the theater on Piaţa Teatrului, at the north end of Bd. Eroilor; and in July the **Golden Stag International Pop Music Festival** is held outdoors in Piaţa Sfatului. Buy tickets for concerts and theater at the booking office on Strada Republicii 4.

Old Braşov has many restaurants and cafes. Around Piaţa Sfatului, you will find the *Cerbul Carpatin, Chinezesc, Orient, Gustări, Casata* and *Stradivari,* among others. **Pasajul Saşului,** at Strada Republicii 53-55, is a skylit atrium with several restaurants, developed by a Saxon family who had fled Romania, and has since returned to Braşov. Restaurant *Butoiul Saşului*, on the lower level, has multiple dining chambers, brick walls and a piano player; *Casa Vinului,* on street level, is a wine-tasting café; *Café Noblesse* is a coffee and drink bar that is half old-style and half-modern. The *New York-New York* Restaurant Club is also located downstairs, with photos of New York City lining its walls. In the Pasaj atrium, there's also a snack bar and bright umbrella tables and chairs.

There's also *Pergola* restaurant in the Aro Palace hotel, and *Restaurant Cetate* on Citadel Hill. For pizza, go to *Pizza Julia* on St. Balcescu, a block north of Strada Republicii via the side street Strada D. Coresi.

Braşov is also the perfect base for exploring the surrounding countryside; close by are Bran and Râşnov, Hârman and Prejmer, and the mountain resorts of Prahova Valley (Poiana Braşov, Predeal, Buşteni and Sinaia). It's also the starting point for traveling the medieval route (Sighişoara, Mediaş, Prejmer, Sibiu); or roving north into Szekely land (Sfântu Gheorghe, Miercurea-Ciuc, Târgu Mureş, and Bistriţa).

Braşov is 166 km (100 miles) north of Bucharest and can be reached in 2.5 hours by express trains running several times each day. In fact, it is the main transportation crossroads of Romania. The train station is north of the old town. A taxi ride to your hotel costs only a few dollars equivalent in lei, or the #4 bus will bring you to Parc Central. The Agenţia CFR is at Bd. 15 Noiembrie #43, near Piaţa Teatrului (open Mon-Fri, 7am-7:30pm).Braşov's tourist office is in the lobby of the Aro Palace hotel; it's mainly useful for planning excursions to Bran, Poiana Braşov or other Transylvanian sites.

Hotels in Braşov are: **Aro Palace**, Bd. Eroilor 27, a 4-star luxury hotel with conference rooms and casino, in the old center, Tel: (40-268)14.28.40, fax: (0268)15.04.27; **Hirscher Residence Hotel**, Apollonia Hirscher 14, a new apartment hotel just off Piaţa Sfatului, with kitchens and Internet access, Tel: (40-268)10.12.12; **Ambient**, Str. Aninoasa 5, a short stroll from the center, some rooms with balconies, Tel: (40-268)47.08.56; **Capitol**, Bd. Eroilor 19, a modern 3-star hotel in old Brasov, Tel: (0268)41.89.20, fax: (0268)15.18.34; **Helis**, Strada Memorandului 29, west of the old town, a somewhat appealing area just south of Strada Lungă, but a pleasant 3-star hotel with a multi-lingual staff, Tel: (40-268)41.02.23; **Corona**, Strada Republicii 62, a 2-star hotel with old-world design, best location, Tel: (40-268)14.43.30, fax: (40-268)15.44.27; **Postăvarul,** Strada Politehnicii 2, the low-budget wing of Coroana hotel, a no-frills hotel, rooms have washbasins, but some shared bathrooms, no credit cards, Tel: (40-268)14.43.40; **Aro Sport**, Strada Sfântu Ioan 3, low-budget rooms like Postăvarul, a short walk from Piaţa Sfatului, Tel: (40-268)14.28.40.

Pensiuni (Guesthouses)**: Casa Mureşan,** Str. Nicopole 54, a 3-star pensiunea in Old Brasov, 16 rooms (3 singles, 9 doubles, 4 apartments); rooms have TV, good bathrooms; conference room and small bar on-site, Tel/fax: (40-268)41.43.73 or (0721)30.64.40, E-mail: casamuresan@cazareturisti.ro. **Casa Ţepeş**, Str. Ţepeş 14, off Bd. 15 Noiembrie, charming villa, five large rooms with huge beds, good bathrooms, TVs (attic rooms best); large living room and dining table, buffet breakfast included; Tel/fax: (40-268)41.39.17 or (40-722)66.39.66, www.hotelrestaurant.ro/casatepes. **Casa Cristina**, Str. Curcanilor 62A in Schei district, 6 lovely rooms, Tel: (40-268)51.25.80, (40-722)32.20.21; fax: (40-722)19.00.06, E-mail: rezervari@casa-cristina.ro**,** www.casacristina.ro. **Curtea Braşoveană**, Str. Băilor 16, pension in the Schei district, all rooms are nicely furnished with good bathrooms, TVs and Internet access; small conference room and sauna onsite; VAT and breakfast included; 10 rooms (4 singles, 2 doubles, 1 suite, 1 apartment, 2 Junior suites); Tel. (0268)47.23.36; fax: (0268)47.21.45, E-mail: curteabrasoveana@rdsbv.ro, www.curteabrasoveana.ro. **Stefan's Guest House,** Str. Pajiştei 22, a cobblestone street, 15-minute walk from Piaţa Sfatului; recently remodeled and converted to an apartment; great for a couple, Tel: (40-722)290 680, E-mail: steve.willis@atcglobal.com, www.brasovcottage.home.ro. **Pensiunea Montana,** Str. Stejeriş 2A, on the road to Poiana Braşov; 7 rooms with bathroom and TV and a 2-room apartment for 4 persons with bathroom and TV; terrace overlooks Braşov, breakfast included, Tel: (40-268)47.27.31 or (40-723)61.45.34, E-mail: info@montana.ro, www.montana.ro. **Pensiunea Stejeriş**, Str. Stejerişului nr.15, on the road to Poiana Brasov, 6 rustic rooms, a terrace view over the city; restaurant open 24 hours a day; a wine cellar available for small private parties or meetings; Tel: (40.268)47.62.49 or (40-744)35.42.31; fax: (40.268)47.62.49.

Campground: Camping Darste, Calea Bucureşti 285, northeast of Brasov, shower and electricity, market and restaurant; no dogs. Tel: (40-268)31.58.63.

If arriving by train, you may be approached by someone at the station offering a private room in their home, usually

an apartment bloc not far away from the center. This is a common practice and may be a good option if you're on a limited budget.

Special service phone numbers: **Ambulance/Emergencies**: 21 Victor Babeş, Tel: 961 or 41.09.99; **Police**: Str. Nicolae Titulescu, Tel: 955; **Train times**: Tel: 952.

Poiana Braşov

An easy and popular day-trip is to Poiana Braşov, at the foot of **Mount Postăvarul**, just 12 km (7 miles) south of Braşov. This great mountain surrounds half of the resort, which sits at an altitude of 1,000 meters (3,300 feet), providing some of the best skiing in Romania. It is one of Romania's most popular winter resorts, with twelve ski slopes of various degrees of difficulty (one run for slalom, an olympic run, three downhill and giant slalom runs) with lifts and cable transport. The skiing is good from December to April. Lessons can be arranged at the ***Complex Favorit*** tourist office, which also provides hiking guides. Equipment can be rented at the Sport, Ciucas and Teleferic hotels.

Poiana Braşov offers year-round recreation. It's a terrific place for hiking, camping, horseback riding, mountain biking (rentals available) or all-terrain motorcycle riding, with routes for various skill levels. It also has tennis courts, a roller-skating rink, a minigolf course, medical gyms, saunas and indoor swimming-pools.

There are plenty of restaurants and night spots, both chic and casual in the town. In addition to the restaurants in the hotels, checkout the very rustic *Şura Dacilor* (Dacian's Shed), *Coliba Haiducilor* (Outlaw's Hut), *Vânătorul* (Hunter), *Capra Neagră*, *Poiana Ursului*, and *Ruia*. Most serve traditional Romanian food in a rustic atmosphere and have a folk music band.

If you choose to stay overnight in Poiana Braşov, you have a choice of 11 hotels, plus villas, cabanas and bungalows. Some hotels: the **Alpin** has an indoor pool, massage and sauna, Tel:

(40-268)26.23.43, fax: (40-268)26.21.11; **Piatra Mara** has a sauna and disco, Tel: (40-268)26.22.26; **Ciucas** also has a sauna, a disco and a sports shop, Tel/fax: (40-268)26.21.81; **Bradul** has a disco, Tel: (40-268)26.23.13); and **Sport** has a sauna, Tel: (40-268)26.23.13, fax: (40-268)26.21.30. Ask about other accommodations at the local tourist office or at tourist agencies in Braşov or Bucharest. In winter its best to reserve rooms ahead. You might also consider accommodations in local villas or mountain chalets, such as **Postăvarul**, at 1,602 m (3,266 ft.), or **Cristianul Mare**, at 1,704 m (5,590 ft.).

Bus #20 leaves every half-hour from Braşov's *Livada Poştei* bus stop on Bd. Eroilor. Tickets can be bought at the RATB kiosks. You might also visit the fortified churches of Prejmer and Hârman, Bran castle or the peasant fortress at Râşnov.

Râşnov

An interesting day-trip for history buffs is to the ruins of **Râşnov Fortress**, an ancient peasant refuge set atop a hill. Its first documentary mention was in 1331. Raised in the 14th–17th centuries, Râşnov's two precincts were surrounded by 5 m (16 ft.) high walls. It was built on a calcareous rock, and had an entrance tower and an outpost bastion with firing outlets. The fortress' interior wall contained cells where the peasants could take refuge at times of siege. The complex also has a 98 m (321 ft.) deep draw-well. Although the fortress is in ruins, its remains are vast and fascinating, and include the shells of several old houses. An inscription in stone reveals the ancient Dacian name of the land: *Cumidava*. Climbing to the top of the hill can be a bit challenging, but the view of the countryside from the top is stupendous. About halfway up, there is a tiny café where you can stop for coffee, sit outside and imagine life on that spot 500 years ago.

If you're coming from Bran on the bus, get off at the second stop in Râşnov and walk to your right until you get to Unirii Square. Look for a stairway inside the courtyard. Râşnov is

15 km (9 miles) southwest of Braşov, on the Braşov-Bran road. Buses marked 'Moieciu-Bran' depart Braşov from bus station *Autogara 2* every half-hour, stopping at both villages. There's an admission charge to visit the fortress ruins.

Bran

The most popular day-trip from Braşov is a 25-km (15-mile) bus ride to **Bran Castle**, the medieval fortress most often associated with the legend of Dracula. Although Prince Vlad Dracula never really stayed there, it was the favorite summer refuge of **Queen Marie** between 1920 and 1937. The castle was built in 1377 to protect Braşov from invading Hungarians and later, from the Turks. Made of stone blocks and boulders, the imposing structure stands atop a hill overlooking the picturesque village of Bran. You must buy a ticket at the kiosk (there's a small extra charge for cameras) and then climb a steep path leading up the hill to the castle.

The castle has four towers and surrounds an inner courtyard with a sculpted stone fountain. The first floor consists of five vaulted halls and the castle's prison. The second floor, the landlords' dwellings, is decorated with Baroque furniture. The third level has an open hallway that overlooks the castle's interior courtyard. On the top level is the watch platform where the guards oversaw the countryside. Narrow winding stairways lead you through the rooms, which house collections of furniture, weapons and armor dating from the 14th to the 19th century. The castle grounds below include a lovely garden and an open-air **Ethnographic Museum** of old village buildings with household objects, furnishings and costumes on display. Local peasants sell their handicrafts in the parking lot at the entrance to the castle grounds. The castle is open Tues-Sun from 9am-5pm, Strada Principală 498, Tel: (0268)23.67.20.

Catch the same 'Moieciu-Bran' bus from Braşov's Autogara 2, as mentioned above; pay the fare in lei (about $2). Plan at least 4 hours for this excursion, as the bus ride takes 40 minutes

each way. (You might also stop and see the fortress at Râşnov on your way to or from Bran.) To return to Braşov, you'll catch the same yellow bus at the bus stop just across the road from where it dropped you off, going the opposite direction. If necessary, ask someone "*Unde este autobuzul spre Braşov/Bran?*" ("Where is the bus toward Braşov/Bran?") They run about every 40-60 minutes and can get crowded, so you may have to stand. The best time to go is in the morning, before the tour bus crowds arrive.

If you'd like to stay overnight, you can contact ANTREC in Braşov: Tel: (0268)236 355, (0788)422 097, (0788)411 450 or (0268)236 917; or in Bucharest, at Tel: (021)223.70.24, fax: (021)222.80.01 to arrange accommodations in a villager's home or an organized tour with guide of Bran and the surrounding areas. They are part of Romania's rural tourism program, providing guest rooms in private homes where hotels are scarce. Participating hosts provide breakfast and sometimes evening entertainment. Guests may even contribute to the household chores, such as milking goats and drying wool, if they like. Campground: **Vampire Camping**, Str. Sohodol 77C, Bran (31-062)50.83.909, www.vampirecamping.com.

Moeciu de Sus & Moeciu de Jos

Moeciu de Sus (upper Moeciu) and Moeciu de Jos (lower Moeciu) are two small villages in an idyllic setting, deep inside the green mountain valley, amid rolling, terraced hillsides. They are also becoming very popular places to stay overnight, as homes are being converted into cozy pensiuni by the local owners. They are especially popular during the Halloween celebrations at Bran Castle. Some hosts will transport guests to Bran Castle, and may include a little tour of the area, possibly in their horse-drawn wagons. They might not speak any English, however.

Pensiuni (guesthouses) can be booked in Bucharest through Arrow International Travel, Str. Franceză 44, Tel/fax:

(021)313.32.84, (021)313.32.6, E-mail office@arrowintravel.ro, www.arrowintravel.ro; or Cultural Romtour, Tel: (021)316.67.65, fax: (021)316.67.64, E-mail: office@culturalromtour.ro, www.culturalromtour.com. ANTREC can also arrange accommodations at its many guesthouses in this area; Tel: (021) 223.70.24, fax: (021)222.80.01, E-mail: antrec@antrec.ro, www.antrec.ro. Another online option is www.hotelrestaurant.ro/romanian/judete/bv/moeciu.htm.

Take the same 'Moieciu-Bran' bus from Braşov. You can probably hitch a ride with a local farmer (perhaps in his horse-cart) to get around the area.

Prejmer

Fifteen kilometers (9 miles) northeast of Braşov, lies the village of Prejmer (German: *Tartlau*), and the **largest fortified church in southeastern Europe**. It was built by Teutonic knights and Saxon villagers, with walls 3-4m. (11 ft.) thick and 12m (39 ft.) high, strengthened by several cylindrical bastions. The watch way has openings where arrows, cannon balls or hot tar could be thrown down upon the attackers.

The village church it surrounds and protects is of an early Gothic style with Cistercian influences, built in 1250. It has a cross-like plan, with Baroque decorations and the remains of mural paintings both inside and outside. But this 14th-century citadel also has double walls and a dungeon.

The interior side of its red-roofed walls provided each village family with one small room where they could be sheltered if the village was attacked. Its 275 rooms were stacked over four-storeys and linked by wooden staircases. There was also a secret, subterranean passage through which food supplies could be transported. In peaceful times, the rooms were used for storage. Now, only one family lives here and takes care of the citadel. A few years ago, a complete restoration of Prejmer was done with the help of the village community.

Prejmer's church is the easiest of the Saxon churches to visit; it has a concierge's lodge in the entrance passage, and there is a small museum with some signs in English. Prejmer is a UNESCO World Heritage site.

Hârman

Hârman (German: *Hönigburg,* literally "honey castle") is 10 km (7 miles) north of Braşov or west of Prejmer. This tiny Saxon village rests in a large and beautiful valley, with a 15th-century **peasant citadel** at its center. The **church**, built in 1241 in a Romanesque style, but later restored in the Gothic style, is surrounded by a high, round perimeter wall with seven square bastions; the wall is surrounded by a large, water-filled moat. The church has an organ, backless bench seats, wide-plank wood floors and is decorated with hanging oriental carpets. Attackers laid siege on the church 47 times without success.

The interior side of the fortified walls has wooden staircases leading to rows of small rooms where each peasant family stored essential supplies for use in times of siege. At that time the number of Saxons in Hârman was 1,500, but today there are fewer than 150. The colorful houses facing the main square are typical of the Saxon era, with large rounded doors and few windows. The local **Bed & Breakfast**, at Strada Mihai Viteazu 441, has 3 rooms.

About 18 km (12 miles) northeast of Braşov lays **Mlaştina de la Hârman**, a nature reserve that contains rare animals, carnivorous plants and glacial relics.

Sighişoara

This beautiful medieval city looks much as it did 700 years ago. It is famous as the birthplace of the real Dracula, **Prince Vlad Ţepeş**, born in 1431. His house, where he lived with his father Vlad Dracul until 1435, when they moved to Târgovişte, still stands at the foot of the **Clock Tower** on the fortress hill. The simple yellow building is now the **Berărie restaurant**, with medieval furnishings and a tavern. You'll know it by the wrought-iron dragon (*dracul*) hanging above its door.

The **fortress**, built on the hill in the 13th and 14th centuries is reached by a long path with 172 steps from the lower town. It is one of the original *Siebenburgen* fortresses. The citadel originally had 14 towers, nine of which are still standing. These were built by Saxon and Magyar craft guilds that controlled the town. The most dominant bastion is the 210-foot-high (64 meters) **Clock Tower**, which now houses the **Museum of History**. Inside you can climb the narrow winding staircase and see displays of furnishings and artifacts from the medieval era. Peek inside the small clock window where, since 1648, 3-foot high (1 meter) carved wooden figurines have mechanically presented themselves to the town when the clock chimes the hour.

From the lookout balcony circling the top of the tower, you get a magnificent view of the old town with the red-tiled roofs of 16th-century Saxon houses lining narrow cobblestone streets. The museum is open Tues-Fri, 9am-5:30pm and Sat-Sun, 9am-3:30pm. Other bastions surrounding the hill are the **Skinners' Tower**, the **Tailors' Tower**, the **Jewelers' Tower**, the **Shoemakers' Tower**, the **Tinsmiths' Tower** and the **Butchers' Tower**.

Across from the Clock Tower is the 13th-century **Monastery Church**. Its white interior is decorated with hanging oriental rugs, a baroque altar and a bronze font from 1440. If you're lucky, you might catch a wedding procession leaving the church, making the traditional walk under the Clock Tower arch.

The surrounding cobblestone streets are lined with enchanting old houses painted yellow, blue, green, and pink. Especially interesting are the yellow 15th-century house near the clock tower, where the real Dracula, **Vlad Ţepeş**, was born in 1431, the 16th-century **Venetian House**, the 17th-century **House with Stag** (now a hotel) and the 18th-century **Schuller House**. Follow the narrow street back to ***Piaţa***

Cetăţii (Citadel Square) where local residents sell their handiwork. There are several charming hotels and restaurants around the piaţa, housed in historical old buildings. Sighişoara is one of the few citadels in the world where the business of day-to-day living still continues within its walls. In fact, the yellow house where Dracula was born is a busy restaurant.

The **Covered Stairway**, erected in 1656, has 175 steps leading up the hill from Strada Şcolii, south of Piaţa Cetăţii. It is covered by a pointed wooden roof and sides loosely slatted to let in light. At the top of this hill stand the 14th-century **school house**, still in use, and the ***Bergkirch*** (Church on the Hill) built in 1309, which has recently undergone restoration. If you can find the keeper of the school or the church, they will let you inside for a look. (Communication may be tricky though, as they speak only German, Hungarian or Romanian.) The school has a wonderful interior of tall, arched windows, iron chandeliers, decoratively painted walls, muraled ceilings and carved wood balconies. On one classroom wall an old photograph of Albert Einstein as a very young man still hangs.

The heart of the lower town is **Piaţa Hermann Oberth**, reached from the hill via the ancient cobblestone **Strada Turnului** under the Clock Tower. Piaţa Oberth is at the south end of Strada 1 Decembrie. In its center is a little park filled with flowers. Around the piaţa are colorful **16th-century houses**, shops and cafes. More small businesses, including the Agenţie CFR and the Post & Telephone office line, Strada 1 Decembrie.

North of the citadel, on the way to the train station, the **Orthodox Cathedral** stands overlooking the river. Built in the Byzantine style, its white exterior is in stark contrast to its dark interior.

Sighişoara was one of the fortified cities that the Saxons founded in Transylvania. It was mainly inhabited by Germans and Hungarians (Magyars). Its German name was *Schassburg;* Hungarians called it *Segesvar*. Today there are 40,000 inhabitants and the modern town has expanded beyond the original medieval settlement. UNESCO has named medieval Sighişoara as a **World Heritage Site**.

Sighişoara has several new *hotels*: **Casa Wagner**, Cetăţii Square 7, charming hotel in two medieval buildings, furnished with antiques; rooms have TV, phone, minibar; hotel has a restaurant, crama (wine cellar restaurant), summer terrace, conference room; buffet breakfast; Tel: (40-265)50.60.14, fax: (40-265)50.60.15, E-mail: office@casa-wagner.com, www.casa-wagner.com. The **Sighişoara**, Strada Şcolii 4-6, medieval building with garden and terrace bar, 2nd-floor balconies, 3-room rustic wine cellar; conference room; beauty center; sauna and jacuzzi; every room different, Tel: (40-265)77.10.00, fax: (40-265)77.77.88, E-mail: hotelsighisoara@elsig.ro, www.sighisoara.com. **Casa cu Cerb** (House with Stag), Strada Şcolii 1, a restored medieval building at Cetăţii Square with crama-style restaurant, Tel: (40-265)77.46.25, fax: (40-265)77.73.49, E-mail: info@casacucerb.ro, www.casacucerb.ro. The new **Korona**, Strada Zaharia Boiu 12-14, behind the citadel in the lower town, has restaurant, bar, conference rooms, patio and garden with fountain, parking lot; rooms have shower or jacuzzi-tub, in-room safe, Tel: (40-265)77.04.80, fax: (40-265)77.04.83, E-mail: hotelkorona@zappmobile.ro, www.hotelkorona.ro. The **Claudiu**, historical building in lower town with restaurant and bar; rooms have TV, phone, Internet access, Tel: (40-744)82.31.01, tel/fax: (40-265)77.98.82, E-mail: office@hotel-claudiu.com, www.hotel-claudiu.com. The **Hotel Rex**, Strada Dumbravei 18, a modern building just east of the center off Strada Mihai Viteazul, Tel: (40-265)77.76.16, fax: (40-265)77.74.31, E-mail: hotelrex@elsig.ro, www.sighisoara.com/hotelrex. **Casa Legenda**, Strada Bastionului 8 bis., Tel. (40-744)63.27.75. The **Hotel Steaua** on Strada 1 Decembrie 1918 #12 has a restaurant and bar, conference room; rooms have cable-TV; cash only, Tel: (40-265)77.19.30, fax: (40-265)77.33.04, E-mail: printuldracula@elsig.ro, www.hotelrestaurant-steaua.home.ro. The small, renovated **Hotel Chic**, directly across from the train station at Strada Libertăţii 44 has nice rooms with shared bath; cash only, Tel: (40-265)77.59.01. For drivers (or anyone else) the **Motel Poieniţa** is a lovely villa in a rural neighborhood, a 20-minute walk east from the center on Strada Dimitrie Cantemir 24; it has a small pool and restaurant, Tel: (40-265)77.27.39). Reservations are wise in summer, though the hosts at hotels Chic and Poieniţa don't speak much English.

For hostellers, there's the **Gia Hostel**, at Strada Libertatii 41, just 50 m west (to the right) of the train station; rooms with 2, 3 or 4 beds, and 1 private room; all rooms have private bathrooms; a multi-lingual staff, 24-hour reception, Tel/fax: (40-265)77.24.86 or (072)249.00.03, international: (40-722)49.00.03, E-mail: giahouse@myx.net.

Sighişoara is 119 km (74 miles) northwest of Braşov and 393 km (244 miles) from Bucharest, located on the Târnava Mare River. It is reached by train from Braşov, or Bucharest on the same line. The train station is situated across the river, about a .8 km (1/2 mile) north of the center of town. You can walk from the station via Strada Garii until you cross the river by the Orthodox Cathedral; then follow Strada Morii south (left) until you reach the main street, Strada 1 Decembrie. The Steaua hotel and the tourist office are across the street; the CFR agency and Piaţa Oberth are to the south (right). The steps up to the Citadel will be to your right, *before* you reach Strada 1 Decembrie.

Along route 14, between Sighişoara and Sibiu, there are three historical places well worth a visit:

Biertan

The 13th-century town of Biertan was a flourishing crafts and trade center during the Middle Ages. High on a hill in the center of town stands the most famous **fortified church** in the region, protected by walls more than 10 m (35 ft.) high. The fortress consists of three fortified precincts, their walls built in several stages, and each with a gate tower. The inner enclosure was built in the 14th century to protect the old basilica; the second wall was erected in the 15th century; and the third one,

The Truth about Dracula

The real Dracula was Vlad Ţepeş, a Wallachian prince and son of Vlad Dracul, so named when he was knighted by King Sigismund of Hungary into the Order of Dracul (the Dragon). Dracula means "son of the dragon". Young Vlad was born in Sighişoara, but spent his youth in Târgovişte and under Turkish custody in Istanbul. As Voivode, or Prince, of Wallachia from 1456-1462 and again in 1476, he was a fierce defender of his country against the Turks.

In the forests around Braşov, Vlad impaled his prisoners with long poles and propped them up on the hills for all to see. Legend says he dined amidst his human forest. He also spent years imprisoned by Hungarian King Matthias Corvinus, Hunyadi's (Iancu de Hunedoara's) son. Vlad Ţepeş (the Impaler) eventually lost his head in battle. His headless body is said to lie in the Snagov Monastery, in the middle of Snagov Lake, 40 km (25 miles) north of Bucharest. He is still honored by Romanians as one of their greatest rulers.

as well as the 8 towers and bastions, were built during the 16th century.

The **church** within was built from 1492-1515 in the late Gothic style with Rennaissance elements on some portals. Its pulpit sculptured in stone is one of the most important Transylvanian sculptures. The altar is made-up of 28 pre-Reformation plates, dating from 1483 and attributed to the Vienna "*Schottenmeister*" school. The altar's crucifix was made by Polish painter and sculptor Wit Stwosz. The **Sacristy door**, made of oak with wrought iron and inlaid work, dates from 1515 and is considered a masterpiece of Transylvanian arts and crafts; it received an award at the Paris World Exhibition in 1937 for the engineering of its huge iron lock with two bolts and 13 other bolting systems that operate simultaneously. The church also has an earthenware fireplace decorated with blue flowers and furniture with inlaid decorations from 1514.

Biertan was the residence of the Lutheran bishops from 1572 to 1867 and seat of the Transylvanian Diet. Their fine gravestones can be seen inside the **Bishops' Tower**. Legend says that a room in the church was kept for couples who wished to divorce; they were locked up together for two weeks so that they might discover the folly of their ways. Biertan was designated a UNESCO **World Heritage** town in 1995.

Biertan is about 30km (18 miles) west of Sighişoara via main road DN14 (toward Mediaş), then south about 8 km (5 miles) on a lesser road. To book a local ANTREC guesthouse room, contact the Sibiu branch: Tel: (0269)23.35.03 or the main Bucharest office, Tel: (021)223.70.24.

Mediaş

Mediaş is a charming medieval town of 63,000 inhabitants, built by Saxon tradesmen in the 13th century on the site of an old Roman camp. It is one of the original *Seibenburgen* fortresses. The heart of town is a large square park surrounded by **colorful medieval houses**. A stately **clock tower** at the entrance to its 14th-century fortress stands guard over **Saint Margaret's Evangelical** church. This 15th-century Gothic cathedral has some Romanesque elements, painted murals, and a 14th-century bronze font. Its wooden altar, painted between 1480 and 1490, features scenes from the life of Christ.

The surrounding hill sides are covered with age-old vineyards that produce Mediaş' famous wine. In Bram Stoker's "*Dracula,*" Jonathan Harker enjoyed "Medias wine" at a Transylvanian inn. There is even a bunch of grapes engraved on the city's coat of arms.

Mediaş is 39 km (19 miles) west of Sighişoara and 55 km (34 miles) north of Sibiu on road DN14. It can also be reached by train from either city. Mediaş's only hotel is in the center of the town, near the train station and bus station. **Hotel Central**, Str. Mihai Eminescu 4-7, has 9 single rooms and 107 doubles, 4 triples and 8 apartments; all rooms have color TV, radio, modern bathroom, phone, 24-hour room-service. It also has a restaurant with 3 rooms, a brasserie, an Internet bar-café, summer terrace, travel agency, and beauty center. Tel: (0269)81.17.87; fax: (0269)82.17.22. To book a local ANTREC guesthouse room, contact the Sibiu branch: Tel: (0269)23.35.03 or the main Bucharest office, Tel: (021)223.70.24.

Cetatea de Baltă

Northwest of Mediaş, on the left bank of the Tarnava Mic River (near Blaj) is Cetaţea de Baltă. For a century Cetatea de Baltă was a possession of the princes of Moldavia, beginning with Stephen the Great (1457-1504) and ending with Alexandru Lăpuşneanu (1564-1568). Its name came from the old 12th-century fortress that Matthias Corvinus modernized in the 15th century; it was restored between 1615 and 1624. Its main body is rectangular, but with large circular towers at each corner. The towers have no defensive function; this castle was meant to be lived in, rather than as a fortress. The building resembles a small version of the Chambord in France.

The surrounding countryside is the wine-growing district of ***Jidvei*** vineyards. Some tourism agencies offer wine-tasting tours combined with a visit to Cetatea de Baltă and other area sights.

Sibiu

Sibiu is possibly the loveliest of all the Transylvanian cities. A stroll along Strada Nicolae Balcescu, between **Piaţa Unirii** and **Piaţa Mare**, immediately reveals why. Its colorful buildings with their gingerbread-house designs are a treat for the eyes. Throughout the town you will find old medieval houses painted in hues of blue, green, gold, turquoise and pink. Doorways and gates have carved wood designs and intricate iron-work figures, also painted in vivid colors. Look up toward the roofs to see faces and flower garlands carved into the stone facades. Notice too, the tiny roof windows that look like sleepy eyes peeking out at you.

Sibiu is the largest medieval site in Romania. It is in southern Transylvania on the banks of the Cibin River, just north of the Făgăraş mountains. The town was first recorded in 1191 as Roman *Cibinium.* In the 12th century, Saxons settled here and renamed the town *Hermannstadt.* They built most of its buildings and made it a prosperous trade city. Medieval Sibiu was surrounded by a fortress wall built in the early 13th century that was destroyed by the Tatars in 1241, rebuilt a century later, and three times assaulted by the Turks during the1400s.

In 1699 Transylvania became part of the Austro-Hungarian empire, and the Hungarian population renamed the city *Nagyszeben.* Today it is an industrial, commercial, cultural, scientific, and tourist center with a mixed population of 200,000 Romanians, Hungarians, and Germans. The city's cultural value was confirmed on May 27, 2004, when a decision by the European Union's Council of Ministers of Culture designated medieval Sibiu as the **Cultural Capital of Europe for 2007**.

The city's main activity was, and still is, concentrated around its three historic squares. ***Piaţa Mare*** (Great Square) is the focal point of Sibiu. It was mentioned in 1411 as a cereal market, and then, in the 16th century, it became the center of the old citadel. The **Council Tower** stands watch over the piaţa; it was one of the city's original defenses, first erected in 1366 and rebuilt in 1588.

Sibiu always had a busy commercial and handicraft life, and surrounding Piaţa Mare are 16th- and 17th-century **merchants' homes** that today house small shops, cafes and businesses. As in the other Saxon towns, Sibiu's craftsmen belonged to guilds. The large arcaded building at no.20 was the **Furriers' and Skinners' Hall**. The former **Butchers' Hall** stands at no. 2. The southern side of the Piaţa Mare is now protected by UNESCO as a monument of architecture.

Another clock tower rises above the 18th-century **Catholic Cathedral,** with its interior of pink marble colonnades, gold-laced walls, and ceiling frescoes. The cathedral holds weekly organ recitals. The statue in the center of Piaţa Mare is a popular gathering place for Sibiu's young people.

One of the favorite attractions here is the **Brukenthal Palace Museum** at no.5, former home of Samuel von Brukenthal, who was governor of Transylvania from 1777-1787 during the Habsburg rule. Of late Baroque style, it contains paintings, graphics, engravings, and sculptures from 15th-19th-century Flemish, Dutch, German, Austrian, Italian, and French artists. It also has History and Natural Sciences sections, Folk art and a Library with priceless early books and old Transylvanian newspapers. Brukenthal's own personal collection was the basis for forming the museum in 1817. The museum is open Tuesday-Sunday (www.brukenthalmuseum.ro/en).

Adjacent to Piaţa Mare is **Piaţa Huet** where the gothic **Evangelical Church** (Lutheran), built during the 14th to 16th centuries as a Catholic basilica, contains the tomb of Mihnea the Bad, the son of Vlad Ţepeş. He was stabbed to death by a political opponent after mass in 1510. The church choir performs on Sundays. The ancient **Passage of Steps** connects ***Piaţa Huet*** with *Strada Turnului* in the lower town, along a medieval wall with brick and tiled overhead arches.

North of Piaţa Huet is **Piaţa Mica** (Little Piaţa) and the **Iron Bridge**, also called **Liars Bridge**, built in 1850. One of its legends says that no one can tell a lie while standing on it, without the bridge collapsing. Running alongside is **Fingerling's Ladder**, a steep staircase that leads from the lower town's artisans area up to Piaţa Mica. The old, arcaded Market Hall, built in 1789, still stands in this piaţa.

The **Museum of Transylvanian Civilization "ASTRA"** is also in Piaţa Mica at no. 11; it was founded in 1993 to exhibit the multi-ethnic culture and civilization of the people in Romanian Transylvania. It displays collections of national costumes, textiles and embroideries, pottery, wooden and iron objects. Tel: (0269)21.80.60, www.itcnet.ro/sibiu/engl/civili_e.htm. Next door, at Piaţa Mica 12, the **Transylvanian Saxon Ethnography Museum** displays the contributions that the Saxon settlers have contributed to the forming and enrichment of the Romanian culture during their more than 800 years of living in Transylvania. The museum contains almost 7,000 objects. Tel: (0269)21.81.95, fax: (0269)21.80.60, E-mail: astra@sbx.logicnet.ro, www.itcnet.ro/sibiu/engl/sigher_e.htm. Open daily, except Mondays.

Southwest of Piaţa Huet, at Strada Mitropoliei 2, is the **Old Town Hall**, built from 1470-1491 and now the home of Sibiu's **History Museum.** The museum's 250,000 exhibits include medieval money pieces, seal-making tools, medals, antique and medieval jewelry and a collection of medieval weaponry (open Tuesday-Sunday). Farther down this street is the **Orthodox Metropolitan Cathedral,** built in 1906 to resemble Istanbul's Hagia Sofia. It is decorated in the Byzantine style, its interior dominated by an enormous gold chandelier.

The most famous building on Strada Balcescu is the 200-year-old **Împăratul Romanilor** Hotel (The Emperor of the Romans) at no. 4. It has hosted guests since 1773, and has housed some outstanding personalities, such as Emperor Franz Joseph II of the Austro-Hungarian Empire, Franz Liszt, Johann Strauss, Johannes Brahms and poet Mihail Eminescu.

The former **Hermannstadt** was the most powerful of the Saxons' fortress cities. It was strategically located not far from the Turnu Roşu gorge, which links Wallachia to Transylvania, and it became the main trading route between the two regions. To protect the town against Turkish invasion, the guilds built a **fortified brick wall** and **40 bastions** around the city in the 15th century. Along Strada Cetatii, three blocks southeast of Piaţa Mare and Strada Balcescu stands the best preserved stretch of the wall and three of its red-roofed bastions. A narrow park lines the high ground inside the wall; stairs lead you down through its arched doorway to the low ground outside the walls, where modern Sibiu resides.

Restoration works being carried out in Sibiu's historical squares have uncovered remnants of its **ancient citadel**. Citadels were strongholds, usually made up of defensive walls surrounding the church. Built into the inside wall was a room for each family in the community, where they could take refuge during an attack and store their most valuable things. Several of these store rooms were also discovered underground. Old texts refer to supply holes to be used in case Sibiu was besieged. Workers have found both empty and full supply holes under Piaţa Mica. One access hole is 60 cm (24 inches) wide, while the deposit itself is 4-5 meters (13-16 ft.) deep, widening like a pear underground. Five of the 13 holes discovered will be equipped with a lighting system and visitors in 2007 will have the opportunity to see the archaeological site.

Sibiu also has one of the best open-air museums in Romania. The **ASTRA Museum of Traditional Folk Civilization** is situated in the Dumbrava Forest, 4 km (2½ miles) south of the city. Covering almost 100 hectares (245 acres) and with almost 6 km (4 miles) of exhibition space, the outdoor museum displays real peasant houses brought from various Romanian regions, peasant tools, wells, and industrial constructions, including an impressive number of mills (wind, water, saw, etc.), as well as some old traditional means of transportation. ASTRA's outdoor museum is on Calea Răşinarilor, open daily (except Mondays) between April 15th and November 1st. From the train station or Piaţa Unirii, trolleybuses T1 and T4 both run to Hanul Dumbrava; or take bus 17 (to Răşinari), or bus 15 (to Păltiniş). Trams run past the museum from Calea Dumbrăvii and from Răşinari. The museum also has a minibus that ferries visitors from Piaţa Mare. For more information, ask at the ASTRA museum on Piaţa Mica. Tel: (0269)42.02.15, fax: (0269)21.80.60, E-mail:astra@sbx.logicnet.ro, www.itcnet.ro/sibiu/engl/astra_e.htm.

Sibiu's **State Philharmonic** is at Strada Cetatii 3-5, Tel. 20.65.08, E-mail: filarmo@rdslink.ro, www.filarmonicasibiu.

The **"Radu Stanca" National Theater** is on Bulevard C. Coposu at no. 2; tickets are available from the Theater Agency on Nicolae Balcescu 17, weekdays and Saturday mornings, or at the theater before the show begins.

Sibiu can be reached by air or train from Bucharest, and by train from Braşov, Sighişoara and Cluj. The train station is northeast of the center. Train services are relatively frequent; from Bucharest the trip takes about three hours. You can easily walk from Piaţa 1 Decembrie, by the station, down Strada G. Magheru to Piaţa Mare, or take a taxi to your hotel. You can buy train tickets at the *Agenţia CFR* at Strada Balcescu 6, Monday-Friday, Tel: (0269)21.20.85. The TAROM airline office is also on Strada Balcescu at no.10 (open Mon-Fri). TAROM runs buses to the airport an hour before each flight.

International Bus Companies serving Sibiu: AtlasSib: scheduled bus service to Germany, Italy, France, Sweden, Tel: (0269)22.92.24, www.atlassib.ro; Kessler: scheduled bus service to Germany, Tel: (0269)22.81.18; Trans Europa: to Germany, Tel: (0269)21.12.96; all buses leave Turnişor Bus Terminal. Amad Touristik: scheduled bus service to Italy, France, Spain and Portugal, Tel: (0269)23.27.32; all buses leave from Calea Poplăcii 56-58.

Sibiu has more than 30 hotels, motels and guest houses able to accommodate over 2,000 visitors. Some hotels are: the elegant **Împăratul Romanilor**, Strada N. Balcescu 4, Tel: (40-269)21.65.00, fax: (40-269)21.32.78; the stately **Bulevard**, at Piaţa Unirii 10, at the south end of Strada Balcescu, Tel: (40-269)21.60.60, fax: (40-269)21.01.58; the **Continental**, Calea Dumbrăvii 4, a block south of Piaţa Unirii, Tel: (40-269)21.81.00, fax: (40-269)21.01.25; **Parc**, on Strada Scoala de Înot 3, south of the center near the Municipal Stadium, Tel: (40-269)42.61.15, fax: (40-269)42.35.59; **Silva**, at Aleea Mihai Eminescu 1, next to the Parc hotel, Tel: (40-269)44.21.41, fax: (40-269)21.79.45; **Hotel 11Euro**, Str. Tudor Vladimirescu 2, a small hotel with 11 rooms, a restaurant, a night club and a guarded parking lot in the inner courtyard, each room is decorated in an individual style (rustic, royal, etc.) to a high standard with 1 or 2 beds, a TV, telephone, and shower. Tel: (40-269)22.20.41, fax: (40-269)21.42.21, Email: contact@11euro.ro or traian.oprean@11euro.ro, www.11euro.ro.

Sibiu's only hostel is the **Black Cat Youth Hostel**, on Piata Mica 26, in a 450-year-old Saxon building; founded in 2004; large old windows make a bright upstairs, contrasting with the dark brick arcade basement; a homey ambience; breakfast (vegan/vegetarian) costs 2 euro. Tel: (40-269)43.12.16 or (0742)75.14.50, Email: hostelsibiu@rdslink.ro.

All of Sibiu's hotels have restaurants, but there are also several small restaurants, cafés and bars along Strada Balcescu and around the old center, where you can listen to Romanian folk or jazz music. Some restaurants: *Sibiul Vechi*, Str. Al. Papiu Ilarian 3; *La Turn*, Piaţa Mare 1; *Rustic*, Calea Răşinarilor; *Crama Ileana*, Str. Gimnasticii; *Egreta,* Str. Orzului 2[a]; *Butoiul de Aur,* Pasajul Scărilor; *Cârciuma din Bătrâni*, Muzeul Civilizaţiei Transilvane ASTRA.

Sibiu's post office is on Strada Mitropoliei, open weekdays 7am-7pm.

Sebeş

The small Saxon town of Sebeş (pop. 30,000) was founded in the 12th century on the site of an ancient Daco-Roman settlement at the foot of the Cândrel mountain. Its German name was *Muhlbach*. After invasions by the Tatars and the Turks, it was rebuilt by its German settlers and became an important political and administrative town during the 14th to 17th centuries. Parts of the town's **14th-century citadel**, including wall fragments and some towers (the most famous being the **Student Tower**), have been preserved. Its 13th-century **Evangelical Church** has a unique architectural history: first built as a Roman basilica with three floors in the Romanesque style, it later took on a Gothic style with Renaissance elements. The church contains valuable paintings and carvings, Anatolian carpets and the largest Gothic altar in Transylvania, made in 1518, with beautiful painted and sculpted figures. Sebeş also has a 14th-century citadel and tower. The 16th-century **Princely House** of Ioan Zapolya now serves as the district **museum**, with sections on history, fine arts, Romania and Saxon folk arts and natural sciences. You'll also find many typical 19th-century Transylvanian houses throughout the town.

Sebeş is just 17 km (10 miles) south of Alba Iulia, via road E81. The train and bus stations are 3 km (1 mile) from the city center. Public buses provide transportation to and from the stations. Taxis can be called at: Pronto, Tel: 731.419. The town has two Youth Hostels: **Dacia**, Tel: (0258)73.27.43 and **Lutsch**, Tel: (0258)73.32.73. Emergency phone numbers are: **City Hospital**, Tel: 73.17.12, 731.045. **Ambulance**, Tel: 73.44.33.

Nearby are the ruins of **Vântu de Jos**, a 17th-century castle built by Gabriel Bethlen, prince of Transylvania in 1613 and king of Hungary from 1620–1634. It was built on the site of a former 14th-century Dominican monastery. The ruins of the castle became associated with fearful stories devised by the local folk about Austrian Empress Maria Teresa's love affairs and the subsequent violent murder of her lovers.

Alba Iulia

One of the oldest settlements in Romania, the site was selected first by the Romans for a military camp, then it became *Apulum*, one of the greatest cities in Roman Dacia. Many important chapters of Romanian history were written here in Alba Iulia, as the town became the center of Romanian nationalism and an important Romanian language printing center.

In the heart of Transylvania, the city has been an object of dispute for most of its existence, which explains its many names: *Karlsburg* (German), *Gyulafehehérvár* (Hungarian), and *Balgrad* (Slavic). Regardless of language, its name always meant "The White City," because of the white walls of the fortress that were visible from afar.

Alba Iulia was always a leader in the fight for a united Romania. It was here that the Romanian provinces were united for the first time in the modern era, in 1599, under the reign of Michael the Brave. Likewise, the second union of Transylvania with Romania was pronounced here on December 1, 1918. Throughout the city, there are numerous monuments related to the Union. Romania's King Ferdinand and his wife Queen Marie were crowned in the city's **Orthodox church**.

The city has a 13th-century Romanesque-style **Roman Catholic cathedral**, an **18th-century fortress**, the grand **Batthyáneum Library** and the **Regional Museum** displaying a rich collection of Roman antiquities from the remains of Roman Dacia's cities.

Plans are underway to build a new airport in Aurel Vlaicu, a town midway between Alba Iulia and Deva, about 35 km (22 miles) from each. In the meantime, the closest airports to Alba Iulia are in Sibiu, (90 km), Caransebeş (110 km), Cluj-Napoca (140 km), Timişoara (160 km) and Arad (180 km). Hotels include: the **Transilvania**, Tel: (40-258)81.25.47; the **Cetate**, Str. Unirii 3, Tel: (40-58)82.38.04; and the **Parc**, Str Primăverii 4, Tel: (40-258)81.17.23.

Deva

Deva (German name: Diemrich or Schloßberg) was originally settled by the Dacians. King Decebalus built his fortress on a nearby hill, overlooking the Mures River Valley. Later, in the 13th and 14th centuries, Citadel hill became the base of a fortified construction, meant to shelter the residents of Deva from Mongol invasions. The citadel was destroyed by an explosion in the early 19th century, but its ruins remain. The hilltop also offers a magnificent view of the Mures River Valley below.

Bethlen was built at the foot of the hill in 1621 by ruling prince Gabriel Bethlen in Renaissance and Baroque styles, and was restored in the 18th century. Also known as ***Magna Curia***, today it houses **Deva's History Museum**.

Deva is best known for its **School of Gymnastics**, where some of the world's best gymnasts were trained, including Olympic gold medalist Nadia Comaneci and Lavinia Miloşovici.

Deva is accessible by train. The airports closest to Deva are at Sibiu (90 km), Caransebeş (110 km), Cluj-Napoca (140 km), Timişoara (160 km), and Arad (180 km). www.world66.com/europe/romania/deva.

Hotels include: The **Decebal**, Bd. 1 Decembrie 37a, rooms, telephone, TV, fridge, restaurant, meeting and conference rooms, disco-bar, Tel: (40-254)21.24.13, fax: (40-254)21.42.45 96. The **Deva**, Bd. 22 Decembrie 110, 120 rooms with telephone, TV, fridge; hotel has a restaurant, summer-terrace, bar, Tel/fax: (40-254)21.12.90, (40-254)22.59.20. The **Sarmis**, Piaţa Victoriei 3, Tel/fax: (40-254)21.47.30, (40-254)21.47.31, 118 rooms with telephone, TV; restaurant, summer-terrace, bar. The **Beno Oil**, Str. Santuhalm 7 (toward city's East exit), Tel/fax: (40-254) 23.42.12, 8 Rooms. **Venus B&B**, Str. M. Eminescu 16, Tel/fax: (40-254)21.22.43, 3 flats with TV and telephone; bar. **Vila Paradis B&B**, Aleea Crişului 1A, Tel/fax: (40-254)22.01.30, 8 rooms and flats with TV, telephone and fridge. **Motel Oil Glat Exim**, Calea Zarandului 1, Tel/fax: (40-254) 21.28.21, 29 rooms with telephone and TV; restaurant and bar.

Hunedoara

Set in a region scattered with ancient ruins and steel mills, the town of Hunedoara rises on the remains of a Dacian settlement. Since its earliest inhabitants, the mineral-rich surrounding areas have been exploited by mining, some mines are still in operation today. During the Communist era, Ceauşescu insisted on building his factories here, destroying the once-beautiful landscape. Remarkably, a bamboo grove grows nearby in Mintia.

The city's main tourist attraction is the Gothic 14th-century **Castle Corvineşti**, a gift from Hungarian King Sigismund to Transylvanian prince Iancu of Hunedoara (in Hungarian:

Janos Hunyadi). Hunedoara was a military genius who played a vital role in defeating the Turks in their attempt to expand into Europe. The castle was built atop an old fortification overlooking the Zlaşti River. It is huge and imposing, yet it has a distinctive elegance. It has three soaring, pointed towers, colorful red roofs, and a drawbridge; the windows, balconies and towers are all adorned with lacy stone carvings.

During his rule, Iancu de Hunedoara turned this strategically placed stronghold into a lavish palace. The castle's successive masters modified its appearance by adding towers, halls and guest rooms. But the Gallery and the donjon—the last defense tower, named "***Ne boisa***" ("Do not be afraid")—have remained unaltered since Iancu de Hunedoara's time. They, and the **Capistrano Tower**, are some of the most significant elements of the structure. The great rooms in the castle are: **the Knights Hall** (a reception hall), **Clubs Tower** and the **White Bulwark** (a food storage room); the **Council Hall**'s walls are adorned with painted medallions including portraits of Matei Basarab, a ruler of Wallachia, and Vasile Lupu, a ruler of Moldavia. In the castle wing, called **the Mantle**, a painting portrays the legend of the raven (corb), from whence came the name of Iancu de Hunedoara's descendants: *Corvini*.

Outside, in the castle yard near the **Chapel,** there is a 30-meter (98 ft.) **deep well**. Legend says that it was dug by three Turkish prisoners, to whom liberty was promised if they reached water. But after 15 years, when they finished the well, their masters did not keep their promise. It's said that an inscription on the well wall reads "You have water, but not soul." The castle is now a museum, open to visitors Tuesday–Sunday.

The castle was restored in 1952 and today it houses a **feudal art museum**. To get to the castle from the train and bus stations, go south along Bd. Republicii and turn right at Bd. Libertatii.

Hunedoara's hotel is the **Rusca**, Bd. Dacia 10, Tel: (0254)71.75.75, fax: (0254)71.20.02, E-mail: hotel.rusca@comser.ro, www.hotelrusca.ro.

Strei

East of Hunedoara via a minor road is Călan, and just south of Călan is the tiny village of Strei and its small **13th-century Orthodox church** founded by the Romanian boyar Ambrozie. It is built of stone in Romanesque and a rustic Gothic style, with a tall front tower. Inside, on the wall, in the nave and on the altarpiece are magnificent **frescoes**, including a self-portrait, that bear the peasant artist's signature.

Densuş

The small village of Densuş, south of Deva and just southwest of the town of Haţeg on the Caransebeş Road 68, is home to a remarkable **13th-century Orthodox church**. It is built on the site of what archeologists believe to be a 4th-century Roman mausoleum. Of Romanesque and Gothic styles, what makes this church unique is that it was built with stones, tiles, columns, and statues taken from the ruins of the ancient Roman citadel of Ulpia Traian Sarmizegetusa, about 15 km (9 miles) away. Many Latin inscriptions are clearly visible on the church's stone walls. Inside the church there are remnants of **Byzantine murals** painted in 1443 that resemble those in St. Nicholas' church in Curtea de Argeş.

Ulpia Traian-Sarmizegetusa

Continuing southwest from Densuş on the Caransebeş road, you come to Ulpia Traian-Sarmizegetusa and the ruins of an ancient city that was designated the **Roman capital of Dacia** after Traian's soldiers defeated Dacian king Decebal's forces in 106 AD. Its ridiculously long name is the result of the recent combining of the city's original Dacian name with its Roman name, but it is still commonly referred to as Sarmizegetusa.

During the 13th century, many of the stones from the ruins were removed and used by local villagers to build new churches. It was not until the 1800s that the ruins came under the protection of the **Deva Archaeological Society** and the **National Museum of Transylvania**.

For six weeks every summer, from July 21st through August, archaeologists from Cluj-Napoca arrive in Sarmizegetusa to continue the task of unearthing and cataloging the ruins. They have uncovered parts of the **Roman Forum** and its 10 m (33 ft.) tall marble columns, an amphitheatre, the **palace of Augustales**, numerous **temples**, a **mausoleum** and two **villas.** But archaeologists believe they have so far uncovered only 5% of the ancient city that lies buried beneath the earth.

Many of the smaller treasures from Sarmizegetusa, including ceramics, tools, and ivory combs, are now exhibited in the **Deva History museum**.

There's one bus a day, at 11am, from Haţeg, returning at 12.30pm, which gives just an hour to see the ruins. Alternatively, you could choose to stay overnight: the town has a recently refurbished **motel** (Tel: 0254)77.7.60; $6-10), and there are three **cabins** (under $6) at the bar by the entrance to the ruins.

Făgăraş

The small city of **Făgăraş** lies north of the mountains on the Olt River, about 66 km (41 miles) west of Braşov. It has 35,400 inhabitants. Its name is derived from the Romanian "fag," meaning beech. Sitting in the midst of the town's modest houses is a massive **14th-century fortress and castle**. It was originally built as a wooden fortress by ruling prince Ladislau Kan, replacing a 9th-century clay stronghold. In the 17th century, Transylvania's ruling prince Gabriel Bethlen redesigned it as a four-sided castle with an inner courtyard and rounded towers with red pointed roofs at each corner. The fortress wall is made of brick, also quadrilateral, in Vauban style with four broad, jutting lookout points. In the 18th century, a moat was being dug around the fortress, but it was never completed. The fortress now serves as the **Făgăraş County Museum**.

The Făgăraş train and bus stations are side by side on Strada Negoiu. Trains run to Braşov and to Sibiu, with a stop at Ucea, 7 km north of Victoria. Daily buses run to Braşov, Târgu Mureş, Sibiu and Victoria. Victoria is the starting point for hikes into the Făgăraş mountains.

The Făgăraş mountain range separates Transylvania from the southern region of Wallachia. It is the highest section of the Transylvanian Alps, with some of its northern peaks reaching 2,500 meters (8,200 ft.). The Făgăraş are a favorite of summer hikers, for their wild ruggedness and their stunning views. The mountains are mostly exposed, and snow covers the highest slopes all year, with snowstorms often beginning in August. They have over 60 glacial lakes, and are also home to the big brown bear.

The **Transfăgărăşan highway** (route 7C) cuts through the mountains from route DN1 at Arpagu de Sus to Curtea de Argeş. The highway was built by Communist leader Nicolae Ceauşescu in the 1970's—one of his few successful projects. It is one of the highest mountain passes in Eastern Europe, crossing the Făgăraş mountains through 1.5 km (.9 miles) long, unlit **Bâlea tunnel** at 2,200 m (7,218 ft.) and providing exquisite panoramic views of Wallachia and Transylvania from the summit. The drive is long and tiring, but breathtaking, beautiful and scary. Take along some food and drink, as there is little to be found in the mountains. There are no gas/service stations along the route either, so be sure to start off with a full tank of petrol/gasoline.

If you choose to stay overnight, there are two fine hotels at the summit, or a few grittier but more reasonably priced communist-style hotels on the southern leg. The road on the Wallachian side is also full of pot-holes, so extra driving care is necessary.

The Făgăraş range is bordered on the west by the Făgăraş Depression, a valley through which the Olt River flows.

Sâmbăta de Sus

At the foot of the Făgăraş mountains, south of Sâmbăta de Jos, stands a **monastery** founded by Wallachian prince Constantin Brâncoveanu on the family estate. Preda Brâncoveanu built the first church in wood in the Sâmbăta valley. Around 1696, Constantin Brâncoveanu, the ruler of Wallachia, rebuilt the original church in stone, in order to strengthen it and protect it from the encroaching Catholicism that the Habsburg empire was forcing on the people of Transylvania. But in 1785, by order of general Bukow from Vienna, the monastery's monks were driven away and this last bastion of Orthodoxy in the region was partially destroyed. It remained in ruins for 140 years until Metropolitan Nicolae Bălan, Th. D., initiated its restoration in 1926. The work was completed in 1946, but then Nicolae Ceauşescu decided to build a private villa for himself and Elena on the monastery grounds. The restored monastery finally reopened in 1993.

Its architectural style is pure Brâncoveanian. Paintings on the small arcaded porch include scenes from the Old Testament. The entrance from the porch to the narthex is through a thick oak door, framed by sculptured stone. Stones also decorate the windows, the sculptured pillars and the panels of the church. The steeple is octagonal outside and cylindrical inside. On the West-side of the narthex, where the Holy Virgin is painted, there is also a painting of Brâncoveanu's founders. The monastery has five bells cast in Vienna, weighing more than 2,000 kg (4,400 lb).

The surrounding quadrangle is made up of white buildings with red roofs. Three stone-carved towers enhance the precincts both on the inside and on the outside. The northern, two-storey building contains the abbey and the monks cells. On the first floor there is a steeple and a new spacious church. The southern buildings house a large refectory and its kitchens, some cells and a large library. The monastery used to be a center of education and culture, with a grammar school, a painting school and a printing house. In 1954, monk Timotei

Traian Tohăneanu started a school for glass icon painting. The monastery's **museum**, exhibits a painted glass icon collection from the 18th-19th centuries and some very rare and valuable historical documents. They include ancient letters, the first edition of some newspapers, clothes worn by former monks, ecclesiastical objects, and a huge library.

In the monastery's courtyard is a 16th-century fountain known as the **Healing Spring** which, according to legend, has the power to work miracles. A huge **festival** is held each year on the Saturday after Orthodox Easter, when throngs of people come from all around the area to take a little of the water from the spring in hopes that their prayers will be answered.

To reach the monastery from Braşov, take route DN1 66 km (41 miles) west toward Făgăraş town, then another13 km (8 miles) to Sâmbăta de Jos village; from Sâmbăta de Jos village to Sâmbăta de Sus on DJ 105 B is 6 km (3½ miles). Coming from Sibiu, take route DN1 east to Sâmbăta de Jos village, 64 km (40 miles).

EASTERN & NORTHERN TRANSYLVANIA

Sfântu Gheorghe

Sfântu Gheorghe (Saint George) sits in an Olt River valley between the Baraolt and Bodoc mountains in eastern Transylvania, about 30 km (18 miles) northeast of Braşov. It is the capital of Covasna County, with 60,900 people, most of whom are Hungarian. (75% of Covasna County's population is Hungarian.) There are also approximately 5,000 Roma. The town's Hungarian name is: *Sepsiszentgyörgy*.

Sfântu Gheorghe was first documented as a settlement in 1332, and is one of the oldest cities in Transylvania. Back then, it was an economic and administrative center for the Hungarian county *Háromszék*, now Covasna and Braşov counties.

Székely Land

The Székely are a Hungarian ethnic group living in Transylvania. Unlike most other ethnic minorities of Romania, Szeklers are tightly concentrated in an area known as Székelyföld (Szekler land). Approximately 670,000 Szeklers live mostly in Harghita, Covasna and parts of Mureş counties, accounting for an important part of the Hungarian minority in Romania. There is a Székely initiative to attain autonomy for a Székelyföld region, on the model of the Spanish autonomous community of Catalonia.

This group has succeeded in preserving its traditions to an extent unusual even in Central and Eastern Europe. The best description of the Székely land and traditions was written between 1859 and 1868 by Balázs Orbán in his masterpiece, "Description of Székely land."

The Szeklers are of uncertain origins, subject to much debate among themselves and among scholars. A widespread theory asserts that they descend from the warrior tribes settled by the Hungarians in the border mountains to defend against invasions from Tatars and other menacing people from the east. Székely people adhere proudly to a Hungarian identity. They have a slightly distinct Hungarian dialect, but most of the differences from modern Hungarian consist of archaic words and phrase constructions, as well as a particular intonation.

In medieval times, the Szeklers were part of the *Unio Trium Nationum* ("Union of Three Nations") a coalition of the three Transylvanian estates, the other two nations being the (predominantly Hungarian) nobility and the Saxon (ethnic German) burghers. These three nations ruled Transylvania, usually in harmony, though sometimes in conflict with one another. Romanian inhabitants, who largely belonged to the class of serfs (including many Hungarians), were not allowed political representation because they were Orthodox. The Szeklers were considered the best warriors of medieval Transylvania.

Theories suggest a modern Hungarian, Gepid, Scythian, or Hunish ancestry, and some have dated their presence in the Eastern Carpathians as early as the fifth century. Others suggest that the Szeklers, like the Hungarians, are simply descended from the Magyars, and that cultural differences with other Hungarian groups stem from their relative isolation in the mountains.

Many scholars believe in a two-fold Hungarian migration of Transylvania, one prior to the main Magyar conquest of the Pannonian Plain in 896. According to this theory, the Székelys are a Hungarian group that settled in Transylvania during this first migration. Others believe that Szeklers had different origins, such as Turkic origins. A small number of scholars believe that the Székelys are related to the Scythians who may have joined the Magyars on their trek westward.

From Wikipedia

In the second half of the 19th century, the city developed both a textile and a cigarette factory.

Sfântu Gheorghe is a center for the Szeklers in the cultural region known as *Székelyföld*, and is home to the **Székely National Museum**. Its sights include a Gothic style **fortified church** (Hungarian: *Vártemplom*) built in the 14th; the **State Archive**, the former headquarters of the Hussar battalions; the **City Library** built in 1832 as the seat of the county council; the **Theatre**, the former town hall from 1854-1866. The **market bazaar** was built in 1868, and its **clock tower** in 1893. The city hosts two market fairs each year.

Accommodations: **Castel Hotel**, Strada Izvorului 2, Tel: (40-267)31.878.01, fax: (40-267)31.87.00, www.hotelcastel.ro. **Bodoc**, Strada 1 Decembrie 1918 no.1, Tel: (40-267)31.12.91, fax: (40-267)35.17.87, E-mail: bodochotel@planet.ro, www.bodochotel.proturism.ro. **Park** hotel, Strada Gabor Aron 14, Tel: (40-267)31.10.58, fax: (40-267)31.18.26, E-mail: park@planet.ro, www.hotelpark.planet.ro.

Covasna

Covasna (Hungarian: *Kovászna*) is a spa resort town in east central Romania, at the foot of the **Vrancea mountains**, 31 km (19 miles) east of Sfântu Gheorghe. It's a year-round resort at 550-600m (1,887 ft.) elevation. Covasna has about 1,000 springs with carbogaseous, bicarbonated, chlorosodic, ferruginous, iodinated, brominated, hypotonic and hypertonic mineral waters that are recommended in the treatment of cardiovascular diseases, hepatobiliary disorders, digestive disorders and their associated diseases.

Treatments available include warm carbogaseous water baths, mofettes (emanations of dry carbon dioxide), fountains for internal cure, electro-, kineto- and hydrotherapy installations, aerosols and inhalations, gyms. The resort has a **hospital** for cardiac diseases and two **children's sanatoriums** specialized in sequels after hepatitis. It is also a bottling station for mineral waters.

Accommodation: **Căpriora Hotel**, Strada 1 Decembrie 1918 1-2. This large hotel has single and double rooms with satellite TV, direct dial telephone, balcony, room service, newsstand, shops, refrigerator rental, laundry and dry-cleaning, safety deposit boxes, errand service, hair dressing and beauty services, a restaurant with music, a bar, and parking. Tel: (40-267)35.11.23, fax: (40-267)35.19.45, E-mail: tcovasna@rotravel.com., www.rotravel.com/hotels/tcovasna.

Covasna is also the name of the Transylvania *județ* (county). Its capital city is Sfântu Gheorghe (population: 67,108), known in Hungarian as *Sepsiszentgyörgy*. Hungarians comprise 74% of the county's 164,158 people. The Hungarians of Covasna (Hungarian: *Kovászna*) are primarily Székely.

Băile Tuşnad

This spa, also called the "Pearl of Ardeal", is one of the most beautiful spa resorts of the country. Located in the southern part of the Harghita Mountains, on the west side of the Olt River, the spa has been used medically since the second half of the 19th century. Surrounded by mountains and fir trees, the resort's environment offers fresh air, ozone, aerosols, and negative ions.

In 1968, Băile Tuşnad was declared a tourist town. Its many nearby attractions include the baroque **church of Şumuleu** (35 km), with one of the biggest organ installation in Ardeal. The surrounding area includes the ruins of **Balvanyos citadel**, and **Balvanyos's folk festival** in June; **Târgu Secuiesc's City Museum**, with exhibits from the 1848 Revolution and a collection of dolls in traditional costumes; **Santa Ana Lake** (20 km), the only lake in Central Europe on a volcanic crater; **Mohoş preserve** (1,056m), with rare plant species, near Santa Ana Lake; the **Birds Cemetery**; and rock carving at **Tuşnad Sat**. **Miercurea Ciuc** (30 km) with its **Miko Citadel**, the **Ethnographic Museum**, **Lacul Roşu** (115 km), with the largest natural dam in Romania; the **Folkloric Festival** at **Ica Citadel**

(Cernat commune) every December. You can find traditional arts and crafts at **Corund** (enameled ceramics, weavings with floral or geometric models), **Dăneşti** (black ceramics) and **Sâncrăieni** (traditional costumes).

Local gastronomic specialties to try include caraway soup, cabbage soup dressed with cream, filled mushrooms and traditional Hungarian food (paprika, goulash).

Băile Tuşnad can be reached by train via the Bucharest–Baia Mare line; or by car via the Bucharest–Braşov route E60, then toward Miercurea Ciuc on route DN12; it is 67 km (41 miles) north of Braşov, 37 km (23 miles) from Sf. Gheorghe, and 32 km (20 miles) south of Miercurea Ciuc.

Accommodations: SC Tuşnad SA/**Tuşnad Hotel**, Aleea Sfânta Ana 18; Tel: (40-266)33.55.58; fax: (40-266)13.51.08, E-mail: tusnad@topnet.ro, www.tusnad.ro; treatment base; the hotel has 108 rooms, restaurant, bar, phone, fridge, safe, TV, room service, elevator, luggage, gym room, sport field, sauna, parking, cinema, shop, hairdresser and barbershop, tourism agency. The **Ciucaş**, Strada Sfânta Ana 1, has a restaurant with terrace, bar, parking; rooms with fridge, phone, safe, cable TV; room service, laundry, luggage, shop, and a cinema, Tel: (40-266)33.50.04; fax: (40-266)33.52.52, E-mail: hbhotels@hotmail.com, www.spas.ro/tusnad. The **Fortuna Hotel**, Strada Kovacs Miklos 68, has a restaurant, sauna and massage, horse riding, skiing, fishing; in-rooms Internet access, Visa accepted, Tel: (40-266)33.52.16; fax: (40-266)33.52.75, E-mail: office@hotelfortuna.ro, www.hotelfortuna.ro. The **Olt**, Aleea Sf. Ana 2, restaurant, bar, conference room, wheelchair access, Visa accepted, no pets, Tel: (40-266)33.54.74; fax: (40-266)33.52.61. **Vila Astoria**, 74 places; phone, cable TV, sport field, sauna, parking. More info at: www.tusnad.ro.

Miercurea-Ciuc

Miercurea-Ciuc (Hungarian: *Csíkszereda*) is also in the eastern part of Transylvania, surrounded by the volcanic mountains of the

Harghita and Ciuc ranges. It sits at the crossroads of the Vlăhiţa and Ghimeş passes through the Carpathians. The town was founded in the 16th century near the existing villages of **Şumuleu** (1333), **Topliţa-Ciuc** and **Jigodin** (12th-13th century), with which it has since merged. It was the site of the local market (peasant fair), held on Wednesdays (Hungarian name: Szerda).

The first known authentic document certifying the town is a letter of Queen Izabella, mother of János Zsigmond, Prince of Transylvania, dated August 5, 1558, in which the townspeople were exempted from taxes, but not the ones due the Ottoman Empire.

Şumuleu is the oldest district of Miercurea-Ciuc, being mentioned in the papal cashier registers in 1333; its **Franciscan monastery** dates from 1630; it had a school *(gymnasium)* and in 1676 it had a printing shop run by Franciscan monk; the monastery's four chapels are the most well-known buildings of this Catholic pilgrim center. The **parish church** was built in 1758.

The **Miko fortress,** the city's oldest historical monument, has become the symbol of Miercurea-Ciuc. Built by Ferenc Miko of Hidveg (1585-1635), a relative Gabor Bethlen, its building was decisive in the development of the settlement. The fortress was rebuilt twice: in 1623 under Miko's guidance after the Szeklers' outburst in 1595, when it was called *Mikoujvar* ('the new fortress of Miko'); and after the 1661 Tatar's invasion and burning, when Austrian troops fortified it with an external defense ring and ramparts. A copy of the plan of the fortress from 1735 still exists. Today the fortress serves as the **Szekler Museum of Ciuc,** with temporary and permanent exhibitions presenting objects related to history, architecture, natural environment, popular occupations, scholarship and church art. It also holds the **County Library,** including the valuable historical library of the Franciscans with several very old books. Behind the fortress it is the **Ethnographical Museum** containing rural houses typical to the region and 15 Szekler gates. The annual **Old Music Festival** takes place on the fortress grounds.

Another important cultural establishment in Miercurea-Ciuc is the **Márton Áron Grammar School**, which celebrated its 300th anniversary in 1968.

The history of Miercurea-Ciuc has been plagued with devastating raids by the Tatars, Turks, and Habsburg troops. From 1717-1719, it suffered a black pox epidemic that killed two-thirds of the town's population. During the Hungarian Liberation Fight of 1848, patriotic newspapers, such as the *Hadi Lap* and the *Csíki Gyutacs* were printed there.

Today Miercurea-Ciuc, with a population of 50,000, is an important industrial town and continues to be the cultural and ethnic center of the Hungarian Székelys in the Székely-land. Its mountainous environs are an ideal location for several health spas, which take advantage of the area's mineral table waters, mofettes, mountain picturesque landscape.

Some accommodations in Miercurea-Ciuc: **Fenyo Hotel**, Strada Nicolae Bălcescu 11, Tel: (0266)31.14.93; fax: (0266)37.21.81, E-mail: reserve@hunguest-fenyo.ro, www.hunguest-fenyo.ro. The **Flamingo**, Strada Topliței 141 A, Tel/fax: (0266)31.36.00, E-mail: office@hotelflamingo.ro, www.hotelflamingo.ro. **Salvator**, Strada Szek 147, Tel: (0266)31.34.52; fax: (0266)37.21.45, E-mail: montanatours.topnet.ro, www.montanatours.ro.

Gheorgheni

Forty-five kilometers (30 miles) north of Miercurea-Ciuc, just beyond the Izvoru Mureşului pass, lies the town of Gheorgheni (Hungarian: *Gyergyószentmiklós*), jumping-off point for **Lacu Roşu**. **Piața Libertății**, the town's central square, is ringed with tatty buildings redolent of the era of Austro-Hungarian rule. At the north side of the square, the pedestrianized **Strada Miron Cristea** leads to Bulevardul Lacu Roşu and the splendid high school (*liceu*), completed in 1915; to the east, Strada Márton Arón leads past the Catholic church to **Piața Petofi** and the **Museum** (open Tuesday-Saturday, and Sunday mornings) at Strada Rácóczi 1, on the far side of the square.

Housed in a former Armenian merchants' inn, and run by a young couple, the museum contains artifacts of both the Székely and Magyar communities, including Székely fence posts, bark salt-baskets and weatherboards carved with shamanistic motifs brought by the Magyars from Asia. In the garden there's a derelict narrow-gauge steam locomotive that used to work the line towards Lacu Roşu. Just north of the museum is the **Armenian church**. Armenians fled here in the 17th century to escape Turkish persecution, and are now almost wholly assimilated into the Hungarian population. The church's interior is standard Baroque; it is locked, but if you want to see inside, the key can be gotten at Bd. Lacu Roşu 23.

Near Gheorgheni, in a meadow by a forest, is a castle **Lăzarea**, former residence of the Szeckler noble family of the Lazars. This castle precinct is surrounded by stone and brick walls flanked by defense towers at its corners. Its decoration is inspired by traditional Szeckler embroideries. Inside, the castle contains art exhibits.

Trains arriving at Gheorgheni are met by buses to spare passengers the twenty-minute hike east into the town center. Getting back to the station is not so easy and you'll probably end up having to walk. The **bus station** is immediately south of the train station, but you can also board eastbound buses on Bulevardul Lacu Roşu just north of the center; there are no buses on the DN13B west to Praid. Its **tourist office** is on its south side, with a *Bancomat* nearby.

Gheorgheni's hotels include: The lovely **Rubin**, Strada Gabor Aron 1, Tel:(0266)36.55.54, E-mail: rubinhotel@email.ro, www.rubinhotel.ro. The **Mureş,** at Bd. Frăţiei 5, opposite the **Trade Union House of Culture,** the road to the train and bus stations, Tel: (0266)16.19.04. The modest **Szilagyi hotel,** Piaţa Libertăţii 17, Tel: (0266)36.45.91. And the **Sport Hotel Avântul,** Str. Stadionului 11, off Strada Balcescu (the Topliţa road), Tel: (0266)16.12.70. There's also a **campsite** 4 km (2□ miles) east of town on the *Lacu Roşu* road, near the **Motel Patru,** Tel/fax: (0266)16.42.13.

Lacu Roşu

Lacu Roşu Resort, an all-season health and holiday resort, is connected to the town of **Gheorgheni,** in Harghita County. It sits in a valley surrounded by the Suhard, Tarcău, Hăşmaş and Giurgeu mountains, elevation 980 m (3,215 ft.), about 73 km (45 miles) north of Miercurea-Ciuc. The main draw of the resort is **Lacu Roşu**, the only natural reservoir in the country, which was formed in 1837 when the Ghilcos peak of the Suhard Mountains slid down and barred the Bicaz River upstream. The lake is 10.5 m (35 ft.) deep and 12.6 hectares (31 acres) in area. Its name, *Lacu Roşu* (Red Lake), comes from the reddish alluvia deposited in the lake by its main tributary, *Pârâul Roşu* (Red Creek).

In winter the resort draws skiers, having medium-difficult **ski runs**. **Suhardul Mare Massif** has one of the best ski runs at 2,400 m (8,600 ft.) with a 600 m (1,970 ft.) slope. Summer visitors use the sports sites and outdoor pool, or go boating and fishing in Lacu Roşu. There are several marked hiking routes around the lake and in the surrounding mountains, plus mountaineering in the **Bicaz Gorge**, 3 km from the resort.

By the lake, at the foot of **Suhardul Mare** peak, is the **Lacu Roşu Hotel**, Strada Principală 32, Tel: (40-266)38.00.08, fax: (40-266)38.00.20, E-mail: euroturism@nextra.ro. Next to the Hotel is **Lacu Roşu restaurant**, available for conferences, professional meetings and other group events. There are other villas, restaurants, bars and camping places around the lake. Some of them are: the **Raza Soarelui Vila**, with a beautiful view on the *Suhardul Mic*. **Hotel Turist/Vila Bradu**, Strada Lacu-Roşu 14, Tel: (40-745)60.11.133; Tel/fax: (40-266)36.40.49; hotel reception: (40-266)38.00.42. **Vila no. 46**, has 83 beds in 2-3 beds rooms and in 4-5 beds apartments, each with own bath. **Vila no. 30**, phone (40-266)16.44.44.

Bicaz Gorges & Lake

The **Bicaz Gorges** were carved by the waters of the Bicaz River into the Jurassic limestone of Hasmas massif over a length of 6 km (3.7 miles) and a depth of 300 m (984 ft.). It is a spectacular site and its massiveness is even more impressive if walking along the river; the gorges are also a favorite destination for mountain wall climbing.

Lake Bicaz, also known as lake ***Izvorul Muntelui*** is the largest artificial lake on the interior waters of Romania, created by a dam built on the Bistriţa River, a few kilometers north of the town of Bicaz. Built between 1950 and 1960, the dam generates hydroelectricity at the Bicaz-Stejaru hydro-plant. The lake is 40 km (25 miles) long, 119 meters (390 ft.) at its widest point, and has a maximum volume of 1,250 million m3.

The lake is also a popular tourist destination in the region, especially during summer, when visitors can take a ferryboat from Bicaz port for a short trip on the lake, enjoying a magnificent view of Mount Ceahlău.

At **Potoci**, a few kilometers north of Bicaz town there is a **biological research facility**, equipped with a small submersible craft used for underwater explorations. The facility was visited by the marine biologist Jacques-Yves Cousteau in 1984.

Accommodations: **Brad Arginţiu Hotel**, Strada Principală 50 B, Tel/fax: (40-266)37.26.59.

Durău

Durău is a year-round health and holiday resort nestled in a sunny glade surrounded by fir trees at the foot of the Ceahlău Mountains, just north of Bicaz in northeastern Romania. Its main natural cure factors are its elevation at 800 m (2,625 ft.), and its tonic, stimulant, sub-alpine climate, its clean air, free of allergens, and an ozoniferous atmosphere. The resort is recommended for rest and for the treatment of asthenic neurosis, weak conditions, physical and intellectual overexertion, and secondary anemia.

Outdoor activities in the area include skiing, fishing, treks in the mountains to **Ocolaşu Mare** and **Toaca** peaks, at 1,907 m (6,257 ft.) and 1,904 m (6,247 ft.) respectively, visits to the **Duruitoarea falls** or the **Ceahlău wildlife preserve**; for winter sports, there are **ski runs** of various degrees of difficulty, toboggan runs, and a **skating rink**. Durău is 60 km (37 miles) northwest of the Piatra Neamţ, 9 km (5.5 miles) west of the Izvorul Muntelui reservoir on the Bicaz River and 6 km (4 miles) southwest of the commune Ceahlău.

Durău's hotels are: the **Bradul**, with a conference center, sauna, restaurant, bar, accepts Visa, Tel: (40-233)25.66.34; fax: (40-233)25.65.01. The **Bistriţa**, sports facility, restaurant, bar; accepts Visa, Tel: (40-233)25.65.78; fax: (40-233)25.65.77l. The **Brânduşa**, restaurant, bar, ski lift, wheelchair access; accepts Visa, Tel: (40-233)25.65.73; fax: (40-233)25.65.50.

NORTHERN TRANSYLVANIA

Târgu Mureş

Târgu Mureş is capital of Mureş County and the heart of Hungarian culture in Transylvania. It is located in Mureş Valley and has 163,148 inhabitants, the largest Hungarian population in Romania. Most of the Magyar culture is kept alive by their many schools, festivals and local theatre, which are widely known and appreciated. The pride of the town is the 200-year-old **Teleki Library**, which holds 100 paintings of Imre Nagy, as well as many medical, philosophical and scientific texts dating from the 15th to 17th centuries. Today, Târgu Mureş continues its tradition as a learning center, through the modern Medicine and the Fine Arts Schools.

Târgu Mureş also has a medieval citadel, which shelters the **Evangelical Cathedral**. Its well-preserved old center has many Secession-style buildings gloriously rich with ornamentation. The **County History and Art Museum's** ethnographic section documents the traditional customs of the Transylvanian Magyars. There's also the baroque **Jesuits Monastery, Tholdalagi House**, the **Orthodox Church** from wood, and the **Palace of Culture**.

Accommodations: The **Concordia**, Piaţa Trandafirilor 45, conference rooms, business center, sauna and massage; indoor swim pool, restaurant, bar, in-room Internet access, Tel: (40-265)26.06.02, fax: (40-265)26.96.66, E-mail: reception@hotelconcordia.ro, www.hotelconcordia.ro. The **Continental**, Piaţa Teatrului 5-6, close to theatre square; rooms have cable-TV, hair dryer; hotel has a business center, beauty salon, outdoor pool, laundry service, room service, and a restaurant; wheelchair access. The **Helveţia**, Strada Borsos Tamas 13, small, charming hotel, cable-TV, room service, Tel: (40-265)21.69.54; fax: (40-265)21.50.99, www.villahelvetia.ro.

ANTREC guesthouses: **Tempo**, 4 daisies, Strada Morii 27, Tel: (0265)21.35.52; **Ana**, 3 daisies, Gh. Marinescu Street, Tel: (40-265)21.49.77, (0265)214.684; **Doina & Jeno**, 3 daisies, Strada Evreilor Martiri 25C, Tel: (0265)25.59.26; **Tip Top**, 3 daisies, Strada Plopilor 7, Tel: (0265)22.62.48, fax: (0265)313.015; **Cristina**, 3 daisies, Strada Piatra de Moară 1/A, Tel: (0265)26.64.90; **Villa Helvetia**, 3 daisies, Piaţa Boros Tamas 13, Tel: (0265)21.69.54, fax: (0265)21.50.99, www.antrec.ro.

The **Târgu Mureş Airport** is 13 km (8 miles) from downtown, Tel: (0265)328.259. TAROM Office, 6-8, Piaţa Trandafirilor, Tel/fax: 0265.250.170, Tel: 0265.236.200. Transport to the airport is provided by TAROM, free of charge. The bus stop is placed in front of the TAROM Office. Internal flights provide the connection for the external routes to Budapest, Paris, Istanbul, Athens, Milan, Rome, Vienna, Moscow, Dubai, Larnaca.

The **train station** is at Strada Griviţa Roşie 52, 1.5 km (1 mile) from downtown, Tel: 23.62.84. Public transport from downtown to the railway station is by bus and shuttle #5, 5B. *Agenţia CFR*, is at Piaţa Teatrului 1, Tel: 26.62.03. The bus terminal is at Strada Gh. Doja 143, 2 km (1¼ mile) from downtown,

Tel: 23.77.74. Public transport from downtown to the bus terminal is by bus and shuttle nos. 2, 4, 14, and 18. Taxi numbers are: Siltrans, 204.948; Cornisa, 204.943; Transaldea, 204.94; Royal, 204.942.

Emergency calls: Ambulance, Tel: 961, 215.11; County Hospital, Tel: 212.111; SMURD, Tel: 210.110; Police, Tel: 955 or 233.326, 260.221; Fire, Tel: 981 or 269.660.

Restaurants: **China Blue**, Bolyai Farkas10, Tel: 26.94.01; **Rex**, Strada Poştei 1, Tel: 25.06.15; **Triumf**, Bd. Decembrie 1989 22, Tel: 21.31.20; **Leo**, Piaţa Trandafirilor 43, Tel: 21.49.99; **Venezzia**, Piaţa Trandafirilor 2, Tel: 25.02.55. *Clubs and discos*: **Show Club Jo**, Strada Livezeni 4, Tel: 25.44.70; **Cuba Libre**, Strada Nicolae Grigorescu 17, Tel: 21.74.41; **Apollo**, Strada Nicolae Grigorescu 33, Tel: 21.33.26. *Theatres*: the **National Theatre**, Piaţa Teatrului 1, Tel: 26.48.48; **Ariel Theatre for Children and Young People**, Strada Postei 2, Tel: (0265)22.04.28. *Exhibition Halls*: the **Culture Palace**, Tel: 269.946; **Zoo**, Corneşti Plateau, Tel: 22.14.08.

Bistriţa—*Dracula Country*

Bistriţa is at the foot of the Bârgău Mountains, near the **Bârgău Pass** (Borgo Pass), which connects Transylvania to Bucovina. German colonists were the first to settle in the Bistriţa Valley in the 12th century. They were skilled tradesmen and built fine houses and churches in the surrounding area, which was known as the *Nösnerland*. But in 1241, the Tatars came through on their way east, and destroyed much of the area. The townsfolk rebuilt and organized trade guilds; they erected fortress walls around the city with 18 bastions and towers to protect it from future invaders.

By the 14th century their economy was flourishing and Bistriţa became one of the main cities in Transylvania, along with Sibiu and Sighişoara. In 1353, Bistriţa began holding an annual fair that lasted 15 days. The town of 90,000 people is trying to resume the century-old tradition of the annual Fair, and they have hosted the European Festival of Humor for the past five years.

Bistriţa and the forested **Bârgău valley** around it were the setting for Bram Stoker's book *Dracula*. In the novel, Jonathan Harker travels to Transylvania to finalize a property deal with Count Dracula at his castle in the "Borgo Pass." His journey takes him by train to Bistritz (*Bistriţa*) where he dines on 'robber steak' and drinks 'Golden Mediasch' wine at the Golden Krone Inn. It was here that Jonathan Harker received the first hints that something was amiss. Although Stoker had never visited Romania, he accurately described the surrounding hills covered with fruit orchards and the dark forests of the mountainsides. The landscape includes some of the most beautiful and unspoiled scenery in the Carpathians with its picturesque villages in the valleys. It is also an ideal base for hiking treks, horseback riding or discovering the custom handicrafts and folklore of the area.

Bistriţa is one of the original *Siebenburgen*. Its main square, **Piaţa Centrală**, is dominated by a Gothic style **Saxon church** built in the 14th century; it has a 76 m (246 ft.) tall steeple—the tallest in Romania. On the piaţa's northwest side are the arcaded **Sugalete buildings** (15th-century merchants' quarters). You'll find the **Casa Argintarului**, a stone-framed Renaissance silversmith's house, now housing an **art college**, at Strada Dornei 5. To the northeast, on Piaţa Unirii there is an **Orthodox church**, dating from 1280. Beyond it, at Strada General Bălan 81, is a former barracks turned **County Museum** (open Tues-Sun) which has a collection of Thracian bronzeware, Celtic artifacts, and products of the Saxon guilds, mills and presses.

Bistriţa's surrounding fortifications were destroyed by fires in the 19th century and only vestiges of its **14th-century citadel** remain along Strada Kogălniceanu and Strada Teodoroiu, including the **Coopers' Tower** (*Turnul Dogarilor*), now a museum of **medieval weapons** and fortifications in the Municipal Park.

Bistriţa is the capital city of Bistriţa-Nasaud County. The remains of Neolithic settlements have been found nearby, but the earliest record of the town coincides with the arrival of its Saxon settlers. Its population today is 90,000. The area around the town is noted for its wine and timber. **Năsăud**, a few kilometers northwest of Bistriţa, is also famous for the fine **embroidery** on the traditional peasant clothes. Nearby **Lechinţa** is a well-known **wine region**, and **wine-tasting** can be organized in the town's cellars.

Bistriţa has frequent buses to Nasaud and the Someş Valley, trains to Cluj and an overnight sleeper train to Bucharest. The train and bus stations are about ten minutes' walk to the center, southeast along Strada Garii.

Hotels: **Coroana De Aur**, Piaţa Petru Rareş 4, Tel: (40-263)23.24.70, Tel/fax: (40-263)23.26.67; **Castel Dracula**, Piatra Fântânele, Tel: (40-263)26.68.41, fax: (40-263)26.61.19, E-mail: hotelcasteldracula@bn.ro, www.hotelcasteldracula.bn.ro; the **Diana**, Calea Moldovei 80, Tel: (40-263)23.19.60, fax: (40-263)23.19.61, E-mail: receptie-diana@bistita.astral.ro; the **Bistriţa**, Piaţa Petru Rares 2, Tel: (40-263)23.11.54, fax: 23.10.66, E-mail: hotelbistrita@mymail.ro, www.hotel-bistrita.ro; the **Decebal**, Strada Cuza Vodă 9, Tel: (40-263)21.25.68, fax: (40-263)23.35.41.

Cluj-Napoca

The Roman city of Napoca was built over an old Dacian settlement and recognized as a municipality by Emperor Hadrian in A.D.124, and a Roman colony by Marcus Aurelius (A.D.161-180). In A.D.173 it became known as "*Castrum Clus.*" The region was under Hungarian rule from the 11th century until 1918. When the Germans were invited to settle the lands of Transylvania during the 12th and 13th centuries, they named this site *Klausenburg*. In the 1400's Klausenburg was jointly governed by Saxons and Magyars (Hungarians). A century later, the Magyars took control and changed its name to *Kolozsvar*. After World War I, when borders were redrawn and all of Transylvania became part of Romania, it was renamed Cluj. In 1974 Ceauşescu added Napoca to the name in recognition of the city's Dacian forbears.

Today the city is an important industrial center with over 325,000 people. It is also a scientific, cultural, university and tourist center and the capital of the county. Cluj retains the architectural charm of its historical Hungarian buildings. In the center of town is **Piaţa Unirii**, dominated by **St. Michael's Catholic Church**. This gothic edifice was built from 1321-1444. Its 19th century tower stands 79 meters (260 feet) high. A statue of **Matthias Corvinus** on horseback overlooks the piaţa. A controversial archaeological dig searching for Roman ruins mars the south end of the piaţa.

Across the street, in the former Banffy Palace, is the **National Art Museum**. **Banffy Palace** is an 18th-century baroque mansion that was built for Gyorgy Banffy, who was the Habsburg Governor of Transylvania. The museum's collection ranges from the 16th century to modernity and includes paintings and sculptures by Romania's main artists, Grigorescu and Andreescu among others, as well as Dutch and Flemish masters. It also contains furniture, silverware, carpets and weaponry exhibits.

Stroll east along Strada Iulia Maniu to get to the **Orthodox Cathedral**, and a block south of that is Piaţa Ştefan cel Mare and the **Romanian National Theatre and Opera.** Str. Iuliu Maniu is sometimes called the "mirror street" because the buildings on both sides of the street are symmetrical.

Just west of Piaţa Unirii, at Strada Memorandumului 21, is the **Ethnographic Museum of Transylvania** in an 18th-century palace where Hungarian Franz Liszt performed. A museum since the 1920s, it holds a fine collection of Romanian traditional costumes, textiles, pottery, tools, photographs and documents (open Tues-Sun, 9pm-5pm). The museum has an **open-air branch** northwest of the center on **Hoia Hill** consisting of peasant houses and wooden churches from the region (open Tues-Sun, 9am-4pm).

A couple of blocks north of the church, on Strada Matei Corvin, stands the house where Corvinus, the future king of Hungary, was born in 1440. He was the son of Iancu de Hunedoara, a Romanian.

The **Babes-Bolyai University** is south of Piaţa Unirii on Strada Kogalniceanu. The students' club and medical faculty are farther west at Piaţa Păcii and beyond. South of the University are the **Botanical Gardens** on Strada Republicii (open 9am-7pm in summer, closing at 5pm in winter). The gardens cover 35 acres over three hills and contain plants from all over the world, including desert flora from Africa and Mexico. There are greenhouses with subtropical plants and succulent flowers, an aquarium that houses the Amazon lily, and a Japanese garden.

There are several nice restaurants and pizza places in the center of town. Some suggestions: *Escorial* at Piaţa Unirii 23, Tel: 59.14.41; *Matei Corvin*, Str. Matei Corvin 3, Transylvanian cuisine, Tel: 59.74.96; *Continental*, Str. Napoca 1, in the Continental hotel, Tel: 59.41.41; *Napoca 15*, on Strada Napoca, southwest of the piaţa, has a small terrace; *Paradis*, Str. Ciocârliei 47, within Paradis hotel, Transylvanian and Hungarian cuisine, Tel: 41.39.40; *Victoria*, Bd. 21 Decembrie 1989 56, within the Victoria hotel, vegetarian and Romanian cuisine; *Ciuleandra*, St. Septimiu Albinii 10, rustic atmosphere, Transylvanian cuisine, live music, in the Topaz hotel, Tel: 41.40.21; *P&P Ristorante* on Bd. Eroilor. *Diesel Club,* at Piaţa Unirii 17, is a good place for a drink, with live jazz and blues in the cellar at night; *Café Mozart*, Strada Pavloc7, top class non-smoking café.

Cluj can be reached by train or air. Taxis are the easiest way to get to the city center, although buses travel from both train station and airport. The tourist office is on Strada Memorandumului, west of St. Michael's church. The TAROM office and CFR ticket agency are just north of the center at Piaţa Mihai Viteazul. Walk up Strada Gheorghe Doja from Piaţa Unirii, passing Banc Post, until you reach the piaţa on your right. On its far side is the TAROM office and around the corner is the Agenţia CFR. Across the street from CFR there's a McDonald's and the bustling farmers' market. There's a Banca Romana Comercială on Piaţa Unirii.

Some hotels in Cluj are: **Best Western Topaz**, Septimiu Albini 10, Tel: (40-264)41.40.21, fax: (40-264)41.40.66, E-mail:

receptie@bestwesterntopaz.ro, www.bestwesterntopaz.ro; **Transylvania**, Strada Călăraşi 1, a modern luxury hotel, north of city center, atop Cetăţuia hill, Tel: (40-264)43.20.71, fax: (40-264)43.20.76, E-mail: office-cluj@unita-turism.ro, www.turismtransilvania.ro; **Continental Cluj**, Strada Napoca 1, an elegant old building at the southwest corner of Piaţa Unirii, Tel: (40-264)59.14.41, fax: (40-264)59.39.77, E-mail: cluj@continentalhotels.ro, www.continentalhotels.ro; **Confort Hotel**, Calea Turzii 48, a new hotel, wheelchair access, no pets, Tel: (40-264)59.84.10, fax: (40-264)59.20.20, E-mail: hotelconfort@yahoo.com, www.hotelconfort.ro; the renovated **Melody Central**, at Piaţa Unirii 29, has restaurant, Tel: (40-264)59.74.65, fax: (40-264)59.74.68, E-mail: melodyhotel@yahoo.com, www.cm.ro; **Fulton**, Strada Sextil Puşcariu 10, Tel/fax: (40-264)59.78.98, Tel: (40-264) 59.77.66, E-mail: hotelfulton@pcnet.ro; **Meteor**, Bd. Eroilor 29, Tel: (40-264)59.10.60, fax: (40-264)59.10.61, E-mail: receptiehotelmeteor@ro, www.hotel-meteor.ro; **Sport**, Strada G. Cosbuc 15, a modern hotel west of city center, by the sports stadium and swimming pool in Parc Tel: (40-264)19.39.21, fax: (40-264)19.58.59, Tel: (40-264)59.74.65; **Déjà vu**, Strada Ion Ghica 2, near stadium and parc, a 5-star pensiune-hotel with restaurant, café, conference room, terrace, Tel/fax: (40-264)35.49.41, E-mail: office@deja-vu.ro, www.deja-vu.ro; **Paradis hotel**, Str. Ciocârliei 47, is just outside the city center.

CHAPTER 7

MOLDAVIA

Moldavia is in northern Romania, bordering Ukraine and Moldova. It is an historical province of Romania, founded by Prince Bogdan I in 1356, but its history can be traced back to 6,000 BC and its Thracian-Dacian-Roman settlements. Moldavia's hero is Stephen the Great (*Stefan cel Mare*), who fought back the Turks in the 15th century and built churches and monasteries throughout the region. Unfortunately, there was no hero to fight off the Soviets when they annexed its most northern and eastern sections. Today the northern half of Bucovina remains part of Ukraine; Bessarabia, the easternmost section is now the Republic of Moldova. Luckily, the churches built centuries ago still stand, and they are some of the most fascinating sights in all Romania.

Bucovina

Dotting the green hills of northern Moldavia are the **Painted Monasteries** of Bucovina. Built in the 15th and 16th centuries, some served as fortresses against invaders. The exteriors of these small Byzantine churches are decorated with colorful frescoes depicting dramatic religious scenes. The intent was to teach Christianity to the illiterate peasantry by way of pictures. Their artwork has stood the test of time, still remarkably vivid despite 500 years of exposure to the elements. The artists worked in isolation, guarding their trade secrets, and the composition of the paint is still a mystery.

The five main painted monasteries dotting the hills west of Suceava are **Voroneţ**, **Humor**, **Suceviţa**, **Moldoviţa** and

Arbore. Also nearby are **Dragomirna** and **Putna** monasteries, Putna housing the tomb of Stephen the Great. If you haven't the time or the means to travel to all of them, Voroneţ and Humor are good ones to see. In 1993 the painted churches were designated a World Heritage Site by UNESCO, and in 1995, Bucovina was awarded the "Pomme d'Or" (Golden Apple) by the International Federation of Tourist Journalists and Writers for its beautifully preserved monuments, folklore and landscape.

Voroneţ was founded by Stephen the Great in 1488 to celebrate a victory over the Turks. Its exterior frescoes were added between 1547 and 1550. The predominant color of Voroneţ's artwork is a vivid blue which serves as background to all other designs. A depiction of the Last Judgment covers the entire west wall of the church showing devils and angels casting sinners into the fire beneath Jesus' feet. The southern wall displays the Tree of Jesse, the genealogy of Jesus, with nearly 100 personages. The church is maintained by a group of nuns who periodically perform a traditional religious board-tapping ritual dating from the days when the ringing of church bells was banned. (Voroneţ is 38 km [23 miles] from Suceava.)

Humor, founded in 1530, is distinguished by its wide open porch, spireless roof and dark reddish hues. Its southern wall is painted with 24 scenes from the poem *Hymn to the Virgin*, written by Patriarch Sergius of Constantinople in honor of the defeat of the Persians. The Return of the Prodigal Son is also depicted. The porch is painted with another Last Judgment scene where the devil is represented as an evil woman.

Suceviţa Monastery is a fortified compound with guard towers at the corners of its surrounding wall. Built in 1582, the church is covered with thousands of pictures, more than any of the others, but the west wall is blank. Legend has it that the painter fell off his scaffolding and was killed, thus this wall was left unfinished. The brilliant frescoes of this church are painted on a background of emerald green.

Moldoviţa was founded in 1532 by Petru Rareş, Ştefan the Great's illegitimate son. Set against a deep blue background, the red, yellow, blue and brown frescoes present a panoramic view of the siege of Constantinople; it also has the Tree of Jesse and the Hymn to the Virgin. The complex is surrounded by ivy-covered walls which enclose several white stone buildings where the nuns reside. Inside, some of the 16th-century furniture survives, including Prince Petru Rares' princely chair with a seatback 2 meters (6 ft.) high.

Arbore is the smallest of the churches, built in 1503. Its predominant color is green in five shades, combined with red, blue and yellow in its frescoes. Arbore's most interesting painting is the story of Genesis on its western wall. There are also scenes from the lives of the saints, depicting them in motion, lively and graceful.

Two other famous monasteries—though without exterior paintings—are **Dragomirna** and **Putna**. Dragomirna is just 12 km (7 miles) north of Suceava. Reaching 138 ft. (42m) high, the church towers above its surrounding fortress wall, yet it measures only 9.6 m (30 ft.) wide. Its unusual proportions are assuaged by a decorative motif of twisted rope made of carved stone that circles the outer walls halfway up. The church was built by Metropolitan Anastasie Crimca and the boyar Luca Stroici between 1602 and 1609. Crimca was also an artist and teacher of miniatures and icons. Some of his work is displayed in the monastery's museum. In 1627, the surrounding fortress was added by Voivode Miron Barnovski Movila to protect it against attack.

Putna monastery is the farthest west from Suceava, near the Ukrainian border. The idyllic landscape of village houses and orchards, with the Carpathian mountains rising in the background, makes for a pleasant drive. This monastery was erected in 1468 by Stephen the Great and designated as his burial place. Its museum contains many religious artifacts, including painted manuscripts, Byzantine embroideries and shrouds.

On the road, about 32 km (20 miles) before Putna, you will pass through the town of **Rădăuţi**, a market town and former home of one of the region's largest Jewish communities. Its **Bogdana Church** is the oldest stone church in Moldavia, built according to a Romanesque basilica plan. Rădăuţi's ethnographic museum, the **Muzeul Tehnicii Populare din Bucovina** is on Strada Piaţa Unirii 63; it holds collections of Kuty ceramics, household objects, furniture and local costumes. The town's market place is filled with fruits and vegetables and various miscellaneous items. As in any crowded public marketplace, beware of local pickpockets.

Suceava

Suceava is the largest city in Bucovina province and the main transportation connection to the Painted Monasteries with direct air and train links from Bucharest. It was once the capital of Moldavia and is mentioned in documents from the 14th century. Inhabited by the Dacians since the 2nd century AD, today's city has 116,000 residents. The center of town is Piaţa 22 Decembrie, reached by taxi or by trams #2 and 3 from the train station.

The ***Cetatea de Scaun*** (Scaun Citadel), on **Cetatea Hill**, east of the city center, is Suceava's main tourist site. It was first built by Prince Petru Muşat I in 1388, and fortified by Stephen the Great to defend against Mehmed II in 1476 (open Tues-Sun, 10am-6pm). The ruins of Stephen's **Princely Court** are on Bd. Ana Ipătescu, next to Petru Rareş' 16th-century **St. Dumitru's Church**. The **Zamca Medieval Complex**, on a plateau in the northwest part of the city, was a monastery fortress for the invading King Jan Sobieski of Poland in 1691, though little remains of it today.

Also of interest in Suceava is the **Bucovina History Museum** at Strada Stefan cel Mare 33, which displays medieval armor, coins, tools, and ancient documents. Its **Hall of Throne** is a re-creation of Stephen's court with furniture, weapons and costumes (open Tues-Sun, 10am-6pm). The **Folk Art Museum** (Princely Inn) at Strada Ciprian Porumbescu 5 is in a 16th-century building; its displays include pottery, folk dresses, handmade rugs and wooden objects. There's also the **Village Museum of Bucovina**, on Strada Cetatii. The most notable churches are the 14th-century **Mirăuţi** in Strada Mirăuţilor and the 16th-century ***Sfîntu Gheorghe Nou*** (New Saint George), in Aleea Ion Voda. Suceava's post office and telephone center are at the corner of Strada Balcescu. Banca Comercială Romana and its ATM (*Bancomat*) are at Strada Stefan cel Mare.

To reach the Painted Monasteries, you can either fly to Suceava's Salcea Airport, 17 kilometers from the town center, via TAROM Air Transport from Bucharest's Băneasa Airport or take a train, a 6-7 hour trip from Bucharest's Gara de Nord; half that time from Cluj. In Suceava, you can hire a car and driver with a guide from the local tourist agency, Bucovina Estur on Strada Ştefan cel Mare 24, to show you the monasteries: Tel: (0230)22.32.59 or Tel/fax: (0230)52.26.94, E-mail: bestur@assist.cccis.ro or bestur91@warpnet.ro. Rates are per kilometer, plus a charge for the guide. They organize excursions to the monasteries and arrange comfortable overnight accommodations in private homes. You might also check with the APT Bucovina Information Center, Strada Universităţii 15-17, Tel: (0230)53.19.77, E-mail: contact@bucovinaturism.ro, www.bucovinaturism.ro. To telephone for a taxi in Suceava call: Canon Taxi: 52.55.22; Cristaxi: 53.00.13; or Eurotaxi: 51.11.11.

More adventurous travelers can get a sleeper car (*vagon de dormit*) on the overnight train from Bucharest direct to **Gura Humorului**, arriving at about 4:30am. Hang out in the tiny train station until daylight and then walk into town. From the town's bus station, coaches transport tourists to **Voroneţ** and **Humor** monasteries. You can also walk to Voroneţ, about 3.2 km (2 miles) south of town. It's an easy walk and the scenery through the village and pastoral countryside is idyllic. From the bus station, follow Strada Stefan cel Mare away from town for about 750 m (½ mile) until you see the road sign to Voroneţ (you'll turn left). If you beat the bus groups to the church, it's a much more pleasant experience. Humor is slightly farther, at 5.6 km (3.5 miles) north of Gura Humorului.

You might also visit Gura Humorului's **Museum of the Traditions of Bucovina**, at Piaţa Republicii 12. Afterward, you can catch the 1:30pm train to Suceava, or choose to stay overnight in Gura Humorului at the new **Best Western Bukovina Club de Munte** at Bd. Bucovina 4, Tel: (40-230) 20.70.00; business center, gym, conference facilities, Internet access, disabled access, non-smoking areas, pets allowed. There is also a 4:00pm train that will take you back to Bucharest, if your time is limited.

Suceava's Agenţia CFR is at Strada N. Balcescu 8, open weekdays. TAROM's office is at Strada Balcescu 2. By car, Suceava is 447 km (280 miles) from Bucureşti and 325 km (200 miles) from Cluj Napoca. Driving national road DN2 - E 85, Bucureşti – Buzău – Bacău – Suceava from Bucureşti to Suceava, the trip will take about six hours. Driving from Cluj, take route E576 through Bistriţa to Suceava.

Hotels in Suceava: the **Classic**, Strada Universităţii 32, Tel/fax: (40-230)51.00.00, E-mail: classic@assist.ro; **Balada**, Strada Mitropoliei 3, a small private hotel near the **Monastery of St. John the New**, breakfast included, Tel: (40-230)52.21.46, fax: (40-230)52.00.87, E-mail: balada@balada.ro, www.balada.ro; **Hotel Continental – Suceava**, Strada Mihai Viteazul 4-6, near the center, Tel: (40-230)21.09.44, fax: (40-230)22.62.66, E-mail: suceava@continentalhotels.ro, www.continentalhotels.ro; the renovated **Gloria**, Strada Mihai Vasile Bumbac 4-8, breakfast is included, Tel: (40-230)52.12.09, fax: (40-230)52.11.63, E-mail: srp@suceava.ro; the **Bucovina**, Strada Ana Ipătescu 5, a high-rise on the edge of the center, breakfast included, Tel: (40-230)21.70.48, fax: (40-230)52.02.50; the **Albert**, Bd. 1 Decembrie 1918 58, Tel: (40-230)51.17.82, fax: (40-230)55.01.49, E-mail: classic@assist.ro, www.classic.ro; the **Suceava**, Strada Nicolae Balcescu 4, in the center, Tel: (40-230)52.10.79, fax: (40-230)52.10.80, E-mail: office.suceava@unita-turism.ro.

To telephone for a **taxi** in Suceava call: Canon Taxi: 52.22.22; Cristaxi: 53.00.13; or Eurotaxi: 51.11.11.

Câmpulung Moldovenesc is in Suceava County. The town of 21,862 people is located on the banks of the Moldova River.

Câmpulung Moldovenesc is the largest town in the county, after Suceava. Its main industries are dairy products, lumber, and ecotourism. Câmpulung Moldovenesc is accessible by both car and train. There are many places of interest located in and around Câmpulung, such as **Rarău** and **Giumalău**, which at 1,650m and 1,586m are the highest peaks in the region. One can also enjoy the forests which surround Câmpulung or visit a monastery in one of the nearby towns.

Hotel Eden, Strada Bucovinei 148, Tel/fax: (40-230) 31.47.33 or (0722)27.17.47, E-mail: office@hotel-eden.ro, www.hotel-eden.ro.

Vatra Dornei

Vatra Dornei is a year-round health resort situated at the confluence of the Dorna and Bistriţa rivers. This is one of the most beautiful depressions of the eastern Carpathians, the *Ţara Dornelor*, surrounded by forest-covered mountains. The town of 19,000 residents sits at an elevation of 805 meters (2,641 ft.), just about 110 km (68 miles) southwest of Suceava.

The resort is favored primarily for the treatment of cardiovascular diseases; but visitors can also take cures for treatment of degenerative and abarticular rheumatic diseases, post-traumatic physical conditions, peripheral and central neurological diseases, endocrine disorders, gynecological, respiratory, neurotic, metabolic and nutrition, digestive and other disorders.

Its natural cure factors are the tonic-stimulative climate, the clean air, free of dust and allergens and rich in resinous aerosols; natural springs of carbonated, ferruginous, slightly bicarbonated, sodic, calcic, magnesian, hypotonic mineral waters; and the peat mud (from *Poiana Stampei*).

The two treatment compounds—**Hotel Călimani** and the **Dorna Balneal Complex**—offer a variety of therapeutic procedures: warm mineral-water baths in tubs, application of warm mud and paraffin, electrotherapy, hydrotherapy, massage, medical gymnastics, sauna, artificial mofette, and kynetotherapy. There are special fountains for internal cures of mineral water.

Vatra Dornei is also an ideal place for leisure activities during the winter holidays, like mountaineering and skiing. A chair lift extending 3,200 meters (10,000 ft.) connects the town to ***Dealul Negru*** (Black Hill, elevation 1,300 m). Some other tourist draws are the natural park in the resort, famed for its many squirrels and for the brass band concerts given here in summer; the chalet on Runc Hill; the **Hunting and Natural Science museum**; the **Bucovina Ethnographic Museum**.

The travel agency in the resort organizes trips by coach on several routes, including visits to the painted monasteries in Bucovina, as well as other nearby places of ethnographic and folkloric importance.

Accommodations are available in hotels, villas, private homes. Some *hotels* are: **Călimani-Bradul**, Strada Republic ii 5 A, Tel: (40-230) 37.53.14, fax: (40-230) 371778, E-mail: dornaturismrezervari@yahoo.com, www.dornaturism.ro; **Bucovina**, Tel: (40-230)37.30.22; **Lucex**, Strada Republicii 35, Tel: (40-230)37.42.06, fax: (40-230)375005, E-mail: depa@k.ro, www.turismcfr.go.ro; **Intus**, Strada Republicii 5B, Tel: (40-230)37.50.21, fax: (40-230)37.50.20, E-mail: intus12@hotmail.com; **Silva**, Strada Dornelor 12, Tel: (40-230)37.10.33, fax: (40-230)37.55.11, E-mail: pinarcris@assist.ro.

Botoşani

Botoşani is both a *judet* (county) in northeastern Moldavia, as well as a city. Botoşani County occupies 4,965 sq. km (1,946 sq. miles) of green rolling hills. It is a rich farming area bounded on the north by Ukraine and on the east by the Republic of Moldova. The Prut and Siret rivers are, respectively, the county's eastern and western borders. It is a rural area of small towns and villages, but its total population is almost 462,000. Cereal growing and livestock raising are the primary agricultural activities, but Bucecea town also has a sugar refinery.

Botoşani city is the county's capital and its largest town, with 129,000 people. It was first documented as a settlement in 1439. Its **St. Nicholas Church** (*Popăuţi*) was built by Stefan the Great in 1497. It is a handsome example of the Moldavian style, combining Gothic, Byzantine and local elements. Most of its interior painting dates from the 16th century. **St. George's church**, built in 1551 by Lady Elena, the wife of Petru Rares (son of Stefan), is a more typical Moldavian building.

On the central piaţa in the heart of old Botoşani, there is also a **memorial** to the Romanian soldiers who lost their lives in World War I. The city's **museum** tells the history of the city and its region from prehistoric times until the recent history.

In the beginning of the 20th century, more then 15,000 Jews lived in Botoşani. Most of them were professionals or shop owners. At that time, the city had about 70 synagogues. Today there are only a few of them left, and only one still functions as a **synagogue**. Located south of Strada Marchian, it was built in 1834, but today it is surrounded by dull apartment blocks. Nevertheless, its interior is well worth seeing, as it is one of the few frescoed synagogues in Romania. Its ceiling paintings depict the tribes of Israel.

Long known as a market center for agricultural produce and wines, Botoşani has also become an industrial center, particularly in textiles. The city is also an important **market town** for the surrounding agricultural region. On Fridays, its markets are bustling with the buying and selling of flowers, vegetables and clothes.

Botoşani city's luxury hotel, the **Maria**, is at Strada Unirii 16, Tel: (40-231)53.77.78, fax: (40-231)51.43.34, E-mail: mariahotel@petar.ro, www.mariahotel.ro. The **Rapsodia**, Strada Cuza Voda 4, at Piaţa Revoluţiei, is comfortable, with a friendly and helpful staff, Tel/fax: (40-231)51.49.20, E-mail: hotelrapsodia@botosani.rdsnet.ro, www.hotelrapsodia.botosani.ro. Another budget option is the **Rares** hotel, Piaţa 1 Decembrie 1918 65, Tel: (40-231)53.64.53, fax: (40-231)52.97.12.

Verona lies 4 km (2½ miles) from Botoşani city on the way to Fălticeni. It was initially a complex of four churches;

the oldest was built in 1600, but has been destroyed. Of the remaining three, the most interesting dates from 1835. Vorona and the village of **Tudora**, 7 km (4.3 miles) away, belong to an area that has its own specific traditions, and near Tudora, there is a **nature reserve** that contains yew forests.

The **Dragomirna Monastery**, located near **Iţcani** village on road 29 toward Suceava, was built in 1609 by Anastase Crimca, metropolitan of Moldavia and a painter of miniatures. The monastery, fortified in 1627 by Prince Miron Barnevschi, contains a collection of manuscripts decorated by illuminators who were trained in the school that Crimca founded.

Several of Romania's great artists were born in Botoşani County. In **Dorohoi**, northwest of Botoşani city, a museum is dedicated to the composer **Georges Enesco** (1881-1955), who was born in the commune of Liveni (now Georges Enesco town). A 15th-century church and the **Adâncata Forest** are other features of Dorohoi. **Ştefăneşti** village, east of Botoşani, is the birthplace of **Stefan Luchian** (1868-1916), the painter.

Romania's revered poet **Mihail Eminescu** (1850-1889) was born in **Ipoteşti** village, a suburb of Botoşani, and the house where he was born was made a museum commemorating his life. The **Mihai Eminescu Memorial House** is at Strada 1 Decembrie in Ipoteşti, and it will soon have a complete collection of the poet's manuscripts and a large documentary library. In its courtyard, there is a small church that contains the tombs of Eminescu's family. (Mihai Eminescu's grave is in Bellu Cemetery in Bucuresti.)

There are highways and railway connections to Botoşani city and to Dorohoi. Botoşani has a tram line that connects the city center and the railway station, or there are plenty of taxis. There is a daily direct train from Bucharest's Gara de Nord to Botoşani, it departs mid-morning. The trip takes seven hours on *Rapid* train, stopping only at the larger stations along the way. There is also an overnight train. There are also seven daily buses from Botoşani city to Suceava, plus buses to many other Romanian towns and cities, including Iaşi, Bucharest and Târgu Mureş.

Târgu Neamţ

The 14th-century **Neamţ Fortress (*Cetatea Neamţului*)** was built by Petru 1st Muşatinul on a hill overlooking the town. It originally had a square plan and its first walls were 12 m (40 ft.) high. But in the 15th century, Stephen the Great enlarged the fortress, adding another precinct with four circular towers for artillery, and raised the sheer walls to 20 m (65 ft.). He also had a defensive moat dug that was 10 m (33 ft.) deep and 25 m (82 ft.) wide. After this the fortress became virtually invincible. In 1476 it held against a Turkish army of 200,000 that Mahomed II sent into Moldavia after conquering Constantinople 23 years earlier. In 1650, during the Tatar invasion, Vasile Vodă's family sheltered here. But in 1691, the fortress was besieged by Jan Sobieski, King of Poland, and it finally gave way. Follow the signs for Cetatea Neamţului along Bd. Ştefan cel Mare.

Târgu Neamţ's **History and Ethnographic Museum** is at Bd. Stefan cel Mare 37. A statue honoring writer Ion Creangă stands in **Piaţa Mihai Eminescu**. Creangă attended school in Târgu Neamţ (and was a close friend of Eminescu's).

The only hotel in Târgu Neamţ is the **Doina**, at Strada M. Kogalniceanu 6-8, Tel: (40-233)79.02.70, fax: (40-233)79.08.43, E-mail: trustdoina@xnet.ro, www.trustdoina.ro. But 4 km (2½ miles) north of town, on route 15C to Suceava, is the **Hotel Oglinzi,** Tel: (40-233)79.01.11, fax: (40-233)79.03.17, E-mail: iuliana2001@yahoo.com, www.hotelrestaurant.ro.

The countryside of Neamţ County has many interesting places to visit. **Ion Creangă's Memorial House**, mentioned in his "Childhood Memories," was built in 1830 at Humuleşti village. It is a small single-storey cottage, made of beams coated in clay, with a clay porch and a wooden roof with large eaves. Its interior is typical of 19th-century design and is exactly as he described in his writings. Many of the objects on display actually belonged to him. Among them is the breviary of Nică, son of Ştefan a Petrei, and the toys with which his cats used to play.

Neamţ Monastery is 15 km (9 miles) west of Târgu Neamţ. This is Romania's oldest and largest monastery, built by Stephen the Great in 1497. Some 70 monks live within its fortified compound. The bell tower which forms the entrance to the monastery courtyard was partly built by *Alexandru cel Bun* (Alexander the Good, 1400-1432). Look up at its ceiling and you can still see parts of an old painting representing scenes from the story of Varlaam and Ioasaf. Although the church has an ungainly extension at the west end, it is the most interesting of Stephen's architectural monuments because of its plan (which contains a tomb chamber), its interior structure and the decoration of the facades. The naos and the **tomb chamber** were painted in fresco during the reign of Stephen the Great or his son Bogdan III.

This monastery was a great intellectual and cultural center. Monk Gavril Uric ran a school of miniature painting and calligraphy at Neamţ, where superb illuminated manuscripts were created. One of its most famous products was a parchment copy of the Four Gospels from 1429; it is now at the Bodleian Library in Oxford, England. The monastery's **library** has over 11,000 volumes, including 594 manuscripts in Romanian, Slavonic and Greek. The monastery also owns a **600-year-old icon** of the Virgin Mary, which is believed to have miraculous powers. This icon is never taken out of the church, but thousands of pilgrims come to worship it every year. The monastery **museum**'s displays are spread throughout three spacious rooms.

Not far from Neamţ monastery is the **Dragoş Voda Buffalo Reserve**, which covers 16 hectares (38 acres) on the south side of the highway from Târgu Neamţ. These buffalo are wild European oxen descended from the aurochs, which were hunted to extinction in the 19th century. The reserve has four buffaloes: Rodion, Rodiona, Rochita and Rodica.

Agapia Monastery is 4 km (2½ miles) south of Târgu Neamţ. Agapia was built by Hatman Gavril Coci between 1642 and

1644. It stands in a lovely setting in the foothills of the Carpathians. Its church was painted by Nicolae Grigorescu in 1858, when he was just 18, before he went to study in Paris and Barbizon. Grigorescu left his self-portrait here in the figure of Daniel, one of the saints in the upper left-hand side of the iconostasis. The monastery's museum opened in 1922 and it displays religious objects from the 19th and 20th centuries. The monastery **library** has 12,000 volumes, including manuscripts and old books from the 16th and 17th centuries. Agapia also has a **miracle-working icon** of the Virgin Mary. It was one of several icons given to Alexandru cel Bun by the Byzantine Emperor Manuel Paleolog. The others are kept at Neamţ and Bistriţa.

Văratec Monastery has three churches and a chapel, and is home to 600 nuns. Its most important church is dedicated to the Death of the Virgin (August 15th), and was built by a nun called Olimpiada. Traditionally many of the nuns who entered Văratec came from noble families, bringing with them fine pieces of furniture and other valuable objects. Some of these are kept in the **museum** of the monastery. Its library has 6,000 volumes, 1,600 of which are manuscripts and old books. Văratec monastery is 7 km (4 miles) south of the Agapia turn-off from route 15C. About 43 km farther south on route 15C (or east of Durau via 15B) is the city of Piatra Neamţ.

SOUTHERN MOLDAVIA

Piatra-Neamţ

Piatra-Neamţ is set in a valley surrounded by mountains, making it one of the loveliest towns in Moldavia. Its name means "German Rock." Over 500 years ago, Stephen the Great built a royal court here. Archaeologists excavating its ruins have found arcades, staircases, and door and window frames belonging to Stephen's court. Most of the items discovered during these digs are now in the county **History Museum**. The **Church of the Birth of Saint John the Baptist** is the only surviving building from the old Royal Court. It bears an inscription relating that it was built by *Stefan cel Mare* from 1497-1498. On the church's north wall there is a marble plaque listing names of men from Neamţ who died in the War of Independence (1877-1878). Just northeast of the church is a stately bell tower.

Piatra-Neamţ is the capital of **Neamţ County** (pop. 585,000) and was initially called *Piatra lui Crăciun* (Crăciun's stone). Today, Piatra-Neamţ is a modern city and a cultural center, with a **State Theater (*Teatrul Tineretului*)**, a **Natural History museum (*Muzeul de Ştiinte Naturale*)** at the northern end of Strada Petru Rares, and the **History Museum (*Muzeul de Istorie*)** at Bd. Mihai Eminescu 1. The city's main square is **Piaţa Ştefan cel Mare**. On its west side is a **small park** with a statue of Stephen the Great. From the park, some steps take you to the remains of the old **Royal Court**. Every year in late May, the city hosts an **International Theatre Festival**. Piatra-Neamţ is also the starting point for summer hikers of the picturesque **Ceahlău mountains**.

Piatra Neamţ's hotels: **Ceahlău**, Piaţa Ştefan cel Mare, Tel: (40-233)21.99.90, fax: (40-233)21.55.40, www.hotelceahlau.ro; and the **Central**, Piaţa Petrodava 1-3, Tel: (40-233)21.62.30, fax: (40-233)22.35.28, E-mail: rezervari@hotelcentral.ro, www.hotelcentral.ro.

The **Bistriţa River** flows along the southern edge of Piatra Neamţ, and about 20 km (12 miles) west of the city, a dam was built on the river creating a huge lake. This is a tourist base for the **Bicaz Gorges**, an impressive area of eroded limestone that cuts through the mountains to the south. Bicaz Gorges are the gateway to Transylvania and was recently designated a natural reservation. In 2 hours driving time through a majestic landscape you will reach the Transylvanian plateau.

Cotnari Vineyards

Moldavia is the largest wine producing region in Romania, with plantations covering 180,000 hectares (432,000 acres), almost two-thirds of the country's vineyard area. The Cotnari vineyard is also connected to the 15th-century Romanian prince Stephen the Great. Not only did Stephen fight the Turks, but he loved his wine. He commissioned bridges and paved roads for the transport of wine, and deep cellars to keep it cool.

The leading wine of the vineyard is *Grasă de Cotnari*, described as having the bitterish taste of a nutshell and a strong flavor. It is an excellent white wine, similar to Tokay, and referred to as "golden nectar." In 1900, at the World Exhibition in Paris, *Grasă de Cotnari* was awarded a gold medal, and has since acquired the name of "Romania's Bloom."

Accommodations: **Casa Bilius**, in the village on the hill, overlooking the vineyards; owned by a family of wine specialists, who will prepare a delicious meal for you upon request; you can also buy some wine there, Tel: (0232)73.01.54. Several of Romania's tourism agencies offer wine tasting tours to the area (see Appendix).

Iaşi

Located southeast of Suceava and bordering the Republic of Moldova, Iaşi is the cultural capital of Moldavia and the hub of intellectual life in Romania. The third most populous city in Romania with 337,600 inhabitants (30,000 of them students), it is home to the country's oldest public **University**, founded in 1860. Called *Jassy* in German, it was also the home of many important literary figures, including Romania's national poet Mihai Eminescu. Iaşi has museums of history, art, literature, ethnography, theatre and sound technology. It also has memorial houses of famous Romanians, churches and monasteries from the 16th-19th centuries, a botanical garden and a fine theatre and philharmonic.

The major landmark in Iaşi is the magnificent neo-gothic **Palace of Culture** (http://home.dntis.ro/~palatis/uk/index.htm) built between 1900 and 1926. It has 365 rooms and houses four museums: the **Polytechnical Museum**, with old pianolas, music boxes and gramophones among other interesting gizmos; the **Ethnographic Museum** exhibiting costumes, handicrafts and tools of the region; the **Art Museum**; and the **Moldavian History Museum** (open Tues-Sun, 10am-5pm). The bells of the central tower ring out every hour. Next door is the **Church of St. Nicholas**, first built by Stephen the Great in 1492 and restored in 1904.

Iaşi's most famous monument is the beautiful **Trei Ierarhi Church**, built in 1639, at Strada Stefan cel Mare 62. Its entire stone facade is chiseled with intricate patterns resembling traditional wood carving designs. It houses the tombs of Princes Alexandru Ioan Cuza, Vasile Lupu, and scholar Dimitrie Cantemir, whose *Descriptio Moldaviae* is the first history and tourist guide to Moldavia. Elected Prince in 1710, Cantemir was deposed in 1711 for his alliance with Tsar Peter the Great in opposing the Turks. He was exiled at the Russian court. The church is open mornings and from 3pm-7pm; services are held Monday-Saturday at 5:30am and 5:30pm, and on Sundays at 8am.

Continuing north on Str. Stefan cel Mare, at no.46 is **St. George Church**, built in 1761 with its 30 m (99 ft.) high bell tower; it was once gilded in 18-carat gold. Next, you will find the enormous **Metropolitan Cathedral**, built in the 1830s, and the **Metropolitan's Palace**.

Across the park to the east, on Strada G.I. Bratianu is the **National Theatre**, considered one of the most beautiful halls in all Europe. Built by Viennese architects in 1895, the theatre is small, every seat having a fine view of the stage. Its floors and walls are of a rich red, and its magnificent ceiling is a 25 meter (82 ft.) wide vault with a huge mosaic portraying Greek and Roman actors. Its season runs September to April, with a few summer performances. Check with the tourism office for a schedule.

Two blocks southeast of the National Theatre is the **Golia Monastery**, hidden behind a huge stone gate tower, at Str.

Cuza Voda 51. The monastery complex is surrounded by a high wall with rounded turrets built in 1667 at the corners. There is also a bell tower 30 meters (100 ft.) tall with 120 steps to its top; the base is square-shaped (5 meters long on the side), the tower has a ground floor, two vaulted stories, a belfry, an upper gallery and terraces, is one of the symbols of Iaşi. It used to be higher around 1890, and had a balcony at the upper part. In past times, a fireman used the tower to patrol for fires across the city. Damaged in the fires of 1687, 1732, 1822 and by a 1738 earthquake, the church has undergone numerous restorations. Its exterior is of Renaissance design, but its interior is traditional Moldavian. The roof consists of multiple towers, turrets and domes. Tsar Peter the Great visited the monastery in 1711 and commented on its combination of Moldavian, Greek and Russian design. The Golia church is also known as a church of weddings, ever since the 17th-century princely weddings of Constantin Duca and Maria Brâncoveanu in 1693, and of Antioh Cantemir and Catrina in 1696 were perfomed here by the Patriarch of Tsarigrad, James.

At the north end of Str. Stefan cel Mare is **Piaţa Unirii** with its bronze statue of Alexandru Ioan Cuza, who arranged the unification of Moldavia and Wallachia in 1859. Cuza also founded universities in Iaşi and Bucharest, and made education compulsory for both sexes. Just north of Piaţa Unirii is the **Union Museum** in Cuza's old house (open Tues-Sun). Built in 1806 in the Empire style, it contains original documents, sculptures and other items relating to the 1859 union.

Northwest of Piaţa Unirii is **Piaţa Eminescu,** where a statue of the poet Mihail Eminescu stands in its center. Surrounding the square are the **University Libraries**, the **British Council Library** and the Student Cultural House. A block north, behind the Students' House is the **Voivodes Statuary**, eight of Moldavia's princes overlooking a tiny students' park. Just past the statuary, turn right onto Strada Vasile Pogor; the **Junimea Literary Society** founder Vasile Pogor held meetings in this 1850 house which is now the **Pogor House Literary Museum**. The grounds contain rows of busts of literary society members, such as Eminescu, Creangă and Caragiale.

Farther up Bulevard Copou is the **Eminescu Library** and **Cuza University**. This is the **Copou district**, the university district. Along with the university buildings there are the lovely **Copou Gardens,** where poet Mihai Eminescu wrote under his favorite linden tree. It contains the **Alley of Statues** of Romanian cultural notables, an **obelisk** from 1834, several ponds, and a **museum** of paintings and Eminescu memorabilia.

Back in the center, at Bd. Independentei 72, is the **National History Museum**, and across the street, the **Old University,** built in 1795 and now the **University of Medicine and Pharmacology**.

Tucked away in the northern suburb of **Ţicău**, is the rustic cottage of Romania's beloved writer **Ion Creangă**. Unbelievably tiny, Creangă lived there with his son and wife from 1872 to 1889, when he died. When the cottage opened to the public in 1918, it was the first memorial house ever in Romania. Its two little rooms and vestibule still hold some of Creangă's writing materials and personal effects. The porch behind the house looks out on the Şorogari vineyards and the Ciric ponds. The documentary portion of the exhibit is now in a larger, modern building in the cottage garden. In the garden there is a small amphitheatre, which is used for celebrating traditional customs and holidays. The most popular of these, *Mărţişor*, is on March 1st, when a little object is tied with a red and white string that in Romania symbolizes the coming of spring.

Iaşi can be reached by direct trains and by flights from Bucharest. The Bucharest-Iaşi Intercity train runs on weekdays only (trips on regular trains take 6-hours). An overnight train with *vagoane de dormit* (sleeping cars) runs from Iaşi to Timişoara, via Suceava/Cluj/Oradea. The *Gara* (train station) is

Jewish Heritage

Jews have lived in Moldavia since the 15th century. In the mid-19th century one-third of Iaşi's population was Jewish and there were many synagogues in the city. Iaşi was the headquarters of Hacham Bashim in the 17th century, and one of the great European centers of Jewish learning during the 19th century. The world's first **Yiddish theatre** was opened here in 1876 by Avram Goldfaden, who later founded the first Jewish Theatre in New York. Iaşi's Jewish theatre, *Pomul Verde* (Green Tree) was closed in 1963. But now, the European Festival of Yiddish Culture is celebrated in Iaşi in October; more info at www.ccf.tuiasi.ro.

The **Israeli national anthem** was also born here, of an 1878 poem by Naftali Herz Imber, entitled "*Hatikvah*" (Hope) and set to a Moldavian folk tune by Samuel Cohen.

Iaşi's one remaining synagogue, the ***Sinagoga Mare*** (Great Synagogue), built in 1671, can be found at Str. Sinagogelor (across Str. Sărăriei from Golia monastery via Str. Cucu). It serves Iaşi's remaining 500 Jews and houses the **Jewish History museum** (by appointment only, Tel: 25.97.87). The Jewish Community of Iaşi, is at Str. Elena Doamna 15, Tel: (40-32)11.44.14.

Moldavia was also the center of Romanian nationalism and was extremely anti-Semitic. The leader of the fascist Legion of the Archangel Michael, Corneliu Codreanu, was from Iaşi. His Iron Guard's pogroms killed many of the Jews, now buried in the **Jewish cemetery** (*Cimitirul Evreiesc*) on ***Dealul Munteni*** on Şoseaua Păcurari. After WWII, most of Iaşi's remaining Jews fled to Israel.

2 km (1.3 miles) from downtown; the CFR ticket agency at Piaţa Unirii 4 is open weekdays. The airport is 6 km (3.7 miles) from city center; TAROM airline's office is at Strada Arcu 3-5, open weekdays and Saturday mornings, Tel: (0232)21.70.27. There are direct flights between Iaşi and Bucharest on weekdays.

Buses also have daily connections to Bucharest and other main towns. Atlassib and Eurolines coaches travel to western Europe; there are also buses to Chişinău, Istanbul, Athens. The *Autogara* (bus station) is 4 km (2.5 miles) from the center, at Şoseaua Moara de Foc. Minibuses provide services to the local area and nearby towns. To phone for taxis, dial: Euro: 21.72.17, Pro: 21.12.11, Delta: 22.22.22, Tico: 27.22.22 or For You: 22.24.44.

Iaşi's tourist office is located at the *Centru Civic* at Bd. Stefan cel Mare 69, open 9am-3pm. BCIT, at Bd. Ştefan cel Mare 12, is open weekdays 8:30am-1:30pm for changing travelers checks and cash advances.

Some *hotels* in Iaşi: the **Europa**, Str. Anastasie Panu 26, a modern circular high-rise, Tel: (40-232)24.20.00, fax: 24.20.01, E-mail: clientservice@hoteleuropa.ro, www.hoteleuropa.ro; the **Grand Hotel Traian**, Piaţa Unirii, an historical building in the center, Tel: (40-232)26.66.66, fax: (40-232)21.21.87, E-mail: rezervari@hoteltraian.ro, www.hoteltraian.ro; the **Astoria**, Str. Alexandru Lăpuşneanu 1, Tel: (40-232)23.38.88, fax: (40-232)24.47.77, E-mail: reservation@hotelastoria.ro, www.hotelastoria.ro; **Moldova**, Str. Anastasie Panu 31, a modern high-rise at *Centru Civic* near the Palace of Culture with pool and tennis court, Tel: (40-232)25.02.40, fax: (40-232)25.59.75; the **Unirea**, Piaţa Unirii 2, another modern high-rise with a casino and cabaret, breakfast included, Tel: (0232)14.21.10, fax: (0232) 21.28.64; the **Unirea**, Piaţa Unirii 5, Tel: (40-232)24.04.04, fax: (40-232)21.28.64, E-mail: office@hotelunirea.ro, www.hotelunirea.ro; the **Orizont**, Strada Grigore Ureche 27, near the Palace of Culture, behind the Moldova hotel, Tel/fax: (40-232)25.60.70; the **Ceramica**, Str. Tudor Vladimirescu 103A, cash only, Tel/fax: (40-232)27.14.27, E-mail: office@hotelceramicaiasi.ro, www.hotelceramicaiasi.ro.

Some local *restaurants* include: **Bolta Rece**, Str. Rece 10, a turn of the century tavern with vaulted wine cellar, former favorite of Junimea intellectuals, Tel: 21.22.55; **Ginger Ale**, Str. Săulescu 23, an Irish Pub with some of the best food in town, Tel: 27.60.17; **Hanul Trei Sarmale**, Şos. Bucium 50, at the foot of Bucium hill, a 17th-century place where Eminescu and Creangă hung out, traditional food, Tel: 23.72.55; **Expo**, parcul Expoziţiei 21, in Copou park, Tel: 21.36.55.

Galaţi

Galaţi is an unattractive, but hard-working city, home to Romania's largest steel mill and a busy river port. Inhabited since 500 BC, today's population reaches 330,000, most of who work in the steel mill or the shipyards. Galaţi **port** handles all of Europe's river barge shipping, with convoys coming up the Danube from Germany, Austria, Slovakia, Hungary, Yugoslavia, Bulgaria, and Ukraine. From Galaţi one can reach Constanţa's seaport either via the Danube River and Black Sea (189 miles), or by going through the Danube-Black Sea canal (135 miles).

Some of the city's interesting sights include the **Navigation Palace**, an imposing building, designed by Peter Antonescu in 1912. The **Palace of Justice** is an architectural monument from 1905, the work of renowned architect Ion Mincu. The **Dramatic Theatre** built in a Doric style, was named after the great actress Fani Tardini. The **Visual Art Museum** was built at the beginning of the century by architect Ion Cerchez. It incorporates the work of Romania's famous painters: the Arama brothers, Theodor Aman and Corneliu Baba. The **University** has an architectural monument built between 1911 and 1913, after the architects Grigore Cerchez and Anton Vârnav's plans.

Galaţi's **Orthodox Cathedral**, built between 1906 and 1917, is also an Antonescu design. The church is of the Wallachian style and has a narthex spire (the cupola and the sustaining pillars) with no lateral apse. The 17th-century **Precista**

Church also served as a place of shelter and defense; its bell tower is included in the structure and its attic is fortified.

Some places to shop in Galaţi are the **Galeriile de Artă**, Strada Domnească 9; **Vox Maris Shopping Center**, Strada Brăilei.7-9; and **Modern Shopping Center**, Strada Domnească 2.

Just 12 km (7.5 miles) from Galaţi, is the **Gârboavele Garden-Park** and oaks forest preserve. Its **Tuluceşti Stables** were founded in 1987 and house the famous "*Ghidrani*" horses. About 60 km from Galaţi, **Lake Vlădeşti** is a great place for fishing and boating, or a picnic in a beautiful environment.

Vladimireşti Monastery sits on the Gurgueta hills, 4 km (2½ miles) from Tudor Vladimirescu village on the Galaţi-Tecuci road, at 46 km (28 miles) from Galaţi. It was built in 1938 in the same style as the Romanian monastery Prodomu in the Athos Mountain. There are 200 nuns at the monastery, making it the third largest monastery in Romania, after Agapia and Văratec. The **Holy Cocoş Church** is an old historical monument 61 km (40 miles) from Galaţi and 7 km (4 miles) from Niculiţel village. In 1841 the church became a spiritual center for the Romanians in Dobrogea with the approval of the Turkish Empire.

Celic Dere Monastery derives its name from the small river Celic Dere, which in Turkish means "the steel river," due to the large amount of ancient weaponry found there. In the 18th century, monks from Ardeal built a small wooden church here, which was later destroyed by fire. In 1901 the church was rebuilt. The monastery is 55 km (34 miles) from Galaţi.

Situated at 80 km (50 miles) from Galaţi on the Bujorului hills, the **Târgu Bujor Vineyard** is known for its award-winning wines. **Panciu Vineyard** is the largest vineyard in Vrancea County. It is 125 km (78 miles) from Galaţi, bordered by Trotuş Valley to the north and by Putna Valley to the south; it is 30 km (19 miles) from Focşani, the capital of Vrancea County. The **Odobeşti Vineyards** and **Niculiţel Vineyards** are also nearby.

There is no scheduled air service to Galaţi, but the Galaţi Airport is open for charter flights to and from any city in Romania.

Galaţi Train Station (*Gara Galaţi*), at Strada Gării 1, is 6 km (0.4 miles) from downtown. There are daily train connections to and from any city in Romania. Several bus routes connect Galaţi's main areas and tourist attractions. T*axi Companies*: Delta Car, Tel: 320.000; Ace, Tel: 940; Leonardo, Tel: 947. Galaţi's *hotels* include: the **Galaţi, Faleza, Alex**; the **Dunărea**, Bulevard Republicii 15, Tel: (40-236)41.80.41; **Turist**, Bd. George Cosbuc, (40-236)43.36.00; budget hotels are the **Sofin** and **Sport**.

Brăila

Brăila is a city of 230,000 on the Danube River, 28 km (13.5 miles) south of Galaţi, in southeast Romania. It is the second largest port in the country and a leading center of the grain export trade of the country. Tourists can visit the numerous cultural places like the **St. Gheorghe church**, built at the beginning of the 16th century and improved by King Şerban Vodă and his wife Doamna Bălaşa in 1656. Located in downtown, it is one of the oldest buildings of the city. There's also the **Museum of Ethnography**, the **House of Collections**, the **Museum of History**, **"Maria Filotti" Theatre**, **St. Archangels Church**, the **Greek Church**, the **Quay and Wharf** of the port, **Perpessicius Memorial House**, and the **Pile of Kinetic Fountains** on the Esplanade in Brăila.

The **Danube River** is the main attraction for tourists to Brăila country. One can arrange **river cruises** on the Danube with overnight accommodation and special tourist activities like fishing and hunting.

A meadow of the Danube River, the **Small Island of Brăila** is a joint zoological and botanic reservation protected by EarthVoice-Romania and the Wildlife Land Trust. Its 16,446 hectares (40,640 acres) of marshes, cattail swamps, grasslands, and forests are home to 34 species of birds that are internationally protected through the Berne Convention. This wetland is an important ornithological halfway point between the breeding sites of northern Europe and winter refuges of Africa. Over 300 different species of birds have been identified on the island, including the threatened red-breasted goose, breeding colonies of pygmy cormorants, bitterns, loons, red-crested grebes, white pelicans, red herons, little egrets, night herons, black storks, spoonbills, mute swans, and white-tailed eagles. This historic agreement ensures that the island will remain free from recreational and commercial hunting and trapping, deforestation, and development.

Only 5 km (3 miles) from Brăila city, on the bank of the lake, is the ***Lacu Sărat*** (Salt Lake) **Spa**. At 16 m (50 ft.) above the sea, it is surrounded by forest. The bottom of this salt lake is covered with a highly mineralized mud. The therapeutic value of the water and mud from Lacu Sărat is well-known and each year, tourists come to the spa seeking a cure.

Brăila, formerly *Ibrăila*, once had a thriving Jewish community. By 1860, the Jewish population reached almost 10,000. But in 1941, only about 5,100 Jews remained. After WWII, the community grew to about 6,000, but most of the Jews eventually emigrated to Israel.

Brăila can be reached by direct train from Bucharest; coming from Iaşi requires transfers at Bârlad and Galaţi. There are regularly scheduled buses from Galaţi. Accommodations at **Hotel Traian**, Piaţa Traian, Tel: (40-239)61.46.85.

CHAPTER 8

MARAMUREŞ

Beautiful Maramureş is the most remote of our destinations, located in northwest Romania, bordering the Ukraine along the Tisa River. This is the most isolated and undeveloped land in Romania. It is also the only region never occupied by Romans, and its rural inhabitants pride themselves on their ancient Dacian heritage. The region consists of low mountains, green hills and long river valleys extending across northern Romania to Bucovina.

Many of its inhabitants are simple peasants living in small villages in the Iza and Vişeu valleys, still abiding by the same traditions as did their ancestors hundreds of years ago. Many still have no electricity or running water; few own telephones or automobiles. The region is famous for its hand-built wooden churches and elaborately carved gates, its colorful peasant costumes of red, white and black, and beautiful hand-dyed and woven rugs.

Satu Mare

Based on discoveries by archeologists, Satu Mare had settlements back in the Stone and Bronze ages. Control of the community has been fought over for two thousand years. The invading Romans inhabited the area, as well as the Geto-Dacians. In 1006, Teutonic settlers came by invitation of Queen Gisela. In 1543 Hungary's Bathory family took control; they later had to fight the Ottoman's for the land. Then the Habsburgs attacked and destroyed the city's ancient fortress, but later they rebuilt it. In 1721, the town of Mintu united with Satu Mare and they became one city.

In the 18th century the city developed into an important industrial center and became urbanized; many of its fine buildings and its first park were built, roads were paved; steam, brick, lumber and wood-processing factories went up and railways were laid to several cities. After WWI and Transylvania's union with Romania, Satu Mare boomed with new business and investment. Today it has a population of 336,000. Sights around Satu Mare include: the **Old City Hall**, the **Roman Catholic Cathedral**, the **Episcopal Palace**, the **"Ormos" House**, the **White House**, the House of the **Shoemakers' Guild**, **St. Michael's Orthodox Cathedral**, the **Firefighters' Tower**, the **Museum of History**, the **Museum of Ethnography**.

Satu Mare was the birthplace of **Satmar Hasidim**; today a community of just 80 Jewish families keeps up its magnificent **Synagogue**, whose interior walls are completely covered with frescoes depicting biblical scenes.

For local art and handicrafts, visit: **FolkArt,** Strada I.C. Bratianu 3; **Galeriile de Artă**, Strada I.C. Bratianu 10; and **Uniunea Artiştilor Plastici**, Piaţa 25 Octombrie 3-7. The **Dinu Lipatti Philharmony** holds concerts at the **"North" Drama Theater**. Other nearby attractions include**:** **Karoly Castle** in Carei, 32 km (20 miles); **Museum of Oaş Land,** 48 km (30 miles); **Poiana Codrului Glass Factory**; and the **Merry Cemetery** in Sapânţa, 80 km (50 miles).

Satu Mare International Airport is 14 km (9 miles) from downtown Satu Mare. There are daily flights to and from Bucharest. The Satu Mare train station (*Gara Satu Mare*) is at Strada Griviţei 1. There are daily connections to and from most cities in Romania, as well as to and from Hungary. The Agenţia CFR (ticket agency), Tel: (0261)71.10.02. To phone for a taxi, dial: Galant: 942 or 947, Nova: 946 or 76.85.60, Cielo: 944 or 76.18.61.

Some hotels in Satu Mare: the **Dacia**, Piaţa Libertăţii 8, in the old center, Tel: (40-261)71.57.73, E-mail: office@hoteldacia.ro, www.hoteldacia.ro; the **Aurora**, Piaţa Libertăţii 11, in city center, Tel: (40-261)71.41.99, E-mail: aurora@aurora-sm.ro, www.aurora-sm.ro; the **Dana**, Drumul Careiului 128, Satu Mare's newest hotel, Tel: (40-261)76.87.16, E-mail: receptie@dana-hotel.ro, www.dana-hotel.ro; the **Strand**, Strada 24 Ianuarie 17, Tel: (40-261)73.04.72, E-mail: agtabere@p5net.ro, www.classoft.ro/atttssm/sm.htm; the **Sport**, Strada Mileniului 25, Tel: (40-261)71.29.59. There are also two Bed & Breakfasts: **Perla**, Strada L. Rebreanu 2, Tel: (40-261)71.07.94; and **Vila Bodi**, Piaţa Libertăţii 5, in the historical center, a renovated 19th-century villa, Tel: (40-261)7.08.61, E-mail: villa_bodi@datec.ro, www.villabodi.ro.

Baia Mare

Baia Mare sits at the foot of the Gutâi mountains. It is an old gold mining town, known in the 12th century as ***Neustadt;*** and in the 14th century, when it became the home of Iancu de Hunedoara, it was called by its Hungarian name ***Nagybanya*** (Great Mine). Today it best serves as the southern gateway to the Maramureş countryside.

The center of Baia Mare's historical section is **Piaţa Libertăţii** and its charming park. The house at Piaţa Libertăţii no.18 was the home of Iancu de Hunedoara, called **Casa Elizabeta**, built in 1416 for his wife. The **History Museum** near the northeastern part of the piaţa tells the story of Hunedoara and Baia Mara. The **County Museum,** at Strada 1 Mai and the ***Hanul Veche*** (Old Inn) also on Strada 1 Mai are also on the piaţa. Just west, at Piaţa Cetăţii, stands **Ştefan's Tower**, a Gothic clock tower built in the 15th century as part of the town's fortifications, and the **Sfânta Treime** (Holy Trinity) **Cathedral**, built by Jesuits in 1720. At the mining museum, **Muzeul de Mineralogie**, at Bd. Traian 8, you can learn about gold mining. And since you are in the only region not invaded by the Romans, you can learn something about the original Dacian people at the **Ethnographic Museum**, located east of the football stadium, across the footbridge over the Sasar River.

The post office and telephone center are at Bd. Bucuresti 9, open weekdays. Banca Comercială Română, at Bd. Unirii 15, cashes traveler's checks and gives cash advances on Visa/MasterCards.

You can fly to Baia Mare from Bucharest, Braşov or Cluj, or come by train. The train station is west of the center at Strada Garii 4; the bus station is next door at Strada Garii 2. The CFR Agency is at Strada Victoriei 5-7. TAROM's office at Bd. Bucureşti 5 is open Monday-Friday; TAROM runs a shuttle between its office and the airport around scheduled flights.

To get to **Sighetu Marmaţiei** from Baia Mare, however, you must either take a bus (6 daily) or rent a car. Local tourist agencies may be able to arrange a van and driver to tour you through the Maramureş countryside. Because this trip would require a couple of days, you would be responsible for the driver's overnight lodging, but it's absolutely the best way to see the Iza and Vişeu valleys. Contact **Nord Nord-Vest** (North North-West) Agency, Bd. Republicii 15/A/2, Tel: (40-262)22.65.08, (40-722)34.86.91, fax (40-262)22.75.18, E-mail: nnv@mail.alphanet.ro. They arrange personal tours of the Maramureş region and accommodations in village homes; they also arrange for a car and driver or rent you a car and sell maps. The **Mara Intl.** tourism agency on Bd. Unirii 5, Tel: (0262)41.67.41, also arranges accommodations in rural homes as part of Romania's rural tourism progamme. ANTREC's local agent is at Tel: (0262)43.35.93 or (0262)43.35.93. For ANTREC's main Bucharest office, Tel: (021)315.32.06. A Bucharest tourism agency may also be able to make the arrangements for you.

Hotels in Baia Mare: the **Bucureşti**, Piaţa Revoluţiei at Strada Culturii, standard modern, Tel: (40-262)41.63.01; the **Maramureş**, Strada Şincai 37A, caters to businessmen and groups, Tel: (40-262)41.65.55, fax: (0262)43.25.82, E-mail: hotelmm@mail.ro, www.hotemaramures.ro; the **Carpaţi**, Strada Minerva 16, across the river, Tel: (40-262)41.48.12, fax: (40-262)41.54.61, E-mail: office@hotelcarpati.ro, www.hotelcarpati.ro; the **Mara**, Bd. Unirii 11, a large, modern high-rise hotel, Tel: (40-262)22.26.60, fax: (40-262)22.20.08, E-mail:

office@hotelmara.ro, www.hotelmara.ro; the **Minerul**, Piaţa Libertăţii 7, best location but modest accommodations, Tel: (40-262)41.60.56, fax: (40-262)41.60.69.

Sighetu Marmaţiei

Referred to simply as Sighet, this is the northernmost town in Romania, 60 km (37 miles) north of Baia Mare and barely a mile from the Ukrainian border. It lies at the conflux of the Tisa, Ronişoara and Iza rivers. First mentioned in writing in 1328, Sighet is a quiet farming town with 40,000 people and the starting place for your exploration of the valleys of Maramureş. The town has a charming old center around **Piaţa Libertăţii** with shops, restaurants, and the 18th-century **Prefecture**, now the State Archives. Nearby are the 16th-century **Reformed Church** and **Roman Catholic Church**.

Just off the piaţa, at Strada Basarabia 10, is the **Synagogue**. Sighet was the birthplace of 1986 Nobel Prize winner, writer **Elie Wiesel**, and the house on Strada Tudor Vladimirescu where he spent his childhood is a **memorial museum**. There is also a large monument commemorating the Jews who were deported in 1944 by the ruling Hungarians on Strada Mureşan, off Piaţa Libertăţii.

Sighet's former prison on Strada Corneliu Coposu is now the **Museum of Arrested Thoughts & International Study**. It once housed Romania's intellectual and government elite who were tortured and killed by the communists between 1948 and 1952. Though cleaned up now, it displays photographs and you can visit the cells and torture chambers. Plaques list the names of its prisoners. Open Tues-Sun, 9:30am-1pm and 3pm-5pm.

The **Maramureş Ethnographic Museum** at Strada Bogdan Vodă 1 contains examples of local handicraft, including handmade rugs, woodcarving, icons painted on glass, costumes, masks and household objects. It also has a fabulous open-air **Village Museum** of old rural architecture on **Dobales Hill** to the east, overlooking the valley, open Tues-Sun, 10am-6pm. The first Monday of each month is the **livestock market day**, when peasants come in from the surrounding villages with their horse-carts and cows. From December 24 to January 6, Sighet holds its **Winter Carnival** and the local folk dress up in costumes and masks.

One of the most unique sights is in the nearby village of **Săpânţa**, 12 km (7 miles) west of Sighet. Săpânţa is the home of the **Merry Cemetery**, where the deceased are represented by decorative wooden grave markers, carved and painted with their images depicting them at their trades and inscribed with humorous rhymes (in Romanian) about their lives. This was the project of Stan Ion Pătraş from 1935 until he died in 1977. His delightful idea is continued by two of his former apprentices. Buses from Sighet's town center take visitors to Săpânţa.

The Tourist Office at Piaţa Libertăţii 21 is open weekdays 8am-4pm, Sat 9am-1pm. The local CFR agency is at Piaţa Libertăţii 25, open weekdays 8am-6pm. The train and bus station are at Piaţa Gării. Banca Comercială Română on Strada Iuliu Maniu is open weekdays from 8:30-12:30pm and gives cash advances on Visa.

Sighetu Marmaţiei can be reached by train from Bucharest, Braşov or Cluj. (If traveling overnight, get a sleeping car, or *vagon de dormit*.) Coming from Cluj, you can also take a train to Baia Mara, and then take a bus or rent a car or driver. There are no trains from Baia Mare to Sighet, but buses run between the towns every day. Buses also run down the valley daily, stopping at various villages.

Hotels in Sighet: The **Tisa**, Piaţa Libertăţii 8, across from the tourist office has a restaurant and bar, breakfast included, Tel: (40-262)31.26.45, fax: (40-262)51.54.84; the lodge-like **Marmaţia**, Strada Parcul Mihai Eminescu 1, in Grădina Morii park by the river, Tel: (40-262)51.22.41, fax: (40-262)51.54.84; the **Motel Perla Sigheteană**, Tel: (40-262)31.06.13; the **Motel Flamingo**, Tel: (40-262)31.72.65; and the bare-bones **Ardealul** hotel with communal toilet but no bath, Strada Iuliu Maniu 91, Tel: (0262)31.21.72.

The Iza Valley

The Iza Valley crosses the heart of Maramureş, following the Iza River from Sighetu Marmaţiei, 60 km (37 miles) to its source in the Rodna Massif. The valley is lined with small villages where daily life has not changed for centuries. They are famous for their old hand-built houses, elaborately carved gates and tall wooden churches. When not at work in the fields or at home, the villagers like to sit on the benches of their fancy carved gates to socialize, and on Sundays everyone promenades along the streets. A very religious people, the women all wear black flowered headscarves, the traditional black skirts and colored sweaters; the local men all wear hats, styles varying from village to village, and sport sheepskin vests. Their fancy folk costumes of white blouses, red and black striped aprons (*catrinţe*) and multi-colored vests are saved for festivals. (Tourists visiting the churches should dress respectfully, meaning no shorts or sleeveless shirts.)

The first village south of Sighet is **Vadu Izei** which has a tourism information office, the Fundaţia Turistică Agro-Tur, Tel: (0262)33.01.72, housed at no. 161. Here you can buy maps of the region, crafts or hire a local guide for the day to show you the wooden churches and weaving workshops. They also arrange overnight accommodations in private homes.

You'll begin spotting the gates and churches at Năneşti and at **Bîrsana,** whose church was built in 1390 and later moved to its hilltop location. **Strîmtura** was the site of a battle against the Tatars in 1717, and **Rozavlea's** church was made of fir tree trunks, also in 1717.

At **Şieu**, detour south about 7 km (5 miles) off the main road to reach **Botiza**, where the local priest's wife has revived the original vegetable dyes and design motifs of Maramureş' **traditional carpets**. If you stop by the Berbecaru's house next to the church, they may be available to show you inside both churches (old and new), or show you the tiny mill where the **rug weaving** takes place. Mrs. Berbecaru organizes the local rural tourism programme, arranging overnight stays in their home for a reasonable price; you can phone ahead at (062)33.49.91 ext.7, but she doesn't speak English, only French. (One daughter speaks English and another daughter speaks German.)

Back on the main valley road, as you continue south you will reach **Bogdan Vodă**, the birthplace of the first ruler of Moldavia, Bogdan I, who in 1359 led a revolt against the Hungarians. The **wooden church** there dates from 1722. But just before Bogdan Vodă, about 1¼ mile (2 km) south on the Ieud River, is the village of **Ieud**, home of the most famous wooden churches in the valley. The **Church on the Hill** dates from 1364 and contains 15th- and 16th-century paintings on its walls. The **lower church** was built in 1718.

All of the old wooden churches are very small inside, often requiring the women to stand outside if the service gets too crowded with men, but their high, shingled steeples seem to point toward the heavens. To appreciate the craftsmanship of these centuries-old buildings, take a close look at the cantilevered joints and wood-peg nails holding it together. The skill of the local wood carvers is evident on the large **wooden gates** whose intricate designs have symbolic meanings: the rope being the thread of life, spirals representing continuity, and the sun for the harvest.

Continuing southeast on the main road you will pass through **Dragomireşti**, **Săliştea de Sus** and **Săcel**. At Săcel, route DN17C takes you north into the foothills of the Rodna massif, to the large village of Moisei in the Vişeu Valley.

The Vişeu Valley

The Vişeu Valley runs parallel to the Iza Valley, but farther north, along the Vişeu River. It extends from Sighet to the Prislop Pass at the eastern border of Maramureş County. Trains from Sighet run through this valley 6 times a day to Vişeu de Jos, where an eastward branch continues as far as **Borşa**, 9 km

(5½ miles) east of Moisei. (The southern train route from Vişeu de Jos connects with Bucharest.) Borşa has two hotels: the larger **Cerbul**, Strada Brădet 8B, that has a restaurant, bar and skiing, Tel: (40-263)34.41.99, fax: (40-263)34.35.04; and the more modest **Iezer**, on Strada Decebal 2, Tel: (40-262)34.34.30, fax: (40-263)34.40.44. Borşa also has an 18th-century **wooden church**.

Go just 10 km (7 miles) farther east and you'll find the **Borşa Turist Complex**, a spa and ski resort, which also has a hotel and chalets, Tel: (40-262)34.34.66. Just 2 km (1¼ miles) north of the complex is **Prislop Pass**, a 1,416 m (4,645 ft.) corridor between the Maramureş mountains to the north and the Rodna mountains to the south. This is a beautiful area for hiking, and some of the trails through the Rodnas are marked with colored stripes.

Much of the Vişeu valley is uncharted, but explorers who venture into the fir, spruce, oak and beech forests may see bears, stags, roebucks, wild boar, chamois and mountain cocks. There are also glacier lakes, waterfalls, volcanic mountains, caves and the geological reserve **Creasta Cocoşului**, or Cock's Comb.

Traveling northeast, back towards Sighet, you pass through Borşa and Moisei, to **Vişeu de Sus**, which has a small hotel, the **Cerbul**, at Strada Spiru Haret 2. In the morning, an **old steam engine** hauls lumberjacks up the **Vaser Valley** to their camps farther north, and returns them to town in the late afternoon. Tourists can hitch a ride on the train for a small fee, but the trip is long and slow. East of Vişeu de Sus is **Vişeu de Jos**, then **Ruşcova**, and **Leordina** and **Petrova**, picturesque villages known for their **folk costumes** and architecture. The road continues up to the Ukranian border, then cuts south to **Tisa** where there's an interesting **private museum** in the house of the Pipas family. They have a collection of **glass and wood icons, pottery, woven fabrics, coins, paintings, sculptures** and hand-woven rugs. Sighet is just 2.3 km (2 miles) farther west.

Hora la Prislop (Prislop Round Dance)

Every year on the first or second Sunday of August the Hora la Prislop folklore festival takes place at Prislop Pass. Originally a sheep market festival, it has become a celebration of the music, dances and costumes of the region. Thousands turn out for this day of revelry, rain or shine. Locals sell traditional food, like mititei, and artists sell their handicrafts on the hill overlooking the mountains.

CHAPTER 9

CRIŞANA and BANAT

Western Romania consists of a great plain divided by the Mureş River. The territory was ruled by Hungary from the 11th century until 1553 when the Ottomans conquered the region. In 1699 the Turks recognized the Habsburgs' rule of Transylvania (including Crişana), but kept the Banat until 1718 when the Treaty of Passarowitz made Banat and Oltenia part of the Austro-Hungarian empire. In the late 18th century, Swabians from southwest Germany were invited by Empress Maria Theresa to colonize the Banat. The entire territory was under the Habsburg's Austro-Hungarian empire until 1918, when the empire collapsed at the end of World War I. In 1920 the Treaty of Trianon divided the former Habsburg territory among Romania, Hungary and Yugoslavia, awarding Romania Transylvania, Crişana and Banat.

Crişana's Hungarian background is clearly evident, especially in its architecture. The Banat, however, still bears a strong German influence, although most of the descendents of the Swabian Germans fled Romania since WWII and after the collapse of communism. The three major cities in this region are Oradea, Arad and Timişoara.

Oradea

Ornate buildings in eye-popping colors make Oradea a visual delight. Its architecture is the best example of 19th-century Austro-Hungarian design in Romania. The city's history, however, dates all the way back to the 9th century, when it was a feudal state. In 1241, the Tatars passed through on their rampage across Europe and destroyed the town. The city regained its position in the 15th century under the Corvinus dynasty, but then fell subject to Turkish occupation from 1660 to 1692. At the end of the 19th century, Oradea began rebuilding itself in a new architectural style from Vienna called the "Secession." This resulted in the colorful, elaborately designed buildings seen throughout the city today.

Located 16 km (10 miles) from the Hungarian border, Oradea (German: *Grosswardein*, Hungarian: *Nagyvárad*) is a quiet city of 200,000 (one-third of its residents are Hungarian) and the center of the Crişana region. It's a delightful stopping place for travelers going to or coming from Hungary.

Oradea's two main centers of activity are **Piaţa Unirii** and the pedestrianized **Calea Republicii,** separated by the **Crişul Repede River**. North of the river, just across the bridge, is **Piaţa Ferdinand** where the green neoclassical **State Theatre**, built in 1900, dominates the square. Adjoining the piaţa is **Calea Republicii**, a long pedestrian strip lined with shops, bookstores, galleries and cafes. This is the favorite place for Oradeans to stroll on a beautiful day, to meet friends, shop or just hang out in cafes. For a visitor, it's a fabulous place to study Oradea's dazzling architecture. Just a block east, in tiny **Parcul Traian**, there is a pretty little **museum** dedicated to Hungarian left-wing poet **Endre Ady** that also has a nice patio cafe.

As you cross the bridge over the Crişul Repede River, toward Piaţa Unirii, you immediately notice the yellow **Vulturul Negru** (Black Vulture) hotel, overlooking the piaţa. This imposing edifice was built in 1908; its inner shopping **arcade** has a magnificent stained-glass ceiling, and links Piaţa Unirii with Strada Independenţei. Farther down the piaţa is the **Orthodox church** (1784), known as the Moon church because of the 3 m (10 ft.) sphere on its tower which rotates to show the phases of the moon. The **City Library**, built in 1905, dominates the piaţa. East of Piaţa Unirii is lovely **Parcul Central**, the **Casa de Cultură**. Farther east, the **old citadel**, built in the 13th century, has been converted into government offices. You may hear a trumpet tune play out from the old City Hall (1902) at the river's edge, marking every hour.

About a mile (1.6 km) north of Piaţa Republicii, along Strada Stadionului, is **Petőfi Sandor Park.** In its northern section (across Strada Muzeul), is the largest Catholic cathedral in Romania, **Catedrala Romano-Catolică**, built in 1780; painted in three shades of yellows and gold, it has an unusual curved face created by the two tall towers that flank its entrance. Its interior frescoes were painted by Francisco Starno. The cathedral locks its doors promptly at 6pm, so be sure to visit it earlier in the day. In the garden in front of the church is an impressive 1892 **statue of *Szent* (Saint) Laszlo Kiraly**.

Across the garden is the **Episcopal Palace**, built in 1770, and modeled after Vienna's Belvedere Palace, with a U-shape and 100 fresco-adorned rooms and 365 windows. It is serves as the ***Muzeul Ţării Crişurilor*** (**Museum of the Land of the Criş Rivers**) housing history and art exhibits. The palace houses four museums on three floors, with a grand staircase connecting the first and second floors. The first floor has the ornate Hall of Festivities with frescoes from 1879 by Francesco Storni, hallways flanked by Baroque doors, and a chapel. Upstairs is the **Art museum**, with paintings from the 16th century European art to surrealist pre-WWII works; the **History museum** includes a Bronze Age temple from Sălacea, Dacian silver and Greek and Celtic pottery; the **Natural History section** displays dinosaur fossils along with elements and information about the regions nature reserves; and the **Ethnographic museum** exhibits a collection of crafts from around Bihor County, including ceramics, furniture, carved wood doorways and painted glass icons.

The palace's wide green courtyard facing Bd. Dacia displays a very impressive procession of 27 busts of Romania's greatest leaders, beginning with the Dacian Kings Burebista and Decebal (AD 82-107), to Roman emperor Traian (AD 98-117), and 14th-century rulers Basarab and Bogdan I, to the 15th century's Stefan cel Mare and Vlad Tepes, the 16th century's

Constantine Brâncoveanu and Dimitrie Cantemir, and all the way up through the 18th century.

Across Strada Stadionului from the park and cathedral is ***Şirul Canonicilor*** or the **Canon's Corridor**, an arcade of 56 baroque arches from the 18th century that line the sidewalk.

For dining, there are several cafes along the pedestrianized Calea Republicii, such as the *Terasa Café*, with a lovely terrace and *Caffee Cyrano, Pizzaria Kelly's, Lasea Café* or *Marco Polo* restaurants. Casual bites can be gotten at *Segafredo, Zanetti*, and *Fast Food Papa's*.

Just about any shopping needs can be handled at the **Crişul department store**, next door to the McDonalds at the north end of pedestrianized Calea Republicii. The store is not fancy, but it carries everything from jewelry, clothing, electronics, luggage and household items to wines; it even has a delicatessen and a tiny beauty salon (upstairs).

The Post Office at Strada Roman Ciorogariu is open weekdays from 8am-8pm. The Telephone Office is down the alley near Hotel Parc at Piaţa Republicii 5, open daily from 7am-9pm. Banca Comercială Română, at the southern end of Piaţa Independenţei, cashes travelers checks and gives Visa/MasterCard cash advances weekdays and has an ATM outside; it's open weekdays from 8:30am-6:30pm, Saturday 9am-1pm.

The **Agenţia Filarmonică & Teatrală** at Strada Republicii 6 has schedules and sells tickets for performances at the **State Theatre** and **State Philharmonic** (behind the State Theatre on Str. Moscovei 5) weekdays from 10am-4pm, and Saturday morning, Tel: (0265)23.65.92. The **Agenţia de Turism Crişul**, next door to Hotel Crişul at Strada Libertăţii 8, is open weekdays from 9am-4pm, Tel: (0259)13.07.37. The **Automobil Clubul Român** is open weekdays from 8am-3pm, and Saturday morning, Tel: (0259)13.07.25.

Hotels in Oradea: the **Continental**, Aleea Ştrandului 1, on the north riverbank, has conference rooms and business center, a thermal water swimming pool, massage and sauna, a beauty salon, restaurants, terrace, day and night bars; Tel: (40-259)41.86.55, fax: (40-259)41.12.80, E-mail: oradea@continentalhotels.ro, Visa/

MasterCard accepted; the **Atrium**, Strada Republicii 38, a nice intimate hotel in an historic building tucked in a narrow alley off the main street at Bd. Dacia, all rooms face into the bright atrium, restaurant, breakfast included, Tel: (40-259)41.44.21; **Hotel Scorilo**, Parcul Petofi 16, across from the park in a renovated 300-year-old building, rooms with balconies, rustic wine cellar restaurant (*crama*), Tel: (40-259)47.09.10, fax: (40-259)47.09.52; the **Melody**, Strada Transylvania 5, Tel/fax: (40-259)24.30.35, E-mail: melody@rdsor.ro; the 1908 Art-Nouveau **Hotel Vulturul Negru**, Strada Independenţei 1, has rooms with or without bath, Tel: (0259)13.54.17; the **Crişul Repede**, Strada Libertăţii 8, overlooking the river has rooms with or without bath and breakfast included, Tel: (40-259)13.25.09.

Oradea's **airport** is 11 km (7 miles) from the city. TAROM has 8 flights a week to Bucharest, and daily flights to Timişoara and Cluj-Napoca. The TAROM office at Calea Republicii 2 is open weekdays and Saturday mornings, Tel/fax: (0259)13.19.18. Dac Air's office, at Piaţa Independenţei 47, is open weekdays and Saturday mornings, Tel/fax: (0259)13.50.98. It also sells tickets for TAROM, MALEV, JAT, Air France, British Airways, and KLM. Oradea is also linked via Timişoara to Carpatair's 11 destinations in Italy and Germany.

Oradea's *Agenţia CFR* is at the south end of Calea Republicii, next to the TAROM office; it is open weekdays from 7am-8pm. International train tickets must be purchased in advance at the CFR Agency. Express trains run daily to Arad and Cluj-Napoca. The sleek Intercity trains run to Timişoara. Four trains run daily from Oradea to Budapest-Nyugati station: the express trains *Claudiopolis* and *Corona*, and the local *Varadinium* and *Partium* trains. You can check international and domestic train schedules at www.cfr.ro, or call Tel: 41.49.52. Oradea's train station, *Gara Oradea*, is about 2 km (1.2 miles) north of town; an underground passageway takes you across the highway to the station tracks. Trams #1 and #4 run to Piaţa Unirii on the southern bank of the Crişul Repede River.

Oradea is close to several other wonderful places. **Băile Felix** and **Băile 1 Mai**, two famous spas resorts renowned for their geo-thermal waters, can be reached in a ten minute ride from town. To call for taxis: City Taxi: 12.22.22, Fulger: 12.68.00, Pronto: 15.55.55.

Stâna de Vale, just 80 km (50 miles) away, is both a winter holiday resort with skiing tracks for winter sports enthusiasts, and a summer resort, perfect for hiking or driving through a natural environment that includes trees, streams, caves and its picturesque calcareous mountains.

A two-hour drive takes you to the **Apuseni Mountains** and the **Bears Cave**, a treasure for speologists and a delight for tourists, with its unique karstic relief plus relics of *Ursus Spelaeus*, a species that disappeared more than 150,000 years ago, but whose bones and skeletons are spread all over the area.

Băile Felix

Băile Felix is a year-round **health spa** just 8 km (5 miles) southeast of Oradea. The complex of hotels, pools and gardens is a great place to relax, party with the locals, or take a mudbath. It has a large, open-air, **thermal swimming pool** and several smaller thermal pools filled with thermal lotus. The most popular public pools, the **Strand Apollo** and **Strand Felix**, are open daily from 7am-6pm, May to October. Bring your own towel. You can just come for the day or stay awhile at any of several hotels.

Hotels: the **Felix**, Tel: (0259)13.65.32, and the **Lotus**, Tel: (0259)26.13.61, are in the center of the resort; the **Thermal**, Tel: (0259)26.12.15, near the train station has a thermal swimming pool; the **Nufărul**, Tel: (0259)34.39.94, just beyond Strand Apollo, accepts Visa; the **Poeniţa**, Tel: (0259)26.11.72, has a pool and accepts Visa and Amex.

Three trains run from Oradea to Băile Felix every day. The easiest way to go, however, is to take tram #4 (red number) east from Piaţa Unirii, or tram #4 (black number) south from Oradea's railway station to the end of the line at Nufărul. From Nufărul, bus #14 runs directly to the complex (pay on board), stopping first at Staţia Băile Felix, and then passing along the major hotels. To return, board the bus at Staţia Strand Apollo, outside the pool.

Arad

Arad has existed since 400 BC. Today it is a major railroad junction for international trains. The city lies on the **Mureş River**, across which sits its six-pointed **citadel**, built by order of Habsburg Empress Maria Theresa in 1762-1783. In the mid-19th century, Arad's Hungarian population revolted against Habsburg rule but the revolt was crushed in 1848. The Habsburgs executed 13 generals outside the citadel. The citadel is now used as a military barracks and, unfortunately, is off-limits to visitors. A **monument** commemorating the execution stands in front of the **Sub Cetate** camping ground, south of town.

A pleasant town of 190,000 people, there really isn't much happening in Arad. Its main street is Bd. Revoluţiei, where you'll find some impressive turn-of-the-century buildings like the neoclassical **City Hall** (1876) at Bd. Revoluţiei 75, next to the **Cenad Palace**. Behind City Hall, on Piaţa George Enescu, is the **Palace of Culture** (1913); inside, the **History Museum**'s displays recount the entire history of the region. The city's **Philharmonic** is also resident in the Palace of Culture. Adjacent to Piaţa G. Enescu is lovely **Parc Central**. The river runs just west and the parks lining it draw crowds of strollers and sunbathers.

West of City Hall via Strada Horia, on Strada Stejarului 2 is the **National Art Gallery** with furniture from the 17th century on. At the southern end of Bd. Revoluţiei are the huge **Roman Catholic Church** and the **State Theatre** (1874). Behind the State Theatre is broad Piaţa Avram Iancu. Other sites around Arad are: **Buhus Palace**, the **Water Tower**, **Arad Synagogue, St. Simion Monastery**, the **Serbian Church**, the **Museum of Arad County**, the **Museum of Art**, the **Old Theater** and the **Marionette Theater**. The **Agenţia Teatrală**, at the rear of the State Theatre, sells tickets to local performances on Tues-Sun, 11am-1pm.

Arad's main Post Office and Telephone Center is at Bd. Revoluţiei 44, open daily. Change travelers checks and get cash advances at Banca Comercială Română, Bd. Revoluţiei 72, (Mon-Sat, 8:30am-noon). BCR and Banc Post, at the north end of Bd. Revoluţiei, have ATMs or Bancomats. The Agenţia de Turism Zarandul, Bd. Revoluţiei 76, opposite the town hall, sells town maps and international bus tickets.

Some nearby attractions are: **Macea Castle** and **Macea Botanical Garden**, 24 km (15 miles) away; **Bezdin Monastery and Water Lily Preserve**, 24 km (15 miles); **Miniş Vineyard**s and **Siria Fortress**, 24 km (15 miles); **Lipova Spa**, **Lipova Orthodox Church** and **Soimu Fortress**, 32 km (20 miles) from Arad.

Hotels in Arad include: the **Continental-Arad,** Strada Revoluţiei 79-81, Tel: (40-257)28.17.00, fax: (40-257)28.19.94, E-mail: arad@continentalhotels.ro, www.continentalhotels.ro; the **Best Western Central,** Strada Horia 8, has a garden, Tel: (40-257)25.66.36, fax: (40-257)25.66.29, E-mail: central@inext.ro, www.bestwesternhotels.ro/central; the **Marem**, Calea Victoriei 2 C, Tel: (40-257)25.60.11, fax: (40-257)25.71.10; **Parc**, Strada Gen'l. Drăgălina 25, east of Bd. Revoluţiei via Strada Unirii, Tel: (40-257)28.08.20, fax: (40-257)28.07.25, E-mail: parc@inext.ro; and the **President**, Calea Timişoarei 164, Tel: (40-257)27.88.04, fax: (40-257)27.88.18, E-mail: president@rdslink.ro, www.hotel-president.ro; the **Phoenix**, Calea Aurel Vlaicu 267, Tel: (40-257)22.91.10, fax: (40-257)28.92.10, E-mail: rezervari@hotelphoenix.ro, www.hotelphoenix.ro; the **Arad,** Bd. Decebal 9, Tel/fax: (40-257)28.08.94, E-mail: hotelarad@tourconsult.ro, www.hotelarad.tourconsult.ro; and **Ardealul**, Bd. Revoluţiei 98, near the State Theatre, a 1841 neoclassical building whose hall once hosted concerts by Brahms, Liszt,

Strauss and Casals, Tel: (0257)28.08.40 fax: (0257)28.18.45. There are also three **Camping Grounds** nearby: **Voinicul**, **Zori de Zi**, and **Subcetate**.

Restaurants: *Mozart*, Str. Lucian Blaga 7, stylish ambience, live piano music, Tel: (0257)21.48.04; *Coandi Mic*, small and cozy, Romanian and game food, good value for money, in center; *Ratio Beach*, ştrandul Neptun across the river, rustic design, fireplace, intimate atmosphere, Tel: (0257)28.23.28; *Come de Mamma*, Piaţa Avram Iancu, is a small place serving Romanian dishes; the *Corona,* at Bd. Revoluţiei 40, has a nice terrace; *Restaurant International* farther north on Bd. Revoluţiei serves Romanian, French and Greek food and a wide variety of salads from 9am-11pm; *Pizzeria Taverna*, Blvd Revoluţiei 73, has pasta and pizza; *Gornelli* is an Italian-style cafe on the corner of Bd. Revoluţiei and Strada Crişan, open 10am-11pm; the *Gelateria Italiana* nearby offers 28 flavors of ice cream. For fast food, there's *Macul Roşu* on Bd. Revoluţiei and a McDonald's across from the City Hall.

Arad is easily reached by **train** from Romania's main cities. Day trips might include Timişoara (40 miles); the Royal Palace in Savârşin (50 miles); Oradea and Băile Felix Spa (75 miles); Deva and Hunedoara Castle (95 miles). An overnight sleeper train travels the 545 km (339 miles) to Bucharest daily. International express trains to Budapest, just 270 km (168 miles) away, stop at Arad. Reservations are required and international tickets must be purchased in advance from the CFR office. Two daily local trains run from Arad to Bekescsaba There are also daily connections to and from Austria and the Czech Republic. Arad's train station, *Gara Arad*, is at Piaţa Garii nr.8-9, just 1 km ($^1/_2$ mile) north of the center, Tel: 23.71.11. The Agenţia CFR office is at Strada Unirii nr.1 (open weekdays 8am-8pm), Tel: 28.09.77.

Arad's **bus station** (*Autogara*) is two blocks west of the train station. Several buses to Hungary depart every day for Szeged, Bekescaba and Budapest. Buy tickets for Budapest and Bekescaba at the ticket window, but for Szeged, pay the driver. Schedules change, so confirm times with officials. Private bus companies also run to Hungary, Austria, Germany and Poland. Agencies along Bd. Revoluţiei sell tickets for these trips.

Arad Airport is 3.2 km (2 miles) from downtown, Tel: (0257)25.4.44. There are daily domestic flights to and from Bucharest and scheduled international flights to several cities in Italy and Germany. Taxis run to and from the airport. To call for a **taxi**, dial: Getax: 953, Favorit: 28.00.00, or Diesel: 27.55.55. Several local buses and trams cover the main city areas and tourist attractions. Emergency phone numbers in Arad: **Ambulance**: 961or 25.13.13, **Hospital**: 25.11.58 or 25.26.66, **Police**: 955 or 22.39.92.

Timişoara

Timişoara is at the far west of Romania, near the borders of Hungary and Serbia. An ancient Roman fortress, once called *Castrum Temesiensis*, its records date back to 1212. In 1214 it was destroyed by Tatars. A century later, under Hungarian domination it took the name *Temesvar*. In the 15th century the city was rebuilt and enlarged by Transylvanian governor Iancu de Hunedoara and years of prosperity followed. The Turks invaded in 1552 and ruled until they were finally driven out in 1716 by Eugeniu de Savoia. This time the region became part of the Habsburgs' Austro-Hungarian empire, beginning a progressive era that lasted 200 years.

Under Habsburg rule, Swabians from southern Germany and Alsace-Lorraine were invited by Empress Maria Theresa to come settle the territory, and they brought with them their culture and technology. Most of Timişoara's advancements were made during this period. But in 1918, after World War I, the Treaty of Trianon redrew the borders making Transylvania and the Banat part of Romanian territory. The city was then renamed Timişoara.

Timişoara's greatest claim to fame may be its role as the catalyst of the December 1989 revolution which, within 10 days, overthrew Romania's communist dictatorship. It was here on December 15th that a Hungarian minority began protesting the exile of popular Calvinist pastor Laszlo Tokeş for his criticism of the government. Police and the military, unable to control the huge crowds gathered on the piaţa between the Opera House and the Orthodox Cathedral, finally used tanks to clear the square. Protests continued in Piaţa Libertăţii, however. The government in Bucharest then ordered the army to fire on the demonstrators. On December 1st, the army backed off and joined the protesters. On December 20th, Ceauşescu declared martial law in Timişoara, and sent troops to stop the rebellion.

The momentum continued in Bucharest, however, when on December 21st Ceauşescu's speech in the central square (now Piaţa Revoluţiei) was disrupted by the peoples' angry shouting of "Timişoara." The police cleared the piaţa but demonstrators returned the next day. Angry crowds also gathered from Piaţa Romana to Piaţa Universităţii. Unable to stop the advancing protesters, on December 22nd Ceauşescu and his wife Elena fled the city by helicopter. They were caught and arrested in Târgovişte on December 23rd, where they were quickly tried and executed on Christmas Eve.

Timişoara is called the "**garden city**" with good reason. Flower gardens appear everywhere. There is even a large clock made of flowers in the park next to the Hotel Continental. Some of the city's most interesting sights are its elegant baroque buildings, particularly along **Piaţa Victoriei**, which stretches from **Piaţa Opera** to Bulevard C.D. Loga, and in **Piaţa Unirii** a few blocks north.

At the head of the piaţa are the **Opera House** and the **National Theatre**. This is the center of town and its main gathering place, a wide circle where children chase pigeons and locals come to gossip. The promenade is lined with cafes, bookstores, shops and cinemas; manicured gardens and park benches run down its center.

At breaks in the garden are fountains and sculptures including the **Romulus and Remus statue** that was a gift from Rome. At the south end, across the street, stands the towering **Orthodox Cathedral**, founded during the reign of King Michael I, a stately, striped brick edifice with green and red roof tiles in a graphic design. The **Banatul Philharmonic** resides one block east of the cathedral.

East of the Opera stands **Hunyadi Castle**, erected by King Charles Robert of Anjou in 1318 and restored by Iancu de Hunedoara (*Janos Hunyadi* in Hungarian), Voivode of Transylvania. It is home to the **Museum of Banat** (open Tues-Sun).

A block north of the Opera, along pedestrianized **Strada Alba Iulia**, is **Piaţa Libertăţii**, a small green square with flower gardens and park benches. An active little open market operates on its north side, along Strada Eminescu. This was also the execution site of Gheorghe Doja, leader of the Peasant Uprising in 1514. Across the street is the **Old Town Hall**, built in 1734 in the Renaissance style and painted red with white trim. The city's tram line runs along here too. Timişoara was one of the first European cities to use horse-drawn trams in 1869; electrical tramways followed in 1899. Gas lighting was introduced here in 1857, and this was the first city in Europe to use electrical lighting in 1884.

Two blocks north of Piaţa Libertăţii lays **Piaţa Unirii**, a huge open square surrounded by buildings that are gems of architectural design. Painted blue, green, gold, and dark red, they're trimmed with white and beige stripes, window frames and ornamentation. At the east end is the **Roman Catholic Cathedral** (1736) which holds services in German. Opposite, on the west side, is the smaller **Serbian Orthodox Cathedral** (1748). In the piaţa's center are fountains amid grassy plots and stone benches. The **Museum of Fine Arts**, in a 14th-century palace, has works by German, Flemish and Italian artists.

Due east of Piaţa Unirii, at Strada Popa Şapcă 4, is the **Ethnographic Museum** displaying folk costumes and illustrations of regional ethnic diversity (open Tues-Sun). Southeast of Piaţa Unirii and just north of Strada Eugenio de Savoia, is the huge **Dicasterial Palace**. It was built for the Habsburg government and has 450 rooms in neo-Renaissance style.

Timişoara was settled on the northern bank of the **Bega River**, which was canalized to retrieve the marshy land around it. Gustave Eiffel built a bridge across the river. Take a stroll along its banks or through **Parc Central** next to the **Orthodox Cathedral**. South of the canal are Timişoara's **University of the West** and **Technical University**. The city now has 326,000 people, many of them students.

You'll find restaurants and cafes all around town. There's *Cina* at Strada Piatra Craiului 4, and the *Bastion Wine Cellar* at Strada Hector 2. At the head of Piaţa Victoriei is the *Bulevard*, serving traditional Romanian dishes; it also has a patio beer garden. *Lloyd*, at Piaţa Victoriei 2, serves international cuisine, CC accepted, Tel: 29.49.49, www.lloyd.ro; *Timişoreana Club XXI* specializes in beer and traditional Romanian; Contemporary Opera café at Piaţa Victoriei 6 is a place for drinks. For pastries, coffees and good mini-pizzas, there's *Violeta,* halfway down the promenade; inside is off-limits to smokers, but they also have a patio section. The *Casata bakery* and sweets shop is hard to pass up. Pedestrianized Strada Alba Iulia has several cafes and restaurants, like *Casa cu Flori* and the *Sherry Bar*; the casual *LaPizza* serves really good pizza (and beer). *Eclipse* cafe on Piaţa Unirii is a very nice place to rest with a cappuccino or drink, either inside or on the terrace. As usual, all the hotels have restaurants, some with entertainment.

Timişoara's Post Office is at Bd. Revoluţiei 2, open weekdays and Saturday morning. Banca Comercială Română is at Calea Aradului 11, and has *Bancomats* (ATMs) around town for quick cash.

Some *hotels* in Timişoara: the **North Star Continental**, Bd. Revoluţiei 1989 3, a high-rise, east of Piaţa Libertăţii, popular with tour groups and accepts credit cards, Tel: (40-256)449.41.44, fax: (40-256)49.82.37, E-mail: secretariat@hotelcontinental.ro, www.hotelcontinental.ro; the modern **Timişoara**, Strada Mărăşeşti 1-3, is comfortable, and just behind the Opera, accepts Visa, Tel: (40-256)49.88.52, fax: (40-256)49.94.50, E-mail: office@hoteltimisoara.ro, www.hoteltimisoara.ro; the **Central**, Strada Lenau 6 modern, just east off Piaţa Victoriei, accepts Visa, Tel:

(40-256)49.00.91, fax: (40-256)49.00.96; the **Nord,** Strada I. Drăgălina 47, near the train station, is a good choice for budget travelers, Tel: (40-256)49.75.04, E-mail: receptie@hotelnord.ro, www.hotelnord.ro.

Timişoara is 566 km (352 miles) from Bucharest. It can be reached by express and overnight trains (it's a 6-8 hour ride), and by international trains from Hungary, via Arad. They arrive at Timişoara Nord station, a 15-minute walk west of the center along Bd. Republicii. Taxis and trams are available there. The *Agenţia CFR* ticket office is at Strada Măceşilor 3 (downstairs), off Piaţa Operei (open Mon-Fri). Each window handles only certain domestic destinations, so check the posted signs. It's always crowded, so allow ample time.

Timişoara also has an international **airport** 12.5 km (8 miles) east of the city center, at Str. Aeroport 1, Giarmata, Tel: (40-256)49.96.39. Austrian Airlines, Carpatair, Malev and TAROM serve the city. TAROM provides buses into town 30 minutes after each flight and from their office on Bd. Republicii to the airport 90 minutes before each flight. To phone for taxis, dial: 940, 942, 945 or 949. The city's buses, trolleys and trams run from 5am to 11:30pm. There's a route map in the city's free tourist magazine "Timişoara" along with other useful local information.

Buziaş

The mineral springs of Buziaş had been used by the ancient Romans. Around 101 AD it was the site of the Roman fortress *Ahibis*, and before that, the site of a Dacian settlement called *Azizi*. The name Buziaş was first mentioned around 1320. The town sits at an altitude of 128 meters (420 ft.) in Timiş County, (37 km east of Timişoara) in the Banat region of western Romania. Its population is about 7,600.

In 1839 Buziaş was declared a spa. Its waters were used for drinking and bathing as treatment for gastrointestinal, gynecological, urological and venereal diseases and other disorders.

Since then, the quality of the water's natural factors has been recognized in the healing of cardiovascular diseases.

Therapeutic recommendations: cardiovascular affections, arterial hyper-pressure, rheumatism diseases, stress. Natural factors: carbonated, chlorinated, sodium, magnesium mineral waters mofettes (carbon dioxide emanations), sedative, protective bio climate. Treatments include baths in warm, mineral carbonated water; hydrotherapy; mofettes; paraffin packing; kinetotherapy; gym, massage, aerosols, sauna.

Buziaş Spa is at Strada Florilor 1, Tel: (40-56)32.10.60, fax: (40-56)32.15.81, E-mail: tbbbuzias@mail.online.ro, www.online.ro/tbbuzias or www.spas.ro/buzias. The Resort has restaurants, bars, open terraces, a disco, a theatre, a mineral water museum, folk art exhibition, an outdoor swimming pool with mineral water, and a sport hall. Excursions are available to **Silagiu vineyard** for wine tasting, or to Timişoara for a city tour.

By air: Timişoara airport is 40 km (25 miles) from Buziaş. By train: Buziaş station is 2.5 km (1.5 miles) from the center. By road: E 70, Buziaş is about midway between Timişoara (37 km) and Lugoj (25 km).

Hotels: **Parc**, Strada Avram Iancu 12, in the center, Tel: (40-256)32.17.21, fax: (40-256)31.25.81, E-mail: contact@buzias.ro, www.buzias.ro; **Buziaş**, Strada Avram Iancu 3, Tel: (40-256)33.19.20; **Timiş**, Strada Avram Iancu 1, Tel: (40-256)33.23.60.

Lugoj

Lugoj was settled long before its first mention in written history in 1241, after its destruction by invading Tatars. Situated on the left bank of the Timiş River, it was once a great political and cultural center. In 1402, during a time of rapid growth, it built its first Orthodox church. Following the Ottoman rule that began in 1658, in 1718 Lugoj fell under the reign of Austria's Habsburg Empire. During this era, its cultural activity blossomed. In the 19th century, the inhabitants of the left and right banks of the Timiş united to create one large industrial center, which prospered until 1927. But World War I and the political period that followed drastically changed the city, forcing mass urbanization and an end to traditional life. After the fall of Communism in December 1989, Lugoj finally became a free city.

Today, Lugoj has a population of 51,000 and continues as a center of the textile industry, shoemaking, and ceramics production. The city also houses many banking organizations. It is the home of the European Business School C.I. Drăgan and a University with primary focuses on Law and Economics, as well as Cybernetics. Sitting at the crossroads of major trade routes between Bucharest and Timişoara, the city is developing its tourism trade in conjunction with the nearby spa Buziaş, Lake Surduc, the Româneşti Cavern and monastery, all within 30 kilometers of the city.

Some of its sights include: the **Assumption of the Virgin Mary Church**, 1759-1766; the **Paroch's Church** (1733 with restorations in 1796 and 1932) and House (1733), incorporated into the former **Minorit Monastery**; the bell tower of **Sfântu Nicolae Church**; the Greek Catholic Church; the Postal Office restaurant; the "Traian Grozăvescu" Theatre, the **History and Ethnography Museum**, Strada Balcescu 2, Tel: (0256)35.49.03; and the **Pro Arte Gallery**, Strada A. Mocioni 1, Tel: (0256)35.78.86.

Its **Town Hall**, the ***Primăria Municipiului Lugoj***, is at Piaţa Victoriei 4, Tel: (0256)31.14.41, E-mail: plugoj@pcnet.ro. Tourist Office S. C. Dacia Turism SA is at Strada A. Mocioni 7, Tel: (0256)35.27.40/41, fax: (0256)35.06.71. In June 2000, Lugoj held its first beer festival. Since 1989, it has become a "sister-city" with Orléans, France; their friendship pact was ratified in 1994.

Lugoj is accessible by train or bus. Its train station is just 200 m (656 ft.) from city center, Tel: (0256)35.96.79. The *Agenţia CFR* ticket is at Strada A. Mocioni Street 3, Tel/fax: (0256)35.10.59. The Bus Terminal is 2 km (1¼ miles) from the center, Tel: (0256)35.11.02, fax: (0256)35.35.38. Buses go to

Timişoara, Reşiţa, Deva, and Băile Herculane. Taxi companies: Par, Tel: 35.03.50; Getax, Tel: 42.19.33; Pedux Mobel, Tel: 35.11.11. **Emergency calls**: City Hospital, Tel: 35.53.40 or 35.37.31. Ambulance, Tel: 961; Police, Tel: 955 or 35.43.83.

Accommodations: **Union UAP Guesthouse**, Strada Andrei Şaguna 1, Tel: (0256)35.12.04; **Ana Lugojana Camping**, route DN 68 A, km 9, Tel: (0256)35.30.60 or (0744)62.54.26.

Restaurants include: *Baldios*, Romanian and international cuisine, Calea Caransebeşului 89, Tel: (0256)35.83.58 or 35.12.22, fax: (0256)35.12.22; *Ana Lugojana*, Romanian cuisine, route DN 68 A, km 9, Tel: (0256)35.30.60 or (0744)62.54.26; *Dacia*, Romanian and international cuisine, Strada A. Mocioni 7, Tel: (0256)35.27.40, fax: (0256)35.06.71, E-mail: turism.dacia@xnet.ro. **Bars**: *777 FFF*, Strada Gh. Doja 6, Tel: 35.44.21; *Super de Martinis*, Strada J.C. Drăgan 2, Tel: 93.77.72.

Voronet Monastery exterior paintings, Bucovina

Vultural Negru Arcade

Voronet, Bucovina

Crişul Repede River, Oradea

Catholic Cathedral, Oradea

Orthodox Cathedral, Timişoara

Piața Victoriei
Timişoara

Garden Clock,
Timişoara

Mehmud II Mosque,
Constanța

Black Sea Coast

Peleş Castle,
Sinaia

Ancient ruins, Constanța

Danube River

Sinaia
Monastery
fresco

Village Museum, Bucharest

Coral Temple Synagogue, Bucharest

Parliament Palace, Bucharest

Dâmbovița River, Bucharest

Curtea Veche, Bucharest

Pasajul Villacross, Bucharest

Cişmigiu Gardens, Bucharest

Herăstrău Park café, Bucharest

Traditional meal

Piața Sfatului, Brasov

Crama, Brasov

Bran Castle
inner courtyard

Piața Republicii,
Brasov

Borgo Pass,
Transylvania

Medieval Bastion

Sighişoara Clocktower

Sibiu

Sighişoara

Sibiu

Sibiu Rom

Passage of Stairs, Sibiu

Medieval Bastion, Sibiu

Produce Market, Cluj-Napoca

Cluj-Napoca

Merry Cemetery, Sapinta

Hora la Prislop, Maramureş

Maramureş woman

CHAPTER 10

DOBROGEA

Historic Dobrogea

The southeastern province of Romania, between the Danube River and the Black Sea, is called Dobrogea (also called Dobruja). Because of its access to both the sea and the Danube, it has been a region of intense political and military turmoil for over 2,000 years. Today the entire province is a live archaeological site, where ongoing discoveries reveal evidence of its ancient past and people.

Greeks began colonizing the shores of the Black Sea in the late 7th century BC, searching for new trading grounds. They were a progressive society, and brought economic and cultural development to the local people. The colonists dealt in gold and natural products, such as honey, oil and resin, which they exchanged for the fabrics and fine pottery brought from Greece. Business prospered and the small colonies became large permanent settlements. Histria (formerly *Tomis*), just a few kilometers north of Constanta, was the first of the Greek colonies. It was followed by *Callatis* (now Mangalia) and *Argamum*, on the shore of **Lake Razelm**. The small city of Tomis developed into the Greeks' most important settlement and its military capital, and centuries later became the modern city of Constanta.

Today, you can get an idea of the importance of these ancient cities by visiting the ruins at **Histria**. Archaeological digs have revealed part of the city's original layout, its streets, houses and temples. A local museum holds many magnificent sculptures found there, mainly tombstones, temple columns and statues.

Dobrogea later fell under control of the Macedonian Empire, and a few centuries after that it was conquered by the Romans. The Romans, being skilled administrators and engineers, developed a defense system of fortresses along the Danube, the ruins of which are still visible. The best-preserved of these Roman settlements is **Tropaeum Traiani**, near the village of **Adamclisi**. Among the remains of city temples and streets, stands a huge marble monument dedicated by Emperor Traianus to the god Mars commemorating his defeat of the Dacians. An armored faceless warrior sits atop a cylinder 32 m (100 ft.) in diameter; around its base are 49 carved bas-reliefs portraying the Roman conquest. One of the most picturesque of these ruins can be found at **Enisala**, a Heraclea fortress built by Genovese on the foundation of an older Roman-Byzantine stronghold.

Northern Dobrogea

Northern Dobrogea consists of the Măcin Mountain area and the Danube Delta in Tulcea County. The picturesque Măcin Mountains are dotted with volcanic mountain formations. On their western perimeter, the Turcoaia Fortress (Troesmis fortress), located near the Turcoaia village, south of Măcin town, was mentioned as early as the 3rd century BC, during the military conflict between Lysimach and the local king, Dromichete.

In the south-center of the mountains, the **Casimcea Plateau** is one of the oldest geological formations in the country; the **Cheia Gorges** offer beautiful, wild scenery showing geological erosion well-preserved, including sediments and flowers.

On the south bank of the Danube, along route DN22 at Isaccea, you will find ruins of **Isaccea Fortress** (formerly named *Noviodunum*), a Roman Byzantine fortress built in 369 AD. The Emperor Justinian established a bishsopric here. It was declared "*municipium*" for its strategic and commercial importance.

Eight kilometers (5 miles) east of Isaccea via DM2, and then 2 km (1¼ mile) south, is the **Niculiţel Vineyard**, renowned for its red wines, and for the white Aligoté produced here, considered to be the best of its kind in the country. Just 6 km (4 miles) northeast of Niculiţel village, below Cocoşului Hill, is **Cocoş Monastery**, established between the 4th and 6th centuries. In 1971, the bones of some 3rd- and 4th-century Christian martyrs (Zotikos, Attalis, Kamasis and Filippos) were found buried at an archeological site Niculiţel; they were later put into a tomb, the **Niculiţel Martyricon**, in the monastery church at Cocoş. These relics are the oldest testimony to the existence of Christianity in Romania. The present monastery was built in 1833, with parts being added until 1914. There is a chapel and a museum of religious open to the public.

North of Niculiţel is the holy settlement of **Saon**, a monastery established in 1846, during the Ottoman domination, by a group of monks who left the Celic-Dere Monastery. Farther south, on a hill close to the same inner road, is **Celic Dere**, an old orthodox monastery and the preserver of Dobrogea's monastic traditions. The complex includes a museum of religious art and rare books. One of Dobrogea's last windmills stands in the field below the church.

Babadag is 40 km (25 miles) south of Tulcea on route E87 (also 22A). Its history dates from the Thracian Hallstatt culture of the 11th-13th centuries BC. In 1241 Tatars, descendants of the Golden Horde, came with the armies of Mongol emperor Ogedei and established colonies. Between 1262 and 1264, some 12,000 Seljug Turks from Anatolia settled here, led by Sara Saltuk Baba. Today, the town has 10,000 residents, still mostly Turks.

Despite Babadag's shabby condition, its lovely 17th-century Ali-Gazi-Pasha mosque stands in the town center. It is Romania's oldest Muslim monument, with its minaret rising 23 metres (75.5 ft.). Unfortunately, it, too, has been neglected. The tombs of Sara Saltuk Baba and Ali-Gazi-Pasha are decorated with carved flower motifs in a circular pattern; Ali-Gazi-Pasha's is a sacred Muslim place. Still a Turk town, some Muslim women wear the traditional, colorful shalwar (baggy pants).

To get to the small village of **Enisala**, find and take route C east about 7 km (4 miles). In the village center on the main road, there is a traditional **19th-century peasant house** that has become a museum. It has a granary and a stable, and the house's interior is decorated with cotton, woolen and silk hangings. The museum complex is open Tues–Sun.

The **Heracleea citadel** sits atop a rocky hill 5km (3 miles) northeast of the Enisala village. The road to the citadel is very narrow, with no turnaround, so large cars are not advisable. The hill overlooks vast reed marshes and the Babadag plateau. Wallachian prince Mircea cel Bătrân (Michael the Brave) commanded a garrison here at the end of the 14th century until 1417, when Ottomans finally captured Enisala. The Ottoman Empire wanted this section of Black Sea coast as a military and commercial route to northern Europe, and to keep their eye on Moldavia and Wallachia, which were under Turkish suzerainty, but allowed to govern themselves. Archeologists have recovered weapons, tools, coins and glazed pottery from the 13th-16th centuries. At the bottom of the hill, the remains of a 4th-century Roman camp that guarded the bridge over Babadag Lake were uncovered. There are also two large necropolises: one Getic (Dacian) dating from the 4th century BC, and one 15th-century Romanian.

Wines of Dobrogea

Summers in the territory between the Danube and the sea are hot, its soil is dry and water is scarce—ideal conditions for growing grapes. Wine grapes have been grown here as far back as 50 BC, when Dacian King Burebista ruled. Romania has 10 unique grapes that are not found anywhere else in the world. Dobrogea's most famous name in winemaking is **Murfatlar**; another is the **Niculiţel vineyard**. There are several organized tours for exploring Romania's wine culture here, and in the country's other winemaking regions. For information contact the Cultural Romtour, office@culturalromtour.ro or other travel agencies to inquire about tours.

THE DANUBE DELTA

The mighty Danube River flows 2,870 km (1,788 miles) from its beginning in Germany's Black Forest to the Black Sea. But before reaching the sea, the river divides into three main branches: the Chilia arm veers off to the northeast just before reaching the city of Tulcea; the Sulina and Sfintu Gheorghe arms separate just downstream from Tulcea. From there they splinter into a vast network of channels, lakes and brooks creating a magnificent wetland and wildlife sanctuary. Floating reed islands, tropical woods, pastures, sand dunes and waterways cover nearly 5,165 sq.km (3,000 square miles) and shelter over 300 species of birds, countless fish and 1,150 kinds of plants.

A **UNESCO World Heritage Site**, the Danube Delta is made up of a complex system of channels, lakes, sandbanks and forests, and is home to more than 5,500 species of flora and fauna—one of the richest and most diverse nature reserves in the world. In 1990, its 580,000 hectares (1,432,600 acres) were declared a National Biosphere Reservation by UNESCO.

The pristine beauty of the Danube Delta, coupled with its rich bird, animal and plant life makes it the ideal destination for nature lovers, birders, anglers, and eco-tourists. It's also the perfect getaway for an increasing number of travelers whose primary motive is to escape from the hectic city life, to a calm and secluded natural environment.

The Danube Delta's rich heritage extends beyond its natural beauty. The area is home to several cultures. Along with the Romanians, Ukrainians and Macedonians who live here, the Delta has a unique ethnic group called the Lipovans. The Lipovans were originally from the Volga river basin; they left Russia over religious disputes and migrated to the Danube Delta in the 18th century. They are skilled fishermen who know every stream and canal in the delta. The Lipovani have retained their old culture and traditional lifestyle. Also in the area, and easily accessible from the Delta are a number of historic monuments, ancient monasteries, museum's, and other places of tourist interest.

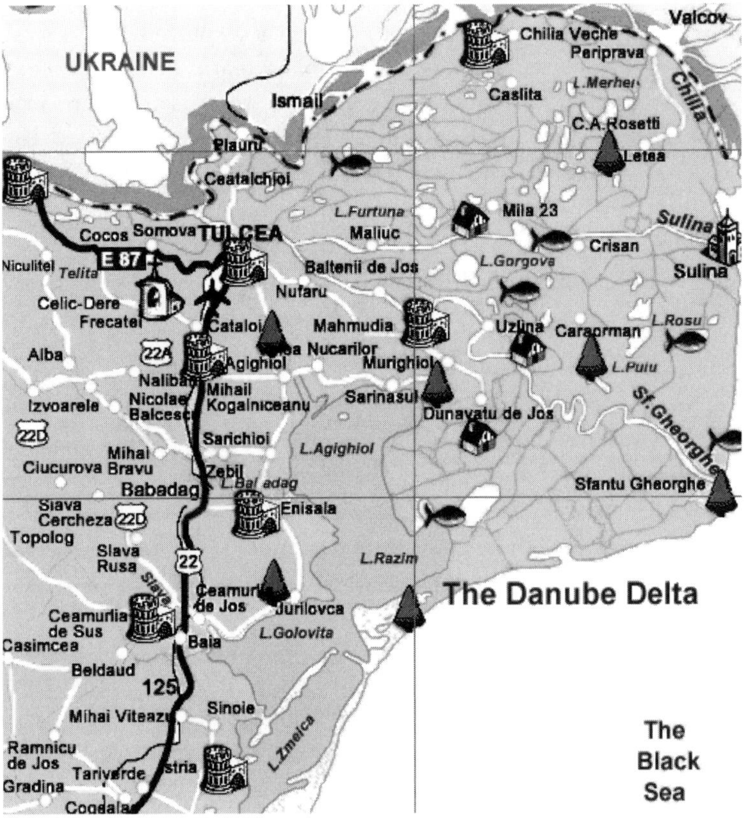
UKRAINE
Valcov
Chilia Veche
Periprava
Chilia
Ismail
Caslita
L.Merhei
C.A.Rosetti
Plauru
Letea
Ceatalchioi
L.Furtuna
Mila 23
Sulina
Cocos
Somova
TULCEA
Maliuc
Crisan
E 87
Niculitel
Telita
Baltenii de Jos
L.Gorgova
Sulina
Nufaru
Celic-Dere
Frecatei
Cataloi
Mahmudia
Uzlina
Caraorman
L.Rosu
Alba
22A
Agighiol
Murighiol
L.Puiu
Nalbant
Mihail Kogalniceanu
Izvoarele
Nicolae Balcescu
Sarinasuf
Dunavatu de Jos
Sf.Gheorghe
22D
Sarichioi
Mihai Bravu
L.Agighiol
Ciucurova
Zebil
Babadag
Sfantu Gheorghe
Slava Cercheza
22D
Enisala
Topolog
Slava Rusa
22
L.Razim
Slava
The Danube Delta
Ceamurlia de Sus
de Jos
Jurilovca
Casimcea
Baia
L.Golovita
Beidaud
125
Mihai Viteazu
Sinoie
L.Zmeica
Ramnicu de Jos
Tariverde
Gradina
The Black Sea

Boat cruises on the three main branches can be made by hydrofoils, river ferry boats or motor boats; and on the smaller channels by rowing boats and tugs. These trips originate at the city of Tulcea and vary in length, some traveling up to 72 km (45 miles) to the end of the Sulina channel, taking one or more days. A two day trip, staying overnight in Crişana or Sulina, is recommended for the best viewing of the Delta flora and fauna. You might also try hiring a local fisherman or a rowboat to take you on a private tour through the narrower waterways.

On your ride you will pass through some of the 16 protected reserves, where pelicans and cormorants fish. The delta is home to more than 325 species of birds, including 60 percent of the world's population of pygmy cormorants, the largest European colonies of the white and dalmatian pelicans and more than half of all the red-breasted geese in the world. The reserve is a winter breeding ground for over 80 species of birds from Asia, Africa and Northern Europe. Purple herons, spoonbills, ospreys, cranes, falcons, eagles, egrets, obis, spoonbills, larks, swans and red-breasted geese all gather in the Delta, as do some rare species, such as the griffon vulture, teal and the sheld duck. The best time for bird watching is April-May and June-September; however, many wintering species can be seen throughout the year.

Delta vegetation includes thousands of white and yellow water lilies floating on the lake surfaces. The Delta is the largest unbroken reed area in the world.

For anglers, the lakes and channels of the Delta offer year-round sport with 45 species of freshwater fish, including carp, pike, zander, perch, catfish, sheat fish and the royal sturgeon. There are also 70 species of clams, shells, and snails, plus microscopic and deep-water species. Some 40 species are to be found exclusively in the Delta. Fishing is allowed year-round except during the spawning period in April and May when sturgeon and sterlets enter the Danube channels from the Black Sea. The fishing seasons are: March 15–April 15 (prime season); April 15–June 15 or July (fishing totally prohibited); June or July 15–August 15 (fishing allowed); August 15–November 1 (prime season).

Fishing areas are established by the National Representative Forum of Hunters and Fishermen (AGVPS) and the Romanian Association of the Biosphere Reservation "*Delta Dunarii*" (ARBDD). Fishing within the Danube Delta Reserve is allowed only for holders of a Fishing Permit, issued by these authorities. Permits can be acquired by contacting the AGVPS, Calea Moşilor 128, in Bucharest, (021)314.21.51, E-mail: agvpsrom@pcnet.ro, open Monday–Friday; or the ARBDD, Strada Portului 34A, Tulcea, Tel: (0240)51.89.45, fax: (0240)51.89.75, E-mail: arbdd@ddbra.ro, www.ddbra.ro.

Tulcea

Guarding the gate of the Delta, Tulcea is a quiet city of 100,000 inhabitants built upon seven hills. The spot was originally settled by Dacians and Romans during the 7th–1st centuries BC. Today it is an important river port, and the tourist and administrative center of the Tulcea County.

City sights include **St. Nicholas' Church** (1865) and the **Azzizie Mosque** (1924); the **Art Museum**, the **Natural History Museum** which tells all about the Delta's eco-system and contains an **aquarium** of regional fish; the **Danube Delta Museum**, a beautiful architectural monument in itself, the museum hosts a 65,000-item collection of botanic, entomology, ornithology and mineralogy exhibits; the **Ethnographic Museum** with exhibits on the different peoples inhabiting the Delta region over history; the **History and Archaeology Museum**, in Independence Park, within an archeological site. It stands next to the ruins of old **Aegysus citadel** (Getic fortress, ancient Roman town and finally, a Romanian settlement) and next to the **Independence War Heroes' monument**, raised in 1899 by citizens of Tulcea. The museum offers a vivid image of the history of this region, from the oldest times to the late Middle Ages.

Outside the city: **The Heroes Monument** at Colnicul Horei-Tulcea, raised to pay homage to the heroes who fought in the Independence War (1877-1878). **Isaccea Fortress**, old ruins of Isaccea fortress (formerly named Noviodunum): Roman Byzantine fortress with a Celtic name, built in 369 AD. It was declared "municipium" for its strategic and commercial importance. **Turcoaia Fortress**, the '*Troesmis*' fortress—located near the Turcoaia village—was mentioned as early as the 3rd century BC, during the military conflict between Lysimach and the local king, Dromichete.

Tulcea also hosts the **International Folk Festival of Danubian Countries** in August, and a winter carnival in December.

Delta tours can be booked at Tulcea's travel agencies: Nouvelles Frontières/Simpa, in the Delta hotel, Tel: (0240)51.57.53; Danubius, Strada Păcii 20, Tel: (0240)51.78.36; and ATBAD SRL, Strada Babadag 11, Tel: (0240)51.76.25, fax: (0240)51.76.25; and at some hotels. Several Bucharest travel agencies specialize in tours to the Danube Delta; there is also a new resort in the area: www.deltaresort.com.

Ferry trips are booked at the NAVROM office on the promenade. A permit must be purchased to enter the Danube Delta Biosphere Reserve. This can be done at the Delta hotel or at the **ARBDD** office at Strada Portului 34A, Tulcea, weekdays between 10am-4pm, Tel: (0240)51.89.45. (Permits are included with tours.) Fishing and hunting permits are sold at the **Fishing and Hunting Association** (AGVPS) on Strada Isaccea 10, Tel: (0240)51.14.04, on Mon-Sat mornings, and on Wed and Fri again from 5pm-8pm. A map in its window shows the areas where fishing is allowed.

Ferry boats to Sulina and Sfîntu Gheorghe operate daily in summer from NAVROM's ferry terminal on the promenade, leaving at 1:30pm, but tickets can only be bought a half hour before sailing time. (Pre-check the departure times, in case they have changed.) The hydrofoils to Galaţi and Sulina are booked here also.

NOTE: If traveling to the Danube Delta in summer, be sure to pack a strong mosquito repellant. If exploring the inner Delta independently, take some food, water, a compass, a knife, a flashlight and binoculars along with you. Do not camp overnight without a tent.

Tulcea's post office and telephone center are at Strada Păcii 6, open weekdays and Saturday mornings. The Agenţia CFR is on Strada Babadag 4, opposite Piaţa Unirii; open weekdays from 9am-4pm. Banca Comerciala Romana, at the top of Strada Babadag, cashes travelers checks and gives cash advances weekdays from 8am-11am, and it has an ATM outside. Banca Agricolă is at Strada Mai 9. Taxi companies: Ace: 941, Alpha: 942, Prima: 943.

Places to eat: *Restaurant Select* at Strada Păcii 6 has a large menu and is open from 10am-midnight; *Restaurant Central* has a terrace on Strada Babadag; *Calypso*, farther up the hill on Strada Babadag, just past the **Synagogue**, has good food; the *Comandor* on the riverfront promenade specializes in fish and is open until 10pm. A pleasant outdoor cafe is the *Union Visa* on Strada Unirii off Strada Isaccea; the *Carul cu Bere* pub is next to the Select.

Hotels in Tulcea: **Rex,** Strada Toamnei 1, Tel: (0240)51.13.51, fax: (0240)51.13.54, E-mail: hotelrextl@x3m.ro, www.hotelrex.ro; **Delta**, Strada Isaccei 2 on the riverfront, Tel: (0240)51.47.20, fax: (0240)51.62.60, E-mail: delta@deltahotelro.com; **Select**, Strada Păcii 6, Tel: (0240) 50.61.80, fax: (0240) 50.61.83, E-mail: office@calypsosrl.ro, www.calypsosrl.r; **Egreta**, Strada Păcii 2, has restaurant and ale house, credit cards accepted, Tel: (0240) 50.62.50, fax: (0240)51.71.03, E-mail: office.tulcea@unita-turism.ro, www.unita-turism.ro; **Europolis**, Strada Păcii 20, has a restaurant, Tel: (0240)51.24.43, fax: (0240)51.66.49; **Casa Albastră**, on Ciuperca lake, Tel: (0240)53.75.06, fax: (0744)25.94.33; **Insula Complex**, on Ciupercă lake, Tulcea, Tel: (0240)53.09.08; **Europolis Ecological Touristic Complex** at Câsla lake, 2 km outside Tulcea, Tel: (0240)53.0.08.

ATBAD runs two floating hotels offering 3-10 day trips through the Delta: **Delta 2** has 8 double-cabins, and **Ibis Delta** has 9 double-cabins. Contact the ATBAD office, Strada Babadag 11, for bookings; Tel: (0240)51.41.14 or (0240)51.24.96; fax: (0240)51.76.25.

Local tourism offices to help you book river trips or Delta hotels: Eurodelta, Strada Isaccei 1, Tel: (0240)51.66.04; Lotus Travel Agency, Strada Portului 26, Tel: (0240)51.12.45; Simpa, Strada Isaccei.2, Tel: (0240)51.57.53; Sind România, Piaţa Independenţei 1, Tel: (0240)51.50.91; Tulcea Strada Isaccei 4, Tel: (0240)51.16.07; Ibis Tours, Tel: (0240)51.12.61; Nouvelles Frontières/ Simpa, Tel: (0240)51.57.53.

On the Sulina channel: In Sulina: the **Sulina Hotel**, Tel: (0240)54.30.17; the **Europolis** and the **Ochis**. In Crişan: the **Lebada**, Tel: (0240)54.37.78, fax: (0240)51.77.09, and the **Sunrise**, Tel: (0240)19.11.92, (0742)06.87.54, fax: (0240)54.71.93, E-mail: dinamic@x3m.ro, www.hotelsunrise.ro.

On the Sfîntu Gheorghe channel: In Uzlina, **Hotel Cormoran** and **Pensiunea Cormoran,** a complex with restaurant, boat hire, transfers, guides and Reserve permits; reached in 20 minutes by boat from Murighiol fishing village (secure parking). In Dunavăţu de Jos: **Hotel Egreta**, Tel: (0722)644.027, (0740)03.73.74, fax: (0722)18.14.45, includes continental breakfast, access to the hotel facilities: swimming pool, sauna, fitness room, billiards. By E-mail: info@hotelegreta.ro, rezervare@ hotelegreta.ro. By mail: Hotel Egreta, Dunavăţu de Jos, Tulcea, ROMANIA, Contact person: Mr. Mihai Costea; www.deltaresort.com.

ANTREC has guesthouses in throughout the area in Caraorman, Chilia Veche, Crisan, Delta Dunarii, Dunavatu de Jos, Murighiol, Sfîntu Gheorghe, Sulina, Uzlina and Vulturul. Local office: (0240)51.92.14; (0721)09.21.50, E-mail: tulcea@ antrec.ro; www.antrec.ro.

For many other hotel, Pensiunea, boarding house and camping options, as well as boats, agencies and general information in the Danube Delta area, visit the **Danube Delta Biosphere Reserve tourism** site: www.ddbra.ro.

Tulcea can be reached by train from Bucharest or Constanţa. An alternative from Bucharest is to take an express train to Galaţi, and then take the hydrofoil down to Tulcea. The train station is at the western edge of the riverfront promenade, a short walk from Piaţa Republicii. There is currently no scheduled air service from Bucharest to Tulcea; however, the airport is open for charter flights to or from any city in Romania. The TAROM office is on Strada Isaccei, near the Delta hotel, Tel: (0240)51.12.27.

THE BLACK SEA COAST

Romania's Black Sea coastline stretches over 245 km (152 miles) from the Danube Delta to Bulgaria. The southern third of this stretch is marked by the ancient port city of Constanţa and numerous modern beach resorts. The region, called Dobrogea, has an intriguing history. Legend has it that Jason's Argonauts anchored on this seashore while searching for the Golden Fleece. Merchants from Hellas arrived here more then 2,700 years ago and founded the flourishing city of Histria, and later the Tomis and Callatis fortresses. The Romans came in the early 2nd century BC and built their own fortresses (castra), as well as roads, defensive walls and the imposing monument at Adamclisi, as well as Adamclisi fortress, to commemorate their conquest over the Dacians. The Genoveses arrived on these shores in the Middle Ages. Vestiges of these early settlers are scattered all throughout the region, from the ruins of Histria fortress on the bank of lake Sinoe to the city of Constanţa, built upon ancient Tomis, where the romantic poet Ovidius died in exile, and all along the southern coastal area to Mangalia, the former Callatis.

Constanţa

Originally settled by Greek merchants in the 6th century BC under the name ***Tomis***, Constanţa was later developed by the Romans and renamed after the Emperor Constantin. In the 7th century AD the city was invaded by Avars. The romantic poet Ovid was exiled here by emperor Octavian Augustus in AD 8, until his death in AD 17. Today all that remains of ancient Tomis is a section of the old city wall and the 6th-century **Butcher's Tower**, plus some **columns and amphorae** in Parc Victoriei.

For 1,200 years after it was destroyed, the city was ignored until King Carol I decided to turn it into an active port and

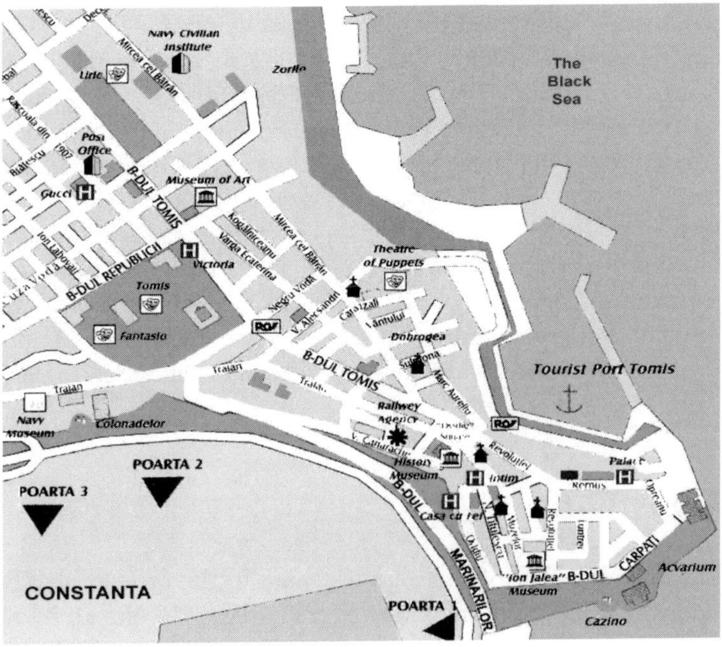
The Black Sea
Navy Civilian Institute
Liric
Zorilo
Post Office
Museum of Art
B-DUL TOMIS
Gucci
B-DUL REPUBLICII
Victoria
Tomis
Fantasio
Theatre of Puppets
Tourist Port Tomis
Traian
Navy Museum
Colonadelor
Railwey Agency
History Museum
POARTA 2
POARTA 3
Casa cu Lei
Intim
Palace
Remus
CARPATI
Acvarium
"Ion Jalea" Museum
Cazino
MARINARILOR
CONSTANTA
POARTA 1

seaside resort at the end of the 19th century. Mansions and hotels were built and a grand rococo casino was erected on the seaside promenade.

Constanţa is now a thriving cultural and economic center in Romania and the largest seaport on the Black Sea (www.constantza-port.ro). With its historical monuments, casino, museums, theatres and shops, it is the focal point of Black Sea Coast tourism. Its population of 345,000 is primarily Romanian, but includes Turks, Gypsies, Russians, Ukrainians, Bulgarians, Armenians, Tartars, Greeks, and Germans. It also has a diverse religious community of Orthodox, Roman Catholic, Greco-Catholic, Protestant, and Muslim sects.

The main street of the old section is Bulevard Tomis. At its intersection with Bd. Republicii are the **Muzeul de Artă,** at Bd. Tomis 82-84, Tel/fax: 61.70.12 and **Muzeul de Artă Populară** (folk art) at Bd. Tomis 32, Tel: 61.61.33, restaurants, hotels, shops, and, in **Parc Victoriei,** the **Fantasio Dance Theater** *(Teatrul de Revistă Fantasio),* Bd. Ferdinand 11, Tel: (0241)61.60.36, and the remaining ruins of Tomis. Just north is the tourist office at no. 69, the TAROM agency and the **Drama Theatre**. Walking southwest along Bd. Tomis you will come to **Piaţa Ovidiu**, dominated by a statue of the exiled Latin poet. The **Archaeology Museum** at no. 12 (open Wed-Sun, Tel: 61.87.63) contains Roman statues that survived the Avars' sacking of the city. Most impressive are the Glykon serpent and the statues of Fortuna and Pontos, the divine protectors of Tomis. They were unearthed in 1962 under an old railway station. It also has a hall devoted to Ovid (43 BC-AD 18). Next door to the museum, in a separate glass building is the **Roman Edifice with Mosaic Inlay**, a gigantic 700 sq.m (2,300 sq.ft.) Roman mosaic floor dated from the 6th century.

Continuing down Bd. Tomis, you'll pass the **Mahmoud II mosque** with its 50 m (164 ft.) high minaret, and finally reach the waterfront promenade and the 13th-century Genovese lighthouse by the yacht harbor.

At the end of the promenade, on Bd. Carpati, sits the city's elegant **Casino**, built in 1904, where you can dine or have a drink on the terrace. Opposite is the **Aquarium**, which displays marine life of the Black Sea (open daily 9am-4pm). If you continue on this road (its name changes to Ovidiu), winding back toward the center of town, you will come upon the ruins of the **Roman baths**, beside the **Orthodox Cathedral**. Constanţa's **Naval History Museum** (*Muzeul Marinei Române*) is at Strada Traian 53, Tel: 61.90.35.

North of Bd. Ferdinand/Bd. Republicii is the modern city with stores, restaurants, galleries and theatres clustered around Strada Stefan cel Mare and Bd. Tomis. Constanţa also has several theatres, including the **Teatrul de Balet "Oleg Danovski"** at Str. Răscoala din 1907 no. 5, Tel: (0241)51.90.45; **Ovidius Theatre**, Str. Mircea cel Bătrân 97, Tel: (0241)70.86.12; **Liric Theatre**, **Opera Constanţa,** also at Str. Mircea cel Bătrân 97, Tel: (0241)61.55.30; and the marionette theater **Teatrul de Păpuşi ELPIS,** Str. Karatzali 16, Tel: (0241)61.89.92 at the north end of Strada V. Alecsandri. At the far north end of the city are the **Planetarium** and **Delfinariu** (*Dolphinarium*), at Bd. Mamaia 255. Dolphins were once numerous in the Black Sea, but their numbers have greatly decreased.

Some places to eat in Constanţa are: *Balada*, Bd. 1 Decembrie 1918 2, Tel: 62.53.27; *Bel Ami*, Tel: 60.95.22; *Bistro Ovidius*, Interioară 2, Tel: 62.90.62; *Boema*, Bd. Tomis 334, Tel: 65.56.40; *Café D'Art*, Bd. Tomis; *Capitol Bar & Crama*, Bd. Mamaia, Tel: 52.05.22; *Casa Rosemarie*, Soseaua Contanţei 23, elegant restaurant, international and Romanian cuisine, Tel: 75.36.05 or (0723)70.27.34, www.rosemarie.ro; *Casa Tomis*, Str. Remus Opreanu 8, Tel: 61.94.86; *Crêperie Tybrezh,* Bd. Mamaia, Tel: 61.62.40; *Dolce Vita,* Str. Mircea cel Bătrân, Tel: 54.77.40; *Irish Pub*, Str. Stefan cel Mare, Tel: 55.04.00; *Joie De Vivre*, Decebal 24, French, Tel: 61.44.48, www.joiedevivre.ro; *Marco Polo*, Pizzerie-Restaurant and Bucătărie Internaţională, Str. Sarmisegetuza 2, Tel: 61.73.57; *Marco Polo Bucătărie Internaţională*, Str. Decebal 24, Tel: 61.73.57, (0722)23.09.76; *Scapino*, Aleea Hortensiei 2A, Italian, Tel. 69.46.89; and *Trattoria d`Angelo*, Str. I.G. Duca 37, Tel: 61.81.81. There are pizzarias all over town and, of course, a McDonalds at the Delfinariu and in **Magazinul Tomis** shopping center.

Banca Comerciala Romana is at Strada Traian 68, between the old city and the train station, open only until 2pm; BCR has an ATM outside. Banca Agricolă at Piaţa Ovidiu 9 also changes traveler's checks and gives cash advances until 2:30pm. Bank Post is at Bd. Mamaia 79-81. There is a Citibank on Bd. Ferdinand 53, for commercial business only, Tel: 55.11.01. The friendly Danubius travel agency on Piaţa Ovidiu also has an exchange office.

Constanţa's Post Office and Telephone Center are on Bd. Tomis 79, at Str. Stefan cel Mare. Constanţa's area code is 241 (0241). Some useful telephone numbers are: Police 955; Ambulance 961; Taxis: General Taxi, tel: 953, Romaris, Tel: 69.00.00.

The **Constanta County Library,** at Mircea cel Bătrân 104A, has 700,000 books and periodicals, maps, video/audio recordings, manuscripts, and iconography, Tel: 616-244, 616-245, fax: 614-48, E-mail: bjc@biblioteca.ct.ro, http://www.bjc.ro. There is also a **British Council Library,** also at Str. Mircea cel Bătrân 104A, Tel: 61.83.65, www.brishcouncil.org/romania, and a **French Library–Alliance Française** at Bd. Ferdinand 78, Tel: 61.94.38.

There are currently no regularly scheduled flights to Constanţa's Mihail Kogalniceanu Airport, but the airport is open daily to charter flights coming to and leaving from Constanţa, Tel: (0241)25.51.77. The airport is 24 km (15 miles) from the city; TAROM runs a shuttle between the airport and their office at Strada Stefan cel Mare 15.

Express trains run to and from Bucharest in 2 hours. The ***Agenţia CFR*** office is on Strada Vasile Canarache 1, behind the Archaeological museum, open weekdays from 7:30am-7pm, Sat. 7:30am-1pm, Tel: 61.49.60. The train station, *Gara Constanta*, and south bus station, *Autogara Sud*, are about 1.6 km (1 mile) west of the center. All of the seaside resorts are easily accessible by train or bus. City bus #40 to/from Mamaia stops in the city center. Private minibuses leave every 30 minutes from the bus stop by the train station for the southern beach resorts.

Hotels in Constanţa: the **Royal**, Bd. Mamaia 191, built in 2002, near the Dolphinarium and Planetarium, on the avenue linking the city to Mamaia beach resort, Tel: (0241)54.26.90, fax:

(0241)54.58.82, E-mail: office@hotelroyal.ro, www.hotelroyal.ro; the **Millenium Constanţa**, Bd. Mamaia 135-137; **Hotel Scala**, Bd. Mamaia 284, built in 2004; the **Bulevard**, Bd. Mamaia 294, renovated in 2002; the **Carmen**, Strada Nicolae Iorga 34; **Hotel Capri**, Str. Mircea cel Bătrân 109, conference room, restaurant and bar, terrace, pool, sauna and jacuzzi, billiards, Tel: (0241)55.30.90, fax: (0241)55.09.93; **Hotel Dali**, Str. Smârdan 6A, 15 rooms, Tel: (0241) 619717, www.hotel-dali.ro; **Oxford**, Alexandru Lăpuşneanu 202 A; **Guci**, Strada Răscoalei din 1907 no. 23, contemporary, Tel: (0241)69.55.00, fax: (0241)63.84.26; **Ibis Constanţa**, Str Mircea cel Bătrân 39-41, pets allowed; the **Palace**, Strada Remus Opreanu 5-7, Tel: (0241)61.46.96, fax: (0241)61.35.32; **Intim**, Strada Nicolae Titulescu 9, elegant, Tel/fax: (0241)61.82.85; the **Maria**, Bd.1 Decembrie 1918 2A; **Tineretului**, Bd. Tomis 24, Tel: (0241)61.35.90, fax: (0241)61.12.90; and the modern **Sport**, at Strada Cuza Voda 2, Tel: (0241)61.75.58, fax: (0241)61.10.09. Nearby **Camping grounds**: Hanul Piraţilor, Mamaia, Pescăresc and Turist.

Black Sea Resorts

The beaches of the southern shores have been developed into summer resorts and are Romanians' favorite holiday spots. The resorts stretch 82 km (50 miles) from Mamaia, just north of Constanţa, all the way down to the Bulgarian border. Beaches are wide and long with a fine, soft sand; the sea is tideless and without fish of prey; it also has a low salinity, almost half compared to other seas. There are resorts tailored to all tastes and ages, with hundreds of hotels in a variety of sizes and price categories lining the seashore. It is mainly a summer playground, offering all sorts of summer activities, sport grounds, swimming pools, boats from yachts to catamarans and ski-jets, live shows and music, and food and beverages available anytime around the clock. Some of the resorts also have **health spas** specializing in therapeutic water, massage and mud cures; these remain open year round. It's best to reserve hotel accommodations through

Crucea
Pantelimon
Capidava
Târguşor
Săcele
Siliştea
Dorobanţu
Nicolae Bălcescu
Corbu
Seimeni
Cernavodă
Mihail Kogălniceanu
Tortoman
Năvodari
Mamaia-Sat
Cocârleni
Saligny
Mircea Vodă
Cuza Vodă
Lumina
Castelu
Ovidiu
Mamaia
Rasova
MEDGIDIA
Murfatlar
CONSTANŢA
Valea Dacilor
Basarabi
Peştera
Aliman
The Black Sea
Abrud
Cumpăna
Ciocârlia
Agigea
Techirghiol
Eforie Nord
Adamclisi
Deleni
Codabia
Mereni
Şipote
Eforie Sud
Petroşani
Topraisar
Amzacea
Independenţa
Costinesti
Dumbrăveni
Chirnogeni
Comana
Pecineaga
Olimp
Neptun
Jupiter
Cap Aurora
Venus
Saturn
Mangalia
Cerchezu
Albeşti
Negru Vodă
Limanu
2 Mai
Vama Veche
BULGARIA

one of Bucharest's tourism agencies before heading to the coast. They can help you decide which resort and hotel best suits your tastes and budget.

Mamaia is the largest resort on the coast and the only one north of Constanţa. Its beach is 8 km (5 miles) long and of extremely fine sand. There are 64 hotels of all price ranges offering diverse recreational activities, restaurants, discos, casinos and cabarets from May through September. Sport facilities include tennis, volleyball, basketball, archery, mini-golf and paragliding. You can hire a bicycle, go sailing on the freshwater **Lake Siutghiol**, scuba dive, surf and water ski. Mamaia's **Aqua Magic** park has nine water attractions, including two for children. The park covers an area of 27,200 sq.m (6.5 acres) and has a capacity of 2,500 visitors. The facilities include a restaurant, a disco, fast food stands and souvenir shops. A new project is a telegondola system running parallel with Mamaia's beach. It will span 2,000 m, from Perla Place to Casino Place; each gondola will have eight seats. Tourists can exit or enter at either station and the ride will last approximately seven minutes, gliding 50 m (164 ft.) above the beach.

There are also spa facilities, and even a beach reserved for nudists. Mamaia is also ideal for family holidays with children; there are kindergartens and children's playgrounds. The **Dolphinarium** offers daily shows for kids, and there is a small train that takes children on trips around the lake.

Eforie Nord, about 15 km (9 miles) south of Constanţa is unique because of its salty therapeutic Techirghiol Lake, rich in curative sapropelic mud and its large natural park. Eforie Nord is known for its balneological treatments and hot or cold mud baths used for healing rheumatic, post-traumatic and dermatologic maladies; these cures are available year round. In summer, many of its 40 hotels offer facilities for aquatic sports, tennis, and volleyball; some also have night clubs. There is a campground in the woods surrounding the beach town. Eforie Nord also has an open market that sells fresh produce, cheese and fish. Smaller **Eforie Sud** has only 18 hotels, but a thriving Bed and Breakfast business whereby local residents offer accommodations in their homes. Together, the two towns have plenty of traditional Romanian restaurants, taverns, fisheries, ale houses and coffee houses.

Costineşti is the favorite of young people who want 24-hour partying. It has three main hotels, plus bungalows and cabins. You can also sleep on the beach, if necessary. It has four sports centers for tennis, basketball, volleyball; there's also aquatic sports and scuba diving. The village holds summer film and theatre festivals, art exhibitions and music concerts. It also has two open-air discos that draw crowds from the other beach resorts. (The resort suffered considerable damage from floods in 2005, so check with a travel agent regarding the status of its facilities.)

Neptun and **Olimp** are twin beach resorts nestled between the sea and the **Comorova forest**. These resorts were designed as playgrounds for rich Communists. Olimp is built on the sea wall with its 10 modern hotels on the beach. Neptun's 28 hotels are set back about 200 meters, separated from the 2 km (1.25 miles) long beach by a lake. Its luxury hotels and fine restaurants make Neptun the priciest of all the resorts. (The Ceauşescu family had their summer villa here.) Sheltered on three sides by the forest, Neptun is the preferred resort of families with children. There is also a modern **balneary clinic** (spa) with therapeutic equipment for rheumatic cures, and Asian organic regeneration therapies. Recreational offerings include sports grounds, indoor pools, a park, bowling, cinema, gambling, discos, and night clubs. Accommodations are also available in private villas, hotels, bungalows and camping sites.

Jupiter, Cap Aurora, Venus, Saturn and **Doi Mai** (2 Mai) are south of Neptun and somewhat less expensive than the resorts to the north, but their beaches are just as large and fine. These four resorts have a total of 60 hotels of various categories, plus bungalows, and caravan and camping sites. **Jupiter** is similar to its northern neighbor, Neptune, but less pricey. Some of its hotels are quite contemporary, having rounded rooms designed by Scoica. This resort also has an open-air cinema. **Cap Aurora** is perched on the tip of a small peninsula; its seven modern hotels are named after precious stones. **Venus** is a youth-oriented resort with modern, high-rise hotels; its beach stretches for 2 km (1¼ miles). The Dana, Raluca and Sanda hotels have lovely gardens and terrace bars. **Saturn** is a suburb of Mangalia and has one of the nicest beaches on the coast. There are sport grounds and a horseback riding center nearby. Entertainments include night clubs, discos and gambling.

Mangalia is the oldest town in Romanian territory, originally settled 2,500 years ago by Greek mariners who called it ***Callatis***. It was eventually conquered by the Romans. The **citadel wall** that surrounded their settlement was built by Emperor Galenius in the 3rd century; its remains jut out of the sea and run west to Strada Mihai Eminescu, then turn north until Aleea Cetăţii, where it turns east again. Its walls, made of stone, are 2 meters (6½ ft.) thick. Along the wall's northeast edge you'll find the remains of a 5th-century complex containing a **Syrian basilica**, atrium and palace. You can enter the complex from Strada Izvor, across from the Mangalia hotel.

Architectural remains of the city's ancient Getai, Greek, Roman and Byzantine civilizations can be found all over the area, but the main sites within the city are: the **Hellenistic cemetery** and **Sarmation burial ground** along Strada Constanţei, between Strada Pârvan and Strada Matei Basarab, and another Sarmatian **burial ground** between Strada Constanţei and the road going to Saturn. In 1994, 1,000 square meters (3,281 sq. ft.) of an ancient Romania-Byzantine district were uncovered. A large collection of ancient artifacts (statues, urns, jewels and coins, tools, etc.) are displayed in the city's **Callatis Archaeology Museum** on Soseaua Constanţei 23. Guided tours in multiple languages are given Tuesday–Sunday. Mangalia's only remaining mosque, the **Sultan Esmahan Mosque** was built in 1590, when the Ottoman Empire controlled the region. It is still in use, as there are substantial Turkish and Tatar communities living here. The mosque is open to non-Muslims from Tuesday–Sunday during the summer; women must cover their heads before entering. It stands at Strada Oituz, about

600 meters (2,150 yards) south of the museum. An area few hundred meters south of the mosque, excavations revealed Callatis' "sacred zone" where a temple and several alters stood.

The ancient city was called *Pangalia* from the 13th to the 16th century, when Genovese traders gave it its present name.

Post-war development has made Mangalia a popular Black Sea resort, with a modern **spa sanitarium** and five hotels, some equipped with conference facilities. Mangalia's sulfurous waters are acknowledged as extremely beneficial for stomach disorders and, combined with its mineral-rich mud treatments, are effective treatments for rheumatism. The city also has a prosperous shipyard that builds cargo ships and oil tankers. Just 3.2 km (2 miles) north is an Arab purebred **stud farm** where visitors can enjoy horse riding in a unique setting by the beach. The two minibuses that shuttle up and down the 45 km (28 mile) resort routes between Constanţa and Mangalia pick up passengers at designated stops along the main street.

South of Mangalia are two small villages. **2 Mai**, a shabby fishing village since the 18th century when Lipovani Russians settled there, used to be frequented only by more adventurous travelers who were happy to spend nights on the beachfront campground in front of a fire. Lately, it has become the new hot spot, despite the lack of hotels and services, much to the dismay of its longtime campers who liked its simplicity and privacy. Now, it has been discovered by the partying set and development is threatening. The local eateries offer homemade wine and traditional food. A wonderful 4 km (2½ miles) walk south, along the beach, will take you to Vama Veche, at the border of Bulgaria.

Vama Veche, just north of the Bulgarian border, has long been a favorite place for the bohemian set who wanted no part of the loud, disco-blaring tourist resorts up the coast. Without hotels, the only accommodations were rented rooms in local villas. It has a wide fine sandy beach, where camping is permitted, as is nude bathing. (Cold showers are available.) But since 2004, it is becoming more popular and entrepreneurs and newcomers want to develop it into another flashy resort. This has led to a campaign to save the village from gentrification and the founding of the **Stufstok music festival**. Its future is uncertain, but the beach and water here are fabulous. Bus #14 travels from the Mangalia train station to Vama Veche six times a day.

CHAPTER 11

THE LANGUAGE

Romanian is the official language of the country, originating from the Latin spoken by Dacia's Roman conquerors in AD 105. It sounds similar to Italian, but remains closest to its original Latin than all of the other romance languages. Migrating and invading tribes over the centuries all contributed words from their own languages, such that about one-fifth of the vocabulary comes from German, Turkish, Greek and Hungarian influence. Today, English is doing the same, particularly with modern technological terms. In fact, English has quickly overtaken French as the country's second language, especially with the young people. In Transylvania, the second language is German. But few people in the rural countryside speak a language other than Romanian. Refer to the English-Romanian translation guide in this book to get familiar with terms and phrases. If you know any Italian, French, Spanish or Portuguese, it should help you to understand Romanian.

Romanians are friendly people and like to talk with visitors. Most, however, do not speak English, so it helps to learn a bit of Romanian. This will not only help you get around—especially in the countryside—but will show respect for the people and their country.

As with other Latin-based languages, Romanian words have **genders**, as well as a polite form and a familiar form of the word "you." The polite forms should always be used in introductions and with older people. Use the familiar forms only with close friends or family. Likewise, on first meeting someone, refer to them by title: Mr. = ***Domnule***, Mrs. = ***Doamnă***, Miss = ***Domnişoară***.

Pronunciation and Grammar The Romanian alphabet contains 26 original letters, plus four that occur only in words borrowed from other languages (k, q, w and y). Romanian is a phonetic language, meaning all letters are pronounced. Most letters sound similar to those in English, but some exceptions are:

Vowels	Consonants
a = ***uh***	**c** before i or e = ***ch***
ă = as in h**ur**t	**ch** = ***k***
â = as the ***o*** in kingdom	**g** before i or e = ***j***
e = as in ten or	**gh** = as in **g**o
e = ***eh*** at the end of a word	**j** = as the ***s*** in lei**s**ure
i = ***ee***,	**r** = rolled as a Scottish ***r***
i = ***y*** at the beginning of a word	**ş** = ***sh***
i at the end of a word is silent	**ţ** with a cedilla under it = ***ts***
î = as the ***o*** in kingdom (same sound as â)	
o = as in p**or**k	
u = ***oo*** as in book	

Diphthongs

ai = ***igh*** as in high	**ia** = ***ya*** as in **yard**
au = ***ow*** as in cow	**ie** = ***ye*** as in **ye**llow
ău = ***oh*** as in go	**io** = ***yo*** as in **yo**nder
ea = something like ***a*** in b**a**t	**iu** = ***ew*** as in f**ew**
ea = at the end of a word, like ***aye*** in l**aye**r	**oa** = ***wha*** as in **wha**t
ei = like ***ay*** in b**ay**	**oi** = ***oy*** as in b**oy**
eu = like the ***e*** in bed followed by ***oo***	**ua** = ***wa*** as in **wa**tch
	uă = ***ue*** as in infl**ue**nce

Romanian nouns have three **genders**: masculine, feminine and neuter. Masculine singular nouns end in **u**, **e**, **i**, or with a consonant; plurals in **i**. Feminine singular nouns end in **a**, **e**, **ea**, or **a**; plurals in **le**, **e** or **i**. Neuter nouns may combine masculine and feminine forms. In their plural form, both masculine and feminine nouns usually end in **i**, while neuter nouns end in **e** or **uri**.

Indefinite articles (a, an) are **un** for masculine and neuter nouns, and **o** for feminine nouns, i.e. **un** ghid = a guidebook, **o** hartă = a map. For plural forms, the invariable article **nişte**, meaning some, is used before the noun, i.e. **nişte** baterii = some batteries.

Definite articles are attached to the end of a word, rather than using a separate, preceding word, i.e. telefon**ul** = the telephone. The definite articles for singular nouns are **ul**, and **a**, and for plural nouns **i** and **le**, as in copac**ul** = the tree, copaci**i** = the trees, and cas**a** = the house, case**le** = the houses.

Similarly, it is not necessary to use **personal pronouns** (I, you, he, she or it) before a verb because Romanian verb endings denote who is doing the action. For example: *Vorbesc englezeşte* = I speak English. *Vorbiţi englezeşte?* = Do you speak English?

Some Grammar Basics

Regular verbs - Present tense:

		a merge (to go)	a vedea (to see)	a face (to make,do)	a vorbi (to speak)
I	eu	merg	văd	fac	vorbesc
you	tu/dumneata	mergi	vezi	faci	vorbeşti
he/she	el/ea	merge	vede	face	vorbeşte
we	noi	mergem	vedem	facem	vorbim
You	voi/ dumneavoastră	mergeţi	vedeţi	faceti	vorbiţi
they	ei/ele	merg	văd	fac	vorbesc

Irregular verbs

	*	a fi (to be)	a avea (to have)	a veni (to come)
I	eu	sunt	am	vin
you (sing.)	tu/dumneata	eşti	ai	vii
he, she, it	el/ea	este/e	are	vine
you (plur.)	noi	suntem	avem	venim
they (masc.)	voi/ dumneavoastră	sunteti	aveţi	veniţi
they (fem.)	ei/ele	sunt	au	vin

*These verbs specify who is performing the action.

Negatives are formed by putting the negation ***nu*** in front of the verb, e.g.: **Nu** vorbesc romaneşte (I don't speak Romanian). For verbs beginning with vowels, as **avea** (to have), the negative is often contracted to **n-** as in **n**-am (I don't have) or **n**-aveţi (You don't have).

Personal pronouns:

	Subject	**Direct Object**	**Indirect Object**	**Reflexive**
I	eu	mă	îmi	mă
you (sing.)	tu/ dumneata	te	îţi	te
he, it	el	îl	îi	se
she	ea	o	ii	se
we	noi	ne	ne	ne
you (plur.)	voi/ dumneavoastră	vă	vă	vă
they (masc.)	ei	îl	le	se
they (fem.)	ele	le	le	se

Romanian has four forms of the word "**you**."

tu	for addressing a close friend or child
dumneata	for addressing a colleague (singular)
voi	for addressing close friends (plural)
dumneavoastră	for addressing strangers or people older than yourself; this is the most respectful term.

The **possessive pronoun** is formed by preceding the possessive adjective with the pronoun article.

	Singular			**Plural**		
	masc.	**fem.**	**neut.**	**masc.**	**fem.**	**neut.**
article	al	a	al	ai	ale	ale
my	meu	mea	meu	mei	mele	mele
your	tău	ta	tău	tai	tale	tale
his/her/its	său	sa	său	săi	sale	sale
our	nostru	noastră	nostru	nostril	noastre	noastre
your	vostru	voastră	vostru	voştri	voastre	voastre
their*						

*Invariable adjectives are used for "their" ***-lor***, and the formal form of "you" – ***dumneavoastră***. When not the subject of a sentence, ***-ei*** "her" and ***-lui*** "his" replace the forms of **său**. Both of these forms are attached to the end of the noun.

Adjectives agree in number, case and gender with the nouns they describe. Most adjectives follow the noun, but exceptions exist.

	Masculine **a good doctor**	**Feminine** **a good map**	**Neuter** **a good hotel**
SINGULAR subject or direct object	un doctor bun	o hartă bună	un hotel bun
possessive object or indirect object	un doctor bun	unei hărţi bune	unui hotel bun

PLURAL subject or direct object	nişte doctori buni	nişte hărţi bune	nişte hoteluri bune
possessive object or indirect object	unor doctori buni	unor hărţi buni	unor hoteluri bune

Demonstrative adjectives can be placed either before or after the noun. When placed after the noun they take the endings of the definite article form (in brackets).

	Masculine	Feminine	Neuter
this	acesta(a)	aceasta (aceasta)	acest(a)
these	aceşti(a)	aceste(a)	aceste(a)
that	acel(a)	acea (aceea)	acel(a)
those	acei(a)	acele(a)	acele(a)

Useful words/phrases *Cuvinte/fraze utile*

Salutations	***Formule de salut***	
Good morning.	**Bună dimineaţa.**	**Boo**-nuh di-mi-**na**-tsa
Hello / Good day.	**Bună ziua.**	**Boo**-nuh **zee**-wa
Good evening.	**Bună seara.**	**Boo**-nuh **sea**-ra
Good-bye.	**La revedere.**	La **rev**-eh-**de**-ray
Good night.	**Noapte bună.**	**Nwap**-te **boo**-nuh
Yes	**Da**	Dah
No	**Nu**	Noo
Maybe	**Poate**	**Pwa**-te
OK / Fine.	**Bine.**	**Bee**-nay
Please.	**Vă rog.**	Vuh-**rog**
Thank you.	**Mulţumesc.**	Mool-tsoo-**mesk**
Thanks very much.	**Mulţumesc foarte mult.**	Mool-tsoo-**mesk** foarte mult
You're welcome. (Lit. With pleasure.)	**Cu plăcere.**	Koo pluh-**che**-re
Excuse me.	**Scuzaţi-mă.**	Skoo-**za**-tsi ma

I beg your pardon? *or* Please, be my guest. *or* Go ahead.	**Poftiţi?**	Pof-**tits**
Do you speak English?	**Vorbiţi englezeşte?**	Vor-**beets** en-gle-**zesht**
How do you say in Romanian?	**Cum se spune pe româneşte?**	**Koom** se **spoo**-ne **peh ro-man-eshte**
I don't know.	**Nu ştiu.**	Noo **shtee-u**
I don't understand.	**Nu înţeleg.**	**Noo** in-tze-**leg**
I don't think so.	**Nu cred.**	**Noo** kred
I think so.	**Cred că da.**	**Kred** kuh **da**
I would like . . .	**Aş vrea . . .**	Osh **vray**-a
. . . and / or . . .	**si / sau . . .**	**shee / sow**
Have you any. . . ?	**Aveţi. . . ?**	Ah-**vetz**
I have / We have	**Am / Avem**	**Ahm** / **Ah**-vum
A little / A lot	**Puţin / Mult**	Pu-**tzin / Moolt**
I want to buy . . .	**Vreau să cumpăr . . .**	Vrau ser coomperr
How much is it?	**Cât costă?**	Kit **kos**-ta
It costs too much.	**Costă prea mult.**	Kos-ta **pray**-a **moolt**
Do you like it?	**Vă place?**	Vuh **pla**-che
It's beautiful.	**E frumos.**	Ye froo-**mos**
It's fine.	**E bine.**	Ye **bee**-nay
Good / Very good.	**Bun / Foarte bun(ă).**	**Boon / Fwar**-tay **boo**-na
Certainly.	**Sigur.**	**Si**-goor
Is it possible?	**Se poate?**	Se **pwa**-te
Really?	**Adevărat?**	A-de-vuh-**rat**
I'm sorry.	**Îmi pare rău.**	ym **pa**-re rau
It doesn't matter.	**Nu face nimic.**	**Noo fa**-che ni-**mik**
I am going to . . .	**Mă duc la . . .**	muh duk la
Come with me.	**Veniţi cu mine.**	Ve-**nits** koo **mi**-ne
Quickly! / Wait!	**Repede! / Aşteptaţi!**	
Be careful.	**Aveţi grijă.**	A-**vets gri**-shuh

Help!	**Ajutor!**	A-zhoo-**tor**
Emergency!	**Urgenţă!**	Er-**jents**-a
Good luck!	**Succes!**	Sook-**ches**
Vocabulary		
breakfast	**micul dejun**	**mi**-kool de-**zhoon**
lunch	**masa de prânz**	**ma**-sa de **prinz**
dinner	**masa de seară**	**ma**-sa de **sea**-ruh
car	**maşina**	muh-**shee**-na
bus	**autobuz**	a-oo-to-buz
bus stop	**staţia de autobuz**	**stat**-zia duh auto-**booz**
hospital	**spital**	spi-**tal**
(the) train	**trenul**	tre-nool
train station	**gara**	ga-ra
fast	**rapid**	ra-peed
above	**deasupra**	da-**soo**-pra
after	**după**	**doo**-puh
and	**şi**	shee
at	**la**	la
before (time)	**înainte**	in-**een**-the
behind	**înapoi**	in-a-**poy**
below	**dedesubt**	de-de-**soobt**
between	**între**	**in**-treh
but	**dar**	dar
down	**jos**	zhos
downstairs	**la parter**	la par-**ter**
during	**în timpul**	in **teem**-pool
for	**pentru**	pen-troo
from	**de la**	deh la
here	**aici**	a-**ich**
there	**acolo**	a-**ko**-lo
in	**în**	in
inside	**înăuntru**	i-ner-**oon**-troo

left	la **stân**-ga	la stinga
right	la **dreap**-ta	la dreapte
near	**lângă**	**lin**-ger
next to	**lângă / aproape**	**lin**-ger / a-**prw**a-peh
never	**niciodată**	**neech**-yo-**da**-tuh
not yet	**nu încă**	noo **in**-cer
not	**nu**	noo
now	**acum**	a-**koom**
on	**pe**	peh
only	**numai**	**noo**-my
or	**sau**	**sa**-oo
outside	**afară**	a-**fa**-ruh
perhaps	**poate**	**pwa**-te
since	**de atunci (încoace)**	deh a-**toonch**' in-**cwa**-cheh
soon	**curând**	koo-**rind**
then	**atunci**	a-**toonch**
through	**prin**	preen
to	**până la**	**pi**-ner la
today	**azi, astăzi**	az'
yesterday	**ieri**	yee-er'
tomorrow	**mâine**	mui-nay
too (also)	**de asemenea**	deh a-**se**-mneh-a
too (excessive)	**prea**	**pray**-eh
towards	**spre**	**spray**
under	**sub / dedesubt**	**soob** / de-de-**soobt**
until	**până**	**pi**-ner
up	**sus**	**soos**
upstairs	**la etaj**	la e-**tazh**
very	**foarte**	**fwar**-te
via (by way of)	**prin**	prin
with	**cu**	**koo**
without	**fară**	**fer**-ruh
yet	**încă**	**in**-keh

Quantities	***Cantităţi***	
a little / a lot	**puţin / mult**	poo-**tsin** / moolt
enough / too	**destul / prea**	des-**tool** / **pray**-uh
few / a few	**puţini / câţiva**	poo-**tsin'** / kitz-i-va
much / many	**mulţi**	moolt / **moolts**
more / less (than)	**mai mult / mai puţin**	**mye**-moolt / mye pu-**tsin**
none	**niciunul** (m) **niciuna** (f)	neech-**oo**-nool (neech-**oo**-na)
nothing	**nimic**	nee-**meek**
some / any	**nişte / oricare**	nisht' / o-ree-car
Questions	***Întrebări***	
Where?	**Unde?**	**oon**-de
Where is . . . ?	**Unde este . . . ?**	**oon**-de **yes**-te
Where is . . . ?	**Unde** e . . . ?	**Oon**-day ye
Where is the bathroom?	**Unde** e w.**c**.ul?	**Oon**-de ye **ve-che**-ool
Where are . . . ?	**Unde sunt . . . ?**	**oon**-de **sint**
How?	**Cum?**	koom
When?	**Când?**	kĭnd
What?	**Ce?**	cheh
Why?	**De ce?**	de **cheh**
Why not?	**De ce nu?**	De chay **noo**
Who?	**Cine?**	**chee**-ne
Which?	**Care?**	**car**-eh
How far . . . ?	**Este departe . . . ?**	**yes**-tah de-**par**-teh
How long?	**Cât timp durează?**	kĭt temp door-**a**-zer
How much / how many?	**Cât / Cîte?**	kĭts / **k**ĭ-teh
How much does it cost?	**Cât costă?**	kĭt **kos**-ta
What is this?	**Ce e asta?**	**Che** ye **as**-ta
What is that?	**Ce e aceea?**	**Che** a-**che**-la
What are you doing?	**Ce faceţi?**	**Che fa**-chets

Descriptives		
It's . . .	***Este . . .***	
beautiful / ugly	**frumos / urât**	**froo**-mos / **oo**-rit
better / worse	**mai bine / mai rău**	ma-i be-neh / ma-i ruh-oo
big / small	**mare / mic**	**mah**-re / meek
cheap / expensive	**ieftin / scump**	yef-tin / skoomp
clean / dirty	**curat / murdar** **pur / obscen**	**coo**-raht / moor/der poor / ob-**sen**
early / late	**devreme / târziu**	de-vrem / tar-zyoo
easy / difficult	**uşor / greu**	**u**-shor / greoo
fast / slow	**repede / încet**	reh-ped / yin-chet
free (vacant) / occupied	**liber / ocupat**	**lee**-ber / **ah**-koo-pat
full / empty	**plin / gol**	plin / gole
good / bad	**bun / rău**	boom / **ruh-u**
heavy / light	**greu / uşor**	gre-u / **u**-shor
here / there	**aici / acolo**	a-**ich** / a-**ko**-lo
hot / cold	**fierbinte / rece** **cald / frig**	feer-bit' / rech cahl-de / freeg
married / single	**căsătorit / necăsătorit**	**kuh**-suh-to-rit / ne- kuh-suh-to-rit
near / far	**aproape / departe**	a-pro-**ap'** / deh-**part'**
next / last (pronouns)	**următorul / ultimul**	oor-muh-to-rool / ul-ti-mool
next (upcoming) / last (most recent)	**viitoare / trecut**	vui-**twa**-re' / treh-**kut**
old / new	**vechi / nou**	**ve**-keh /
old / young	**bătrân / tânăr**	buh-treen / **tee**-nar
open / shut	**deschis / închis**	des-keez / yin-keez
right / wrong	**bine / rău**	reen' / **ruh**-u
loud / quiet	**sonor / liniştit**	**so**-nor / li-nish-tit
with / without	**cu / fără**	koo / **fuh**-ruh
wonderful / terrible	**minunat / groaznic**	mi-noo-nat / **groahz**-nik

Nature Terms		
bridge	**pod**	pode
campsite	**popas, camping**	**po**-pas, **cam**-ping
cave	**peşteră**	pesh-te-ra
cliff	**colţ**	colt
cloud	**nor**	no-ree
crag	**stîncă**	**stan**-ka
field	**câmp**	camp
fog	**ceaţă**	**chatz**-a
forest	**codru**	co-drool
gorge	**chei**	kai
hill	**deal**	del
hut	**cabană**	ca-**ba**-na
ice	**gheaţă**	**gatz**-uh
lake	**lac**	lac
marsh	**mlaştină**	mluh-**stee**-na
mountain range	**masif**	**mas**-sif
meadow	**poiană**	pwoi-**a**-na
mouth	**gură**	**goo**-ruh
pass	**pas**	pas
pasture	**păşune**	puh-soon
path	**potecă, traseu**	po-**te**-ka, tra-eyu
peak	**vârf, pisc**	varf, peesk
rain	**ploaie**	**plo**-ai
ravine	**râpă**	**ra**-puh
ridge	**creastă**	**cres**-tuh-a
river	**râu**	ryoo
rock	**piatră**	pee-**a**-tra
sheepfold	**stână**	**sta**-na
slope	**latură**	la-too-ra
snow	**zăpadă**	zuh-pa-duh
spring (water)	**izvor**	**iz**-vor
stream	**pârâu**	pa-ra-oo
tent	**cort**	kort

valley	**vale**	va-lea
village	**sat**	sat

CONVERSATION

ENGLISH	*ROMÂNĂ*	PRONUNCIATION
Salutations	***Formule de Salut***	
Good morning.	**Bună dimineaţa.**	**Boo**-nuh di-mi-**na**-tsa
Hello/Good day.	**Bună ziua.**	**Boo**-nuh **zee**-wa
Good evening.	**Bună seara.**	**Boo**-nuh **sea**-ra
Good-bye.	**La revedere.**	La rev-eh-**de**-ray
Good night.	**Noapte bună.**	**Nwap**-te **boo**-nuh
My name is . . .	**Numele meu este ...**	**Noo**-me-le **meu yes**-te
What is your name?	**Cum vă numiţi?**	**Koom** vuh noo-**mits**
How are you?	**Ce mai faceţi?**	**Che** may **fa**-chets
I'm fine, thanks.	**Bine, mulţumesc.**	**Bee**-nay, **mool**-tsoo-mesk
Do you speak English? . . . Romanian?	**Vorbiţi englezeşte?** **. . . româneşte?**	Vor-**bits** en-gle-**zesh**-te . . . ro-mi-**nesh**-te
Yes, a little. No.	**Da, puţin.** **Nu.**	**Da**, poo-**tsin** Noo
Please speak slowly.	**Vă rog, vorbiţi mai rar.**	Vuh **rog**, vor-**bits** may rar
How do you say . . . ?	**Cum se spune . . . ?**	**Koom** se **spoo**-ne
Do you understand?	**Înţelegeţi?**	In-tse-**le**-jets
I don't understand.	**Nu înţeleg.**	**Noo** in-tse-**leg**
Please repeat it.	**Vă rog, repetaţi.**	Vuh rog, re-pe-**tats**
I'm sorry.	**Îmi pare rău.**	Im **pa**-re **rau**
Where are you staying?	**Unde staţi?**	**Oon**-de **stats**
I'm at the ... hotel.	**Stau la Hotelul ...**	**Stau** la ho-**te**-lool
Good / Very good.	**Bun / Foarte bun.**	**Boon / Fwar**-tay **boo**-na
Maybe.	**Poate.**	**Pwa**-te

Certainly.	**Sigur.**	Si-**goor**
Is it possible?	**Se poate?**	**Se pwa**-te
Really?	**Adevărat?**	**A-de**-vuh-**rat**
It doesn't matter.	**Nu face nimic.**	**Noo fa**-che ni-**mik**
Thank you.	**Mulţumesc.**	Mool-tsoo-**mesk**
You're welcome.	**Cu plăcere.**	**Koo pluh-che-re**
I don't know.	**Nu ştiu.**	**Noo shtee-u**
I don't think so.	**Nu cred.**	**Noo kred**
I think so.	**Cred că da.**	**Kred kuh da**
I would like . . .	**Aş vrea . . .**	**Osh vray-a**
. . . and / or . . .	**şi / sau . . .**	**shee / sow**
I have / We have	**Am / Avem**	**Ahm / Ah-vum**
What is this?	**Ce e acesta?**	**Che ye as-ta**
What is that?	**Ce acela?**	**Che a-che-la**
What are you doing?	**Ce faceţi?**	**Che fa-chets**
I beg your pardon?	**Poftiţi?**	**Pof-tits**
Excuse me . . .	**Scuzaţi-mă . . .**	Skoo-**za**-tsi ma
Come with me.	**Veniţi cu mine.**	Ve-**nits** koo **mi**-ne
Here . . .	**Aici . . .**	Ah-**eech**
There . . .	**Acolo . . .**	Ah-**ko-lo**
Toward . . .	**Spre . . .**	**Spray**
Be careful.	**Aveţi grijă.**	A-**vets gri**-shuh
Good luck!	**Succes!**	Sook-**ches**
Tickets	**Bilete**	Bi-**le**-te
Entrance / Exit	**Intrare / Ieşire**	In-**trah**-re / Ye-**sheer**-e
Push / Pull	**Împingeţi / Trageţi**	Im-pin-**jets** / Tra-**jets**
Arrive / Depart	**Sosire / Plecare**	So-**she**-re / Ple-**kar**-e

WEATHER	***VREMEA***	
How's the weather today?	**Cum e vremea azi?**	**Koom** ye **vre**-mea **az'**
It's cold. . . . nice / hot . . . sunny / windy	**E frig.** **. . . plăcut / cald** **. . . soare / vânt**	Ye **frig** . . . pluh-**koot** / **kald** . . . **swa**-re / **vint**
Is it raining?	**Plouă?**	**Plo**-wuh
Is it snowing?	**Ninge?**	**Nin**-je
How will the weather be tomorrow?	**Cum o să fie vremea mâine?**	**Koom** o suh **fee**-ye **vre**-mea **mîi**-ne
It will be clear. . . . cloudy . . . cool . . . frosty . . . foggy	**O sa fie senin.** **. . . înnorat** **. . . răcoare** **. . . îngheţ** **. . . ceaţă**	O suh **fee**-ye se-**nin** . . . m-no-**rat** . . . ruh-**kwa**-re . . . in-**gets** . . . **chea**-tsuh
It's spring. . . . summer . . . autumn . . . winter	**E primavară.** **. . . vară** **. . . toamnă** **. . . iarnă**	Ye pri-muh-**va**-ruh . . . **va**-ruh . . . **twam**-nuh . . . **yar**-nuh
MONTHS OF THE YEAR	***LUNILE ANULUI***	
January	**ianuarie**	ya-nwa-rye
February	**februarie**	fe-brwa-rye
March	**martie**	mar-tye
April	**aprilie**	a-pri-lye
May	**mai**	may
June	**iunie**	yu-ny
July	**iulie**	yu-lye
August	**august**	augoost
September	**septembrie**	sep-tem-brye
October	**octombrie**	ok-tom-brye
November	**noiembrie**	no-yem-bry
December	**decembrie**	de-chem-brye

What is the date today?	**Ce dată e azi?**	Che **da**-tuh ye **az**'
It is the sixth of May	**E şase mai.**	Ye **sha**-se may
How old are you?	**Ce vârstă aveţi?**	Che **virs**-tuh a-**vets**'
I'm 33 years old.	**Am treizece şi trei de ani.**	Am **trey**-zech' shi **trey** de an'
NUMBERS	***NUMERE***	
zero	**zero**	**ze**-ro
one	**unu**	**oo**-noo
two	**doi**	**doy**
three	**trei**	**trey**
four	**patru**	**pa**-troo
five	**cinci**	**chinch'**
six	**şase**	**sha**-se
seven	**şapte**	**shap**-te
eight	**opt**	**opt**
nine	**nouă**	**no**-wuh
ten	**zece**	**ze**-che
eleven	**unsprezece**	**oon**-spre-ze-che
twelve	**doisprezece**	**doy** -spre-ze-che
thirteen	**treisprezece**	**trey** -spre-ze-che
fourteen	**paisprezece**	**pay**-spre-ze-che
fifteen	**cincisprezece**	**chinch** '-spre-ze-che
sixteen	**şaisprezece**	**shay**-spre-ze-che
seventeen	**şaptesprezece**	**shap**-te-spre-ze-che
eighteen	**optsprezece**	**opt**-spre-ze-che
nineteen	**nouăsprezece**	**no**-wuh-spre-ze-che
twenty	**douăzeci**	do-wuh **zech**'

twenty-one	**douăzeci şi unu**	do-wuh-**zech'** shi **oo**-noo
twenty-two	**douăzeci şi doi**	do-wuh-zech' shi **doy**
thirty	**treizeci**	trey-**zech'**
forty	**patruzeci**	pa-troo- **zech'**
fifty	**cincizeci**	chinch'- **zech'**
sixty	**şaizeci**	shay- **zech'**
seventy	**şaptezeci**	shap-te- **zech'**
eighty	**optzeci**	oot-**zech'**
ninety	**nouăsprezece**	no-whu-**zech**
one hundred	**o sută**	o **soo**-tuh
two hundred	**două sute**	**do**-wuh **soo**-te
the first one the second one the third one the fourth one	**primul** **al doilea** **al treilea** **al patrulea**	pri-**mool** al **do**-i-lea al **tre**-i-lea al **pa**-troo-lea
once	**odată**	o **da**-tuh
twice	**de două ori**	de **do**-wuh **or'**
ten percent	**zece la sută**	**ze**-che la **soo**-tuh

TIME	***ORA***	
What time is it?	**Cât e ceasul?**	**Kit** ye **chea**-sool
It's one o'clock.	**E unu fix.**	Ye **oo**-noo **fix**
It's ten to five.	**E cinci fărăz ece.**	Ye **chinch**' fuh-ruh **ze**-che
It's a quarter past nine.	**E nouă şi un sfert.**	Ye **no**-wuh shi oon **sfert**
It's half past one.	**E unu si jumatate.**	Ye **oo**-noo shi zhoo-muh-**ta**-te
a second	**o secundă**	o se-**koon**-duh
two seconds	**două secunde**	d**o**-wuh se-**koon**-de
a minute	**un minut**	oon mi-**noot**
five minutes	**Cinci minute**	**chinch**' mi-**noo**-te
an hour	**O ora**	o **o**-ruh
three hours	**trei ore**	**trey o**-re
It is early . . . late	**E devreme** **. . . târziu**	Ye de-**vre**-me . . . tîr-**ziu**
I leave today. . . .tomorrow . . .the day after tomorrow . . .this week . . .next week	**Plec azi.** **. . . mâine** **. . . poimâine** **. . . săptămâna asta** **. . . săptămâna viitoare**	**Plek** az' . . . **mîi**-ne . . . **poy**-mîi-ne . . . suhp-tuh-**mî**-na **as**-ta . . . suhp-tuh-**mî**-na vi-i-**twa**-re
I arrived yesterday. . . . the day before yesterday . . .last week	**Am ajuns ieri.** **. . . alaltăieri** **. . . săptămâna trecută**	Am a-zhoons **yer**' . . . a-lal-tuh-yer' . . . suhp-tuh-**mi**-na tre-**koo**-tuh
Shall we meet . . . at noon? . . . at midnight . . . tomorrow at ten . . . this evening . . . tonight . . . in the afternoon	**Să ne întâlnim** **. . . la prânz?** **. . . la miezul nopţii** **. . . mâine la zece** **. . . în seara asta** **. . . deseară** **. . . după masă**	Suh ne îin-tîl-**nim** . . . la **prînz** . . . la **mye**-zool **nop**-tsiy . . . **mîi**-ne la zece . . . în **sea**-ra **as**-ta . . . di-**sea**-ruh . . . **doo**-puh **ma**-suh

DAYS OF THE WEEK	***ZILELE SĂPTĂMÂNII***	
Monday Tuesday Wednesday Thursday Friday Saturday Sunday	**luni** **marţi** **miercuri** **joi** **vineri** **sâmbătă** **duminică**	**loon'** **marts'** myer-**koor'** **zho'** **vi**-ner' **sîm**-buh-tuh doo-**mi**-ni-kuh
everyday	**în fiecare zi**	in **fi**-e-ka-re **zi**
PERSONAL COMFORT	***COMFORT PERSONAL***	
What's the matter?	**Ce s-a întâmplat?**	**Che** sa în-tîm-**plat**
Are you feeling well?	**Vă simţiţi bine?**	Vuh sim-**tsits' bi**-ne
I'm <u>cold</u>. . . . hot . . . hungry . . . thirsty	**Mi-e frig.** **. . . cald** **. . . foame** **. . . sete**	Mye **frig** . . . **kald** . . . **fwa**-me . . . **se**-te
I'm fine. . . . angry (male) (female) . . . happy (male) (female) . . . sad (male) (female) . . . tired (male) (female)	**Sunt bine.** **. . . supărat** **. . . supărată** **. . . fericit** **. . . fericită** **. . . trist** **. . . tristă** **. . . obosit** **. . . obosită**	Sint **bi**-ne . . . soo-puh-**rat** . . . soo-puh-**ra**-tuh . . . fe-ri-**chit** . . . fe-ri-**chit**-tuh . . . **trist** . . . **tris**-tuh . . . o-bo **sit** . . . o-bo-**si**-tuh
Please leave me alone.	**Vă rog, lăsaţi-mă-n pace.**	Vuh **rog**, luh-**sa**-tsi-muhn **pa**-che

AT THE HOTEL	***LA HOTEL***	
I have a reservation.	**Am o rezervare.**	**Am** o re-zer-**va**-re
Do you have a double room? . . . single	**Aveţi o cameră pentru două persoane?** **. . . o persoană**	A-**vets** o **ka**-me-ruh **pen**-troo **do**-wuh per-**swa**-ne . . . o per-**swa**-nuh
Do you have a room with a bath? . . . a shower . . . air conditioning . . . twin beds	**Aveţi o cameră cu baie?** **. . . duş** **. . . aer condiţionat** **. . . două paturi**	A-**vets** o **ka**-me-ruh cu **ba**-ye . . . **doosh** . . . **a**-er kon-di-tsyo-**nat** . . . **do**-wuh **pa**-toor'
What is the rate per day?	**Cât costă pe zi?**	**Kit kos**-tuh pe **zi**
Is breakfast included?	**Micul dejun e inclus?**	**Mic** de-**jun** ye in-**kloo**-suh
I'll be staying four nights.	**Stau patru nopţi.**	**Stau pa**-troo **nopts'**
Is there a better room? . . . cheaper . . . larger . . . smaller . . . quieter	**Aveţi o cameră mai bună?** **. . . ieftină** **. . . mare** **. . . mică** **. . . liniştită**	A-**vets'** o **ka**-me-ruh may **boo**-na . . . **yef**-ti-nuh . . . **ma**-re . . . **mi**-kuh . . . li-nish-**ti**-tuh
Your name, please? . . . address	**Numele dumneavoastră, vă rog?** **Adresa . . .**	**Noo**-me-le doom-nea-**vwas**-truh, vuh-**rog** A-**dre**-sa . . .
Please wake me up at 6 am.	**Vă rog, treziţi-mă la şase dimineaţa.**	Vuh **rog**, tre-**zi**-tsi-muh la **sha**-se di-mi-**nea**-tsa
The key to my room, please.	**Cheia camerei, vă rog.**	**Ke**-ya **ka**-me-rey, vuh **rog**
On what floor is my room?	**La ce etaj e camera mea?**	La **che** e-**tazh** ye ka-**me**-ra **mea**
Take the elevator.	**Luaţi liftul.**	**Lwats' lif**-tool
Go up the stairs. . . . down	**Urcaţi pe scări.** **Coborâţi . . .**	Oor-**kats'** pe **skuhr'** Ko-bo-**rîts'** . . .
There is no hot water.	**Nu e apă caldă.**	**Noo** ye **a**-puh **kal**-duh

I need ice, please. . . . another blanket . . . an electric fan . . . a heater . . . an iron . . . a light bulb . . . a pillow . . . shampoo . . . soap . . . toilet paper . . . a towel	**Am nevoie de gheaţă, vă rog.** **. . . încă o pătură** **. . . un ventilator** **. . . un reşou** **. . . un fier de călcat** **. . . un bec** **. . . o pernă** **. . . şampon** **. . . săpun** **. . . hârtie igienică** **. . . un prosop**	Am ne-vo-ye de **gea**-tsuh, vuh rog . . . **in**-kuh o **puh**-too-ruh . . . oon ven-ti-la-**tor** . . . oon re-**shoh** . . . oon **fyer** de kuhl-**kat** . . . oon **bek** . . . o **per**-nuh . . . sham-**pon** . . . suh-**poon** . . . hîr-**tee**-ye i-ji-**e**-ni-kuh . . . oon pro-**sop**
At what time is breakfast served?	**La ce oră se serveşte micul dejun?**	La **che o**-ruh se ser-**vesh**-te mi-**kool** de-**zhoon**
Where is the dry cleaner?	**Unde e curăţătoria chimică?**	**Oon**-de ye koo-ruh-tsuh-to-**ree**-ya **ki**-mi-kuh
When will the clothes be ready?	**Când sunt gata hainele?**	**Kind** sint **ga**-ta **hay**-ne-le
I'm leaving today.	**Plec astăzi.**	**Plek as**-tuhz'
I shall return tomorrow.	**Mă întorc mâine.**	Muh în-**tork mîi**-ne
I wish to speak to the manager.	**Aş vrea să vorbesc cu şeful.**	Ash **vrea** suh vor-**besk** koo **chef**-ool
Please call a taxi.	**Vă rog, chemaţi-mi un taxi.**	Vuh **rog**, ke-**ma**-tsim'oon ta-**xi**

ENTERTAINMENT	***AGREMENT***	
Would you like to see the town?	**Doriţi să vedeţi oraşul?**	Do-**rits'** suh ve-**dets'** o-ra-**shool**
I would like to go to the pool. . . . beach . . . mountains . . . sea . . . country	**Aş vrea să merg la piscină.** **. . . plajă** **. . . munte** **. . . mare** **. . . ţară**	Ash **vrea** suh **merg** la pis-**chi**-nuh . . . **pla**-zhuh . . . **moon**-te . . . **ma**-re . . . **tsa**-ruh
Would you be kind enough to take a photo of us? (to a male) (to a female)	**Sunteţi amabil să ne faceţi o fotografie?** **Sunteţi amabilă să ne faceţi o fotografie?**	Sîn-**tets'** a-ma-**bil** suh ne **fa**-chets' o fo-to-gra-**fee**-ye Sîn-**tets'** a-ma-**bi**-luh suh ne **fa**-chets' o fo-to-gra-**fee**-ye
We'd like to see a traditional dance. . . . village festival	**Am vrea să vedem un dans tradiţional.** **. . . festival sătesc**	Am **vrea** suh ve-**dem** oon **dans** tra-di-tsyo-**nal** . . . **şat** fes-ti-**val**
A ticket for the ballet, please. . . . opera concert	**Un bilet la balet, vă rog.** **. . . operă**	Oon bi-**let** la ba-**let**, vuh **rog** . . . **o**-pe-ruh kon-**chert**
There are no tickets left.	**Nu mai avem bilete.**	Noo may a-vem bi-le-te.
I like to go to the theater. . . . movies . . . museum	**Îmi place să merg la teatru.** **. . . film** **. . . muzeu**	Îm' **pla**-che suh **merg** la **tea**-tru . . . film . . . moo-zeu
At what time does the play begin? . . . film tour	**La ce oră începe piesa?** **. . . filmul**	La **che o**-ruh în-**che**-pe **pye**-sa . . . **fil**-mool **too**-rool
What film is playing tonight?	**Ce film e în seara asta?**	**Che** film **ye** în **sea**-ra **as**-ta
Where is the ticket office?	**Unde e casa de bilete?**	**Oon**-de ye **ka**-sa de bi-**le**-te
I'd like two tickets, please.	**Aş vrea două bilete, vă rog.**	Ash **vrea do**-wuh bi-**le**-te, vuh **rog**

Is there a night club nearby? . . . a discoteque	**Există un bar de noapte în apropiere?** **. . . o discotecă**	E-**xis**-tuh oon **bar** de **nwap**-te pe a-**prwa**-pe . . . o dis-ko-**te**-kuh
AT A RESTAURANT	***LA RESTAURANT***	
Could you recommend a good restaurant? . . . an inexpensive restaurant . . . a traditional restaurant	**Îmi puteţi recomanda un restaurant bun?** **. . . un restaurant convenabil** **. . . un restaurant tradiţional**	Im' poo-**tets'** re-ko-**man**-da oon res-ta-**oo**-rant **boon** . . . res-**ta-oo**-rant kon-**ve**-na-**bil** . . . oon res-**ta-oo**-rant tra-**di**-tsyo-**nal**
I prefer to sit in the non-smoking area. . . . by the window	**Prefer să stau în secţia pentru nefumători.** **. . . la fereastră**	Pre-**fer** suh **stau** in **sek**-tsya **pen**-troo ne-**foo**-muh-**tor'** . . . la fe-**reas**-truh
I'm on a diet.	**Sunt la regim.**	**Sînt** la **re**-jim
Do you have anything without meat?	**Aveţi ceva fără carne?**	A-vets' **che**-va fuh-ruh **kar**-ne
May I see the menu? . . . wine list	**Pot vedea meniul?** **. . . lista de vinuri**	Pot ve-**dea meni**-ool . . . lis-ta de vi-noor'
I'd like to order this.	**Aş vrea să comand acesta.**	Ahsh **vray**-ah suh cah-**mahnd** a-**ches**-tah
Some butter, please.	**Vă rog, nişte unt**.	Vuh rog, nişte unt
A bottle of this wine, please.	**O sticlă din vinul acesta, vă rog.**	O **sti**-kluh din **vi**-nool a-**ches**-ta, vuh **rog**
Please bring me a knife. . . . a fork	**Vă rog, aduceţi-mi un cuţit.** **. . . o furculiţă**	Vuh **rog**, a-doo-**che**-ts im' oon **koo**-tsit . . . o **foor**-koo-**li**-tsuh
Coffee with milk, please.	**Vuh rog, o cafea cu lapte.**	Vuh **rog**, o ka-**fe** koo **lap**-tuh
a Turkish coffee	**o cafea turcească**	o ka-**fea** toor-**cheas**-kuh
an instant coffee	**un nes**	oon **nes**
Some tea, please. . . . with lemon	**Vă rog, un ceai** **. . . cu lămîie**	Vuh **rog**, un **chie** . . . koo **luh**-mwy

Do you like lemonade? . . . fruit juice . . . red wine . . . white wine	**Vă place limonada?** **. . . sucul de fructe** **. . . vinul roşu** **. . . vinul alb**	Vuh **pla**-che **li**-mo-**na**-da . . . **soo**-kul de **frook**-te . . . **vi**-nool **ro**-shoo . . . **vi**-nool **alb**
The check, please.	**Vă rog, nota de plată.**	Vuh **rog**, **no**-tuh de **plah**-tuh
Thank you.	**Mulţumesc.**	Mool-tsoo-**mesk**
FOOD AND DRINK	***MÂNCARE şi BĂUTURI***	
Where's the market place? . . . the food store . . . the bakery	**Unde e piaţa?** **. . . alimentara** **. . . magazinul de pâine**	**Oon**-de ye **pya**-tsa . . . a-li-men-**ta**-ra . . . ma-ga-**zi**-nool de **pîi**-ne
Where can I buy. . . ?	**De unde pot cumpăra. . . ?**	De **oon**-de pot koom-**puh**-ra. . .
Fruit	***Fructe***	**frook-te**
. . . apple	**. . . mere**	. . . **me**-re
. . . apricot	**. . . caise**	. . . kaes
. . . banana	**. . . banane**	. . . ba-**na**-ne
. . . cherries	**. . . cireşe**	. . . chi-**re**-she
. . . grapes	**. . . struguri**	. . . **stroo**-gur'
. . . lemons	**. . . lămâi**	. . . luh-**mîi**
. . . olives	**. . . măsline**	. . . muhs-**li**-ne
. . . melons	**. . . pepeni**	. . . **pe**-pen'
. . . oranges	**. . . portocale**	. . . pr-to-**ka**-le
. . . peaches	**. . . piersici**	. . . **pyer**-sich'
. . . pears	**. . . pere**	. . . **pe**-re
. . . plums	**. . . prune**	. . . **proo**-ne
. . . raisins	**. . . stafide**	. . . sta-**fi**-de
. . . raspberries	**. . . zmeură**	. . . **zme**-oo-ruh
. . . strawberries	**. . . căpşuni**	. . . kuhp-**shoon'**
. . . watermelons	**. . . pepeni verzi**	. . . **pe**-pen' **verz'**

I would like meat.	**Aş vrea carne.**	Ash vrea **kar**-ne
. . . beef	**. . . carne de vacă**	. . . **kar**-ne de **va**-că
. . . chicken	**. . . carne de pui**	. . . **kar**-ne de **pui**
. . . ham	**. . . şuncă**	. . . **shoon**-kuh
. . . lamb	**. . . carne de miel**	. . . **kar**-ne de **myel**
. . . pork	**. . . carne de porc**	. . . **kar**-ne de **pork**
. . . salami	**. . . salam**	. . . sa-**lam**
. . . sausages	**. . . cârnaţi , mezeluri**	. . . **kîr**-nats' meh-zuh-**loo**-ree
. . .stuffed cabbage rolls	**. . . sarmale**	. . . sar-**ma**-le
. . . skinless sausages	**. . . mititiei**	. . . **mee**-tee-tsey
. . . veal	**. . . carne de vit**	. . . **kar**-ne de vi-**tsel**
I like fish and seafood.	**Îmi plac peştele şi moluştele.**	îm' **plak pesh**-te-le şi mo-loosh-te-le
. . . anchovies	**. . . ansoa**	. . . an-**shwa**
. . . carp	**. . . crap**	. . . **kra**-pool
. . . crab	**. . . racii**	. . . **ra**-chiy
. . . salmon	**. . . somonul**	. . . so-**mo**-nool
. . . shrimp	**. . . creveţii**	. . . kre-**ve**-tsiy
I prefer . . .	**Prefer . . .**	Pre-**fer** . . .
Vegetables	***Legume***	. . . le-**goo**-me
. . . asparagus	**. . . sparanghel**	
. . . beans	**. . . fasole**	. . . fa-**so**-le
. . . cabbage	**. . . varză**	. . . **var**-zuh
. . . carrots	**. . . morcovi**	. . . **mor**-kov'
. . . cauliflower	**. . . conopidă**	. . . ko-no-**pi**-duh
. . . celery	**. . . ţelină**	. . . tse-**lee**-ne

. . . cucumbers	**. . . castraveţi**	. . . kas-tra-**vets**
. . . eggplant	**. . . vinete**	. . . **vi**-ne-te
. . . garlic	**. . . usturoi**	. . . oos-too-**roy**
. . . green beans	**. . . fasole verde**	. . . fa-**so**-le **var**-de
. . . leeks	**. . . praz**	. . . **praz**
. . . lettuce	**. . . salată**	. . . sa-**la**-tuh
. . . mushrooms	**. . . ciuperci**	. . . chyu-**perch**'
. . . onion	**. . . ceapă**	. . . **chea**-puh
. . . peas	**. . . mazăre**	. . . **ma**-zuh-re
. . . peppers	**. . . ardei**	. . . ar-**dey**
. . . potatoes	**. . . cartofi**	. . . kar-**tof**
. . . radishes	**. . . radichi**	. . . ri-**dik**
. . . spinach	**. . . spanac**	. . . spa-**nak**
. . . tomatoes	**. . . roşii**	. . . **ro**-shiy
Dairy		
butter	**unt**	unt
ice cream	**îngheţată**	yin-geh-**ta**-tzuh
sour cream	**smântână**	**smen**-ti-na
milk	**lapte**	**lahp**-tah
yogurt	**iaurt**	**yaort**
Eggs	***Ouă***	
. . . boiled	. . . **fierte**	. . . **fyer**-the
. . . scrambled	. . . **jumări**	. . . yu-**ma**-ree
. . . fried	. . . **prăjite**	. . . prah-**jee**-teh
omelet	**omletă**	om-**let**-tah

Miscellaneous	***Diverse***	
bread	**pâine**	**pui**-neh
ice	**gheaţă**	**ga**-ta
rice	**orez**	**o**-rez
pancake	**plăcintă**	pluh-**chin**-tuh
soup	**supă/ciorbă**	**zu**-puh / **chor**-ba
cheese	**brânză/caşcaval**	**brin**-za / kah-ska-**vul**
Condiments	***Condimente***	
catsup / ketchup	**ketchup**	**ket**-chup
mustard	**muştar**	**moo**-shtar
oil	**ulei**	**oo**-lee
pepper	**piper**	**pih**-pair
salt	**sare**	**sah**-ray
vinegar	**oţet**	**o**-tset
Sweets	***Dulciuri***	
cake	**tort**	**tort**
donut	**gogoşi**	go-**gosh**
candy	**bomboane**	bom-**bwon**-e
honey	**miere**	mi-**her**-e
chocolate	**ciocolată**	chock-o-**lah**-tuh
jam	**gem**	**jem**
cookie	**biscuiţi**	bis-**kwi**-te
pastry	**prăjitură**	pra-ji-**too**-ruh
crepe	**clatite**	klah-**tit**
sugar	**zahăr**	zah-**har**

Drinks	***Băuturi***	
Cheers!	**Noroc!**	**Nor**-auk
To health!	**Sănătate!**	**Sah**-nuh-**tah**-teh
coffee	**cafea**	kah-**fey**-uh
. . . with milk	**. . . cu lapte**	**. . . koo lahp**-tah
. . . without sugar	**. . . fără zahăr**	**. . . fah**-ruh zah-**har**
tea	**ceai**	**chei**
mineral water	**apa minerală**	**ah**-puh mi-ner-**ah**-luh
fruit juice	**suc de fructe**	**sook** de **frook**-teh
milk	**lapte**	**lahp**-tah
lemonade	**limonadă**	**lee**-mon-**ah**-duh
A bottle of ...	**o sticlă ...**	o **stik**-luh . . .
. . . red wine	. . . **vin roşu**	. . . **vin** ro-**shoo**
. . . white wine	. . . **vin alb**	. . . **vin alb**
. . . beer	. . . **bere**	. . . **beh**-reh
a wine glass	**o pahar de vin**	o pah-**har** de **vin**
a plate	**o farfurie**	o **far-foo**-ry
a cup	**o ceaşcă**	o **chesh**-kuh
a bowl	**o castron**	o kas-**tron**
a bottle	**o sticlă**	o **stik**-luh
Tableware		
a fork	**o furculiţă**	o **foor**-ku-**li**-tsuh
a napkin	**un şervetel**	un **sher**-ve-**tel**
a teaspoon	**o linguriţă**	o **ling**-oo-**ri**-tsuh
a water glass	**pahar de apă**	o pah-**har** de **ah**-puh
a spoon	**o lingură**	o **ling-oo**-ruh

SHOPPING	***LA CUMPĂRĂTURI***	
Excuse me . . .	**Scuzaţi-mă . . .**	Skoo-**za**-tsi **ma** . . .
I'd like a dozen eggs.	**Aş vrea douăsprezece ouă.**	Ash **vrea do**-wuh-spre-**ze**-che **o**-wuh
Where can I buy . . .	**De unde pot cumpăra . . .**	De **oon**-de pot koom-**puh**-ra . . .
. . . souvenirs?	**. . . suveniruri?**	. . . soo-ve-**ni**-roor'
. . . camera film	**. . . film foto**	. . . film **fo**-to
. . . magazines	**. . . reviste**	. . . re-vis-te
. . . an English newspaper	**. . . un ziar englezesc**	. . . oon **zi**-ar en-gle-**zesk**
I am going to the . . .	**Mă duc la . . .**	Muh **dook** la . . .
. . . pharmacy.	**. . . farmacie.**	. . . **far**-ma-chee-ye
. . . bookstore	**. . . librărie**	. . . li-**bruh**-ree-ye
. . . florist	**. . . florărie**	. . . flo-**ruh**-ree-ye
. . . stationer's	**. . . papetărie**	. . . pa-pe-**tuh**-ree-ye
. . . department store	**. . . magazinul universal**	. . . ma-ga-**zi**-nool oo-ni-**ver**-sal
I need to buy . . .	**Trebuie să cumpăr . . .**	Tre-**boo**-ye suh koom-**puhr** . . .
Have you any. . . ?	**Aveţi. . . ?**	Ah-**vetz** . . .
I'd like to buy . . .	**Aş vrea să cumpăr . . .**	Ash **vrea** suh koom-**puhr** . . .
. . . a Romanian blouse.	**. . .o bluză românească.**	. . . o **bloo**-zuh ro-ma-**neas**-kuh
. . . craft items	**. . .obiecte de artizanat**	. . . o-**byek**-te de ar-**ti**-za-**nat**
Do you like it?	**Vă place?**	Vuh **pla-che**
A little / A lot	**Puţin / Mult**	Pu-**tzin** / **Moolt**
It's beautiful.	**E frumos.**	Ye froo-**mos**
It's fine.	**E bine.**	Ye **bee**-nay
How much does it cost?	**Cât costă?**	Kit **kos**-tuh
It costs too much.	**Costă prea mult.**	Kos-ta **pray**-a moolt

I bought a pair of pants. . . . a jacket . . . a shirt . . . a sweater . . . a skirt . . . a coat . . . a bathing suit . . . a pair of shoes	**Am cumpărat o pereche de pantaloni.** **. . . o jachetă** **. . . o cămaşă** **. . . un pulover** **. . . o fusta** **. . . un palton** **. . . un costum de ba**ie **. . . o pereche de pantofi**	Am **koom**-puh-**rat** o pe-**re**-ke de pan-ta-**lon** . . . o zha-**ke**-tuh . . . o kuh-**ma**-shuh . . . oon **poo**-lo-ver . . . o **foos**-tuh . . . oon **pal**-ton . . . oon **kos**-toom de **ba**-ye . . . o pe-**re**-ke de **pan**-tof
I like this color.	**Îmi place culoarea asta.**	Îm' **pla**-che koo-**lwa**-rea **as**-ta
COLORS	***CULORI***	
What color is it?	**Ce culoare e?**	**Che** koo-**lwa**-re **ye**
It is black.	**E negru / neagră.**	Ye **ne**-gru / **ne**-gruh
blue brown gray green pink purple red white yellow	**albastru / albastră** **maro** **gri** **verde** **roz** **mov** **roşu / roşie** **alb / albă** **galben / galbenă**	al-**bas**-troo / al-**bas**-truh ma-**ro** **gri** **ver**-de **roz** **mov** **ro**-shoo / **ro**-shee **alb** / **al**-buh **gal**-ben / gal-**be**-nuh

MONEY	***BANI***	
Do you accept traveler's checks? this credit card?	**Acceptaţi cecuri de călătorie?** **cartea asta de credit?**	Ak-chep-**tats' che**-koor' de kuh-luh-to-**ri**-ye . . . **kar**-tea **as**-ta de **kre**-it
Where is the foreign currency exchange? . . . the bank	**Unde e biroul de schimb valutar?** **. . . banca**	**Oon**-de ye bi-ro-**ool** de **skimb** va-loo-**tar** . . . **ban**-ka
What is today's exchange rate?	**Care e cursul de schimb astăzi?**	**Ka**-re ye **koor**-sool de **skimb as**-tuhz'
Please change this to lei.	**Schimbaţi-mi în lei, vă rog.**	Skim-**bats** 'm in lay, vuh-**rog**
THE POST OFFICE	***LA POŞTĂ***	
Can I have money wired to me here?	**Se pot primi bani telegrafic?**	Se pot pri-**mi ban'** te-le-**gra**-fik
I'd like stamps, please. . . . air letters . . . post cards . . . an envelope	**Aş nişte vrea timbre, vă rog.** **. . . plicuri par avion** **. . . vederi** **. . . un plic**	Ash **vrea tim**-bre, vuh **rog** . . . **pli**-koor' par a-vi-**on** . . . ve-**der'** . . . oon **plik**
I want to send this registered mail. . . . air mail . . . parcel post . . . first class	**Vreau să trimit o recomandată.** **. . . plicuri par avion** **. . . un colet poştal** **. . . cu avionul**	Vryau suh tri-**mit** o re-ko-man-**da**-tuh . . . **pli**-koor par a-vi-**on** . . . oon ko-**let** posh-**tal** . . . koo a-vi-**o**-nool
I want to send money.	**Vreau să trimit bani.**	**Vryau** suh tri-**mit ban'**
When will it arrive?	**Când ajunge?**	**Kind** a-**zhoon**-je
How much is the postage?	**Cât costă expedierea?**	Kit **kos**-tuh ex-pe-di-**e**-rea
Where is the mail box?	**Unde e cutia poştală?**	**Oon**-de ye koo-**ti**-ya posh-**ta**-luh
When will the mailman arrive?	**Când vine poştaşul?**	**Kind** vi-ne posh-**ta**-shool

Is there any mail for me?	**Aveţi corespondenţă pentru mine?**	A-**vets'** che-va **posh**-tuh **pen**-troo **mi**-ne?
This contains food. . . . printed matter . . . fragile material	**Conţine alimente.** **. . . text tipărit** **. . . obiecte fragile**	Kon-**tsi**-ne a-li-**men**-te. . . . **text** ti-puh-rit . . . o-**byek**-te fra-ji-le
AT WORK	***LA SERVICIU***	
Where can I make a photocopy?	**Unde pot să fac o copie?**	**Oon**-de **pot** suh **fak** o **ko**-pye
Can I use the computer? . . . fax machine	**Pot folosi computerul?** **. . . faxul**	**Pot** fo-lo-**si** kom-**pyu**-te-rool . . . **fa**-xool
How much do you charge per page?	**Cât costă pagina?**	**Kit kos**-tuh **pa**-ji-na?
ON THE TELPHONE	***LA TELEFON***	
May I use the telephone?	**Pot să dau un telefon?**	**Pot** suh **dau** oon te-le-**fon**
Where is the phone directory?	**Unde e cartea de telefoane?**	**Oon**-de ye **kar**-tea de te-le-**fon**?
I'd like to make . . . a collect call. . . . an international call	**Aş vrea o convorbire** **. . . cu taxă inversă.** **. . . cu străinătatea**	Ash **vrea** o kon-vor-**bi-re** . . . koo **ta**-xuh in-**ver**-suh . . . koo struh-i-nuh-**ta**-tea
What is the code for Bucharest?	**Care este codul pentru Bucureşti?**	**Ka**-re **yes**-te **ko**-dool **pen**-troo Boo-koo-**resht'**
The line is busy.	**Sună ocupat.**	**Soo**-nuh o-koo-**pat**
Hello (*used only on the phone*)	**Alo.**	A-**lo**
Who's speaking?	**Cine e la telefon?**	**Chi**-ne ye la te-le-**fon**
Could I leave a message?	**Pot lăsa un mesaj?**	Pot **luh**-sa oon me-**sazh**

TRANSPORTATION	***CĂLĂTORIE***	
Have a good trip!	**Drum bun!**	Droom **boon**!
Where is the . . . ? . . . metro station . . . train station . . . bus stop . . . ticket office . . . information desk . . . exit to the street	**Unde e . . . ?** **. . .staţia de metrou** **. . . gara** **. . . staţia de autobuz** **. . . casa de bilete** **. . . biroul de informaţii** **. . . ieşirea spre stradă**	**Oon**-de ye . . . . . . **sta**-tsya de **me**-troh . . . **ga**-ra . . . **sta**-tsya de a-oo-to-**booz** . . . **ka**-sa de bi-**le**-te? . . . bi-**ro**-ool de in-for-**ma**-tsiy . . . ye-**shi**-rea spre **stra**-duh
I need a porter.	**Am nevoie de un hamal.**	Am ne-**vo**-ye de oon **ha**-mal
I'd like a schedule, please.	**Aş vrea un orar, vă rog.**	Ash **vrea** oon o-**rar**, **vuh** rog
How much is a . . . ticket? one-way round-trip first-class second-class tourist-class	**Cât costă un bilet, . . . ?** **dus** **dus şi întors** **la clasa întâi** **la clasa a doua** **la clasa turist**	**Kit kos**-tuh oon bi-**let**, . . . **doos** **doos** shi în-**tors** la **kla**-sa yn-**tyi** la **kla**-sa a **do**-wa la **kla**-sa too-**rist**
Is there a special . . . rate? . . . mid-week . . . weekend . . . high-school students . . . college students . . . senior-citizens	**Există tarif redus pentru . . . ?** **. . . mijlocul săptămânii** **. . . weekend** **. . . elevi** **. . . studenţi** **. . . pensionari**	E-**xis**-tuh ta-**rif** re-**doos pen**-tru . . . . . . **mizh**-lo-kool suhp-tuh-**mi**-niy . . . **wik**-end . . . e-**lev**' . . . stoo-**dents**' . . . pen-syo-**nar**'
Smoking or non-smoking?	**Fumători sau nefumători?**	Foo-muh-**tor**' sau **ne**-foo-muh-**tor**'

TRAIN TRAVEL	***CU TRENUL***	
Is there a . . . ? . . . dining car . . . sleeping car	**Există . . . ?** **. . .vagon-restaurant** **. . .vagon de dormit**	E-**xis**-tuh . . . . . . va-**gon** res-ta-oo-**rant** . . . va-**gon** de dor-**mit**
At what time does the train leave for lasi?	**La ce oră pleacă trenul spre Iaşi?**	La **che o**-ruh **plea**-kuh **tre**-nool spre **Yash**'
At what time does the train get to Sibiu?	**La ce oră ajunge trenul la Sibiu?**	La **che o**-ruh a-**zhoon**-je **tre**-nool la Si-**biu**
Is it on time?	**Ajunge la timp?**	A-zhoon-je la timp
Does this train go to Timişoara?	**Trenul ăsta merge la Timişoara?**	**Tre**-nool **uhs**-ta **mer**-je la Ti-mi-**shwa**-ra
What is this place called?	**Ce localitate e asta?**	**Che** lo-ka-li-**ta**-te ye **as**-ta
How long do we stop here?	**Cât ne oprim aici?**	**Kit** ne o-**prim** a-**ich**
AT THE AIRPORT	***LA AEROPORT***	
Which gate must I go to for . . . flights? . . . domestic . . . international	**Care e poarta pentru zboruri** **. . . interne?** **. . . internaţionale**	**Ka**-re ye **pwar**-ta **pen**-troo **zbo**-roor' . . . . . . in-**ter**-ne . . . in-ter-**na**-tsyo-**na**-le
How long will the flight to Sibiu be delayed?	**Cu ce întârziere pleacă avionul de Sibiu?**	**Koo** che in-**tir**-zi-e-re **plea**-kuh **a**-vi-o-nul de Si-**yu**
Please call the flight attendant.(male) (female)	**Vă rog, chemaţi . . .** **stewardul.** **stewardesa**	Vuh **rog**, ke-**mats**' . . . styu-**ar**-dool styu-ar-**de**-sa
AT CUSTOMS	***LA VAMĂ***	
Here is my passport.	**Poftiţi paşaportul.**	Pof-**tits**' pa-sha-**por**-tool
This is my luggage.	**Acesta e bagajul meu.**	A-**ches**-ta ye ba-**ga**-zhool meu
This is my . . . . . . suitcase. . . . briefcase . . . handbag	**Aceasta e . . . mea.** **. . . valiza** **. . . servieta** **. . . sacoşa**	A-**cheas**-ta ye . . . mea . . . va-**li**-za . . . ser-**vye**-ta . . . sa-**ko**-sha

Do you have anything to declare?	**Aveţi ceva de declarat?**	A-**vets'** che-**va** de de-kla-**rat**
I have nothing to declare.	**Nu am nimic de declarat.**	**Nu** am ni-**mik** de de-kla-**rat**
I have some . . . . perfume . . . cigarettes . . . personal belongings . . . a gift	**Am nişte . . . .** **. . . parfum** **. . . ţigari** **. . . obiecte personale** **. . . un cadou**	Am **nish**-te . . . . par-**foom** . . . tsi-**guhr'** . . . o-**byek**-te per-so-**na**-le . . . oon ka-**doh**
IN THE CAR	***CU MAŞINA***	
Where can I rent a car?	**Unde pot închiria o maşină?**	**Oon**-de pot in-**ki**-rya o ma-**shi**-nuh
Do you know the road to Brasov?	**Ştiţi drumul spre Braşov?**	**Shtiu droo**-mool spre **Bra**-shov
Is the road good? . . . bad	**Drumul e bun?** **. . . prost**	**Droo**-mool ye **boon** . . . **prost**
Which town does this road lead to?	**Spre ce oraş duce drumul ăsta?**	Spre **che o**-rash **doo**-che **droo**-mool **uhs**-ta
How many kilometers is it to Cluj?	**Câţi kilometri sunt până la Cluj?**	**Kits'** ki-lo-**me**-tri sint **pi**-nuh la **Kloozh**
Could you direct me . . . ? . . . to the next town . . . to the highway . . . to the parking lot	**Cum se ajunge . . . ?** **. . . în următorul oraş** **. . . pe autostradă** **. . . la parcare**	**Koom** se a-**zhoon**-je . . . . . . in oor-muh-**to**-rool o-**rash** . . . pe a-oo-to-**stra**-duh . . . la par-**ka**-re
Is it far?	**E departe?**	Ye de-**par**-te
It's dangerous.	**E periculos.**	Ye pe-ri-koo-**los**
Please draw me a map.	**Vă rog, faceţi-mi o schiţă.**	Vuh **rog**, **fa**-che-tsim' o **ski**-tsuh
Could you direct me to . . . ? . . . a garage . . . a gas station	**Cum se ajunge la . . . ?** **. . . un garaj** **. . . o benzinărie**	**Koom** se a-**zhoon**-je la . . . . . . oon ga-**rash** . . . o ben-zi-nuh-**ree**-ye

I need gasoline.	**Am nevoie de benzină.**	Am ne-**vo**-ye de ben-**zi**-nuh
Please fill the tank up.	**Vă rog, faceţi plinul.**	Vuh **rog**, **fa**-chets' **pli**-nool
Where can I find a mechanic?	**Unde pot găsi un mecanic?**	**Oon**-de pot guh-**si** oon me-**ka**-nik
This doesn't work.	**Nu funcţionează.**	Noo **foonk**-tsyo-**nea**-zuh
Please repair . . . . . . the tire . . . the headlight	**Vă rog, reparaţi . . .** **. . . cauciucul** **. . . farul**	Vuh **rog**, re-pa-**rats**' . . . . . . ka-oo-**chyu**-kool . . . **fa**-rool
How much will it cost?	**Cât costă?**	**Kit kos**-tuh
When will it be ready?	**Când e gata?**	**Kind** ye **ga**-ta
HEALTH	***SANATATE***	
I'm feeling ill.	**Mi-e rău.**	Mye **rău**
I need to go to the dentist.	**Trebuie să merg la dentist.**	**Tre**-boo-ye suh **merg** la den-**tist**
I need some aspirin.	**Am nevoie de nişte aspirine.**	Am ne-**vo**-ye de **nish**-te as-pi-**ri**-ne
I'm allergic to penicillin. (male) (female)	**Sunt alergic la penicilină.** **arahidă** **peste** **Sunt alergică la penicilină.**	Sînt a-**ler**-jik la pe-ni-chi-**li**-nuh uh-ruh-**hee**-duh **peh**-shtuh Sînt a-**ler**-ji-kuh la pe-ni-chi-**li**-nuh
I'm diabetic. (male) (female)	**Sunt diabetic.** **Sunt diabetică.**	Sînt di-a-**be**-tik Sînt di-a-**be**-ti-kuh
My . . . hurts. . . . arm . . . back . . . foot or leg . . . hand . . . head . . . neck . . . stomach	**Mă doare . . . .** **. . . braţul** **. . . spatele** **. . . piciorul** **. . . mâna** **. . . capul** **. . . gâtul** **. . . stomacul**	Muh **dwa**-re . . . . . . bra-tsul . . . spa **spa** -te-le . . . pi-**chyo**-rool . . . **mi**-na . . . **ka**-pool . . . **gi**-tool . . . sto-**ma**-kool

My . . . hurt. . . . knees . . . ankles . . . eyes	**Mă dor . . . .** **. . . genunchii** **. . . gleznele** **. . . ochii**	Muh **dor** . . . . . . je-**noon**-kiy . . . **glez**-ne-le . . . **o**-kiy
Thank you for your help.	**Mulţumesc pentru ajutor.**	**Mool**-tsoo-mesk **pen**-tru a-zhoo-**tor**
GETTING HELP	***AJUTOR***	
I need a translator.	**Am nevoie de un traducator.**	Am ne-**vo**-ye de oon tra-doo-kuh-**tor**
I've lost my passport.	**Mi-am pierdut paşaportul.**	**Myam** pyer-**doot** pa-sha-**por**-tool
My wallet has been stolen.	**Mi s-a furat portmoneul.**	Mi sa foo-**rat** port-mo-**ne**-ool
How can I get to the hospital?	**Cum pot ajunge la spital?**	**Koom** pot a-**zhoon**-je la spi-**tal**
Please call . . . ! . . . a doctor . . . an ambulance . . . the police . . . the fire department	**Vă rog, chemaţi . . . !** **. . . doctorul** **. . . salvarea** **. . . poliţia** **. . .pompierii**	Vuh **rog**, ke-**mats**' . . . . . . **dok**-to-rool . . . sal-**va**-rea . . . po-**li**-tsya . . . pom-pi-**e**-riy
Fire!	**Foc!**	**Fok**
Help!	**Ajutor!**	A-zhoo-**tor**
This is an emergency!	**E o urgenţă!**	Ye o oor-**jen**-tsuh
It's dangerous.	**E periculos.**	Ye per-ri-koo-**los**
IMPORTANT SIGNS	***SEMNELE***	
Caution	**Atenţie**	A-**ten**-tsye
Men	**Bărbaţi**	Buhr-**bats**'
Railroad	**Cale ferată**	**Ka**-le fe-**ra**-tuh
Right Turn	**Curbă la dreapta**	**Koor**-buh la **dreap**-ta
Left Turn	**Curbă la stânga**	**Koor**-buh la **stîn**-ga
Dangerous Curve	**Curbă periculoasă**	**Koor**-buh pe-ri-koo-**lwa**-suh

Women	**Femei**	Feh-**mey**
No Smoking	**Fumatul interzis**	Foo-**ma**-tool in-ter-**zis**
Weight Limit: 5 Tons	**Greutatea maximă: cinci tone**	Gre-oo-**ta**-tea **ma**-xi-muh **chinch**' **to**-ne
Exit	**Ieşire**	Ye-**shi**-re
Emergency Exit	**Ieşire de incendiu**	Ye-**shi**-re de in-chen-dyu
Closed	**Închis**	Yn-**kis**
Automobiles Prohibited	**Interzis pentru automobile**	In-ter-**zis pen**-troo a-oo-to-mo-**bi**-le
Vehicles Prohibited	**Interzis pentru vehicole**	In-ter-**zis pen**-troo ve-**hi**-ko-le
Entrance	**Intrare**	In-**tra**-re
No Entry	**Intrarea interzisă**	In-**tra**-rea in-ter-**zi**-suh
No Admittance	**Intrarea oprită**	In-**tra**-rea o-**pri**-tuh
Speed Limit	**Limită de viteză**	**Li**-mi-tuh de vi-**te**-zuh
Subway	**Metrou**	Me-**troh**
Detour	**Ocol**	O-**kol**
Parking	**Parcare**	Par-**ka**-re
Parking	**Parcare interzisă**	Par-**ka**-re in-ter-**zi**-suh
Overpass	**Pasaj superior de nivel**	Pa-**sazh** soo-pe-ri-**or** de ni-**vel**
Underpass	**Pasaj inferior de nivel**	Pa-**sazh** in-fe-ri-**or** de ni-**vel**
This Way	**Pe aici**	Peh a-**ich**'
Danger	**Pericol**	Pe-**ri**-kol
Bridge	**Pod**	**Pod**
First Aid Station	**Post de prim ajutor**	**Post** de **prim** a-zhoo-**tor**
Reduce Speed	**Reduceţi viteza**	Re-**doo**-chets' vi-**te**-za
Main Road ahead	**Şosea principală înainte**	Sho-**sea** prin-chi- pa-luh î-na-in-te
Keep Right	**Staţi pe dreapta**	**Stats**' pe **dreap**-ta

Keep Left	**Staţi pe stânga**	**Stats'** pe **stîn**-ga
No Standing	**Staţionarea interzisă**	Sta-tsyo-na-rea in-ter-zi-suh
One Way Street	**Stradă cu sens unic**	**Stra-duh** koo **sens** oo-nik
Railroad Crossing	**Trecere peste calea ferată**	Tre-**che**-re pes-te **ka**-lea fe-**ra**-tuh
Tunnel	**Tunel**	Too-**nel**
Sharp Turn	**Viraj brusc**	Vi-**razh broosk**
Toilet	**W.C.**	Ve-**che**

APPENDIX

ROMANIAN NATIONAL TOURIST OFFICES WORLDWIDE:

www.romaniatourism.com/worldwide.html

United States of America
355 Lexington Avenue, 19th Floor, New York, NY 10017
Tel: 212-545-8484, Fax: 212-251-0429
E-mail: infoUS@RomaniaTourism.com
www.RomaniaTourism.com

Austria
Wahringerstrasee 6-8, 1090 Vienna
Tel: (43-1) 317.31.57, Fax: (43-1) 317.31.574
E-mail: rumaenien@aon.at

Belgium
17 A Avenue de la Toison d'Or, 1050 Brussels
Tel: (32-2) 502.46.42, Fax: (32-2) 502.56.22
E-mail: tourisme.roumain@skynet.be

China
9G Oriental Kenzo Office Building
48 Dongzhimenwai Street, Dong Cheng 100027 Beijing
Tel: (86-10) 65.66.01.36, Fax: (86-10) 65.66.01.37
E-mail: info@RomaniaTourism.cn

Czech Republic
Ul. Mikulandská 2/213, 110 00 Prague 1
Tel: (420-2) 249.111.60, Fax: (420-2) 249.305.76
E-mail: romaniatourism@volny.cz

France
7, Rue Gaillon, 75002 Paris
Tel: (33-1) 40.20.99.33, Fax: (33-1) 40.20.99.43
E-mail: roumanie@office-tourisme-roumanie.com

Germany–Berlin
Budapesterstrasse 20a, 10787 Berlin
Tel: (49-30) 241.90.41, Fax: (49-30) 24.72.50.20
E-mail: berlin@rumaenien-tourismus.de
www.rumaenien-tourismus.de

Germany–Munich
Dachauerstr. 32-34, 80335 Munchen
Tel: (49-89) 515.67.687, Fax: (49-89) 515.67.689
E-mail: muenchen@rumaenien-tourismus.de
www.rumaenien-tourismus.de

Holland
183 Weteringschans, 1017 XE Amsterdam
Tel: (31-20) 623.90.44, Fax: (31-20) 626.26.60
E-mail: romaniantourist@site.nl
www.romanian-tourist-office.site.nl

Hungary
9 Hercegprimas Utca, H-1244 Budapest
Tel: (36-1) 269.49.61, Fax: (36-1) 269.49.57
E-mail: romaniatourism@axelero.hu

United Kingdom
22 New Cavendish Street, London WIM 7LH
Tel: (44-207) 224.36.92, Fax: (44-207) 935.64.35
E-mail: infoUK@RomaniaTourism.com
www.VisitRomania.com

Israel
135 Ben Yehuda Street, Tel Aviv
Tel: (972-3) 527.67.46
E-mail: rominfo@zahav.net.il

Italy
Via Torino 95, Galleria Esedra, 00184 Rome
Tel: (39-06) 488.02.67, Fax: (39-6) 4898.62.81
E-mail: romania@progleonard.it
www.romania.it

Japan
Hanawa Bldg. 4F
1-8-5 Kamezawa Sumida-ku Tokyo
Tel: (81-3) 5819.1929, Fax: (81-3) 5819.1928
E-mail: romania@jmail.co.jp

Poland
Ul. Marszalkowska 84/92, 00-514 Warsaw
Tel: (39-06) 488.02.67, Fax: (48-22) 621.03.46
E-mail: info@rumuniatur.org.pl

Republic of Moldova
Bd. Stefan cel Mare 4, Chisinau
Tel: (37-32) 27.35.55
E-mail: romtur@ch.moldpac.md

Russia
Ul. Bolshaya Marinskaya 9, off. 313
129085 Moscow
Tel: (7-095) 215.95.57
E-mail: mt@futures.msk.ru

Spain
Calle Alcantara 49-51, 28006 Madrid
Tel: (34-91) 401.42.68, Fax: (34-91) 402.71.83
E-mail: oficina@rumaniatour.com
www.rumaniatour.com

Sweden
Gamla Brogatan 36-38, 111 20 Stockholm
Tel: (46-8) 21.02.53, Fax: (46-8) 21.02.55
E-mail: rotoscand@telia.com

Turkey
Lamartin Cad. No. 7, kat 1, Taksim, 80090 Istanbul
Tel: (90-212) 238.25.880, Fax: (90-212) 256.84.17
E-mail: info@romaniatravel.org
www.romaniatravel.

International Embassies in Bucharest

Albania (40-21)211.87.43
Algeria (40-21)211.51.50
Argentina (40-21)233.91.75
Armenia (40-21)321.56.79
Australia (40-21)320.98.02
Austria (40-21)210.93.77
Belarus (40-21)222.42.88
Belgium (40-21)212.36.80
Brazil (40-21)230.11.30
Bulgaria (40-21)210.52.48
Canada (40-21)307.50.00
Chile (40-21)312.73.11
China (40-21)232.97.44
Columbia (03936)617.09.73
Congo (40-21)315.33.71
Croatia (40-21)311.26.12
Cuba (40-21)211.87.95
Czech Republic (40-21)303.92.38
Denmark (40-21)312.03.52
Egypt (40-21)211.09.38
Finland (40-21)230.75.04
France (40-21)312.02.17
Germany (40-21)230.25.80
Great Britain (40-21)201.73.00
Greece (40-21)209.41.90
Hungary (40-21)312.00.73
India (40-21)222.87.15
Indonesia (40-21)312.07.42

Iran (40-21)312.04.93
Israel (40-21)330.41.49
Italy (40-21)223.33.12
Japan (40-21)210.07.90
Jordan (40-21)210.47.05
Korea, North (40-21)232.96.65
Korea, South (40-21)230.71.98
Lebanon (40-21)230.10.80
Macedonia (40-21)210.08.80
Malaysia (40-21)211.38.01
Mexico (40-21)210.44.17
Moldova (40-21)410.98.26
Morocco (40-21)210.29.45
Netherlands (40-21)230.06.17
Nigeria (40-21)312.79.37
Norway (40-21)210.02.77
Pakistan (40-21)222.57.36
Peru (40-21)223.12.53
Philippines 224.80.70
Poland (40-21)230.23.30
Portugal (40-21)230.41.36
Quatar (40-21)230.47.41
Russia (40-21)222.31.70
Slovakia (40-21)312.68.22
South Africa (00361)392.09.99
Spain (40-21)230.17.39
Sweden (40-21)230.21.84
Switzerland (40-21)607.92.51
Syria (40-21)212.41.86
Thailand (40-21)311.00.31
Turkey (40-21)210.02.79
Ukraine (40-21)211.69.86
Uruguay (40-21)222.58.74
United States (40-21)210.40.42
Vatican (40-21)313.94.90
Venezuela (40-21)222.58.74
Vietnam (40-21)311.16.04
Yugoslavia (40-21)211.98.71

International Airlines to Romania

AF	Air France	(40 21) 210.11.76	www.airfrance.ro
KL	KLM	(40 21) 231.56.19	www.romania.klm.com
LH	LUFTHANSA	(40 21) 315.75.75	www.lufthansa.ro
AZ	ALITALIA	(40 21) 210.41.11	www.alitalia.ro
BA	British Airways	(40 21) 204.20.01	www.ba.com
OS	Austrian Airlines	(40 21) 312.05.45	www.austrianairlines.ro
LX	Swiss Air Lines	(40 21) 312.02.38	www.swiss.com
LY	El-Al	(40 21) 330.87.60	www.elal.co
MA	Malev	(40 21) 326.80.72	www.malev.ro
OA	Olympic Airways	(40 21) 316.63.60	www.olympic-airways.com
OK	CSA	(40 21) 315.32.05	www.czechairlines.com
LO	LOT	(40 21) 212.83.65	www.lot.com
SU	Aeroflot	(40 21) 315.03.14	www.aeroflot.ru
RB	SyrianAir	(40 21) 315.32.93	www.syrianairlines.co
DU	HemusAir	(40 21) 312.30.26	www.hemusair.bg
9U	Air Moldova	(40 21) 312.12.58	www.airmoldova.md
TK	Turkish Airlines	(40 21) 311.24.10	www.turkishairlines.com
CIM	Cimber Air	(40 21) 204.19.00	www.cimber.com
6P	Club Air Sixgo	(40 21) 201.47.30	www.clubair.it
SX	Air Europa Lineas Aereas	(40 21) 204.19.00	www.air-europa.com

Romania's RomTelecom Country + Area Codes

When calling from abroad, dial your international access code, then Romania's country code 40 and the three-digit area code (except for Bucharest, which has a two-digit area code (21), e.g. xx + 40 + 230 + number.

When dialing within Romania, omit the first digit of the country code (4) and just dial the **zero + the two or three-digit area code**, e.g. 0230 + number.

40	**Romania**	40 256	TIMIŞ
40 21	BUCHAREST	40 257	ARAD
40 230	SUCEAVA	40 258	ALBA
40 231	BOTOŞANI	40 259	BIHOR
40 232	IAŞI	40 260	SALAJ
40 233	NEAMŢ	40 261	SATU MARE
40 234	BACAU	40 262	MARAMUREŞ
40 235	VASLUI	40 263	BISTRIŢA
40 236	GALAŢI	40 264	CLUJ
40 237	VRANCEA	40 265	MUREŞ
40 238	BUZAU	40 266	HARGHITA
40 239	BRĂILA	40 267	COVAŞNA
40 240	TULCEA	40 268	BRAŞOV
40 241	CONSTANŢA	40 269	SIBIU
40 242	CALARAŞI	40 72	Mobile Connex-Vodafone
40 243	IALOMIŢA	40 721	Mobile Connex-Vodafone
40 244	PRAHOVA	40 722	Mobile Connex-Vodafone
40 245	DAMBOVIŢA	40 723	Mobile Connex-Vodafone
40 246	GIURGIU	40 724	Mobile Connex-Vodafone
40 247	TELEORMAN	40 74	Mobile Orange
40 248	ARGEŞ	40 740	Mobile Orange
40 249	OLT	40 742	Mobile Orange
40 250	VĂLCEA	40 744	Mobile Orange
40 251	DOLJ	40 745	Mobile Orange
40 252	MEHEDINŢI	40 76	Mobile Cosmorom
40 253	GORJ	40 766	Mobile Cosmorom
40 254	HUNEDOARA	40 78	Mobile Telemobil
40 255	CARAS-SEVERIN	40 788	Mobile Telemobil

Metric Conversions—Romania uses the metric system of weights and measures.

Speed and distance are measured in kilometers; goods in kilograms and liters; temperatures are in Celsius/Centigrade.

Length conversion	**Weight & Volume conversion**
1 centimeter = 0.4 inches	100 grams = 3.5 oz
1 inch = 2.54 cm	1 oz = 28.35 grams
1 meter = 3.3 feet = 1.1 yards = 100 centimeters	1 kilogram = 2.2 lbs = 1,000 grams
1 foot = 0.3 meters	1 lb = 454 grams
1 kilometer = 0.62 miles = 1,000 meters	100 milliliters = 3.4 fl.oz
1 mile = 1.61 km	1 fl. oz. = 28.4 milliliters
1 hectare = 2.4 acres	1 liter = 1/4 gallon = 1,000 milliliters
	1 gallon = 3.78 liters

Temperature conversion °C to °F

°C	-18	-12	-7	**0**	4	10	16	21	27	32	38
°F	0	10	20	**32**	40	50	60	70	80	90	100

(°C multiply by 9, divide by 5, and add 32; or double °C and add 30.)

Speed conversion (kilometers divided by 1.6 = miles)

KmPH	10	30	50	60	80	90	110
MPH	6	21	31	39	50	56	70

ANTREC—National Association of Rural, Ecological and Cultural Tourism

Bucharest main office: Strada Maica Alexandra 7, sector 1, Bucharest; Tel: (40-21)223.70.24; fax: (40-21)222.80.01; E-mail: office@antrec.ro, www.ANTREC.ro.

ANTREC County branches and telephone contacts:

ALBA	Emil Anton Comşa	(0258)833.064, (0722)683.340
ARGES	Ana Vorovenci	(0248)542.689, (0744)370.666
BACAU	Beatrice Grigoraş	(0234)170.826, (0744)584.176
BIHOR	Maria Tatar	(0259)406.313, (0723)125.936
BISTRIŢA	V. Sanmihaian	(0263)212.056
BRAŞOV	Maria Stoian Vişan	(0268)236 355, (0788)422.097, (0788)411 450, (0268)236.917
BUCHAREST	Daniela Diţoiu	(021) 223.70.24
BUZAU	Poliana Partal	(0238)710.735; (0238)451.255
CLUJ	Ioana Tamas	(0264)406.363, (0723)655.119, (0743)146.362
CONSTANŢA	Florentina Dospinescu	0241 759 473; 0722 745 987
COVAŞNA	Attila Dărăguş	0267.361.130, 0744.380.000
DAMBOVIŢA	Şerban Constantin	(0245)206 336, (0721)84 55 99, (0744)38 68 74
DOLJ	Marian Nicola	(0251)415.071, (0722)527.762
GALAŢI		(0236)319.011, (0723)235.756
GORJ	Radu Ciobanu	(0253)223.081, (0722)542.764
HARGHIŢA	Elisabeta Reisz	(0265)570.484, (0722)601.464
HUNEDOARA	Rodica Csanadi	(0254)770.796, (0746)273.652, (0722)952.584
IAŞI	Ana Onica	(0232)216.227, (0721)223.710
ILFOV	Cristina Zamfir	(021)236.02.53, (0744)36.104
MARAMUREŞ	Livia Sima	(0722)377.766, (0262)215.543
MEHEDINŢI	Daniel Amza	(0252)318.076
MUREŞ	Mihai Ranca	(0265)269.343, (0721)992.878
NEAMŢ	Lucia Muj	(0233)234.204, (0722)608.431
PRAHOVA	Alexandru Sult	(0244)592.915, (0722)664.216
SIBIU	Radu George Lazăr	(0269)233.503
SUCEAVA	Corina Cubleşan	(0230)371.306, (0745)615.320
TIMIŞ	Codruţa Dobrescu	(0256)191.027, (0722)45.79.88
TULCEA	Silviu Gheorghe	(0240)519.214, (0721)092.150
VĂLCEA	Simona Veteleanu	(0250)73.32.40
VRANCEA	Vasile Bostiog	(0237)673.049, (0722)491.665

Romanian Festivals Schedule

Name	Date	Type	Region	Details
Mihai Eminescu Day	January 15	culture	Botosani, Ipoteşti	National Poet
Union of Romanian Principalities	January 24	history	all country	Iaşi city
The Winter Festival	February	Mountain sports, fun	Mountain resorts	Ski resorts
Valentine's Day	February 14	fun	in cities and villages	imported from western culture
Dragobetele (The Lovers Day)	February 24	fun, traditions	all country	older than Valentine's Day
Boulder Cup	end of April	mountain sports	Retezat Mountains	oldest ski cup in Retezat Mountains
Catholic Easter	-	religious	all country	Banat and Transylvania
Orthodox Easter	-	religious	all country	holiest day
International Jazz Festival	May	culture	Sibiu	a festival tradition
Tanjana	May 5	tradition, folklore	Maramureş	very old tradition
Catholic Rusalii	May	religious	Transylvania	Miercurea Ciuc
Balvanyos	June 1-2	folklore	Balvanyos Spa	a folk marathon
Saint Ioan cel Nou from Suceava	June 2	religious	Suceava	an important holy day
Cireşar	June 2	folklore	Cisnădie (Sibiu)	
The Wine Holiday	June	tasting wines, fun	Cotnari (Iaşi)	also history
La Cetate	June	folklore, market	Cernat (Covasna)	

The Raising Day (*Înălţarea*), The Heroes Day	June 14	religious, history	all country	celebration of all Romanian heroes
Sânzienele	June 24	religious, traditions	all country	Suceava Town
National Flag Day	June 26	history	all country	Cluj-Napoca
Holda de Aur	June 29	folklore	Tudora (Botoşani)	
Artisans Market	June	folklore, market	Bucharest	The Village Museum
Folk Pottery Market	June	folklore, market	Iaşi	Parc Copou, pottery market in Romania
Saint Stephen the Great	July 2	religious	Putna (Suceava)	the most important ruler of Moldavia
Pottery Day	July	folklore, market	Lungeşti (Vâlcea)	
Medieval Art Festival	July	culture, fun	Sighişoara	a very popular festival
The Cherries Fair	June - July	folklore, market	Brăniştea (Bistrita)	regional holiday
Maidens' Fair from Găina Mountain	July	folklore, market	Găina Mountain	very popular holiday
Calattis Festival	July - Aug	fun, pop music	Mangalia resort (Black Sea Coast)	a big and new festival
Hora de la Prislop	August	folklore, market	Prislop Pass	song, dance, food, crafts Maramureş and Bukovina
National Pop Music Festival	August	pop music, fun	Mamaia (Black Sea Coast)	a traditional pop music festival

International Motorcyclist Festival	August	fun, market	Sibiu	very popular
Virgin Maria sleeping	August 15	religious	Nicula (Cluj Region)	pilgrimage from all Romania
Bran Festival	August	folklore, fun	Bran (Braşov)	
Dole Hora (Hora de Pomană)	August	folklore, market, traditions	Lunca Cireşului (Mehedinţi)	
The Garlic Festival	end of August	folklore	Copalău (Botoşani)	a new festival
The Motorcyclist Festival	Aug. - Sept.	fun, motor sports	Bucharest	a new festival
The Autumn Festival	September	traditions, fun	Sinaia Spa	old cars and old fashions
The Forest Celebration	September	folklore, market, religious	Vorona (Botosani)	folklore festival
The Cross Day	September 14	religious	Voroneţ (Suceava)	
The Golden Stag International Festival	September	pop music	Braşov	hugely popular
George Enescu International Festival	September	culture (music)	Bucharest	appreciated all over Europe
Artisans Market	September	folklore, market	Piteşti	
Bucharest Days	September	culture, history	Bucharest	
Fechetaului Market	beginning of October	folklore market	Negreni (Cluj)	one of the biggest folklore markets in region
The Fortress Festival	October	medieval history, fun	Rupea (Braşov)	medieval festival
Popasul Ţapinarilor	October	folklore	Bistriţa mountains	professional holiday

Iaşului Days and Saint Parascheva Day	October 12-15	traditions, religious	Iaşi	Pilgrimage day
The Mushroom Festival	October	fun	Predeal	a new and funny festival
The Harvest Day	October	traditions, market	Comăneşti	also a holy day
Saint Dimitrie Basarabov	October 26	religious		Protector of the city
The Wine Holiday	October	tasting wines	Focşani	
Sanmedru Fire	October 26	traditions, religious	Poiana Mărului (Braşov)	
Romania National Day	December 1	history	all country	Alba Iulia, Bucharest, Cluj-Napoca
Christmas	December 25	religious, traditions	all country	traditional village fests

ARCHAEOLOGICAL SITES

1. **Adamclisi,** *Tropaeum Traiani* , Constanţa County; a monument built by the Roman Emperor Traianus in AD 109; the funerary tower and altar; the ruins of 1st–6th centuries town; streets, walls, towers, gates, and Paleochristian churches (4th–6th centuries).
2. **Arutela**, Poiana Bivolari, Vâlcea County, a Roman stone castrum built during Hadrian, on Olt River, north of Cozia Monastery.
3. **Barboşi**, near Galaţi, Galaţi County, on terrace of Siret River's left bank, Tirighina Hill, the vestiges of Getae and Roman settlement (1st–6th centuries), connected to Dinogetia, on right side of Danube.
4. **Basarabi,** Murfatlar, Constanţa County, in southern part of the village, the vestiges of a quarry and a monastic community with churches (10th–12th centuries) sculptured in chalk.
5. **Beroe**, Piatra Frecăţei, Ostrov Village, Tulcea County. Ruins of Roman and Byzantine stronghold (1st–6th centuries and 10th–12th centuries); Paleochristian church (5th–6th centuries) beside former cemetery of the settlement (1st–12th centuries).
6. **Blidaru**, Dacian stronghold from Orăştie Mountains.
7. **Bumbeşti-Jiu**, Gorj County, on the left side of the river, vestiges of two Roman castra (2nd–3rd centuries); other discoveries from this area displayed in the museum at Târgu Jiu.
8. **Topalu Village**, Constanţa County, Capidava, stronghold on high bank of the Danube River. Roman ruins (1st–6th centuries); defense walls, towers and gates with Byzantine vestiges (10th–12th centuries) nearby.
9. **Dolojman Cape**, Jurilovca, Tulcea County. Ruins of Greek Roman fortress *Argamum* (the 7th century BC–AD 6th century) in the steep bank of the lake. Known as *Orgame*, it is the first settlement in Romania mentioned in an ancient written document; fortress gate with defense wall, streets, Paleochristian Basilica.
10. **Căşeiu**, Cluj County, on Someş River bank, ruins of Roman stone castrum *Samum*, a square stronghold with a side 165 m in length (2nd–3rd centuries).

11. **Celeiu**, Corabia, Olt County. On the terrace of Danube, the defense walls with eight towers, once part of Roman town *Sucidava* (4th–6th centuries). It covers, part of a lesser known Roman town (2nd–3rd centuries); Roman baths (*thermae*), a paleochristian basilica (5th–6th centuries), paved streets, underground fountain built by Romans; foundation of foot bridge on the Danube during the time of Constantin the Great.
12. **Constanta**, Constanta County. Greek-Roman town *Tomis*, a colony founded by Milet, in the 6th century BC; vestiges date from Roman times (1st–AD 6th centuries), and covered by the modern town; defense wall with towers and gates, a few street segments, Roman baths, the great Roman building with a polychromatic mosaic near the port, paleochristian baths, a Roman grave with a fresco, a Christian tomb with a fresco, many architectural pieces and inscriptions.
13. **Costesti**, Dacian stronghold in Orăştie Mountains.
14. **Cotnari**, Iaşi County, on Cătălina hill. A Thracian–Getae stronghold from the Iron Age (4th–2nd centuries BC), defense systems have been partly preserved.
15. **Covasna**, on Cetatea Zânelor hill. Almost entirely revealed ruins of a large Dacian stronghold with stone walls arranged in terraces (1st century BC–AD 1st century).
16. **Garvăn**, Tulcea County, Dinogetia. Getae settlement covered by a Roman one, preserving a defense wall with 14 towers, partly restored, streets and interior buildings, headquarters and Roman house of the commander, a paleochristian basilica; outside, to the south, ruins of the Roman thermae from the 1st–6th centuries; Byzantine discoveries from 10th–12th centuries; most visible are southern gate and little Byzantine church, the oldest of this kind known on Romania's territory.
17. **Drobeta-Turnu Severin**, Mehedinţi County. Ruins of the Roman town Drobeta with a defense wall, streets, interior buildings; ruins of the main pillar on the left bank of the bridge built by Apollodor of Damascus, for Roman Emperor Trajanus.

18. **Enisala**, Tulcea County. Heracleea Fortress. Genovese stronghold built on the foundation of a Roman and a Roman-Byzantine stronghold.
19. **Gilău**, Cluj County. Vestiges of a Roman castrum and of a Roman civilian settlement south of the village; the first *castrum* in Transylvania where archaeologists have clearly identified the development from a clay and wood castrum to a stone one (200 x 140 m).
20. **Grădiştea Muncelului**, Hunedoara County. Most important among Dacian strongholds in Orăştie Mountains, was King Decebalus's capital *Sarmizegetusa Regia*, meaning the Royal Sarmizegetusa (see Orăştie Mountains).
21. **Murighiol**, Tulcea County. Ruins of ancient Roman town *Halmyris* (1st–6th centuries), a former port on the Sfîntu Gheorghe arm in the Danube Delta, and a sacrificial place for martyrs Epictet and Astion at the beginning of Christianity; a strong defense wall with towers and gates, Roman thermae, a paleochristian basilica with vault for martyrs' bones.
22. **Istria Village**, Constanţa County, Histria. A defense wall with towers and bastions from Greek and Roman periods; used to enclose the smaller surface of a late Roman town (7 hectares, plus the former acropole of the Greek town), west of Sinoe Lake. Well-preserved ruins of Greek temples, paved streets and residential districts, workshops, thermae, civilian and Christian basilicas, and one of the greatest Christian basilicas in the area (50 m length), dating from the 6th century AD.
23. **Jupa**, Caraş-Severin County. Ruins of a Roman *castrum* and of civilian settlement *Tibiscum* on Timiş river bank, partly preserved.
24. **Mangalia**, Constanţa County. A Greek-Roman town called *Callatis*. Northern side and part of western side of the wall that protected the former Roman town from the sea. Also, ruins of a basilica, a piece from the southern gate, and a small urban segment preserved near the entrance and in the basement of President Hotel.

25. **Moigrad**, Mirsid Village, Sălaj County. The partly revealed ruins of the Roman *castrum Porolissum*, the most important military and civilian headquarters in the northwestern Roman Dacia, are to be found here. Also preserved are a gate and a piece from the fortress wall.
26. **Orăştie Mountains**, Hunedoara County. Dacian strongholds from King Decebalus' times, earlier stages of inhabitance and fortification (1st century BC–AD 106) in the Sebeşului Mountains. In Grădiştea Muncelului, *Sarmizegetusa*, King Decebalus' capital at 1,200 m altitude. In the forest, stone walls of terraces, ruins of the buildings, paved roads and vestiges of stone Dacian sanctuaries are still visible. To the east, Piatra Rosie stronghold; to the west, Căpâlna and Tilişca.
27. **Niculiţel**, Tulcea County. Bones of Christian martyrs from the 3rd–4th centuries were found here and put into a tomb under the shrine of a paleochristian basilica from the 5th–6th century.
28. **Ocniţa**, Ocnele Mari, Vâlcea County. Preserved on a hill the vestiges of a stronghold built by the Dacians from this area, called "*bur,*" named local settlement *Buridava*. Also the name of a Roman settlement at Stolniceni, in Olt River Valley.
29. **Păcuiul lui Soare**, Ostrov Village, Constanţa County. Ruins of a Byzantine fortress from the 10th–13th centuries on an island cut in pieces by the Danube River; a gate, parts from the port and a piece from the fortress.
30. **Piatra Craivii**, Alba County. Vestiges of a fortress and a Dacian settlement from the 2nd century BC–the 1st century AD; the stone precinct and the sanctuaries.
31. **Popeşti**, Mihăileşti Village, Giurgiu County. Vestiges of settlements from the first and second Iron Age; last settlement said to be *Argedava*, Getae King Burebista's Court. (2nd–1st centuries BC.)
32. **Roşia Montana**, Alba County. Vestiges of Roman gold mine Alburnus Maior; galleries, human traces, necropolis; many inscriptions are now in local museums or in Alba Iulia and Cluj.

33. **Sarmizegetusa Regia**, King Decebalus' Capital (see Orăştie Mountains).
34. **Slava Rusă**, Tulcea County. This village partially covers one of the biggest Roman urban areas in Dobrogea, *Libida* (called *Ibida* in some publications and guidebooks), 24 hectares. Today, some pieces from the defense wall with towers, a gate, etc.
35. **Turda**, Cluj County. Ruins of the Roman castrum *Potaissa*; precincts wall, gates, towers, important interior buildings.
36. **Ulpia Traiana Sarmisegetusa**, Hunedoara County. A Roman town founded by the Emperor Traianus after his conquest of Dacia, as the capital of the new province. The square shape, typically Roman, covers a surface of 32.4 hectares. Pieces from the defense wall, towers, paved streets, the largest part of forum and ruins of residential districts are still preserved. In the northern area, the Roman amphitheatre, surrounded by the ruins of other buildings, some sacred.
37. **Veţel**, Hunedoara County; inside the village, on Mureş River bank. Vestiges of the Roman castrum and *Micia* settlement. On both sides the modern railway, ruins of the castrum (to the south); closer to Mureş, the Roman thermae and traces of an amphitheatre.

NOTE: For more information, visit the local museums of historic sites or the museums in Alba Iulia, Bucharest, Cluj Napoca, Constanţa, Deva, Galaţi, Tulcea, Zalău.

CASTLES and MEDIEVAL FORTRESSES

Moldavia Province

1. **Suceava Fortress**—capital of Moldavia province in the Middle Ages; built in the 14th century by Petru Muşat; developed and strengthen by Alexandru the Kind, and later by Stephan the Great, who transformed it into a defense bastion.
2. **Neamţ Fortress**—built in the 14th century on plateau overlooking the Moldavian Valley by Petru Muşat.

Later, Stephan the Great suffered hard sieges laid by Sultan Mehmet the II and by Polish King Ioan Sobieski.

3. **Hotin Fortress**—in northern Moldavia (today within Ukraine) next to Nistru River; was an important Romanian fortress built by Moldavian rulers.
4. **Soroca Fortress**—built in the 14th century, on the site of an older Genovese fortress *Alcionia*, next to Nistru River; strengthened by Stephan the Great and Petru Rares; preserved in excellent condition, with high and massive walls and towers.
5. **Tighina Fortress**—built in the 14th century by Stephan the Great and well-preserved; controlled by the Ottoman Empire from 1535 until 1812. King Carol the XIII of Sweden was a refugee here between 1709-1711 after disastrous expeditions against Russia.
6. **Cetatea Albă Fortress**—medieval fortress built by Moldavian rulers, with a tumultuous history; well-preserved; now within Ukraine borders.

Dobrogea Province

1. Ruins of **Heracleea Fortress**—a Genovese fortress with Byzantine roots; after 1388 it belonged to Wallachian ruler Mircea the Elder; after 1417 it belonged to Ottoman Empire, until 1878.

Wallachia Province

1. **Poienari Fortress**—built in the 14th century on Cetăţuia Mountain by Vlad the Impaler; access via more than 1,000 steps.
2. Ruins of **Fortress of Negru Vodă—Cetăţeni**, one of the first medieval fortresses of Wallachia.
3. Ruins of the **Medieval Fortress—Giurgiu**, built on an island in the front of the town in the 15th century by Mircea the Elder.
4. Ruins of the **Severinului Fortress**—built in 13th century and resisted until 1524, when it was destroyed by Turks. Inside the fortress are ruins of a church.

5. **Ada Kaleh Fortress**—a medieval fortress on Simian Ostrov island, in the Danube River.

Banat Province

1. **Ruins of Caraşova Fortress**—a huge fortress built in 1333.
2. **Bastion of the Citadel—Timişoara**, one of few Vauban-type fortresses, built between 1730-1733, with massive brick walls.
3. **Ruins of Morisena Fortress—Cenad**, built in the 10th century.
4. **Ruins of Ciacova Fortress**—built between 1390-1394; defense tower remains.
5. **Stone Fortress Siria**—built in 1331; was a royal fortress of Iancu of Hunedoara, King Sigismund of Luxembourg, Serbian despot George Brancovici, Bathory Family.
6. **Arad Fortress**—built between 1762-1783 by Empress Maria Theresa in Vauban-style with six corners; inside are ruins of a chapel.
7. **Lipova Castle**—built in the 15th century by Iancu of Hunedoara and his son, Mathias Corvin; a precinct with square corners and defense towers; today it is ruins.
8. **Stone Fortress of Soimuş**—built in 1278, dominating Mureş valley; was ruled by Transylvanians, Turks and Hungarians; after 1688 the fortress became ruins.
9. **Agriş Fortress**—built in 1400 in western part of Apuseni Mountains.

Transylvania Province

1. **Alba Iulia Fortress**—built by ruler Gyla in the 9th–10th centuries, it was the first medieval fortress.
2. **Fortress Aiud**—built from 13th-15th centuries, among the oldest urban fortifications in Transylvania.
3. **Aiud Castle**, Alba County—Voivodes' Palace since the 16th-17th centuries is one of the most beautiful edifices. It was owned by Prince Gabriel Bethlen (1612-1629).

4. **Fortress Tăiuţi**—built in 1276 in the Trascau Mountains; triangular, with a donjon.
5. **Salo Fortress**, Sibiel—built in the 12th-13th centuries.
6. **Calnic Fortress**, Alba County—built in the 13th century; owned by the nobles from the Kelling family; an oval precinct, two defense towers, a chapel, and dungeon (Siegfried tower, 1270). During the 15th-16th centuries, it was a peasant fortress; an exterior belt of walls, a barbacana and a round tower were added.
7. **Cetatea de Baltă** (Bethlen-Haller Castle)—1615-1624, has a quadrilateral plan with corner round towers, with no defensive role; resembles the Chambord Castle; was restored in 1769 and 1773.
8. **Gârbova Castle**, Alba County—built in the 13th century, one of the oldest castles in Transylvania, composed of a dungeon and a circular precinct; today in ruins, but preserves a 13th-century Romanic basilica with three halls, a belfry, and a tribune on the western edge of the central hall.
9. **Săvârşin Castle**, Alba County—a neoclassic style from the 18th century on the foundation of a former hunting manor; the castle was bought by the last king of Romania; today, it is a museum.
10. **Bethlen Castle** (Sanmiclaus)—built between 1668 and 1683; representative of the late Renaissance in Transylvania; the southern façade is treated as a double loggia with six archways in the center of each level.
11. **Episcopal palace**, Blaj—former noble residence in the 16th-18th centuries; Bazilians Monastery during 18th-19th centuries; today it's the Theology Academy building.
12. **Deva Fortress**—built in the 13th century on a volcanic cone that dominates the city center from an altitude of 184m (603 ft.); mentioned in 1269, it was one of the strongest fortresses in Transylvania. It was deserted in 1849 after an explosion of powder reserves blew up the fortress.
13. **Corvin Castle**—a 13th century fortress castle in Hunedoara, built on a rock; very impressive with many towers. Renovated a few centuries later, the castle mixes the

Gothic style with characteristic elements of Renaissance and Baroque.

14. **Ruins of Fortress Tălmaciu**—documentary mentioned in 1370 under the name of "*Castrum Lanchron*", the fortification dominates the Olt Valley where the river enters narrow Turnu Rosu path.
15. **Medieval Fortifications—Sibiu**, remains of the citadel wall with its many towers: the City Hall Tower built in the 12th century and modified in the 15th and 17th centuries and again in 1826; the Stairs Tower, built in the 13th century, one of the oldest constructions of the town; the Gate's Tower, 15th century; the Carpenters' Tower; the Harquebusiers' Tower; Potters' Tower; Soldisch Bastion; and Powder Warehouse Tower.
16. **Ruins of Fortress Mediaş**—still standing are interior walls and defense towers built between the 15th-16th centuries.
17. **Rural Fortress Biertan**—built in the 15th-16th centuries; one of the most impressive constructions of this type in Transylvania; a UNESCO World Heritage site.
18. **Sighişoara Fortress**—beautiful 13th-century city on a high hill; fully preserved and the only inhabited medieval fortress in Europe; the birthplace of Vlad Dracula; remaining bastions: the Clock Tower, the Ropes' Tower, the Tinkers' Tower, the Tanners' Tower, the Cobblers' Tower; hosts a Medieval Art Festival every July. A UNESCO World Heritage site.
19. **Brâncoveneşti Castle**—built in Transylvanian Renaissance style, between 1537 and 1555; strengthened with defense channels between 1599 and 1600.
20. **Criş Castle**—built in 1559 in Transylvanian Renaissance style; a noble residence with a circular archers' tower and a loggia with semicircular vaulted openings, supported by short cylindrical columns; access to the loggia is by the 17th-century honor staircase.
21. **Fortress of Târgu Mureş**—built in the 15th century, was expanded with 7 new towers in 17th century.

22. **Târgu Mureş Castle**—built at the beginning of the 10th century in Secession style; façades decorated with statues and bas-reliefs; it has a Venetian mirrors hall; its concert hall organ is one of the largest in Romania with 4,600 pipes.
23. **Teleky Palace**, Gorneşti—built from 1772-1778, with a U-plan, representative of Baroque architecture; it has a park with Baroque statues.
24. **Bosckay Castle**, Aghireşu—built in 1572, in Renaissance style. Partly in ruins, the castle stone frames are impressive.
25. **Bontida Castle**—castle with round towers at corners, renovated in Baroque style; two wings added; statues decorate the gate and stables from 1750.
26. **Bologa Fortress**—mentioned in 1322, and held by Wallahian ruler, Mircea the Elder, at the end of the 14th century.
27. **Ruins of Colt Fortress**—built in the 14th century in a spectacular place close to Retezat Mountains, it inspired Jules Verne's "The Castle from Carpathians."
28. **Fortress with Roman Basilica—Cisnădioara**, one of the most remarkable monuments of this style in Transylvania.
29. **Prejmer Fortress** (15th century)—a great fortress with many rooms on many levels. The walls are 4 m thick; it was the powerful peasants' fortress in Transylvania.
30. **Fortress of Braşov**—built in 1395 under Sigismund of Luxembourg, King of Hungary; one of the strongest fortresses in Transylvania.
31. **Braşov Towers** (bastions)—many fortified towers (bastions) made by people from Braşov town to protect their family and works. The most important is the Weavers' Bastion (1421-1573) where we find Braşov Fortress Museum.
32. **Râşnov Fortress**—built in the 14th century, it is one of the largest rural fortresses in the country.
33. **Bran Castle**—built between 1377-1382 on a rock mountain, and preserves elements of original Gothic style. Today it hosts a museum of medieval art.
34. **Făgăraş Fortress**—built in the 15th century, in the middle of Făgăraş town; inside the fortress walls is a huge castle, now a museum and library.

35. **Feldioara Fortress**—built between 1211-1225 by the Teutonic Knights; after 1457 it belonged to the peasants.
36. **Ruins of the Rupea Fortress**—built in 14th-16th century upon a big rock. A refuge fortress for the inhabitants of the area, built in the 14th-17th centuries. The defense walls define four precincts, strengthened by defense towers.
37. **Fortress of Ilieni**—a 15th-century fortress with a great history of Szekely people.
38. **Pagans' Fortress—Balvanyoş**, also named the Idolatrous Castle, is a 13th-century Szekely building in a beautiful and wild area.
39. **Miko Fortress,** Miercurea Ciuc—built in1621 by Ferenc Miko on quadrilateral plan around a central courtyard, on the spot of a previous fortress; renovated in 1714 after the invasion of Turks (1661); now hosts the Ethnographic Museum of the province.
40. **Ruins of the Ciceu Fortress**—built between 1203-1204, it was a great fortress in the Middle Ages belonging to Moldavian rulers, like Stephan the Great, Petru Rares, Alexandru Lapusneanu. Now just ruins.
41. **Ruins of Medieval Fortress Almaş**—one of the oldest and impressive medieval fortresses in Transylvania (1247-1278); between 1545-1546, this fortress belonged to Moldavian ruler Petru Rares.
42. **Ruins of the Rodna Fortress**—(10th century) was an important fortress in region.
43. **Medieval Fortress Dăbâca**—has an important place in Transylvania history, special between 10th-14th century, when became a royal fortress.
44. **Fortress of Şimleul Silvaniei**—built in 1532 by Bathory family. Today is ruins.
45. **Ruins of Feudal Fortress Cheud**—an impressive fortress mentioned in 1387.
46. **Fortress Ardud** (Satu Mare County)—built in 1481; one of the strongest senorial fortresses in the north of Transylvania. It has a polygonal plan with bastions on the corners; a Roman Catholic Church from 1482, rebuilt in 1860

and 1959; today only a fortified tower and a few traces of Gothic architecture.

NATURE RESERVES

1. **Bicaz Gorges and Lacu Roşu** (Hasmas Mountains)—The territory of the gorges and the area surrounding the lake has been declared a monument of nature and forms a geological, botanical and wildlife reserve complex.
2. **Bottomless Lake–Ocna Sibiului** (Sibiu area)—geological reserve with a lake created where a salt mine had caved in; the lake is 35m deep and of therapeutic value.
3. **Bucegi National Park**—several natural reserve complexes with abrupt precipices, pointed crests, karst relief, mountain animals, and unique flora.
4. **Călimani Mountains**—the most grandiose volcanic mountains of the country. There is a reserve complex aiming to protect alpine landscapes, and numerous rare species of flora and fauna.
5. **The Caraş Gorges** (Anina Mountains)—botanical, geological and speleological reserve complex with many karst phenomena.
6. **Ceahlău Reserve Complex** (Ceahlău Mountains)—the most beautiful mountain in Moldova preserves rare botanical and geological species.
7 **Cetăţile Ponorului** (Bihor Mountains)—a natural reserve complex made up of the three huge dolina (sinkholes), a cave, waterfalls and an underground river.
8 **Cândrel Mountain Lake**—a reserve including several glacial basins; around these mountain lakes, are varied species of animals protected by law (chamois, bears, wolves).
9. **Cozia National Park**—contains numerous rocks with bizarre forms, beautiful gorges and waterfalls, the diversity of plant species and the interesting fauna.
10. **Danube Delta Biosphere Reserve** (UNESCO site)—5,050 km^2 of geological and biological laboratory; a diverse fauna, home to species unique in the world, including hermine, wild cat, muskrat, raccoon dog and tortoise; 300

species of birds, including pelicans, geese and ducks, storks, cormorants, egrets, flamingo and swan, most protected by law. The Delta is crossed by six flight paths of migratory birds. The Delta's many fish include sturgeon and sterlet—important for their caviar. The unrivaled flora comprises, among other species: white and yellow water lilies, bulrush and bracken; there are also 8,000 hectares (20,000 acres) of forest with giant trees on whose trunks grow climbing plants like lianas.

11. **Domogled–Valea Cerna** (Mehedinţi and Cerna mountains)—an area with many reserves and natural monuments; the Domogled has one of the richest varieties of plant species in Europe.
12. **The Glades with Daffodils from Dumbrava Vadului** (Ţâgla Mountains)—these glades become covered with a glorious carpet of daffodils and represent one of Romania's unique beauties.
13. **The Living Fire** (Vrancea area)—geological reserve on the Upper Milcov; emissions of natural gas spew from crevices in the earth's crust and ignite spontaneously, forming 30-50 cm high flames.
14. **Reserve of Motley Tulips**—(Plopiş Mountains) near Şimleu Silvaniei.
15. **The Mud Volcanoes**—from *Pâclele Mari* and *Pâclele Mici* (Buzău area)—a mixed reserve with one of the most spectacular and rare phenomena in the world.
16. **The Nera Gorges** (Anina Mountains)—one of the most beautiful gorges in Romania.
17. **Piatra Craiului National Park**—in a very beautiful mountain preserve, a great variety of relief, vegetation and animals.
18. **Pietroşul Rodnei Biosphere Preserve** (UNESCO site—Rodna Mountains) the most important nature reserve in the northern region (geological, botanical and wildlife).
19. **Repedea Hill** (near Iaşi)—paleonthological reserve.
20. **Retezat National Park** (UNESCO site—Retezat Mountains)—this 20,000 hectares (950,000 acres) park is the

finest scientific reserve in Romania and includes glacial relief, rare vegetal species, and valuable animal species; the park includes the Zlatna Scientific Preserve (access prohibited).

21. **Saint Ana Lake** (Ciomaţu Mountains)—the only lake in Central Europe formed in a volcano crater; the area surrounding the lake, including *Tinovul Mohoş*, forms a geological and floristic reserve.
22. **The Salt Mountain–Slănic Prahova**—within the perimeter of this mountain there is a karst saline lake.
23. **Secular Forest from Slătioara** (Rarău Mountains)—it is one of the oldest secular forests of Romania and Europe.
24. **The Small Island of Brăila** (on Danube River)—complex reserve where, on over 5,336 ha (13,000 aces), one can see rare species and a lot of birds.
25. **Topolniţa Cave** (Mehedinţi Plateau)—it has numerous karst, spectacular lakes and structures. Speleological reserve, it has been declared monument of nature.
26. **Turzii Gorges Complex Reserve** (Trascau Mountains)—there are about 60 caves in this gorge; there are also various species of butterflies and more than 1,000 species of plants, some unique in the world.

For guided tours to some of these natural reserves, see: www.activtravel.ro.

SPAS

1. **Herculane Spa**—Roman spa (AD 105–107) in forested Cerna River valley, southwest Romania. Air has negative ionization increasing body endurance and stimulating blood circulation; thermal mineral springs (45-55°C) are sulfurous, chloro-sodic, calcic, hypotonic, bicarbonate, magnesian; recommended for treatment of rheumatoid, gynecological and peripheral nervous system diseases, and digestive duct and ductless glands diseases.
2. **Felix Spa**—Suburb of Oradea, at Pădurea Craiului mountains, at 140 m (460 ft.) altitude. The bicarbonate, sulfurous, chloro-sodic, calcic, silicious springs and therapeutic

mud, recommended for rheumatoid and post-traumatic diseases, gynecological afflictions, central and peripheral nervous systems disturbances, and metabolic and nutritional diseases.

3. **Buziaş**—Between Timişoara (37 km) and Lugoj (25 km) via E70. Natural carbonated, chlorinated, sodium, magnesium mineral waters, mofettes (carbon dioxide emanations) sedative, protective bio climate; recommended for cardiovascular affections, arterial hyper-pressure, rheumatism diseases, and stress.
4. **Covasna**—Southeast Transylvania, near Sfântu Gheorghe, amid forests and meadows; Spa of the Heart, known for treatments of cardiovascular diseases and digestive maladies; rich in carbogaseous, bicarbonate, calcic, magnessian mineral springs, in carbon dioxide emanation of the mofettes.
5. **Sovata**—On a salt mountain at the foot of Gurghiu volcanic massif, central Transylvania; heliothermal lakes, condensed chlorosodic and sapropelic mud and mineral springs; recommended for gynecological diseases and sterility; rheumatoid and post-traumatic diseases, peripheral nervous system afflictions; endocrine and cardiovascular maladies; and the asthenic neurosis.
6. **Borsec**—In the northeast Carpathians, west of Durau and Bicaz gorges at 900 m (2,953 ft.) altitude; surrounded by a coniferous forest; natural curing factors are its microclimate and pure air, the healing mineral waters and waters, and the physio-therapeutic procedures to heal or ameliorate nutritional or metabolic illnesses.
7. **Tuşnad**—In the southeastern Carpathians, east of Transylvania at 650 m (2,133 ft.) altitude; air rich in ozone, resinous aerosols and negative ions promote relaxation and stress relief; mineral water springs helpful for cardiovascular, nervous system, digestive (chronic gastritis, enterocolitis) and endocrine diseases.
8. **Vatra Dornei**—Certified since 1592; northern Transylvania; famous for its mineral water and for treatments

against heart attack, ischemic cardiomyopathy, different forms of valvular–pathy, arterial hypertension; also for degenerative rheumatoid diseases, abarticular rheumatism, post-traumatic and neurologic afflictions.

9. **Slănic Moldova**—In eastern Carpathians, at 530 m (1,740 ft.) altitude; 20 mineral water springs with diverse chemical compositions. Aids digestive and respiratory diseases, nutritional and metabolic disturbances (diabetes, gout, obesity); also treats chronic bronchitis, tracheitis, ORL afflictions, renal and urinary diseases, and chronic and degenerative rheumatism.
10. **Mangalia**—Southeast Romania, on the Black Sea Coast; natural therapeutic agents include sulfurated, chlorinate, bicarbonate, sodic, calcic mineral springs and sapropelic mud from Techirghiol Lake; treats central and peripheral nervous system afflictions (vascular accidents, pareses, neuralgia); the respiratory system (chronic allergic rhinitis, chronic bronchitis, bronchial asthma); dermatological disease (psoriasis, allergohernia); and gynecological diseases (chronic cystitis, secondary infertility).
11. **Eforie Nord**—Black Sea Coast (same treatments as Mangalia).

UNESCO WORLD HERITAGE SITES

The wooden churches of Maramureş:

1. **Bârşana**, 1720, a rectangular plan with a five-sided apse; belfry on the pronave; roof with a double hem.
2. **Budeşti**—Joseni, 1643, a rectangular plan with a separated polygonal apse; mural paintings since 1762.
3. **Deseşti**, 1770, mentioned for the first time in 1360; paintings by master Radu Munteanu in 1780; a collection of icons on wood from the 17th century, and on glass from the 19th century.
4. **Ieud**, *Biserica din Vale*, 1717, a rectangular plan with a polygonal cutout apse; roof with a double hem.

5. **Siseşti**, Plopis village, 1796, a rectangular plan with a cutout apse; porch on the western side; a very tall belfry.
6. **Poienile Izei**, 1604, a rectangular plan with a square apse of the shrine; a porch with wooden pillars; a mural painting since 1794.
7. **Târgu Lăpuş**, Rogoz Village, 1663, set on fire by Tatars and rebuilt in 1717; it is remarkable due to the beauty of the silhouette and the decoration; mural paintings made by many masters at the end of the 17th century and the beginning of the 18th century.
8. **Siseşti**, Surdeşti village, 1767, the church was made from oak-tree beams on a stone foundation; the tower, 54 m tall, is guarded by four smaller towers; interior paintings since the 18th century.

The monasteries & churches of Moldavia:

9. **Arbore**, built in 1503 by Boyar Luca Arbore; has a longitudinal plan with no tower; two niches in the wall as apses are in the nave; a large apse for the alms table is outside (a feature found in only one other church); painting dated 1541.
10. **Humor**, built in 1530 by boyar Toader Bubuiog, on the foundation of a 14th-century settlement. An harmonious architecture, it has no tower; has vault and an open porch—the first from Moldavian architecture. The exterior painting's main theme is the siege of Constantinople. Contains a portrait of founder Voivode Petru Rareş's family.
11. **Moldoviţa**, rebuilt by Voivode Petru Rareş on an older foundation; one of the most important monuments from the old Romanian art; mural paintings since 1537, both inside and outside; the main theme is the siege of Constantinople.
12. **Pătrăuţi**, built by Steven the Great in 1487; small but well-proportioned; a triconic plan with a tower on the nave; it uses an element specific to the Moldavian architecture—the oblique archways; the interior painting is extremely valuable—a portrayal of the "the Deploration" and "the Cavalcade of the military saints" scenes.

13. **Probota**, founded by Petru Rareş in 1530; interior painting (restored) and the exterior (destroyed) since 1532; a representative piece of architecture for Moldavia's 16th century.
14. **Suceava**, built in 1514-1522; remarkable mural paintings; on the exterior facades, fragments of painting can be seen; the silver tomb of Sf. Ion cel Nou.
15. **Suceviţa**, built by Movilă brothers between 1583 and 1586. The plan of the church is specific to that period. Pronave, nave and shrine; porch and vault added later; richly painted decoration, inside and outside, and elegant shape.
16. **Voroneţ**, built by Steven the Great in 1488; it has a triconic style with a tower on the nave; original paintings in the nave; a close porch and the exterior paintings (the famous Voroneţ blue) dated since 1547; the main theme of the painting is Doomsday.

Saxon fortified churches in Transylvania:

17. **Biertan**, hall-type church, 1492-1515; late Gothic with Rennaissance elements on some portals; pulpit sculptured in stone is one of the most important Transylvanian sculptures; a precious polyptic shrine made in 1483-1524; the door to the Sacristy room is considered a masterpiece.
18. **Calnic Fortress**, first certified in the 13th century; a peasant fortress renovated in the 15th–16th centuries; has a donjon, Siegfried's Tower, mentioned in 1270.
19. **Dârjiu**, a Unitarian hall-type church, 14th–15th centuries, strengthened in the 16th century; it has very valuable interior mural paintings.
20. **Prejmer**, the strongest peasant fortress in Transylvania; Evangelist Church an early Gothic with Cistercian influences built in 1250, has a cross-like plan, a valuable polyptic shrine, Baroque decorations, fragments of murals, both inside and outside.
21. **Saschiz**, Evangelist Church, 1493-1496, remarkable due to the way the building was strengthened, plan with a single hall, an oblong quire and polygonal apse.

22. **Valea Viilor**, Sf. Petru Church, 13th century, extended and strengthened in the 15th–16th centuries; the church looks like a strong tower, surrounded by fortified walls.
23. **Viscri**, built in the end of the 15th century, it has a double precinct, the Evangelist Church in Gothic style, it suffered many changes in the 15th–17th centuries.

Dacian fortresses in Orăştie Mountains:

24. **Blidaru** (*Costeşti Blidaru*), fortress from the 2nd century BC–AD 106, was the permanent residence of Dacian King Burebista; the fortress has two precincts with walls of limestone blocks; surrounded by a clay wall.
25. **Căpâlna**, Dacian fortress located on La Cetate cliff (610 m altitude).
26. **Costeşti**, a fortress with defense towers on Cetăţuia Hill (561m altitude).
27. **Luncani Piatra Roşie**, a Dacian stone-made fortress located in Boşorod Village. It has five towers and a gate since the 1st century BC and the 1st century AD it was destroyed after the Dacian-Roman War in 106; discovered objects: an iron sword of Celtic origin, the cover of a parade shield, a Bronze chandelier.
28. **Sarmizegetusa Regia**—*Grădiştea de Munte*, former political, administrative and military capital of the Dacian State from the end of the 1st century BC to the beginning of the 1st century AD. It was one of the largest refuge fortresses in Transylvania, of a polygonal plan, stone walls with two gates and many terraces; a paved alley between the fortress and two sanctuaries, a large rectangle (six rows, each with ten limestone cylindrical rolls), and a large circular (the Dacians Calendar, when the year was 360 days).

Other World Heritage Sites:

29. **Mănăstirea Horezu Horezu Monastery** (Horez, Hurez)—The largest medieval monument preserved in Wallachia. It was Voivode Constantin Brâncoveanu's main foundation and includes many buildings and the church

(1690-1693). It has a triconic plan with the tower on the nave and pronave. It also has a large porch with archways supported by ten stone-made pillars, sculptured in Rennaissance motives. Contains a portrait of the founder and his family. The other buildings include the belfry, the chapel, and the trapeze.

30. **Centrul Istoric Sighişoara**—Sighişoara historic center. It is the most beautiful and complete medieval urban center in Romania. The fortress dates from the 14th–17th centuries; narrow streets, massive brick houses, defense walls and towers. Most interesting tower, the Clock Tower or the Council's Tower, is a museum. Important monuments: the Monastery Church (13th–15th centuries), Biserica din Deal (14th–16th centuries), the house where Vlad Dracul lived, and Vlad Tepes (the Impaler) was born.
31. **Delta Dunarii**—The Danube Delta. The lowest territory of Romania, with a relief permanently changing; also the second largest delta in Europe. The minimum altitude is –36 m on Chilia Arm, and the maximum +13 m on the dunes from Letea Sand Bank. With a surface of 2.590 km^2, the Danube Delta includes both dry land (about 15%) and swamps with lakes and streams. The main arms of the Danube—Chilia, Sulina and Sf. Gheorghe—are the results of the water separation at *Ceatalul Izmail.*

    More details at www.cimec.ro

VINEYARDS

1. **Cotnari vineyard**—was royal Moldavian vineyard; centers in Cotnari, Hârlau and Rădeni.
2. **Bucium vineyard**—on the hills south of Iaşi. Riesling, White Fetească, Aligot and Muscat Ottonel.
3. **Huşi vineyard**—medieval history, Stephan the Great drank this wine.
4. **Odobeşti vineyard**—smaller vineyards, with great traditions: Panciu, Odobeşti, Zariştea, Coteşti, Nicoreşti and Iveşti.

5. **Niculiţel vineyard**—Tulcea County; a very old wine from same period as ancient Greek fortress.
6. **Murfatlar vineyard**—Dobrogea, west of Constanţa; the oldest wine in Romania, more than 2,000 years.
7. **Ostrov vineyard**—old vineyard in Dobrogea province, near the Danube River.
8. **Dealu Mare vineyard**—Odobeşti, Vrancea County, northeast of Bucharest. In medieval times it was a royal Wallachian vineyard, with a monastic administration; smaller vineyards in Pietroasele, Mizil, Valea Călugarească.
9. **Piteşti vineyard**—Two centers on the Argeş River, at Ştefăneşti and Topoloveni.
10. **Drăgăşani vineyard**—A large vineyard, principal center in Drăgăşani, beside the Olt River in Oltenia Province.
11. **Aradului vineyard**—The most important wine growing region in Banat province; main centers are Teremia Mare, Buziaş, Pâncota, Siria, Ghioroc, Pauliş.
12. **Alba vineyard**—On the southeast Apuseni Mountains.
13. **Târnave vineyard**—The most famous vineyard in Transylvania. Vineyard centers in Cetatea de Baltă, Mediaş, Jidvei, Târnăveni, Băgaciu.
14. **Bistriţa vineyard**—The vineyard centers are Lachinta and Viişoara.
15. **Valea lui Mihai vineyard**—Vineyard in northeast, on West Hills with centers in Zalău, Marghita and Valea lui Mihai.

Agencies offering Wine Tasting tours:

Arcadia Tour, Tel: (40-21)312.67.89, E-mail: arcadia@starnets.ro, www.rotravel.com/agencies/arcadia

Apsa Tour, Tel: (40-21)311.36.21, E-mail: office@apsatravel.ro, www.apsatravel.ro

Atlantic Tour, Tel: (40-21)312.77.75, E-mail: office@atlantic.ro, www.atlantic.ro

Atlantic Tourism, Tel: (40-232)21.38.72, E-mail: Atlantic@mail.dntis.ro, www.atlanticturism.ro

CMB Travel, Tel: (40-21) 210.52.44,
E-mail: mircea@cmbtravel.ro, www.cmbtravel.ro
Cultural RomTour, Tel: (40-21)316.67.65;
E-mail: office@culturalromtour.ro, www.culturalromtour.ro
Karpaten Turism, Tel: (40-21)322.04.35,
E-mail: karpaten@seftnet.ro, www.karpaten.ro
Prestige Tours, Tel: (40-21) 659.77.31,
E-mail: prestige@moon.ro, www.prestigetours.ro
Ro Team Tour, Tel: (40-21)313.19.09,
E-mail: office@roteamtour.ro, www.roteamtour.ro

RECOMMENDED BOOKS ABOUT ROMANIA

Fiction

The Land of Green Plums, by Herta Muller, 1996
Trouble in Transylvania: a Cassandra Reilly Mystery, by Barbara Wilson, 1993
Stalin's Nose: Travels Around the Bloc, by Rory MacLean, 1992
The Balkan Trilogy (Fortunes of War), by Olivia Manning, 1981

Non-Fiction

Romania: An Illustrated History, by Nicolae Klepper, 2003
Transylvania and Beyond, by Dervla Murphy, 1993
Balkan Ghosts, by Robert D. Kaplan, 1993
Exit Into History, by Eva Hoffman, 1993
Roumanian Journey, by Sacheverell Sitwell, 1993 (orig. 1938)
Transylvania: History and Reality, by Milton G. Lehrer, 1986
The Last Romantic: Biography of Queen Marie of Roumania, by Hannah Pakula, 1984
Athenee Palace Bucharest, by R.G. Waldeck, 1943
Raggle Taggle: Adventures With a Fiddle in Hungary and Roumania, by Walter Starkie, 1933
Eastern European Narrow Gauge, by Keith Chester, 1994
The Railways of Romania, by Chris Bailey, 2002

Cookbooks

Taste of Romania, by Nicolae Klepper 1997, 2000

Illustrated

For They Are My Friends, by Tom Marotta (b&w photography); text by Mihail Eminescu, et al

INDEX

Other Titles of Interest from Hippocrene Books

ALL ALONG THE DANUBE

Marina Polway

Expanded Edition

For novices and gourmets, this unique cookbook offers a tempting variety of Central European dishes from the shores of the Danube River, bringing Old World flavor to today's dishes. Along with a special chapter, "Christmas Along the Danube" which covers holiday specialties of all the countries, the book also includes black and white photographs of menus.

Paperback • 360 pages • 5½ x 8¼ • ISBN: 0-7818-0806-5 • $14.95

TASTE OF ROMANIA

Nicolae Klepper

Expanded Edition

Here is a real taste of both Old World and modern Romanian culture in a unique cookbook that combines over 140 traditional recipes with enchanting examples of Romania's folklore, humor, art, poetry and proverbs.

Hardcover • 330 pages • 6 x 9 • photos/illustrations •
ISBN: 0-7818-0766-2 • $24.95

ROMANIAN-ENGLISH/ENGLISH-ROMANIAN DICTIONARY & PHRASEBOOK

Mihai Miroiu

From the monasteries of northern Moldovia to the Danube Delta to Dracula's homeland, Transylvania, Romania offers many activities to its visitors.

The aim of this Dictionary & Phrasebook is to supply the American tourist or businessperson with certain conversational formulas indispensable for starting a conversation and carrying it on in a natural manner.

Paperback • 250 pages 3¾ x 7½ • 5,500 entries •
ISBN: 0-7818-0921-5 • $12.95

ROMANIA: AN ILLUSTRATED HISTORY

Nicolae Klepper

As a state, Romania has only been in existence since 1859, but the history of its people stretches to the late Bronze Age and early Iron Age, to the Geto-Dacians and Romans.

This concise history tells the fascinating story of the evolution of the Romanian people, the creation of the Romanian Principalities, their struggle against empire-building powers, and their eventual unification to form the state of Romania. For a fuller appreciation of Romanian history, each chapter (beginning with Chapter 3) includes a section called "Perspective," which gives a bird's eye view of events occurring simultaneously in other parts of Europe.

Paperback • 225 pages 5 x 7 • 70 black & white illustrations • ISBN: 0-7818-0935-5 • $14.95

BEGINNER'S BULGARIAN WITH 2 AUDIO CDs

Mariana Raykov

2 80-MINUTE AUDIO CDs

This series is for the businessperson, tourist or student traveling in Bulgaria. It will help in common situations such as going through Customs, checking into hotel, making phone calls, going to the post office. Also included is information on history and cultures, driving tips, social customs, restaurant practices. Language skills cover a good vocabulary, fundamental grammar and phrases.

Paperback • 212 pages • 5½ x 8½ • ISBN: 0-7818-1101-5 • $27.95

BYZANTIUM: AN ILLUSTRATED HISTORY

Sean McLachlan

Long after Rome fell to the Germanic tribes, its culture lived on in Constantinople, the glittering capital of the Byzantine Empire. For more than a thousand years (A.D. 330-1453) Byzantium was one of the most advanced and complex civilizations the world had ever seen. As the Mediterranean outlet for the Silk Route, its trade networks stretched from Scandinavia to Sri Lanka; its artists created somber icons and brilliant gold mosaics; its scholarship served as a vital cultural bridge between the Muslim East and the Catholic West; and it fostered the Orthodox Christianity that is the faith of millions today. In *Byzantium: An Illustrated History*, more than 50 photos and maps show the innovative art that inspired French kings and Arab emirs. It includes a gazetteer of historic Byzantine sites and monuments that travelers can visit today in Greece, Italy, Turkey, and the Middle East. A chronology of Byzantine history and a list of emperors complete this ideal resource for the student, traveler, or generally curious reader.

About the author: Sean McLachlan earned his master's degree in archaeology from the University of Missouri-Columbia, where he specialized in the medieval period. He has worked on excavations in Israel,

Cyprus, Bulgaria, and the United States. Now a full-time writer, he has published hundreds of articles in newspapers and magazines, specializing in history and travel. He resides in Tucson, Arizona.

Paperback • 200 pages • 5½ x 8½ • 50 b/w photos, illustrations, maps • ISBN: 0-7818-1033-7 • $14.95

LANGUAGE AND TRAVEL GUIDE TO SICILY

Giovanna Bellia La Marca

Giovanna Bellia La Marca is a native of Ragusa, Sicily, and the author of Hippocrene's Sicilian Feasts cookbook. She came to the United States at the age of 10, and has kept alive her love of the island with frequent trips there. Here she takes us through the beauties of her native country's people, landscapes, and architecture.

ONE 80-MINUTE AUDIO CD • 200 PAGES • 5½ x 8½ • 0-7818-1149-X • $21.95